A Taste for
Comfort and Status

Christine Adams

A Taste for
Comfort and Status

A Bourgeois Family
in
Eighteenth-Century France

The Pennsylvania State University Press
University Park, Pennsylvania

Library of Congress Cataloging-in-Publication Data

Adams, Christine, 1962–
    A taste for comfort and status : a bourgeois family
in eighteenth-century France / Christine Adams.

        p.   cm.
    Includes bibliographical references and index.
    ISBN 0–271–01955–7 (cloth : alk. paper)
    ISBN 0–271–01956–5 (pbk. : alk. paper)
    1. Lamothe family.   2. Bordeaux (France)—Social life and
customs—18th century.   3. Middle class families—France—Bordeaux—
History—18th century.   I. Title.
DC801.B72A33   2000
305.5'5'0944714—dc21   98-54961
                                                                        CIP

Copyright © 2000 The Pennsylvania State University
All rights reserved
Printed in the United States of America
Published by The Pennsylvania State University Press,
University Park, PA 16802-1003

It is the policy of The Pennsylvania State University Press to use acid-free paper for the first
printing of all clothbound books. Publications on uncoated stock satisfy the minimum
requirements of American National Standard for Information Sciences—Permanence of
Paper for Printed Library Materials, ANSI Z39.48–1992.

In memory of Bridget Bernadette Phillips, 1966–1989

Contents

Acknowledgments

The Lamothe family has been a part of my life for the past ten years, first as I worked to turn this family's story into my dissertation at Johns Hopkins University, then into a book. Naturally, there are many people who helped to bring this work to fruition. The staff of the Manuscripts Division of the Library of Congress helped me in the early phases of my research when I first located the Lamothe family letters. A travel grant from the Frederick Jackson Turner Society at Johns Hopkins University in August 1990 allowed me to conduct preliminary research in the archives of Bordeaux, and a *bourse Chateaubriand* from the French government financed my stay in Bordeaux from November 1990 through May 1991.

During my stay in France, a number of people made my work immeasurably easier, as well as more enjoyable. Jean-Paul Avisseau, *conservateur* of the Archives municipales, and his staff sent me information on the Lamothes back in December 1988, and did everything they could to facilitate my research there. At the Archives départementales de la Gironde, Director Jean Valette showed me every kindness, accompanying me to the archives of Sainte-Foy-la-Grande and taking me for a tour of the region. Hélène Avisseau and Jean-Pierre Bériac also assisted my project enormously, and the rest of the staff of the Archives départementales searched high and low for documents that I hoped existed, seeming as disappointed as I when they could not be located. Steve Peterson, a fellow American also doing research in the Archives départementales, provided companionship as well as several notarial references. Going above and beyond the call of duty, M. Botineau and the staff of the Bibliothèque municipale opened the library to me for two weeks, despite the fact that it was officially closed during the 1990–91 academic year for its move to a new location at Mériadeck. Mlle. Guesnon, the archivist at Sainte-Foy, found numerous documents concerning the Lamothes for me, and provided friendship as well as assistance. Claude Bayle, whose wife is descended from a branch of the Lamothe family, obligingly sent me genealogical material, and Jean-Eugène Borie, the eminent *propriétaire* of Château Ducru-Beaucaillou, sent out several letters of inquiry on my behalf.

Back in the United States, many friends and colleagues helped with my project. Toby Ditz offered suggestions for this dissertation in its early stages, and Caroline Hannaway provided her expertise on the French medical world. Julie Hardwick, and my sister, Tracy Adams, provided useful and critical comments on the work in progress. Michael Scally helped with the tedious work of proofreading at the end. Robert Forster, my advisor, and his wife, Elborg, provided both scholarly and emotional support during the long process of research and writing. Orest Ranum gave me the benefit of his insight and creativity in his reading of my work, and Cissie Fairchilds and Jonathan Dewald offered many useful suggestions. Peter Potter and Cherene Holland, my editors at Penn, have always been a pleasure to work with, as was Romaine Perin, my copyeditor.

Paul DeLaHunt provided the "emotional underpinnings" for my work, and offered support and understanding, as well as practical assistance when computer difficulties threatened to stymie my progress. Loki, our faithful keeshond, accompanied me to France, and patiently listened as I sorted out my ideas on our many walks. Our daughters, Sylvie, who arrived midway through the composition of the dissertation, and Julia, who came along while I was revising the material for this book, helped me to keep my priorities straight, and to appreciate the importance of families, both past and present.

Introduction

On 17 January 1757, Alexandre Lamothe wrote to his brother Victor, who was studying medicine in Paris: "I have never doubted, my very dear brother, your amity for me, I have always received too much strong proof, but this letter that you had the goodness to write me would have removed any suspicion in case I had any, however small. In it, you demonstrate your sentiments in terms so energetic that one would have to be unfeeling not to be moved."[1] This letter, with its protestations of affection and tender sentiments, is typical of the mail that passed back and forth between Paris and Bordeaux during Victor Lamothe's ten-year absence from his provincial home and from his family. It also illustrates one of the most powerful elements in the lives of all members of the Lamothe family—complete and utter devotion to their parents, children, and siblings.

The Lamothe family of Bordeaux represent on many levels an "ordinary" family of eighteenth-century France.[2] A well-to-do and well-respected professional family, the Lamothes made a mark in pre- and even postrevolutionary Bordeaux, but their apparent merit and talent did not bring them wider or lasting recognition. Their "fame" was as local notables.

The Lamothes were also representative of a specific social class: that of the provincial professional family. The male members of the family were well educated, well to do without being ostentatious, dedicated to creating

---

1. Lamothe Family Letters, Manuscripts Division, Library of Congress. Alexandre to Victor, 17 January 1757. All translations are my own, unless indicated otherwise.
2. According to Robert Forster, *ordinary* does not mean a "statistical 'average family,' nor in every case, the 'menu peuple,' but families, rich or poor, who have not left a special mark on history." See "Family Biography," in Wolfdieter Bihl and Gernot Heiss, eds., *Biographie und Geschichtswissenschaft: Aufsätze zur Theorie und Praxis biographischer Arbeit* (Vienna: Verlage für Geschichte und Politik, 1979), 111.

a local milieu both in opposition to and in imitation of the dominant culture of Paris. They were only moderately ambitious for themselves, convinced of their own merit and talent, but harboring few notions of glory and splendor in imitation of a noble house, *les grands* of Old Regime France.[3] Their sense of self-worth and identity was not linked to illustrious ancient title and imposing outward display; rather, it was dependent on family ties, professional expertise, and satisfaction, cultural contribution and personal cultivation, and a sense of local status based on their respected achievement and position in the community.

"Identity" is a term that varies from individual to individual and from social group to social group. Highlighting a key element of identity, whether familial, professional, or intellectual, can illuminate core values of a specific social group. For example, in a recent study of the Parisian bourgeoisie, David Garrioch focuses on political behavior as central to the formation of class identity.[4] The question that is relevant in the case of the Lamothe family, as representative of their specific social group, the provincial *bourgeoisie à talents*, or professional classes, is, Did they possess a group consciousness reflected in their attitudes, values, and behavior?[5] Was their sense of identity securely bound to their family life, their professional status, and their cultural activities, which carried them to the threshold of elite culture?

This study examines the many factors that contributed to the identity of the members of the Lamothe family in an effort to uncover the values and norms that governed their social group in eighteenth-century France. In doing so, it explores new ground, for despite growing interest in the French "bourgeoisie," there have been few family studies of the middle classes or professionals in early modern France.[6] Historians have studied

---

3. Robert Dietle, in his study of the *bon bourgeois* of Paris, suggests that the bourgeoisie of the eighteenth century possessed its own culture, one that was separate from, and that they indeed considered preferable to that of the idle nobility. See Robert Dietle, "Salvaging the Everyday: The *Bon Bourgeois* of Paris" (Ph.D. diss., Harvard University, 1991).

4. David Garrioch, *The Formation of the Parisian Bourgeoisie, 1690–1830* (Cambridge: Harvard University Press, 1996).

5. *Bourgeoisie à talents*, as used by Michel Peronnet, includes "les avocats, les procureurs et les hommes de loi, les professeurs, les médecins et les chirurgiens et les membres dirigeants du clergé." See "Bourgeois et bourgeoisie d'après les textes contemporains," in Michel Vovelle, ed., *Bourgeoisies de province et Révolution* (Grenoble: Presses Universitaires de Grenoble, 1987), 21.

6. A notable exception is Robert Forster's *Merchants, Landlords, Magistrates: The Depont Family in Eighteenth-Century France* (Baltimore: Johns Hopkins University Press, 1980). However, even Forster's Depont family became nobles in the second generation.

members of the upper nobility extensively, and the *Annales*-style social historians have carried out research on the "inarticulate masses," the peasantry and the urban popular classes.[7] But the urban middle classes, even the elite of this group, the liberal professionals, have been somewhat neglected until quite recently.[8] In contrast, there have been extensive studies of middle-class families of the nineteenth century.[9]

This is due in part to the traditional historical focus on the "making of the middle classes" in the nineteenth century, and the formation and domination of what can be called a "bourgeois" mentality.[10] It is also due to difficulties in definition.[11] Sarah Maza goes so far as to deny the

7. For works on noble families in English, see, for example, Jonathan Dewald, *Pont-St-Pierre, 1398–1789: Lordship, Community, and Capitalism in Early Modern France* (Berkeley and Los Angeles: University of California Press, 1987); and Robert Forster, *The House of Saulx-Tavanes: Versailles and Burgundy, 1700–1830* (Baltimore: Johns Hopkins University Press, 1971). The bibliography of Jean-Pierre Labatut's *Les Ducs et pairs de France au XVIIe siècle* (Paris: Presses Universitaires de France, 1972), 24–29, lists more than one hundred titles of studies concerning the history of ducal families. Works on the popular classes include Olwen H. Hufton, *The Poor in Eighteenth-Century France, 1750–1789* (Oxford: Clarendon Press, 1974) and Daniel Roche, *The People of Paris: An Essay in Popular Culture in the Eighteenth Century*, trans. Marie Evans (Berkeley and Los Angeles: University of California Press, 1987), to name just two. For an overview of the *Annales*-style history, see Robert Forster and Orest Ranum's seven-volume edition of *Selections from the Annales, E.S.C.*, trans. Elborg Forster and Patricia Ranum (Baltimore: Johns Hopkins University Press, 1975–82).

8. See, for example, Sarah Maza, "Luxury, Morality, and Social Change: Why There Was No Middle-Class Consciousness in Prerevolutionary France," *Journal of Modern History* 69 (June 1997): 199–229; and Garrioch, *Formation of the Parisian Bourgeoisie*. Jean Nicolas's older study examines the elite of Savoy more generally, including both nobility and bourgeoisie. *La Savoie au 18e siècle: Noblesse et bourgeoisie*, 2 vols. (Paris: Maloine, 1978). Among German historians, the upper middle classes have become an area of intense research efforts in recent years. See Jonathan Sperber's review article, "Bürger, Bürgertum, Bürgerlichkeit, Bürgerliche Gesellschaft: Studies of the German (Upper) Middle Class and Its Sociocultural World," *Journal of Modern History* 69 (June 1997): 271–97. Jonathan Barry's review article, "The Making of the Middle Class?" *Past and Present*, no. 145 (November 1994): 194–208, attests to the increasing interest in the "middling sort" among historians.

9. Julie Hardwick points this out in *The Practice of Patriarchy: Gender and the Politics of Household Authority in Early Modern France* (University Park: Penn State Press, 1998), xiii n. 10

10. For two works that place the creation of a middle class identity in the nineteenth century, see Leonore Davidoff and Catherine Hall, *Family Fortunes: Men and Women of the English Middle Class, 1780–1850* (Chicago: University of Chicago Press, 1987); Mary Ryan, *Cradle of the Middle Class: The Family in Oneida County, New York, 1790–1865* (New York: Cambridge University Press, 1981). Most of the books reviewed by Jonathan Barry in "The Making of the Middle Class?" focus on the nineteenth century. On the ascendancy of the "bourgeois mentality" in nineteenth-century France, see Roger Magraw, *France, 1815–1914: The Bourgeois Century* (Oxford: Oxford University Press, 1983).

11. Robert Forster, "The Middle Classes in Eighteenth-Century Western Europe: An Essay," in Jürgen Schneider, ed., *Wirtschaftskräfte und Wirtschaftswege*, vol. 3: *Auf dem Weg zur Industrialisierung* (Bamberg: Hermann Kellenbenz and Jürgen Schneider, 1978), 16. Garrioch also highlights some of these problems of definition in *Formation of the Parisian Bourgeoisie*, 3–5; as do Pamela M. Pilbeam in *The Middle Classes in Europe, 1789–1914: France, Germany, Italy, and Russia* (Basingstoke: Macmillan, 1990),

relevance of the term "middle class" for eighteenth-century French society, while David Garrioch argues that there was no eighteenth-century bourgeoisie.[12] Both Maza and Garrioch stress the absence of class consciousness among those we would consider the "middle classes" of the eighteenth century. Maza argues that "a decisive factor in determining the presence and role of a middle class is the discourse about it—whether and how it is named and invested with social, political, moral, or historical importance."[13] Garrioch further emphasizes that "the political and social institutions of the city [of Paris] served to fragment rather than to unite the middle classes," and that while there were "merchants and lawyers, teachers, manufacturers, rentiers, bourgeois de Paris," there was no bourgeoisie.[14]

However, in denying the existence of a budding French bourgeoisie in the eighteenth century and placing its formation on the other side of the revolutionary divide, perhaps both Garrioch and Maza are looking in the wrong place. Garrioch's work examines the city of Paris, but the quintessential French bourgeoisie—as illustrated by Balzac, Zola, and Flaubert—lay in the provinces. Indeed, a key aspect of provincial bourgeois identity was regional pride and resistance to the lure and dominance of the capital. Maza seeks a discourse of "middle class-ness" in the published documents of both celebrated and obscure writers—but perhaps the lived reality of a family such as the Lamothes can bring us closer to understanding the stirrings of a middle-class or bourgeois consciousness. The case of the Lamothe family suggests that the provincial professional family of eighteenth-century France had a cultural style of its own and embodied values and goals not unlike those of its better-documented nineteenth-century counterpart.[15] Specifically, they displayed the moral rectitude, fiscal conservatism, family-centeredness, desire for public esteem though not glory, professional ambition tempered by caution, and cultural awareness height-

chap. 1; and Nicolas, La Savoie au 18e siècle, 1:3 and 47. Nicolas's definition encompasses a rural as well as urban bourgeoisie.

12. Maza, "Luxury, Morality, and Social Change"; Garrioch, Formation of the Parisian Bourgeoisie, 1.

13. Maza, "Luxury, Morality, and Social Change," 202. In his Imagining the Middle Class: The Political Representation of Class in Britain, c. 1780–1840 (New York: Cambridge University Press, 1995), Dror Wahrman also highlights discourse and changing political configurations in the creation of the middle class.

14. Garrioch, Formation of the Parisian Bourgeoisie, 1.

15. Dietle, in "Salvaging the Everyday," especially the introduction, suggests that this urban bourgeois culture was clearly developed in the eighteenth century, and included respectability, thrift, productivity, and respect for tradition. See also Nicolas, La Savoie au 18e siècle, 1:3.

ened by the desire to serve the public good that we associate with the respectable bourgeois of the first three generations of nineteenth-century France.[16] And in a very real sense, it is these social and cultural values, even more than economic and political activity, that we associate with the bourgeoisie.[17]

The parallel should not be pushed too far, for the eighteenth century was a different era, with a different *mentalité*, and different issues of concern—although certain historians have emphasized continuities between eighteenth- and nineteenth-century France rather than focusing on the disruptions caused by revolution.[18] But the *bourgeoisie à talents*, the class of professional notables, was making its mark in the eighteenth century, and their values and worldview were beginning to crystallize.[19] This was a social group with a specific personal, professional, and cultural identity, bound up with issues of family, friendship, religion, professionalism, provincial loyalty, and personal cultivation. The Lamothes are representative, if not typical, of this social group.

The question of typicality always arises when we try to make assumptions based on the study of one family. But an in-depth study of one provincial professional family demonstrates how its members responded to the demands and challenges in both their public and private lives and suggests how other members of their social group may have responded.[20] We see the family and the individual as active agents rather than as passive before the forces of history. A study of this nature also illustrates the interplay of social structures and values and mentalities, and allows us to draw broader conclusions about such important issues as family life, social

16. Theodore Zeldin succinctly describes "the ambitions of the ordinary man," the good bourgeois professional of the nineteenth century, in his *France, 1848–1945: Ambition and Love* (New York: Oxford University Press, 1979), esp. 10–22 and 87–112.

17. Margaret R. Hunt makes a similar argument in *The Middling Sort: Commerce, Gender, and the Family in England, 1680–1780* (Berkeley and Los Angeles: University of California Press, 1996).

18. The best-known exposition of the continuity in pre- and postrevolutionary France is Alexis de Tocqueville's *The Old Regime and the French Revolution*, trans. Stuart Gilbert (New York: Doubleday, 1954). For historiographical issues, see Christine Adams, Jack R. Censer, and Lisa Jane Graham, eds., introduction to *Visions and Revisions of Eighteenth-Century France* (University Park: Penn State Press, 1997), 1–18.

19. Robert Forster has noted the existence of a certain professionalism and devotion to public service among royal administrators and other French elite of the late eighteenth century, traits that became characteristic of nineteenth century professional culture. "The French Revolution and the 'New' Elite, 1800–1850," in J. Perlenski, ed., *The American and European Revolutions, 1776–1848* (Iowa City: University of Iowa Press, 1980), 182–207.

20. Nicolas makes a similar attempt in his broader study, *La Savoie au 18e siècle*.

networks, professionalism, material concerns, and participation in the social and cultural trends of the time.[21] These issues comprise the themes of this study.

The warm family life of the Lamothe family and the importance of their social networks are illuminated by a particularly rich source of materials, a collection of more than three hundred personal letters that were written by the members of the family over a period of twenty-five years. The bulk of the letters were written to Victor, one of the younger sons of the family, while he was studying medicine in Paris and Montpellier in the 1750s and 1760s. These letters form the basis of our knowledge of the Lamothes' family life and their network of friends and relations. This is the focus of the first three chapters (Part I).

Part I, then, examines the conjugal family of Daniel de Lamothe, a barrister at the Parlement of Bordeaux, and his wife, Marie de Sérézac. Their large family included three lawyers (Simon-Antoine-Delphin, Alexis, and Alexis-Alexandre), one doctor (Simon-Victor), one priest (Jules-Bertrand), and two unmarried daughters (Marie and Marianne), as well as several children who died in infancy or childhood (see Chapter 1, section 1). The lives of this large family were tightly interwoven, as its members shared financial resources, emotional support, and a home.[22]

The personalities of the various men of the family emerge clearly in the letters: the stern but devoted father, Daniel, constantly nagging Victor to keep more careful account of his spending; Delphin, the perfect eldest son, relaying his father's orders to Victor and slipping easily into the role of *chef de famille* after the death of his father in 1763; Alexis, the elegant *honnête homme* of the eighteenth century, composing his letters to Victor with a

21. In a defense of case studies, Robert Forster notes that they "may not undermine an accepted interpretation of a large social group or a period of history," but goes on to argue that "it is likely to refine or qualify that interpretation. Even in instances where the case study confirms an old generalization, the personal example presents an immediacy and specificity that descriptions of general trends and conditions can rarely attain. More than simply an illustration of a general development, a family biography can elucidate the mediation process, that is, recapture precisely how individuals cope with the larger pressures and influences playing upon them." See "Family Biography," 111. Although his focus is on the aristocracy of Naples, Tommaso Astarita also makes a compelling argument for the usefulness of the family monograph as a vehicle to study "the importance of community ties, networks of obligations and symbols, attitudes and beliefs." See his introduction to *The Continuity of Feudal Power: The Caracciolo di Brienza in Spanish Naples* (New York: Cambridge University Press, 1992).

22. Jules Delpit, *Notes biographiques sur les Messieurs de Lamothe* (Bordeaux: Balarac Jeune, 1846), 9–10.

romantic flourish. Jules, the sober priest, laced his letters to his brother living in the wicked city of Paris with moral exhortations and pleas that he maintain his pious habits. Alexandre's letters to Victor were filled with affection and admiration for his older brother, and reflect his sweet and pious nature. Although the letters from Victor are fewer in number, his stubbornness in trying to persuade his family that he should stay in Paris to practice medicine comes through as Delphin and Alexis admonished him about his "too great attachment" to the capital.

The women in the family also emerge through their letters. Marie de Sérézac, the much loved and respected matriarch of the family, wrote only a few laborious and poorly spelled letters.[23] But she dearly loved her sons, frequently preparing jams and articles of clothing to send to the two in Paris. Marie and Marianne modeled themselves on their mother, and focused on the care of their father and brothers and on maintenance of the household. The salient quality of their letters to their brother is intense religiosity, as devotional exhortations filled their missives to Victor.[24]

The gendered nature of familial roles is evident, even if issues of "appropriate" feminine and masculine spheres were not made explicit in the letters. The males of the family emphasized their public roles, their professional and cultural pursuits, while the lives of the women, with their domestic tasks, religious practice, and charitable work at the hospital, yield nothing to the "ladies of the leisure class" of nineteenth-century France (see Chapter 1, section 5 below).[25] Daniel and his sons apparently treated the women of the family with affection and respect, and Delphin carried these attitudes to his marriage to Elisabeth de Brulz in 1772. His letters to her serve as a touching testament to a companionate marriage and suggest that perhaps his close and loving relations with his sisters served as a model for his married life.[26]

The Lamothes also sought to possess the symbols of status important to the eighteenth-century provincial French. They owned several properties, both urban and rural. The rural properties of Goulards and Muscadet were

23. Marie to Victor, 11 August 1760.

24. Religious concerns often filled the letters of early modern families. Forster, "Family Biography," 113–14.

25. See Bonnie G. Smith, *Ladies of the Leisure Class: The Bourgeoises of Northern France in the Nineteenth Century* (Princeton: Princeton University Press, 1981).

26. See Delphin's letters to Elisabeth de Brulz, November 1780. In his letters to Alexis in 1773, Delphin also speaks of his wife with great tenderness. For a more detailed analysis of the brother-sister relationship, see Christine Adams, "Devoted Companions or Surrogate Spouses? Sibling Relations in Eighteenth-Century France," in Adams, Censer, and Graham, *Visions and Revisions*, 59–76.

especially important in lending the cachet of *propriétaire* and *seigneur* to their public image. Like the *parlementaires* of Bordeaux's "high society," the Lamothes retired to their rural properties each year for the vintage. But they never allowed their desire for social prestige and *éclat* to push them beyond the bounds of fiscal conservatism and restraint. While the male members of the family, most notably Delphin and Victor, demonstrated clear professional ambition, and the others were determined to maintain a respectable position in the community, they were unwilling to take risks that might threaten the financial, and indeed the emotional, underpinnings of the family.

Each member of the Lamothe family relied heavily upon family and friends for both emotional and practical support. The first three chapters of this book point to the importance of both the family and the wider circle, as well as the interconnections between emotional and material concerns in the relations of everyday life. Patronage and connections were key in undergirding both the social and professional position of the Lamothes in Bordelais society, and they participated fully in the web of social favors and exchanges necessary to advancement in their social milieu (see Chapter 3 below).

While the lives of the women of the family remained focused on family and friends, their brothers sought an active role in the professional community. Professionalism in the context of eighteenth-century France is an important theme in this study, and an examination of the meaning of "profession" to the male members of the Lamothe family can illuminate what it meant to exercise a liberal profession in early modern France.[27]

The Lamothes, practicing law, medicine, and theology, clearly considered themselves "professionals," even if they did not use that term—although they frequently employed the word *profession*.[28] They were

27. Jan Goldstein notes that the term *profession libérale* did not appear in French until the nineteenth century, and argues that "from the Old Regime through at least the early nineteenth century, Frenchmen had in their cognitive mappings of the social world, no concept corresponding to the twentieth-century Anglo-American 'profession.' They knew, to be sure, doctors and lawyers, but different categories shaped their understanding of the work of these persons and of their place in the social scheme." See *Console and Classify: The French Psychiatric Profession in the Nineteenth Century* (New York: Cambridge University Press, 1987), 13–14.

28. See, for example, Jules to Victor, 28 January 1758; 8 April 1758; 7 June 1761; Daniel to Victor, 7 April 1760. The *Encyclopédie* defines "profession" as simply "état, métier qu'on embrasse, dont on fait son apprentissage, ses études et son exercise ordinaire," thus encompassing all *métiers*. *Encyclopédie ou Dictionnaire raisonné des sciences, des arts et des métiers, par une société de gens de lettres* (Neuchastel: Chez Samuel

educated elites by the standards of their day and felt entitled to the prestige and status associated with the titles of *avocat, médecin,* and *prêtre.*[29] Doctors, lawyers, and theologians are the only occupational groups that have been accorded professional status and the corresponding prestige since the Middle Ages. Lawrence Brockliss argues that these three occupational groups shared an institutionalized education in the humanities and sciences that gave them a special status as an urban caste, and set them apart socially, culturally, and intellectually from other practitioners of law and medicine—a special status that resulted in a shared personal and social identity.[30] This liberal education—or perhaps more fundamentally, the social background that allowed pursuit of this education—assured a professional identity leading to a respected position in the community.

Traditional sociological theory has held that the specialized body of knowledge associated with law and, most prominently, with medicine, led to professionalization of these occupations and the resultant social and professional privileges.[31] Toby Gelfand, in his study of the professional-

---

Faulche, 1765), 13:426. Even today, the word "professional" does not translate easily into French. "Professions libérales" is the closest equivalent to the American and English notion of "profession." See Gerald Geison, ed., *Professions and the French State, 1700–1900* (Philadelphia: University of Pennsylvania Press, 1984), 3; and Jan Goldstein, *Console and Classify,* 13–14. However, in its definition of the word "professer," Furetière's *Dictionnaire universel* uses as its example "Ce docteur professe la Médecine, L'exercice, la science qu'un avocat professe, est le Barreau." The word "professer" signifies "s'appliquer à l'étude d'un art, d'une vocation," indicating that medicine and law were accorded special status, as specifically identified with the notion "to profess," or "vocation." Antoine Furetière, *Dictionnaire universel contenant generalement tous les mots françois tant vieux que modern, & des termes des sciences & des arts,* vol. 3 (The Hague: Chez Hasson, Johnson, et al., 1727).

29. Studies by Jonathan Dewald, Bailey Stone, and François Bluche that discuss the professional identity and attachments of the magistrates of the Parlements of France suggest that while these men took their legal tasks and professional commitments very seriously, social status and esteem were of equal importance. Jean-Pierre Labatut, in his study of dukes and peers in seventeenth-century France, asserts that for those who pursued the *profession d'armes,* social esteem and *dignité* were the defining qualities. See Dewald, *The Formation of a Provincial Nobility: The Magistrates of the Parlement of Rouen, 1499–1610* (Princeton: Princeton University Press, 1980), 16–68; Stone, *The French Parlements and the Crisis of the Old Regime* (Chapel Hill: University of North Carolina Press, 1986); Bluche, *Les Magistrats du Parlement de Paris au XVIIIe siècle (1715–1771)* (Paris: Les Belles Lettres, 1960); Labatut, *Les Ducs et pairs de France,* 33–37.

30. L. W. B. Brockliss, *French Higher Education in the Seventeenth and Eighteenth Centuries: A Cultural History* (Oxford: Oxford University Press, 1987), 5–7. See also Colin Jones, "Bourgeois Revolution Revivified: 1789 and Social Change," in Colin Lucas, ed., *Rewriting the French Revolution* (Oxford: Clarendon Press, 1991), 95.

31. For sociological works that outline the rise and nature of professionalism in the Anglo-American context, see Eliot Freidson, *Profession of Medicine: A Study of Applied Knowledge* (New York: Dodd, Mead, 1970); and Magali Sarfatti Larson, *The Rise of Professionalism: A Sociological Analysis* (Berkeley and

ization of French surgeons, proposes an alternative theory. He asserts that
the intellectual backgrounds of various professionals in Old Regime France
were remarkably similar, due to their liberal education, and that specialized education was not yet the defining characteristic of the professional.
Rather, "knowledge itself was of secondary importance in defining the
learned professional; social practice, status and privilege, ritual, place of
residence, and even costume were more reliable guides to professional
identity."[32] This argument has a certain validity for an age that prized the
amateur scientist, the amateur historian, and the amateur poet enshrined
by the academies.

At the same time, technical knowledge, along with what might be
termed a "public service ethic," became more highly valued, at least by the
second half of the eighteenth century, as professionals began to eclipse
knowledgeable amateurs in scientific and scholarly writings.[33] Colin Jones
suggests that the professions of the "traditional elite" of France underwent
considerable institutional and intellectual ferment in the eighteenth century, resulting in a development of new "self-esteem, self-definition, and
commitment" on the part of professionals. He argues that the eighteenth
century witnessed a plethora of ongoing debates concerning the nature of
professionalism, in which arguments for professionalization fall into two
broad frameworks: one that he terms corporative, stressing expertise,
internal discipline, and segregation from the wider society; while the other
expressed more civic values of service to the public, to a professional ethic
of the law and natural justice.[34] In their own professional identities, the
Lamothes invoked both these models. Their experience suggests that the

---

Los Angeles: University of California Press, 1977). Howard M. Vollmer and Donald L. Mills, eds,
Professionalization (Englewood Cliffs, N.J.: Prentice Hall, 1966) comprises a series of essays on different
aspects of the professions and professionalization.

32. Toby Gelfand, *Professionalizing Modern Medicine: Paris Surgeons and Medical Science and Institutions in
the Eighteenth Century* (Westport, Conn.: Greenwood Press, 1980), 191.

33. Robert Darnton makes this argument concerning the increasing importance of professional
expertise in his analysis of the professional composition of the contributors to Panckoucke's *Encyclopédie
méthodique*, a group he refers to as the "second generation of Encyclopedists." Doctors, lawyers,
professors, and "savants" replaced the amateurs and generalists who had worked with Diderot and
d'Alembert. Darnton argues that this predominance of specialists shows how far professionalization
had advanced in the second half of the eighteenth century. See *The Business of Enlightenment: A Publishing
History of the Encyclopédie, 1775–1800* (Cambridge: Harvard University Press, Belknap Press, 1979),
437–46.

34. Jones, "Bourgeois Revolution Revivified," 96–103. Goldstein discusses various models of
professionalization in the eighteenth century and also includes a "corporate" model, along with what
she terms a "statist" model and a "laissez-faire" model, in *Console and Classify*, 15–35.

PART I

Identity Through Family and Friends

The circle of friends and kin provided both companionship and practical support to the members of the Lamothe family, buttressing their public position and assisting in both professional and social pursuits. Important as this wider circle was, however, the immediate family, including Daniel Lamothe and Marie de Sérézac, and their children, had first claim on both the affection and the material help of each member of the family. Bound together both emotionally and economically, the Lamothes supported and sustained each other, and the family unit provided firm foundation for the identity of each individual member. This is the subject of the first three chapters.

"En Famille"

The Private Life of the Lamothes

The roots of the Lamothe family can be traced to the region of Sainte-Foy-la-Grande, a town in southwest France about seventy kilometers east of Bordeaux on the Dordogne River. In the early 1630s, Pierre Sanfourche married Judith Guignard, a native of Pineuilh, by whom he had three children, Jean, Anne, and Pierre. Jean Sanfourche, Sieur de Guignard, born around 1635, married Louise Avoyer, a native of Livry, near Meaux. Jean Sanfourche served as *substitut du procureur du roi* and secretary of M. Lecocq, a *conseiller* at the Parlement of Paris, and he owned the property of Goulards in Saint-Avit-du-Moiron, bordering on Sainte-Foy. The only known child of their union was Daniel Sanfourche, Sieur de Lamothe, born around 1683.[1] According to Bordelais genealogist Pierre Meller, Daniel abandoned the name Sanfourche and took that of Lamothe, the "name of a piece of land that had been left to him . . . by a relative, on the condition that he use the name [Lamothe] and take up the family coat of arms."[2]

Sainte-Foy-la-Grande was constructed as a *bastide*, a fortified town, in

---

1. A genealogy of the Lamothe family can be found in Pierre Meller, *Essais généalogiques: Familles du bordelais/recueil factice de brochures concernant des familles* (Bordeaux: Feret et Fils, 1897), 165–72 (brochure numbered 25–32. I will use the brochure numbering in my citations). I thank Claude Bayle, who shared additional genealogical work on the Lamothe family.

2. Ibid., 25. For a description of the family arms, see Pierre Meller, *Armorial du bordelais: Sénéchaussées de Bordeaux, Bazas et Libourne* (Marseilles: Laffitte Reprints, 1978), 2:287. Albert Dujarric-Descombes

1255 under Alphonse of Poitiers. A wine-producing region, it is best known for its Protestant heritage since about 1541. Until 1622, Sainte-Foy referred to itself proudly as "little Geneva" or "Geneva of the Southwest." Even after the "reconquest" by Louis XIII in May 1622 and the forced mass conversion of Protestants in 1685, Sainte-Foy remained heavily Protestant, and the Huguenots continued to hold assemblies "in the desert" throughout the eighteenth century.[3]

Although he retained the family property in Saint-Avit-du-Moiron, Daniel Lamothe chose to advance his career by moving to Bordeaux, a city rapidly growing in size and importance in the eighteenth century. A port city with commercial ties to the West Indies, it was the hub of the most important wine-producing region in France.[4] But Bordeaux was also the judicial center of the Gironde, and Daniel became an *avocat au parlement* there in 1705.[5] In 1724, at nearly forty-one years of age, Daniel married Marie de Sérézac, a young woman from the town of Castillon-sur-Dordogne. Marie was the daughter of Jean de Sérézac, Sieur de Grande Place, a former officer in the regiment of the Poitou infantry and mayor of Castillon, and his wife, Marie Meynard.[6] The two were married in the parish of Belvès, near Castillon, and just west of Sainte-Foy. Marie de Sérézac's maternal grandmother, Delphine Filhol, was a member of a noble Agenais family that had lived in Sainte-Foy since the sixteenth century. Possibly she helped to arrange the marriage of her granddaughter.[7]

supplies a sketch of the Lamothe coat of arms as it appeared in their books in *Deux Ex-libris bordelais: Les Frères de Lamothe et L'abbé Desbiey* (Paris: H. Daragon, 1918), 11.

3. For the history of Sainte-Foy-la-Grande, see Jean Corriger, *Au fil des eaux . . . Au fil des siècles: Mon village du grand coeur, Sainte-Foy-la-Grande. 700 ans de souvenirs* (n.p.: Group Girondin des Études Locales, 1974). I would like to thank Mlle. M.-M. Guesnon, archivist at the Archives municipales of Sainte-Foy, and M. Jean Valette, former *conservateur* of the Archives départementales de la Gironde, for introducing me to the history of Sainte-Foy.

4. The most thorough treatment of eighteenth-century Bordeaux is François-Georges Pariset, ed., *Bordeaux au XVIIIe siècle* (Bordeaux: Fédération historique du Sud-Ouest, 1968). Also useful are Paul Butel and Jean-Pierre Poussou, *La Vie quotidienne à Bordeaux au XVIIIe siècle* (Paris: Hachette, 1980); and Jean-Pierre Poussou, *Bordeaux et le Sud-Ouest au XVIIIe siècle: Croissance économique et attraction urbaine* (Paris: Touzot, 1983).

5. William Doyle's *The Parlement of Bordeaux and the End of the Old Regime, 1771–1790* (New York: St. Martin's Press, 1974) is the best account of Bordeaux's importance as a judicial center.

6. For a history of the town of Castillon, see Fernand Guignard, *Histoire de Castillon sur Dordogne (l'une des filleules de Bordeaux) et de la région castillonnaise* (Paris: Maison Française d'Editions, 1912). M. Sérézac was *maire* of Castillon in 1702, and both the Sérézac and Meynard families had the *droit de banc* at the parish church of Belvès. See 285 and 354.

7. The marriage contract of Daniel Sanfourche de Lamothe and Marie de Sérézac was signed in the home of Delphine Filhol, and she provided Marie with a portion of her dowry. Archives

Daniel Lamothe and Marie de Sérézac were parents to a large family. Marie gave birth at least ten times between 1725 and 1740, but three of the children died at a young age. The eldest, Simon-Antoine-Delphin, was born in 1725. He was followed in quick succession by Marie, Alexis, Marguerite-Rose (who died at the age of six in 1736), Jules-Bertrand, another Marie (who also died young), Julien (who died in 1739 at the age of five), Simon-Victor, Marie-Anne (Marianne), and Alexis-Alexandre.[8] With seven children surviving to adulthood, this was a very large family by all demographic indications.[9]

Three of the children—Delphin, Alexis, and Alexandre—followed in Daniel's footsteps and studied law. The two eldest sons became barristers at the Parlement of Bordeaux, like their father. The youngest joined the Conseil du roi in Paris. Jules entered the priesthood, while Victor became a doctor in medicine. Thus, the Lamothes were members of a small and prestigious group in eighteenth-century France. They were a family of liberal professionals, a social group that played a key role in the cultural life of provincial urban France.[10]

The Lamothes were a loving and tightly knit family. They placed strong emphasis on personal values, including family ties, religious devotion, self-restraint, and domestic comfort, and highly valued their stable and family-centered existence. In their private correspondence, they stressed and encouraged these conservative values.

A deep-rootedness in the family was an essential part of the identity of each member of the Lamothe family. Sometimes, the very traditional attitudes of the family members seem at odds with Delphin, Alexis, and Victor's voracious consumption of Enlightenment literature and thought, indicating that conservatism in personal life and religious orthodoxy did

départementales de la Gironde, Bordeaux (hereafter abbreviated as ADG) 3E 19493, #233, Articles de marriage, Daniel Sanfourche de Lamothe and Marie de Sérézac, 16 December 1723.

8. Pierre Meller's research indicates that Marie Lamothe, *l'aînée*, died in 1769 at the age of forty-two and that Marianne died in 1768 at thirty. However, the Archives municipales de Sainte-Foy, GG 26, 257, Register of Saint-Avit-du Moiron, record the birth of Marie de Lamothe, baptized on 27 September 1733, who appears to be another daughter who died in infancy, although no record of her death appears to exist.

9. See Jacques Dupâquier, *Pour la démographie historique* (Paris: Presses Universitaires de France, 1984), 73–74; and Michael Flinn, *The European Demographic System, 1500–1820* (Baltimore: Johns Hopkins University Press, 1981), 33.

10. On the cultural importance of the educated liberal professionals in urban ancien régime France, see L. W. B. Brockliss, *French Higher Education in the Seventeenth and Eighteenth Centuries: A Cultural History* (Oxford: Oxford University Press, 1987), 1–9.

not exclude interest in the "new ideas" of the eighteenth century. The conduct of their personal life lends insight to the family's values, attitudes, and priorities, values that they surely shared with other members of their social group.

The material life and the patterns of consumption within the Lamothe family also allow us to penetrate the lifestyle of the provincial professional of the eighteenth century. The constant admonition to "watch your purse" and *économiser* offered by Daniel and his daughters warred with any aspirations on the part of the sons to maintain a more brilliant lifestyle. Still, their tastes and consumption priorities betray a determination to lead a comfortable and sometimes elegant life, although certainly not on par with the wealthy *parlementaires* and *négociants* of Bordeaux. Both the material comforts and family attitudes of the Lamothe household reflect those of other professional families living in provincial urban centers attempting to strike a balance between limited resources and fitting signs of status.

1. Family Ties

When Daniel Lamothe died in 1763, his daughter Marianne wrote sadly to her brothers in Paris, "I call to mind . . . our dear father who so often told us to love each other, and the comparison that I make between him and our divine master seems very just to me."[11] This passage eloquently portrays the deep love that the Lamothe children felt for their father, who ruled the household as a somewhat autocratic but always loving and benevolent patriarch.

The patterns of affection and authority within the Lamothe household both challenge and confirm our notions about relations within eighteenth-century families. Historians point to a strengthening of paternal authority between the thirteenth and eighteenth centuries. According to early modern jurists such as Jean Bodin, this patriarchal family was part of the "natural order," ordained by God.[12] In French regions of Roman law, such as the Bordelais, the power of the household head was further enhanced.

---

11. Lamothe Family Letters, Marianne to Victor, 7 May 1763.

12. For Jean Bodin's views on the family and state, see Nannerl O. Keohane, *Philosophy and the State in France: The Renaissance to the Enlightenment* (Princeton: Princeton University Press, 1980), 69–70.

The rights of both wives and children were strictly subordinated to those of the husband and father.[13]

However, in the early eighteenth century, a shift took place in this traditional image of the family. Philippe Ariès argues that a new concept of the family emerged in the seventeenth century in which the child held a central role. The new family was less hierarchical, less formal, indeed, a "modern family."[14] Other historians have confirmed certain aspects of his assessment, while still emphasizing the patriarchal character of family life. In this new family model, the duties of the parents toward their children were emphasized as well as the obligations of the children toward their parents. Still, love rather than duty was the glue binding the new family together.[15]

How well did the patterns of authority within the Lamothe family fit the image of the new domesticated family? Clearly, mutual love and respect were the foundations of family relations within the household. Although Daniel often appeared strict in his letters, he and his wife were affectionate, even doting, parents. Marianne wrote to Victor, "I know the goodness of their hearts, and how much they want to make their children happy, at least to the degree that prudence and economy permit them to."[16] Marie noted the great pleasure her parents took in showing Victor small signs of affection, such as the *poule dinde* and other little treats that they sent to him in Paris each year.[17]

At the same time, Daniel Lamothe and Marie de Sérézac inspired adoration in their children, who considered *ce cher père* and *cette chère maman*

13. Jean-Louis Flandrin, *Families in Former Times: Kinship, Household, and Sexuality in Early Modern France,* trans. Richard Southern (Cambridge: Cambridge University Press, 1979), 112–40. See also Lawrence Stone, *The Family, Sex, and Marriage in England, 1500–1800* (New York: Weidenfeld & Nicolson, 1977) for his discussion of family models in the English context.

14. Philippe Ariès, *Centuries of Childhood: A Social History of Family Life,* trans. Robert Baldick (New York: Vintage, 1962).

15. See, for example, Stone, *The Family, Sex, and Marriage;* Flandrin, *Families in Former Times,* 135–40; Randolph Trumbach, *The Rise of the Egalitarian Family: Aristocratic Kinship and Domestic Relations in Eighteenth-Century England* (New York: Academic Press, 1978); James Traer, *Marriage and the Family in Eighteenth-Century France* (Ithaca: Cornell University Press, 1980). Hans Medick and David Warren Sabean nuance this rather "Whiggish" view of the history of the family by emphasizing the interplay of both interest and emotion in family interactions. See the introduction and chap. 1 in Medick and Sabean, eds., *Interest and Emotion: Essays on the Study of Family and Kinship* (Cambridge: Cambridge University Press, 1984), 1–27.

16. Marianne to Victor, 20 April 1757. See also Marie to Victor, 14 April 1760; 4 July 1761; and Marianne to Victor, 21 April 1760; 19 October 1760.

17. Marie to Victor, 21 January 1758.

worthy of the utmost reverence. Marianne stressed that they must show "respect, affection, and the most exacting submission vis-à-vis such parents."[18] Marie and Marianne considered their mother an admirable role model, and Marie assured Victor that "she's a fine mother who well deserves our respect and our love."[19] Victor planned to dedicate his master's thesis to his father as "an authentic proof of my affection."[20]

This attachment extended to concern for the health of their parents.[21] As their parents grew older, the Lamothe children sometimes tried to protect them by withholding upsetting information, or by reading only portions of Victor's letters if the news contained might be disturbing.[22] They were also determined that Daniel should continue to enjoy the same comforts in his old age that he had in his younger years, despite the financial problems that the family experienced in the early 1760s.[23] This protective attitude seems at odds with the image of Daniel as the stern family patriarch, but his children found it possible to accept simultaneously their father's position of authority and his increasing vulnerability.

Daniel and his wife had high expectations of their children, and demanded both moral behavior and professional expertise. In one of her rare, painstakingly composed letters to Victor, Marie de Sérézac beseeched her son to "always behave *en honete* [sic] *homme*" and warned him to avoid the *écueils* (shoals) of the big city.[24] Daniel urged Victor to demonstrate virtue and probity, and to continue his religious practices.[25] Maître and Madame Lamothe were proud of their children, and took delight in their activities. Marie wrote Victor that "your letters are always read and reread with great pleasure. Our dear father never stops talking about you, I believe that we will soon be jealous that he loves you so much."[26]

At the same time, Daniel and Marie de Sérézac took very seriously the obligation of parents to educate their children and to place each male

18. Marianne to Victor, 24 January 1757.

19. Marie to Victor, 20 October 1757; 18 August 1764.

20. Victor to Delphin, undated 1760.

21. See, for example, Marie to Victor, 20 October 1757; 26 May 1760; 25 November 1761; 6 December 1764; Marianne to Victor, 21 April 1760; 7 August 1762; 27 October 1763.

22. Marie to Victor, 27 November 1760; Jules to Victor, 7 June 1761; Marianne to Victor, 7 August 1762; Delphin to Victor, 9 December 1762; Alexis to Victor, 21 August 1762 and 1 January 1763.

23. Alexis to Victor, 10 October 1762.

24. Marie de Sérézac to Victor, 1 March 1757.

25. Daniel to Victor, 3 February 1759.

26. Marie to Victor, 20 October 1757; see also Marianne to Victor, 24 January 1757.

child in a suitable profession.[27] They provided the two eldest sons with a legal education and paid for Jules's clerical title. More dramatically, they marshaled the family's resources and made important sacrifices to finance Victor's medical education in Paris and Montpellier and to allow Alexandre to work as a lawyer in Paris. Daniel's assistance in his children's education went beyond the financial. He helped his sons with their legal studies and assisted Alexandre in choosing the most suitable law books for his courses.[28] And he urged his sons to profit from every spare moment to improve themselves.[29]

The children were expected to show their gratitude for their parent's contributions both in words and by working hard and advancing in their chosen fields. Marie exhorted Victor, "Try . . . to use your time so that you can profit from the expenditure that my father is making for you," and he was frequently reminded to thank his father for various "little favors" (*douceurs*).[30]

Despite his love for his children and his increasing age, Daniel was the head of the household, the *paterfamilias*, entitled to respect and deference. According to Alexis, "It would not be fitting that he [Daniel] inconvenience himself for his children, who owe him everything."[31] The children were to obey him without question and to acknowledge the wisdom of his counsel. Marie wrote to Victor, "Always accept his advice submissively, you know that it is wise."[32]

Daniel could be a demanding father, and his letters to Victor were sometimes scolding and often critical. He had a quick temper, and on more than one occasion, Marie reassured Victor, "Don't think that he is angry with you, no, I assure you, it is just one of those outbursts of temper that you know he has."[33] After a particularly harsh letter, a sibling was always ready to remind Victor that "it was dictated by his heart," and that the

---

27. Several historians point out the new emphasis on the duty of parents to provide a professional education and a suitable *état* for their children in the eighteenth century. Ariès, *Centuries of Childhood*, 402–4; Flandrin, *Families in Former Times*, 138–40.

28. Alexandre to Victor, 20 April 1757; Delphin to Victor, 18 October 1760.

29. See, for example, Daniel to Victor, 22 November 1757. Margaret R. Hunt notes that the English "middling sort" also emphasized the importance of time discipline in *The Middling Sort: Commerce, Gender, and the Family in England, 1680–1780* (Berkeley and Los Angeles: University of California Press, 1996), 53–56.

30. Marie to Victor, 1 December 1756; Delphin to Victor, 17 December 1757.

31. Alexis to Victor, 10 October 1762.

32. Marie to Victor, 1 December 1756.

33. Marie to Victor, 25 November 1761.

letter was only meant for Victor's benefit.[34] Marie sometimes tried to persuade Victor not to take his father's reproaches too seriously.[35] On other occasions, she tried to make peace between Victor and Daniel when Victor inadvertently offended his father, advising him to "write him a submissive letter filled with affection, and make your apologies to him."[36]

Still, Daniel did not want his children to see him as a tyrant who must always be appeased. After Victor responded humbly to a stern letter, Marie wrote to Victor on Daniel's behalf:

> I have been instructed to tell you something, he [Daniel] was very touched by all the indications of submission that you gave him, but at the same time mortified that the things that he wrote had such an effect on you. He has no poor opinion of you, he always thinks of you as a son whom he loves and cherishes most tenderly. If he wrote to you in a different manner, it was more so that the letter would serve as advice and precepts rather than reproaches . . . it was dictated only by a heart that loves you tenderly and affectionately, more than you can imagine.[37]

Daniel himself tried to disabuse Victor of the notion that he was a taskmaster who must be cajoled into granting his son's wishes: "The beginning of your last letter from the 17th of this month gave us much pleasure, but I could not keep myself from being a bit suspicious; the praise in your sister's letter, was it not to put me into good humor so that I would more willingly grant you the things that you asked for in your letter? However, I will ignore your strategy, which you really do not need, since as long as you make good use of your time and the money that we send you, we pay the cost with pleasure."[38] Despite Daniel's unchallenged position as head of the household, the acknowledged basis of the Lamothe family was affection, and not authority.

The most poignant attestation to the strong emotions that the Lamothe children felt for their father was the letter written by Delphin to Alexandre's landlord in Paris, Me. Marais, upon Daniel's death. In a hand shaky with emotion, Delphin penned: "Render us, I beseech you, the favor of a

34. See, for example, Daniel and Alexis to Victor, 3 February 1759.
35. Marie to Victor, 27 November 1762.
36. Marie to Victor, 25 November 1761.
37. Marie to Victor, 17 February 1759.
38. Daniel to Victor, 31 July 1760.

friend: announce to my brothers some overwhelming news, the death of our father, following an attack of indigestion which we regarded as nothing important . . . he died in my arms this afternoon at four-thirty: they can imagine the condition of our mother and the rest of us by their own."[39] After his death, Daniel's children continued to refer often to "our father . . . whose memory is so precious to us" and to exhort each other to offer frequent prayers for his soul.[40]

Still, the familial bonds of the Lamothes were perhaps more complex than the regular assurances of love and trust would indicate. The large difference in age between the parents and children, as well as between the children themselves, was a factor in their relations. Daniel was nearly sixty years old and his wife forty-one when their youngest son, Alexandre, was born, and fifteen years separated the oldest son, Delphin, from the youngest. The three youngest children—Marianne, Victor, and Alexandre— were close. Alexandre wrote letters to Victor filled with protestations of affection, and Marianne referred to Victor and herself as "childhood companions" who had shared almond *gâteaux*.[41] The eldest children of the family—Delphin, Alexis, and Marie—affected a parental attitude with their younger siblings, offering frequent advice and counsel.

Marie, the oldest daughter, showed strong maternal feelings for her two youngest brothers: "I think of you and Alexandre as my two children, I love you with the love of a mother . . . my title of godmother along with my sentiments gives me, I think, much leeway."[42] She urged Victor to confide in her and delighted in his letters.[43] Alexis and Delphin were full of advice for their younger siblings as well. This created rather unequal relations between the children, especially when the death of Daniel left Alexis and Delphin in charge of the family finances and, consequently, in control of Victor and Alexandre's future careers. Both Delphin and Alexis sometimes took on the harsh tone of their father when writing to their brothers, but the two younger boys submitted to the reprimands of their elder siblings. And Delphin and Alexis were always quick to assure them

39. Delphin to Me. Marais, 7 March 1763.

40. Marianne to Victor, 7 May 1763; Jules to Victor and Alexandre, undated 1763; Marie to Victor, May 1763.

41. For example, Alexandre to Victor, 17 January 1757; Marie to Victor, 19 October 1760.

42. Marie to Victor, 27 November 1760. See also 14 April 1760; 7 September 1762; 11 January 1763; and 22 July 1766.

43. Marie to Victor, 8 May 1759.

that they spoke only as affectionate brothers, who "want very much for you to advance and perfect yourself."[44]

Although their letters stressed the strong bonds of sentiment, tensions sometimes arose among the seven Lamothe siblings. On occasion, Marie or Marianne scolded Victor for not writing more often, or when his letters seemed too impersonal.[45] Victor resisted his family's orders to return to Bordeaux, as he so clearly wished to remain in Paris.[46] Strains also arose between Victor and the *prêtre* Jules. The two wrote frequent and loving letters when Victor first left for Paris, but their correspondence tapered off. Victor sometimes resented Jules's reprimands for certain vulgar expressions in his letters, and expressed frustration with Jules's *trop grande exactitude*.[47] At one point, Victor did not write to Jules for two years.[48] Jules believed that it was because Victor feared having to account for his moral conduct in Paris, which Victor denied.[49] It does appear, however, that Victor's religious fervor had lessened during his years in Paris. Jules may have sensed this, creating stress in their relationship; but this situation, like other potential conflicts, was glossed over.

Areas of contestation were contained beneath declarations of affection and devotion as the siblings constantly reiterated their mutual affection. Alexis thanked Victor for one letter, noting, "It was full of sentiments so tender, so beautiful, so touching, so natural, that one would have to be insensitive to tender feelings . . . not to have been extremely moved by it."[50] Shortly after Victor's departure for Paris, Alexandre wrote to him, "It is wonderful to be loved by you, & especially to be linked by ties of blood."[51]

They requested counsel from each other.[52] Victor, asking for advice on his choice of career, was thrilled with Alexis's reply, "so full of good advice," and "such deep affection."[53] They demonstrated great admiration for each other's skills. The sisters asked for medical advice from Victor on many occasions and praised his expertise. They also respected their elder

44. Alexis to Victor, 9 March 1759.
45. Marie to Victor, 22 August 1758; 17 February 1759; 8 May 1759.
46. Marie to Victor, 13 June 1766; Alexis to Victor, undated 1766.
47. Jules to Victor, 24 October 1761; 6 February 1762.
48. Marie to Victor, 18 August 1764; Victor to Jules, 25 August 1764.
49. Marie to Victor, 18 August 1764; Victor to Jules, 25 August 1764.
50. Alexis to Victor, 27 October 1763.
51. Alexandre to Victor, 17 January 1757.
52. See, for example, Victor to Delphin, undated 1760.
53. Victor to Alexis, 1–5 October 1755; 25 October 1755; Alexis to Victor, 14 October 1755.

brothers' legal proficiency,[54] as well as Delphin's mechanical cleverness.[55]

The family letters testify to the intensity of the brother-brother and sister-sister bonds. As the only two sisters, Marie and Marianne were especially close, with Marie referring to Marianne affectionately as *la petite Marianette*.[56] When Marie spent time in the country due to a severe illness, Marianne wrote to Victor, "Our relationship is so strong that a separation is cause for distress, and our reunion the remedy."[57] Delphin and Alexis, the two eldest, were very attached, and worked well together.[58] When his first child, a son, was born, Delphin turned to his brother for support, expressing the hope that "if the Lord takes away his natural guide, may he find in you a second father, and his mother a second husband."[59] In his last will and testament, Alexis responded with an equally emotional tribute to his brother. Alexis, and Victor as well, lived up to Delphin's confidence, treating their nephews as their own children when their father died in 1781.[60]

It is even possible that the consuming and passionate devotion of the brothers and sisters to their parents and to each other satisfied their emotional needs and attenuated the need or desire for a wife or husband.[61] Their strong family bonds gave the Lamothe family an important foundation in life. Their identities were as firmly grounded in family as in a sense of individuality.

2. Marital Relations

Little direct evidence of the nature of the relationship between Daniel Lamothe and Marie de Sérézac exists, but it seems that they enjoyed an

---

54. Marianne to Victor, 24 January 1757.

55. Marianne to Victor, 2 December 1758.

56. Marie to Victor, 29 April 1766.

57. Marianne to Victor, 17 October 1764.

58. Marie to Victor, 6 December 1764. Much of their legal work, including their book on the *coutume* of Bordeaux, was done together. See Chapter 4 below.

59. Delphin to Alexis, 24 October 1773.

60. ADG 3E 21732, Testament, Alexis de Lamothe, opened 25 March 1790. See also Jules Delpit, *Notes biographiques sur les Messieurs de Lamothe* (Bordeaux: Balarac Jeune, 1846), 23.

61. I develop this theme more fully in "Devoted Companions or Surrogate Spouses? Sibling Relations in Eighteenth-Century France," in Christine Adams, Jack R. Censer, and Lisa Jane Graham, eds., *Visions and Revisions of Eighteenth-Century France* (University Park: Penn State Press, 1997), 59–76.

28

affectionate and mutually respectful marriage. In his letters to Victor, Daniel occasionally conveyed messages from the two of them or mentioned decisions that he and his wife had reached concerning Victor's stay in Paris, suggesting that they discussed the welfare of their children and reached mutual decisions regarding them—although Daniel had the final word.[62] Marie de Sérézac's deep grief at the time of her husband's death is further proof of their tender alliance.

Strangely enough, only one child of this large family married—Delphin, in 1772, at the age of forty-seven.[63] None of the Lamothe brothers chose to wed during the lifetimes of their sisters. Delphin did not marry until three years after the death of Marie and four years after the death of Marianne. This situation elevated the status of Marie and Marianne within the household, allowing them to act as surrogate wives to their unmarried brothers and to manage the household along with their mother.[64] On one occasion, Marie remarked that she had been at Muscadet, one of the family's country homes, "in the company of my *fidel époux* [faithful spouse]," referring to Delphin, and underlining the quasi-marital nature of her relationship with her brother.[65]

The example of his parents and his close relationship with his sisters became the model for Delphin's marriage to Marie-Elisabeth de Brulz in 1772. The marriage was socially advantageous—Elisabeth was the daughter of the *écuyer* François-Marie de Brulz and niece and goddaughter of André-Pierre de Brulz, seigneur of the *maison* of Lyde and *doyen* of the *conseillers* of the Cour des aides in Bordeaux. Elisabeth brought as her dowry the noble property of Lyde, along with the sum of 6,000 livres.[66] Elisabeth was also related by marriage to the family of Joseph de Bacalan, *président* of the Parlement of Bordeaux and professor of French law at the University of

62. Daniel to Victor, 3 February 1759; 16 March 1762. See also Delphin to Victor, 31 March 1759; 13 June 1761.

63. Barristers tended to marry late. In Toulouse, they married an average of 9.4 years after beginning professional practice, and were generally in their mid-thirties when the marriage contract was signed. Lenard R. Berlanstein, *The Barristers of Toulouse in the Eighteenth Century (1740–1793)* (Baltimore: Johns Hopkins University Press, 1975), 42–43.

64. Leonore Davidoff and Catherine Hall analyze the intense relationships of brothers and sisters in nineteenth-century England, noting that sisters frequently filled in as substitute spouses to unmarried brothers. See *Family Fortunes: Men and Women of the English Middle Class, 1780–1850* (Chicago: University of Chicago Press, 1987), 348–51.

65. Marie to Victor, 11 January 1763. See Adams, "Devoted Companions or Surrogate Spouses?"

66. ADG 3E 21696, Contrat de mariage, Delphin de Lamothe and Marie-Elisabeth de Brulz, 21 June 1772.

Bordeaux.[67] In sum, the Brulz were on the margins of the *robe noblesse*. Certainly, the marriage enhanced Delphin's status in Bordeaux.

Although Elisabeth's suitability played a role in Delphin's desire to contract their marriage, it is unlikely that economic and social factors were the sole considerations. With his father dead, and as de facto household head, Delphin was able to freely choose his wife.[68] Elisabeth de Brulz was twenty years younger than her husband, but she was older than the average woman of her social class at the time of a first marriage.[69] The legal background of her family allowed her to share Delphin's professional interests, and her maturity meant that she could be a loving companion to her husband.

Elisabeth moved into the Lamothe family home on Rue Neuve following her marriage, and established a close relationship with her brothers-in-law as well. She quickly became pregnant, an event that elicited tender and sometimes amused commentary from her husband. He wrote proudly to Alexis, "My wife is still nimble and sprightly, although very close to term."[70] As the months of Elisabeth's pregnancy stretched on, Delphin commented: "Births are very late this year, my dear brother; it is all the rage, & my wife likes to be in style too much not to conform, as a result, she has not yet delivered her baby, but she is doing very well, and still takes Delphin or Delphine for walks as often as she can."[71] Elisabeth grew increasingly impatient with the length of her pregnancy, and Delphin wrote to his brother: "My wife came into my office, my dear brother, just as I started this letter to you. She has told me to tell you that you can forget about having a nephew or niece this year, it is not going to happen. She's losing patience, even though she knows that sooner or later, it is going to happen."[72] When his son arrived nine days later, Delphin reported with joy, "At last, at last, my dear brother, I am a father, ergo, you are an uncle."[73] He and his wife's great attachment was evident in her distress at

---

67. Maurice Campagne, *Histoire des Bacalan du XVe au XXe siècle* (Bergerac: Imprimerie Générale du Sud-Ouest, 1905), 199.

68. According to Berlanstein, "The maturity of the barrister at marriage assured him a definite voice in the selection of his wife." See *The Barristers of Toulouse*, 43.

69. Archives municipales de Bordeaux (hereafter abbreviated as AM) GG 96, Baptismal Record, Marie-Elisabeth de Brulz. She was born on 13 July 1744.

70. Delphin to Alexis, 14 September 1773.

71. Delphin to Alexis, 30 September 1773.

72. Delphin to Alexis, 3 October 1773.

73. Delphin to Alexis, 12 October 1773.

his rapid departure to attend to the grape harvest the day following her delivery, and his desire to be with her again as soon as possible.[74]

The letters that Delphin wrote to his wife in 1780, when they were briefly separated during the wine harvest, were equally tender. Delphin was recovering from a bout of ill health, and assured Elisabeth frequently that he was taking good care of himself: "Farewell, my tender friend, I embrace you with all my heart, take care of yourself, set your mind at ease, I am taking care of myself, & I hope to see you again soon, *gros & gras*."[75] He waited hungrily for her letters: "I received that last letter that you wrote to me with the greatest of pleasure, my dear *maman*, as you gave me new proof of your affection."[76] Delphin made clear his impatience to be with his wife again: "Farewell, dear friend, I am longing to tell you how much I love you."[77] During this separation of perhaps three weeks, Elisabeth de Brulz received at least six letters from her spouse.

Delphin's affection for his wife extended to their four children. He took great interest in the activities of his newborn son: "He's nursing very well, cries & sleeps equally well, there you have his three primary functions . . . *hélas*, the tiny creature!"[78] He wrote to Elisabeth of the antics of their children at Goulards, noting proudly that "Lamothe rides his horse like a little cavalier," and that all the neighbors were pleased with the children; "the ladies are mad about them."[79] Delphin found great joy in his family life during his nine short years with Elisabeth de Brulz.

It seems curious that with these two examples of a happy married life before them, the younger Lamothe brothers chose to remain single, reinforcing the possibility that the family members found sufficient contentment within the confines of the immediate family. On the other hand, perhaps Daniel Lamothe and his wife were afraid that to marry seven children would dissipate the family fortune, and they pressed their children to postpone marriage or to forego it entirely.[80] As young men, the

---

74. Victor and Delphin to Alexis, 24 October 1773.
75. Delphin to Elisabeth de Brulz, 1 November 1780.
76. Delphin to Elisabeth de Brulz, 8 November 1780.
77. Delphin to Elisabeth de Brulz, 11 November 1780.
78. Delphin to Alexis, 24 October 1780.
79. Delphin to Elisabeth de Brulz, 11 and 16 November 1780.
80. Well-to-do families often pressured their younger children to remain unmarried in order to prevent excessive division of the family fortune. Margaret H. Darrow, *Revolution in the House: Family, Class, and Inheritance in Southern France, 1775–1825* (Princeton: Princeton University Press, 1989), 109–11; Robert Forster, *The Nobility of Toulouse in the Eighteenth Century: A Social and Economic Study* (Baltimore: Johns Hopkins University Press, 1960), 125–29. The same was true among noble Venetian families, where

Lamothe brothers were explicitly discouraged from marrying. When Victor was approached by his relations in Paris concerning a potential match, Alexis counseled him "to refuse as politely as you can the propositions that they are making, saying that you are too young, and that your parents do not want to hear any discussion of marriage for you for a very long time yet."[81] Alexis later confirmed that the Lamothe sons were discouraged from marrying: "I did . . . not marry: circumstances opposed the possibility in my youth."[82] Thus, except for Delphin, the Lamothe children experienced family life only with their parents and siblings.

3. Conservative Values

Emphasis on a secure and stable familial existence lent balance and calm to the lives of the Lamothe family. However, their private letters reveal other preoccupations as well. The themes of religion, economy, health, and moderation emerge again and again in their correspondence. Their letters reflect a genuine concern with their spiritual lives and personal well-being. Religious beliefs formed the cornerstone in the lives of the Lamothes and permeated every aspect of their days. Their attention to health, and efforts to maintain a moderate lifestyle—the *juste milieu*, or golden mean—were also important in conserving both psychological and physical equilibrium.[83]

Despite evidence of a decline in religious practices in the eighteenth century, especially among lawyers and other members of the urban middle classes, the Lamothe family retained a strong emphasis on piety and devotion in their religious lives.[84] Their religious creed was the quiet,

---

primogeniture was almost unknown. James C. Davis, *A Venetian Family and Its Fortune, 1500–1900: The Donà and the Conservation of Their Wealth* (Philadelphia: American Philosophical Society, 1975), 93–112.

81. Alexis to Victor, 22 December 1761.

82. ADG 3E 21732, Testament, Alexis de Lamothe, opened 25 March 1790.

83. See Christine Adams, "Defining *État* in Eighteenth-Century France: The Lamothe Family of Bordeaux," *Journal of Family History* 17 (Winter 1992): 25–45.

84. Michel Vovelle, *Piété baroque et déchristianisation: Les Attitudes devant la mort en Provence au XVIIIe siècle* (Paris: Plon, 1973); Kathryn Norberg, *Rich and Poor in Grenoble, 1600–1814* (Berkeley and Los Angeles: University of California Press, 1985), 247; Elinor Barber, *The Bourgeoisie in Eighteenth Century France* (Princeton: Princeton University Press, 1955).

introspective faith of the post-Tridentine Catholic church, with its emphasis on reflection, the sacraments, and private acts of piety.[85] The religious practices of the Lamothe family shaped their personal identities, both the public acts of attendance at mass and vespers and work at the hospital, as well as the private exercises of prayer, meditation, and religious retreats.[86] Although Marie Andrieu found in her study of religious life in eighteenth-century Bordeaux that "religious practice was usual even among those who could be hostile to the Church," the members of the Lamothe family appear sincerely religious, in both inner commitment and outward *geste*.[87] Delphin and Alexis, who sometimes exhibited the more skeptical beliefs of the philosophes, were not, perhaps, as religious as their extremely pious parents, brothers, and sisters, but they were practicing Catholics and believing Christians all the same.[88]

The Lamothes lived in the parish of Saint-Michel, the largest church in Bordeaux after the cathedral Saint-André.[89] Daniel Lamothe served as *grand ouvrier* for a time, and the family enjoyed the rights to a pew at the church.[90] Most members of the family were buried in the church at Saint-Michel.[91] Marie de Sérézac and her daughters, as well as Alexandre and Victor, frequently assisted the nuns at Saint-Michel with their hospital

85. On the post-Tridentine church in France, see Philip T. Hoffman, *Church and Community in the Diocese of Lyon, 1500–1789* (New Haven: Yale University Press, 1984), esp. 71–97.

86. Davidoff and Hall discuss the importance of religious belief and belonging for members of the British middle classes in the nineteenth century, and how it gave a distinctive identity to particular communities and classes in *Family Fortunes*, 76–77.

87. Marie Andrieu, "Les Paroisses et la vie religieuse à Bordeaux de 1680 à 1789," 2 vols. (Thèse de troisième cycle, Université de Bordeaux, 1973), 545.

88. In his discussion of "bourgeois emancipation" from religious dogma, Bernard Groethuysen argues that "there might be a weakening of faith without contraction of the content of faith, or the area of faith might be contracted without any diminution in the zeal of the believer." *The Bourgeois: Catholicism Versus Capitalism in Eighteenth-Century France*, trans. Mary Ilford (New York: Barrie & Rockliff the Cresset P., 1968), 37–43. Berlanstein also found that the barristers of Toulouse remained quite conventional in their religious practices and considered themselves orthodox Catholics, despite the fact that many had reassessed their views on Christian morality. See *The Barristers of Toulouse*, 116–17. See Chapter 7 below for a discussion of Delphin and Alexis's philosophical beliefs.

89. Andrieu, in "Paroisses et la vie religieuse," 114–16, discusses the church and parish of Saint-Michel.

90. Charles Marionneau, *Description des oeuvres d'art qui décorent les édifices publics de la ville de Bordeaux* (Paris and Bordeaux: A. Aubry and Chaumas-Gayet, 1861–65), 330; ADG G 2333, Registre, Concession de bancs, Fabrique St. Michel, 3 March 1752, folio 17: Concession en faveur de Daniel Lamothe. The *grand ouvrier* was elected for a two-year term, and helped direct the financial affairs of the church. See Andrieu, "Paroisses et la vie religieuse," 222–23.

91. Meller, *Essais généalogiques*. Burial in the parish church was generally a privilege of the elite, those who had served as an official of the church, contributed funds to the building, or founded masses for

work.[92] Delphin served as legal advisor to the clergy at Saint-Michel, as well as for the Grand Séminaire at Saint-Seurin.[93]

Like many provincial French "notable" families, the Lamothes contributed a son to the priesthood. It was financially advantageous for a middle- or upper-class family to persuade a son to enter the clergy, for the cost of the clerical title was generally less than a son's portion of the family patrimony.[94] However, Jules felt a sincere calling to his vocation and enjoyed the work of a priest.[95]

Jules attended the Séminaire des ordinands, or de la mission, also known as the Grand Séminaire, located in the Bordelais district of Saint-Seurin.[96] He received the title of deacon in early 1758, and was ordained that May.[97] While his family sometimes lamented Jules's lack of personal ambition, his career path subsequently followed that of the typical parish priest.[98] His first position was as vicar at the parish of Saint-Estephe in the Médoc.[99] He later ascended to the post of *archiprêtre* at Saint-Magne upon resignation of the curé there, and received a benefice providing revenues of 3,000–4,000 livres per year.[100] At the same time that he took on his new benefice at Saint-Magne, Jules also received the title of doctor of theol-

themselves and family members. Barbara B. Diefendorf, *Beneath the Cross: Catholics and Huguenots in Sixteenth-Century Paris* (New York: Oxford University Press, 1991), 36.

92. Lamothe Family Letters, passim.

93. Meller, *Essais généalogiques*, 26 and 28; Jules to Victor, 2 August 1757.

94. On the family origins of the clergy, see Timothy Tackett, *Priest and Parish in Eighteenth-Century France: A Social and Political Study of the Curés in the Diocese of Dauphiné, 1750–1791* (Princeton: Princeton University Press, 1977), 54–64; and Olwen Hufton, "The French Church," in William J. Callahan and David Higgs, eds., *Church and Society in Catholic Europe of the Eighteenth Century* (New York: Cambridge University Press, 1979), 22. Forster also found that the church was a common vocation for the cadet sons of the Toulousan nobility in *The Nobility of Toulouse*, 127.

95. Jules to Victor, 5 February 1759; Marie to Victor, 17 March 1758.

96. Letters to Jules were addressed to the Grand Séminaire, St. Seurin. See L. Bertrand, *Histoire des séminaires de Bordeaux et de Bazas*, vol. 1 (Bordeaux: Feret Frères, 1894) on the seminaries of Bordeaux.

97. Victor to Jules, 1 April 1758; Jules to Victor, 27 May 1758.

98. Marianne to Victor and Alexandre, 17 October 1764; Marie to Victor, 12 January 1765. See Tackett, *Priest and Parish*, 96–117, on the typical career path of priests.

99. Jules to Victor, 22 August 1758. "Vicaires" were auxiliary priests who assisted the curé in large parishes. Tackett, *Priest and Parish*, 35.

100. According to Tackett, an *archiprêtre*, or archpriest, was commissioned from the parish priests serving in each *archiprêtré*, or ecclesiastical canton, to serve as director of his colleagues and as the administrative and pastoral link to the bishop. Jules's revenues were substantial, despite the fact that he would owe one-third of the total for the support of the *resignant*. The great majority of priests had a net income of less than 1,000 livres. *Priest and Parish*, 35 and 124.

ogy.[101] He noted with some pride, "I now begin to hold a certain position [*rang*] in the world" but hastened to add that "this would be enough to lead me astray if I were so wretched as to lose sight of the obligations I have toward my God."[102]

Jules's letters reflect a genuinely religious disposition, and a sternly moralistic nature. His admonitions reveal his religious temperament and beliefs, as he advised Victor on how to lead a Christian life: "The best measures you can employ are those that you have always put into practice, that is, to take the sacraments regularly, to be assiduous about your Christian duties, to apply yourself to your studies and to flee bad company."[103] Most of all, he expressed the desire to be a good priest, and to avoid the pitfalls of his profession.[104] He believed that, for a priest, "the essential thing . . . is to experience a true calling [*d'y etre bien appellé*], for it makes pleasant that which would otherwise be intolerable, and one finds a taste for that which is the most tiresome."[105]

The piety of Jules's parents prepared him for the priesthood, and influenced the rest of the children as well.[106] Marie and Marianne in particular were strongly devout, and their letters to Victor were filled with religious exhortations.[107] Victor was urged to conduct himself "as a true Christian," and both of his sisters offered frequent prayers for his soul.

More than anything, Marie, Marianne, and Jules feared the contagion of worldly society, and they urged Victor to hold himself aloof from the corrupt world.[108] As a medical student, Victor was in particular danger, and Marie exhorted Victor, "You know that physicians are often justly accused . . . of not being very religious. I beg you to make a lie of that prejudice."[109] They were especially concerned when Victor moved to Montpellier and was forced to live among the "debauched" medical students. Jules advised, "At this time, you must see yourself as did the

101. Delphin to Victor and Alexandre, 23 April 1765. For a brief summary of Jules's career, see Delpit, *Notes biographiques*, 9.

102. Jules to Victor, 5 May 1765.

103. Jules to Victor, 5 February 1759. See also 9 January 1761.

104. Jules to Victor, 20 April 1757; 28 January 1758; 8 April 1758.

105. Jules to Victor, 8 April 1758.

106. Both Daniel Lamothe's and Marie de Sérézac's letters to Victor were filled with religious admonitions. See, for example, Marie de Sérézac to Victor, 1 March 1757; Daniel to Victor, 3 February 1759.

107. For example, Marie to Victor, 17 January 1757.

108. See Marie to Victor, 3 September 1757.

109. Marie to Victor, 2 April 1757. See also Jules to Victor, 20 April 1757.

Israelites in the land of Babylon," and suggested that Victor avoid students lacking his high moral standards.[110]

While Delphin and Alexis were religious, they embraced more secular values than did the women of the family, or Jules.[111] Alexandre was also very devout, and may have considered the priesthood for a time.[112] However, Victor vacillated between the two extremes. When he first left for Paris in 1756 at the age of twenty, he expressed strongly religious views and fear of the contagion of the less godly people of Paris, and later Montpellier.[113] But it appears that his fervor lessened over the years. In a letter to Jules written after his trip to Marseille, Victor expressed some skepticism about the alleged voyage of Mary Magdalene to Provence and the miraculous efficacy of the relics that he saw there: "One can still see the hair, the earth colored with blood that our Lord saw from the cross, etc., etc., etc., do you believe it then? What do you think of it, what does M. *l'archiprêtre* think of it? Is it really possible that St. Magdalene came by sea, as they say in Provence?"[114] Although Victor assured Jules that his religious sentiments had not changed, more worldly concerns occupied his time as his *séjour* in Paris lengthened.[115]

Religion extended to frequent contact with members of the clergy and the female religious orders. The Lamothes' relations with the clergy were quite warm—the abbé of Sainte-Foy was a frequent visitor and dinner guest at Goulards.[116] Daguille, the precentor at Condom, stayed with the family in Bordeaux while pleading a court case for his religious chapter.[117] M. *l'archiprêtre*, Jules's supervisor, was always a welcome guest of the family, as was the curé of Saint-Avit and other members of the religious orders.[118] The entire family was close to the sisters of Saint-Michel, whom they often visited. Marie, Marianne, and Alexandre shared the contents of

110. Jules to Victor, 23 April 1760. See also 11 October 1760; and Marie to Victor, 14 April 1760; 27 November 1760.

111. See Chapter 7 below.

112. Jules to Victor, 2 July 1757; 7 June 1761.

113. See, for example, Victor to Jules, 26 November 1756; 7 February 1757; 11 May 1757; 14 January 1758; Victor to Delphin, undated 1760.

114. Victor to Jules, 21 October 1760.

115. Victor to Jules, 25 August 1764.

116. Marie to Victor, 20 October 1757.

117. Marie to Victor, 18 February 1758.

118. Marie to Victor, 28 September 1758; 7 October 1758; Alexis to Victor, 9 March 1759; 26 June 1759; Marianne to Victor, 19 October 1760; Victor to Jules, 16 April 1765.

Victor's letters with the nuns, who always sent their warmest regards to the medical student in Paris.[119]

Still, the intense religiosity of the Lamothes did not necessarily indicate fanaticism or extreme intolerance. Sainte-Foy, the region of their country home, was still a heavily Protestant area in the 1750s. Many of the Lamothes' friends, and even relatives, were Protestant, or had Protestant family connections.[120] One of Delphin's closest friends, *avocat* Nicolas de Lisleferme, was a Protestant, forced to marry in Holland.[121] Thus, the Lamothes had social contact with Protestants on an almost daily basis. Both Marie and Marianne still expressed worry about the Protestant assemblies "in the desert," but their concerns did not reflect the fanaticism of an earlier era: "The assemblies of our Protestants were very numerous and very well attended, and made us hope that our new Captain would keep order, God willing. Let us pray with all our hearts for those poor people [the Protestants] who were for the most part prejudiced from childhood, which is a great obstacle to any new doctrine."[122] Marianne referred to Protestants as "our separated brothers," and Victor voiced hope that Catholics could provide them with a better example.[123] Even the abbé Jules seemed as concerned by the nonpracticing Catholics in his new parish community of Saint-Magne as by the Protestants. Upon taking up residence there in 1765, he wrote to Victor, "There is much work to do in this Parish, partly because of the Protestants who make up a little part [of

119. See, for example, Alexandre to Victor, 17 January 1757; 17 May 1757; 10 January 1758; Marie to Victor, 28 May 1757; 24 August 1759.

120. The Archives municipales de Sainte-Foy-la-Grande, Série GG and Série E record the births, deaths, and marriages of the residents of the area of Sainte-Foy. The vital statistics of some members of the families Rigaud de Grandefon, Rossane, Lajonie, Gaussen, Papus, Turcaud, and Jauge are recorded in the Protestant registers. It is likely that many more of the Lamothe friends were closet Protestants, because of the civil disabilities imposed upon professed Huguenots. I thank Mlle. Guesnon, archivist at Sainte-Foy, for allowing me to consult her research on these families.

121. Louis Desgraves, *Evocations du vieux Bordeaux* (Paris: Les Editions de Minuit, 1960), 356; Edouard Feret, *Statistique générale topographique, scientifique, administrative, industrielle et biographique du département de la Gironde* (Bordeaux and Paris: Feret et Fils and G. Masson/Emile Lechevalier, 1889), vol. 3: *Biographie*, 409; Meaudre de Lapouyade, *Impressions d'une allemande à Bordeaux en 1785* (Bordeaux: G. Gounouilhou, 1911), 42.

122. Marianne to Victor, 9 October 1757. See also Marie to Victor, 3 September 1757. The religious fanaticism of the sixteenth and seventeenth centuries has been well documented by Diefendorf, *Beneath the Cross*; Natalie Zemon Davis, "The Rites of Violence," in *Society and Culture in Early Modern France* (Stanford: Stanford University Press, 1975), 152–87; and Orest Ranum, *Paris in the Age of Absolutism* (Bloomington: Indiana University Press, 1968), 35–38.

123. Marianne to Victor, 10 December 1757; Victor to Jules, 14 January 1758.

the community] but also because of the lack of faith that prevails among those who profess Catholicism."[124]

Along with having concern for their souls, the Lamothes worried about their physical health. "Watch your health" was a standard admonition. The letters of the Lamothe family reflect the increasing tendency of individuals to write about their bodies and health.[125] In countless letters, Marie and Marianne recounted their illnesses to Victor in minute detail, reporting their symptoms and the remedies tried and requesting advice from the family's medical student. Marianne apologized for discussing her health so frequently, "I'm falling into the usual fault of the sick . . . which is to constantly talk about illness," but excused herself with, "Who better to discuss [illness] with than a doctor, and especially a brother with equally tender sentiments."[126]

Other family members experienced health problems as well, and took very seriously all bouts of sickness. This concern was not surprising in a time when illness was so often mortal. When Victor became sick in Paris, the family was concerned only for his quick recovery. Alexis wrote, "On behalf of my father, I forbid you . . . to apply yourself to anything until you are completely recovered."[127] Jules also suffered from poor health most of his life. When he took up his position at Saint-Magne, he expressed the hope that the country air would improve his condition.[128] But he was evidently never strong, and was stricken by a severe fever in the summer of 1766.[129] Father Jules died the following September at the age of thirty-four.

As an antidote to ill health, the Lamothes stressed the benefits of a moderate regime. The vigorous Daniel, who lived to eighty, was proof of

124. Jules to Victor, 5 May 1765.

125. Madeleine Foisil traces this to the seventeenth century in "The Literature of Intimacy," in Philippe Ariès and Georges Duby, gen. eds., *A History of Private Life*, trans. Arthur Goldhammer (Cambridge: Harvard University Press, Belknap Press, 1989), vol. 3: *Passions of the Renaissance*, ed. Roger Chartier, 351–55. Robert Forster also notes this tendency in "Family Biography," in Wolfdieter Bihl and Gernot Heiss, eds., *Biographie und Geschichtswissenschaft: Aufsätze zur Theorie und Praxis biographischer Arbeit* (Vienna: Verlage für Geschichte und Politik, 1979), 113–14. The letters of Liselotte von der Pfalz, Duchesse d'Orléans, provide another example of this obsession with health and the body. See Elborg Forster, "From the Patient's Point of View: Illness and Health in the Letters of Liselotte von der Pfalz (1652–1722)," *Bulletin of the History of Medicine* 60 (1986): 297–320.

126. Marianne to Victor, 2 December 1758.

127. Alexis to Victor, 9 May 1758.

128. Jules to Victor, 5 May 1765.

129. Alexis to Victor, 8 July 1766.

the benefits of a temperate lifestyle: "He continues to enjoy very good health, and it seems that he can continue with his work . . . he knows how to treat it as he does all other things, that is, with uncommon moderation, I believe that it is the best medicine one can practice, and if everyone conducted himself in the same manner, MM. *les médecins*, you would not have much work to do."[130] As conscientious professionals, the Lamothe men recognized the necessity for hard work, but knew that relaxation and moderation were also crucial to one's health and mental well-being. Delphin stressed that Victor should "scrupulously follow the precepts of moderation."[131] The *juste milieu* was best.

This belief in moderation extended to other aspects of family life, especially the conservation of resources. In good bourgeois fashion, the Lamothes stressed the need to economize and to avoid extravagance.[132] For them, "watch your purse" was more than a conventional expression—it was a way of life, more a function of self-discipline than an actual need to save. Daniel Lamothe set the tone, urging Victor to keep careful account of his daily expenses.[133] The rest of the family shared Daniel's attitude toward money and joined in the admonitions to economize.[134]

Religion, health, balance, and economy—all members of the Lamothe family stressed their importance. These values provided calm and stability in both their inner lives and family relations, and supplied the foundation of their familial existence.

4. Domestic Amenities and *Douceurs*

The Lamothe family's preoccupation with economy suggests at times a puritanical ethic of austerity. In a letter to Victor in Paris not long after his arrival there, Delphin wrote: "In your last letter to my sister, you spoke of several purchases that you made, I will leave it to her to write to you in more detail about them; there were perhaps some that you could have saved yourself, for example, the umbrella, unless the one that I had given you was so [badly] broken during the voyage that it was not possible to

130. Alexis to Victor, 19 May 1760.
131. Delphin to Victor, 20 May 1758.
132. See Chapter 2 below for a discussion of the family's financial resources.
133. Daniel to Victor, 1 March 1757; 20 April 1757; 22 November 1757.
134. Jules to Victor, 2 July 1757; Marie to Victor, 11 August 1760.

repair it, because as for the size [of the umbrella], it had served me well without being larger. It is even easier to carry it in a bag [*poche*]; but in general, I recommend to you the spirit of economy."[135] At the same time, the Lamothes required a degree of comfort, even elegance, in their style of living. Eighteenth-century Bordeaux was a wealthy city, and according to one observer, "Luxury is the norm in everything."[136] The Lamothes had a position to maintain in society, and were accustomed to a certain refinement in their appearance, furnishings, and food in order to conform to the standard set by Bordeaux's *beau monde*.[137]

It was especially important to the children that Daniel maintain his standard of living, even after his retirement diminished the family's revenues. Alexis observed to Victor, "Certain expenses are always necessary, my father is at an age, having worked to earn a living all his life, to have the right to find in his old age the same comforts that he enjoyed when he was younger."[138] Despite their concern with economy, the family enjoyed many luxuries and owned a number of valuable possessions that suggest an affluent standard of living. They traveled comfortably by horse and carriage.[139] Like all well-to-do families, they possessed substantial supplies of the necessities of everyday life, which they stored in a number of armoires at both their country and city homes.[140] When their country home, Goulards, was robbed, Jules noted to Victor that the major loss the family sustained was two or three dozen napkins and other linens.[141] Their silver chest was well stocked with a wide selection of tableware, candlesticks, a writing case, a water pitcher, assorted boxes, and engraved coffee spoons.[142]

135. Delphin to Victor, 26 March 1757.

136. Letters of F. de la Rochefoucauld, quoted in André Meallet, *Promenade dans le Bordeaux du XVIIIe siècle* (Bordeaux: Archives départementales de la Gironde, 1979), 23. William Doyle also notes the high standard of living in eighteenth-century Bordeaux in *The Parlement of Bordeaux*, 1–3.

137. The Bordelais *parlementaires* enjoyed an extremely luxurious standard of living. Pierre Meller, *Mobilier d'une famille parlementaire sous Louis XIV à Bordeaux* (Bordeaux: Y. Cadoret, 1903), 3–4; Doyle, *The Parlement of Bordeaux*, 127–41.

138. Alexis to Victor, 10 October 1762.

139. See, for example, Marie to Victor, 20 October 1757.

140. ADG Série B, Parlement, Répertoire numérique détaillé provisoire de la Tournelle de Sainte-Foy, Liasse 9, Verbal fait par le Juge dans la maison du Sr. Lamothe, 28 January 1758.

141. Jules to Victor, 28 January 1758. Delphin confirmed that the thieves had taken "quatre balots . . . de notre linge" before they were frightened off. Delphin to Victor, 6 February 1758.

142. Alexis to Victor, 13 September 1757; Delphin to Victor and Alexandre, 11 March 1763; ADG 3E 21732, Testament, Alexis de Lamothe, opened 25 March 1790. Annik Pardailhé-Galabrun attests to the increasing number of objects of comfort and luxury in individuals' homes in eighteenth-century

Family members tried to procure the latest appliances and accessories.[143] Daniel owned a telescope, field glasses, and medals of the place Royale and of Montesquieu.[144] Victor received two guitars, or *guimbardes*, as a present in Paris.[145] Engravings and an expensive set of pistols adorned the walls at Goulards.[146] Delphin was willing to spend up to 200 livres for a watch from Paris.[147] And despite all the talk of economy, neither Delphin nor Alexis, nor their father, was willing to give up the purchase of books, maps, and pamphlets, although they did caution Victor to purchase various books only "if you find them a bargain" or to wait for second printings, which would be less expensive.[148]

The Lamothe brothers were well dressed, and tried to procure the latest fashions, although they acknowledged that the *mode* in Bordeaux was not on par with that in Paris.[149] They chose their clothing with care, and requested items of fashion from Paris, including embroidered silk stockings and shoes made of the finest Moroccan leather.[150] Their *chemises* were meticulously selected and "very smart."[151] Alexis asked that Victor purchase a hat for him similar to that which he was purchasing for a friend, "trimmed in the same manner, which will undoubtedly be the latest style."[152] He and Delphin even sent their black velvet lawyer's robes to Paris to be embossed and trimmed with the most elegant design "to give

Paris, especially among the upper classes, in *La Naissance de l'intime: 3000 foyers parisiens, XVII–XVIIIe siècles* (Paris: Presses Universitaires de France, 1988), 287–302 and 331–65. Sarah Maza also notes that the increasing wealth of the eighteenth century led to changes in consumption and greater luxury even among those of more modest resources in "Luxury, Morality, and Social Change: Why There was No Middle-Class Consciousness in Prerevolutionary France," *Journal of Modern History* 69 (June 1997): 215–16.

143. For example, Marie to Victor, 7 October 1758.

144. Delphin to Victor and Alexandre, 11 March 1763.

145. Marie to Victor, 10 December 1757; Delphin to Victor, 17 December 1757.

146. ADG Série B, Parlement, Répertoire numérique détaillé provisoire de la Tournelle de Sainte-Foy, Liasse 9, Verbal fait par le Juge dans la maison du Sr. Lamothe, 28 January 1758. Death inventories reveal increasing numbers of all these objects among Parisians of the eighteenth century. Pardailhé-Galabrun, *La Naissance de l'intime*, 366–428.

147. Delphin to Victor, 13 November 1766.

148. Alexis to Victor, 4 May 1758; 7 October 1761.

149. Alexis to Victor, 6 August 1765. Daniel Roche found that in the eighteenth century, even the traditionally sober *robins* and professionals demonstrated increasing concern with their wardrobes. Although they still favored the sober *habit noir*, they began to add touches of color and *luxe* to their wardrobes. See *La Culture des apparences: Une histoire du vêtement, XVII–XVIIIe siècle* (Paris: Fayard, 1989), 140.

150. Delphin to Victor, 1 April 1758; Alexis to Victor, 23 June 1758; 31 March 1759.

151. Alexis to Victor and Alexandre, 4 September 1764.

152. Alexis to Victor, 25 August 1759.

them a new look."[153] Although the Lamothes undoubtedly eschewed the bright and colorful finery of the nobility, this concern with fashionable clothing suggests that the urban professional of the eighteenth century was increasingly interested in his appearance. The brothers also owned expensive jewelry, and Alexis left to his nephews and brothers a gold neck buckle, a diamond ring, gold cufflinks, silver cufflinks, and two silver watches, among other pieces of silver and jewelry upon his death.[154]

Despite his brothers' tastes, Jules, as a good post-Tridentine priest, rejected the lure of luxury: "Yet the people of this century just don't understand, ambition passes for a virtue, and it has become an honor to appear rich . . . you meditate . . . on the different shoals that one must avoid in this world. I regard as very serious that of loving finery, beautiful clothing, luxury."[155] Still, even the ascetic Jules appreciated the comforts of home. He relished his well-appointed parish house in Saint-Magne, and looked forward to his family visits.[156]

The family members also demanded a certain degree of comfort, order, cleanliness, and privacy in their surroundings. They always retained at least two servants to help with their daily chores and needs.[157] Before moving to Paris to room with the attorney Me. Marais and his wife, Alexandre expressed concern at the potential loss of privacy and the prospect of sharing a room, and possibly even a bed, with other pensioners.[158] At the beginning of his third year in Paris, Victor was pleased to move into his own apartment, complete with his own furniture and a servant, "a Savoyard" who would make his bed and clean his shoes.[159]

Other physical comforts were important as well. Marie assured Victor

153. Delphin to Victor, 4 May 1765; 12 July 1765; 6 August 1765.
154. ADG 3E 21732, Testament, Alexis de Lamothe, opened 25 March 1790. Annik Pardailhé-Galabrun found that in general these "signes de richesse" did not hold a place of importance in the inventories of professionals, and clearly books and professional items comprised a much larger component of the Lamothes' possessions than did *bijoux*. See *La Naissance de l'intime*, 155.
155. Jules to Victor, 27 May 1758.
156. Jules to Victor, 20 April 1757; 2 August 1757; to Victor and Alexandre, 24 October 1761; 5 May 1765.
157. See Appendix IV, tax records. Also see Lamothe Family Letters, Mémoire of earthquake by Alexis, 10 August 1759; Marie to Victor, 11 August 1759. Maurice Gresset found that the *avocats* of Besançon employed an average of 1.2 *domestiques* and notes that "aucun avocat chef de famille ne se passe de servante, c'est en quelque sorte une obligation de son état." Gresset, *Gens de justice à Besançon de la conquête par Louis XIV à la Révolution française (1674–1789)*, 2 vols. (Paris: Bibliothèque Nationale, 1978), 1:272. Most barristers in Toulouse also employed at least one servant, but seldom more than two. Berlanstein, *The Barristers of Toulouse*, 59–60.
158. Alexandre to Victor, 1 September 1759.
159. Daniel to Victor, 3 February 1759.

that her father would be willing to allow him to change his Parisian lodgings, which were full of bugs and would be too hot in the summertime.[160] Delphin urged him to make sure that his new lodgings would include "water, fire, in short all those little necessities."[161] Clean personal effects were as important as clean surroundings. Marie frequently advised Victor to check his linens and to keep them in good condition.[162]

The entire family enjoyed good food, both that produced at the family's country homes, Goulards and Muscadet, and more elegant tidbits purchased in Paris and elsewhere.[163] Seasons were marked by the consumption of ripe fruits and vegetables, many of which they raised themselves, for example, strawberries, apples, pears, peaches, artichokes, and peas.[164] Gifts of food, especially food made at home by mother and sisters, were greatly appreciated, and constituted a strong mark of affection. Each January, the family sent a *poule dinde farcie*, sometimes with partridges and truffles, to the seminary for Jules and all the way to Paris for Victor, and later for Alexandre.[165] The distances these culinary delights traveled without refrigeration over poor roads is a tribute to the French postal system as well as to family affection.[166] Marie de Sérézac lovingly sent homemade jams to her sons, as well as raisins, nuts, and *cuisses d'oye*.[167] Victor returned the favor by sending the family gifts of cheese, olives, oranges, and other delicacies from Paris and from his voyage to Provence.[168] Gatherings with friends and neighbors involved a sumptuous table as well.[169] Even the austere curé Jules waxed eloquent over his mother's food, and a little poem

---

160. Marie to Victor, 2 April 1757.

161. Delphin to Victor, 19 December 1758.

162. Marie to Victor, 2 April 1757; 8 May 1759.

163. For example, Alexis to Victor, 14 August 1755.

164. Marie to Victor, 28 May 1757; 20 June 1757; 25 September 1761.

165. Marianne to Victor, 24 January 1757; 2 February 1761; Marie to Victor, 21 January 1758; 11 January 1763; 6 February 1765; Delphin to Victor, 6 February 1758; Alexis to Victor, 22 January 1759; 3 February 1759; Alexandre to Victor, February 1766.

166. See Dena Goodman, *The Republic of Letters: A Cultural History of the French Enlightenment* (Ithaca: Cornell University Press, 1994), 140–42, on improvements to the postal system in the eighteenth century.

167. Marianne to Victor, 10 December 1757; Marie to Victor, 6 January 1759; Delphin to Victor, 3 January 1758; Daniel to Victor, 2 December 1758.

168. Marie de Sérézac to Victor, 10 January 1758; Marie to Victor, 21 January 1758; Alexis to Victor, 28–31 August 1760; Delphin to Victor, 24 March 1761.

169. Marie to Victor, 28 May 1757; 20 June 1757; 23 February 1762; Alexis to Victor, 22 December 1761; Marianne to Victor, 11 January 1763.

that Victor composed for Jules vividly demonstrates the family's love of gustatory pleasures.[170]

This appreciation of the accoutrements of status, a respectable standard of living, was critical to both the public image and the private well-being of the Lamothes. Orderliness; cleanliness; material comfort; proper clothing, accessories, and furnishings; and above all, an ample and varied cuisine were essential to both aspects of the identity of a provincial professional family.

5. The Role of the Women

It was the Lamothe women who worked to provide the members of the family with the homey comforts that they all so enjoyed. The role of Marie de Sérézac and her daughters within the family household is an important and complex one, and their story is very different from that of the men in the Lamothe family. Their story is also different from that of women of other social groups of the eighteenth century.[171]

Historians have studied the function of wives and sisters as co-workers within the rural family economy and the urban working-class household, as well as the privileged position of the elite noblewoman in early modern France, but we know much less about the position of the wives and sisters of professional men, and the middling classes generally.[172] The female relatives of lawyers and doctors could not participate actively in the work

170. Jules to Victor, 11 January 1760; Victor to Jules, 1 April 1758.
171. Gerda Lerner, "Placing Women in History: Definitions and Challenges," *Feminist Studies* 3 (1975): 1–14. For my analysis of the Lamothe sisters, see "A Choice Not to Wed? Unmarried Women in Eighteenth-Century France," *Journal of Social History* 29 (Summer 1996): 883–94.
172. See, for example, Olwen Hufton, "Women and the Family Economy in Eighteenth-Century France," *French Historical Studies* 9, no. 1 (1975): 1–22; Samia I. Spencer, ed., *French Women and the Age of Enlightenment* (Bloomington: Indiana University Press, 1984), esp. Cissie Fairchilds, "Women and the Family," 97–110, and Elizabeth Fox-Genovese, "Women and Work," 111–27; Carolyn C. Lougee, *Le Paradis des Femmes: Women, Salons, and Social Stratification in Seventeenth-Century France* (Princeton: Princeton University Press, 1976); Margaret H. Darrow, "French Noblewomen and the New Domesticity, 1750–1850," *Feminist Studies* 5 (Spring 1979): 41–65. David Garrioch, in *The Formation of the Parisian Bourgeoisie, 1690–1830* (Cambridge: Harvard University Press), notes the important role of women in class formation, but does not explore their role in depth. Julie Hardwick's *The Practice of Patriarchy: Gender and the Politics of Household Authority in Early Modern France* (University Park: Penn State Press, 1998), which discusses the wives of notaries, is an exception. For a fine analysis of the role of women in middling families in the English context, see Hunt, *The Middling Sort*, esp. chaps. 3 and 5.

of their menfolk, as could the wives of farmers and artisans.[173] While some would argue that the division between public and private spheres was not so clearly defined in the eighteenth century as it would become in the nineteenth, the evidence suggests that the lives of Marie, Marianne, and their mother seldom crossed the boundaries of domesticity into public life. Except for their work at the hospital and their religious activities, the Lamothe women pursued their lives in the security and isolation of the circle of family and friends.

However, Marie de Sérézac and her two daughters were far from idle, and they strove to create a comfortable home environment for the male members of the family. The division of labor within the Lamothe family household was based on gender. The Lamothe women, unlike the sons, were not expected to earn money by pursuing a profession, but they contributed to the "family economy" with their labor and production of household goods, as well as their careful attention to the household budget.[174] They knitted stockings and slippers. They sewed the family's sheets, handkerchiefs, napkins, shirts, collars, nightshirts, and bonnets, and other articles of clothing. They inquired about Victor and Alexandre's clothing needs and mailed packages of the necessary items.[175] Marie even suggested that Victor and Alexandre "send us . . . your dirty laundry that can be repaired."[176] They went shopping for the family's needs and searched for the best prices.[177] Although the family always employed servants, Marie de Sérézac and her daughters worked constantly, selecting and preparing the family's foods, such as the small delicacies that they sent to Victor and Alexandre in Paris.[178]

In a very real sense, Marie and Marianne filled the functional, as well as the emotional, role of wives to their brothers.[179] When Delphin married, his wife took on the tasks previously attended to by his mother and sisters,

173. However, there are suggestions that Marianne and Marie sometimes attended the sessions of Parlement to watch their brothers plead cases. See Marianne to Victor, 24 January 1757.

174. Hunt outlines the role of middle class women in the family economy in *The Middling Sort*, chap. 3, esp. 80–83.

175. Marie to Victor, 10 December 1757; 4 May 1758; 6 January 1759; 17 February 1759; 8 May 1759; 7 September 1762; 16 July 1763; Marianne to Victor, 1 April 1758; 10 March 1764; Delphin to Victor, 19 December 1758; 11 August 1759; 8 June 1764; 29 June 1764; Alexis to Victor, 13 November 1764; Alexandre to Victor, February 1766.

176. Marie to Victor and Alexandre, 9 July 1765.

177. Marianne to Victor, 24 March 1761; 23 January 1762.

178. See Jules to Victor, 20 April 1757.

179. For more on this, see Adams, "Devoted Companions or Surrogate Spouses?"

including the preparation of food and assistance in the production of wine.[180] The important role of the women during the vintage is underscored by the fact that the help of at least one of them was considered essential at both of the family's country homes during the wine harvest. Marie went to Muscadet with Delphin, while Marie de Sérézac and Marianne accompanied Alexis to Goulards.

The details of the family's household budget, both expenses and revenues, were within the purview of the women's concerns. Marie was always informed on the price and availability of food and other items, both those that the family needed to purchase, and those that they were trying to sell. In 1758, she wrote to Victor: "There is no fish. Eggs are very scarce and very expensive. They're selling for 3# 12 sols per one hundred, cod is prohibitively expensive, cuttlefish is at 14 sols per pound, butt is at 15#, peas are at 28# and 32# per bushel. In short, there is destitution everywhere. We sold our wines from this year for 20# wholesale, we have only loaded six and a half *tonneaux*. We're pleased enough with the price, but revenues are small, and there are a lot of expenses. I'm telling you a lot of tedious details, but you know that I am Madame *l'économe*."[181] As always, Marie was proud of her efforts to maximize the family's resources. The double sense of the word *économe*, which has the meaning of "thrifty and economical," but also refers to the steward, the treasurer, or the housekeeper of an institution, suggests Marie's elevated perception of her role within the household. She considered it her duty to be informed of the family's financial situation: "For a long time now, I've taken notice of our expenses and revenues, I find that one cannot know too much about that subject in order to watch expenses."[182] Marie de Sérézac's role in the management of family finances grew with the death of her husband. Although she deferred to her adult sons in the management of family affairs following Daniel's death, she was definitely the mistress of the household.[183]

Marie and Marianne enjoyed meals with friends, and visiting close companions such as the Laloubie sisters, but they were very selective in their socializing, declining to attend even those public affairs available to them. Their piety and rejection of worldly amusements surely militated

180. Delphin to Elisabeth de Brulz, 5 November 1780; 13 November 1780.
181. Marie to Victor, 18 February 1758. See also 17 March 1758.
182. Marie to Victor, 23 February 1762.
183. Marianne to Victor, 7 May 1763. Also see Chapter 2 below.

against any desire to participate in social events they considered frivolous or even sinful. They refused to appear at a ball hosted by a M. Griau, despite the entreaties of the Laloubie sisters, noting that "to spend maybe a night, dine, go to the ball of a stranger . . . that would hardly be according to our way of thinking."[184] The next year, they refused once again to attend: "Following our praiseworthy custom, we refused them, for, thanks be to God, for five or six years, we have not gone to balls . . . nor have we curled our hair, nor have we been to the fair except by force."[185] Their modesty and religiosity, perhaps mixed with a sense of superiority over more frivolous women, circumscribed their social activities. Marie and Marianne held high standards for women that they considered "of good character," and Marie wrote disapprovingly of the activities of Madame d'Egmont, daughter of the governor of the province of the Guyenne, when she was in town.[186] The two sisters were likely somewhat shocked and critical of the antics of aristocratic women who rejected the religious- and domestic-oriented lives of bourgeois women such as themselves.[187]

Marie's cryptic praise for the wife of a family friend suggests the three qualities that she, her sister, and her mother most admired in a woman: "His wife is charming, of very good character, very thrifty and very pious. I believe that must make for a very happy household."[188] She was also impressed by the wife of one of the *conseillers* at parlement, an "exemplary" and "devout" woman who had spent six weeks working at the hospital "in order to be able to give assistance to the sick peasants in her district."[189] Piety, economy, and service to others were the qualities that the Lamothe women considered most praiseworthy.

Considering their priorities, it is not surprising that the activities that took the Lamothe women into the public realm were religious exercises and charitable work.[190] While much of their religious activity involved

184. Marianne to Victor, 2 February 1761.

185. Marie to Victor, 23 February 1762.

186. Marie to Victor, 7 July 1760.

187. This disapproving attitude toward aristocratic women was quite common among women of the middle and even lower classes. See Darrow, "French Noblewomen and the New Domesticity"; and Davidoff and Hall, *Family Fortunes*, 22.

188. Marie to Victor, 2 April 1757.

189. Marie to Victor, 3 September 1757.

190. The same was true of the "bourgeoises" of northern France in the nineteenth century. Bonnie G. Smith, *Ladies of the Leisure Class: The Bourgeoises of Northern France in the Nineteenth Century* (Princeton: Princeton University Press, 1981), 93–161.

quiet prayer and meditation at home, they also participated in communal activities. Marie attended religious retreats for women organized by Father Danahil, and they were assiduous at Mass and vespers.[191] All three women regularly visited the sisters at Saint-Michel and lent their assistance to the Sisters of Charity at the hospital.[192] Their spiritual and charitable endeavors suggest that Marie and Marianne might have been drawn to a religious lifestyle; neither, however, indicated an interest in taking religious vows. Perhaps the contemplative life did not appeal to them, and their delicate health did not allow them to consider a more vigorous life in a working order. At any rate, as Olwen Hufton reminds us, one could certainly lead a pious life outside a convent.[193]

Perhaps they found equal satisfaction in helping to make a pleasant life for their parents and brothers. Devoted daughters, they spent much of their time caring for their parents, especially their father, as they grew older. Marianne remarked, "Both of them are in very good health, but their age requires the little attentions that we always give them with great pleasure, my dear father appreciates that his children do not neglect him."[194] True, on at least one occasion, Marianne acknowledged that caring for her parents could be a difficult burden.[195] But prescribed gender roles dictated that they fulfill this duty to their parents, and they did so without question.[196]

The activities of Marie de Sérézac and her daughters hint at a lifestyle that lay between the world of the idle elite and that of the working poor. They presaged the middle-class ideal of "domesticity" of the nineteenth

191. Marie to Victor, 28 May 1757; and passim.
192. Marie to Victor, 17 January 1757; 1 March 1757; 2 April 1757; 18 February 1758; 17 March 1758; 16 March 1759; 24 August 1759; 4 March 1760; 23 July 1762; Marianne to Victor, 24 January 1757; 7 August 1759; 2 February 1761. According to Colin Jones, nursing sisters modeled on the Daughters of Charity provided highly effective nursing services in ancien régime hospitals, where they also ran the hospital pharmacies and controlled the distribution of food. *The Charitable Imperative: Hospitals and Nursing in Ancien Régime and Revolutionary France* (New York: Routledge, 1989), 15. See 122–205 for a discussion of the nursing sisters.
193. Olwen Hufton, "Women Without Men: Widows and Spinsters in Britain and France in the Eighteenth Century," *Journal of Family History* 9, no. 4 (1984): 369–70.
194. Marianne to Victor, 23 January 1762.
195. Marianne to Victor, 7 August 1762.
196. Patricia Jalland examines the importance of the role of the "dutiful daughter" for unmarried women, and notes that in nineteenth-century England, many regarded service to a father in his old age as the primary duty of the spinster daughter. See "Victorian Spinsters: Dutiful Daughters, Desperate Rebels, and the Transition to the New Woman," in Patricia Crawford, ed., *Exploring Women's Past: Essays in Social History* (Boston: G. Allen and Unwin, 1984), 137–41.

century. Like the "bourgeoises" of northern France in the nineteenth century, they devoted their lives to their families and the church, and held themselves aloof from the corrupt world.[197] They considered it their task to make the lives of their menfolk free of daily cares, and they took special pride in their ability to carefully manage the household resources of the family.[198]

The lives of the members of the Lamothe family were tightly intertwined, physically, financially, and emotionally. The parents and their children enjoyed loving relationships, despite occasional tensions among family members. Their warm emotional life was enhanced by a secure standard of living and domestic comfort, with Marie de Sérézac and her two daughters playing supportive roles to the six men of the family. The Lamothe style of life was solid rather than ostentatious, expressing an instinctive love of order and comfort, but also reflecting a deeply ingrained religious and social conservatism. The Lamothes achieved "le bonheur bourgeois" in the full sense of the eighteenth-century expression—material security, self-discipline, assignment of family functions, and domestic solidarity laced by strong emotional bonds.[199]

While the members of the Lamothe family never spoke of the "joys of the fireside," their lives were centered on a *home*—not yet the airtight, private home of the nineteenth-century bourgeoisie, perhaps, but still fundamental to their emotional equilibrium. Jules's description of the Lamothe family circle evokes an image of cozy domesticity:

> In the morning, I had the pleasure of dining with the family, we made toast and had chocolate, we laughed, we amused ourselves,

197. Smith, *Ladies of the Leisure Class*. However, the Lamothe women seemed to lack a clear concept of domesticity, with the ideological underpinnings that gave it such resonance by the nineteenth century. For further analysis of this concept, see Darrow, "French Noblewomen and the New Domesticity"; Davidoff and Hall, *Family Fortunes*; and Elizabeth Fox-Genovese and Eugene D. Genovese, "The Ideological Bases of Domestic Economy," in Fox-Genovese and Genovese, *Fruits of Merchant Capital: Slavery and Bourgeois Property in the Rise and Expansion of Capitalism* (Oxford: Oxford University Press, 1983), 299–336.

198. Darrow notes that the domesticity of nineteenth-century French women had a more positive tone than the English equivalent, as the wife was extolled as *maîtresse de la maison* and director and manager of domestic affairs, in "French Noblewomen and the New Domesticity," 57–58. Still, Hunt points to the pride of middling wives in their management of the household in *The Middling Sort*, passim.

199. See Robert Mauzi, *L'Idée du bonheur dans la littérature et la pensée françaises au XVIIIe siècle* (Paris: A. Colin, 1960), 269–89.

then I had a few moments in the company of our good papa, Marianne attacked me for letting her win a few games of cards. Imperceptibly, the morning passed, at dinner, we made the conversation lively as possible, after dinner, we walked, played cards, played backgammon, walked again, played cards again, etc. No one slept after supper, because we did so well that we always had something to say. There you have a sample of my days which, as you see, were nearly engrossed by pleasure.[200]

Surely the domestic existence of the Lamothe family, with due allowance made for family eccentricities, extended to the social milieu in which they lived. These were close emotional family relations, so close indeed that they might seem to leave little space or emotional energy for any commitment to the larger community. Yet for the male members of the family, there was energy in reserve not only for professional application, but also for much wider public activity.

200. Jules to Victor and Alexandre, 24 October 1761.

"Ménager ta bourse"

Management of the Family Fortune

In 1763, the emotional and material underpinnings of the Lamothe family were radically altered. On 11 March, Delphin wrote to Alexandre and Victor, who were living in Paris: "The loss that we have all just suffered, my very dear brothers, must have greatly affected you . . . our dear father died, at a time when we believed that he was out of danger: it is true that for more than a year, his health had declined considerably, that he had almost entirely cut himself off from business, but he always seemed to have the same soundness of spirit, if not the same quickness; he was always able to give us, & in effect gave us good advice, he was a respectable & respected *chef*."[1]

Until his death on 7 March 1763, Daniel Lamothe, *père de famille*, had directed the wealth of the family, in name and in fact. With his death, the family's resources were divided on the basis of a handwritten will dated 26 August 1762.[2] While the division of property specified in the will had little practical impact on the administration of wealth within the Lamothe

1. Lamothe Family Letters, Delphin to Victor and Alexandre, 11 March 1763. Jonathan Dewald traces the disruptions created by the death of the father of a family and the economic impact of the subsequent division of property in *The Formation of a Provincial Nobility: The Magistrates of the Parlement of Rouen, 1499–1610* (Princeton: Princeton University Press, 1980), 294–300.

2. ADG 2C 189, Contrôle des grandes actes, Bureau de Bordeaux, 18 February 1772, 85. Registration of Testament, Daniel Lamothe. The original document was not in the notarial *études* of the

family immediately after Daniel's death, the consequences were greater in later years, following the deaths of mother Marie de Sérézac, daughters Marie and Marianne, and son Jules and the marriage of Delphin.

The division of property outlined in Daniel Lamothe's will, and subsequent divisions based upon Delphin's marriage contract, Alexis's will, Victor's will, and partition documents (*contrats de partage*) also have implications for family relations and strategies. Although customary law controlled the inheritance strategies of French families in the Guyenne, despite the influence of Roman law in this *pays de droit écrit*, and all children had a strong claim to a share of the parental estate, parents still exercised significant control over the distribution of their possessions after death, especially their *acquêts* (acquired goods).[3] Parents could also use the right of *préciput* to substantially favor one child over the others as allowed by customary law, but few in Bordeaux did so.[4]

Daniel Lamothe named his two eldest sons, Delphin and Alexis, as co-heirs to his property, with provision made for the younger children. Daniel and Marie's marriage contract, an *association aux acquêts*, stipulated that all property and goods acquired during their marriage were shared equally by the two spouses, and that each controlled the disposition of his or her portion.[5] Delphin meticulously outlined his father's property arrangements in his letter to his brothers:

> Our dear father had written a will by his own hand last year, and here are the most essential clauses that you should know about. His property & that of my mother are approximately equivalent in value, considering my mother's taking over her goods & their

---

Archives départementales de la Gironde. It was not registered until nearly ten years after Daniel's death in 1763.

3. Stricter rules governed the succession of *propres*. See Robert Wheaton, "Affinity and Descent in Seventeenth-Century Bordeaux," in Wheaton and Tamara K. Hareven, eds., *Family and Sexuality in French History* (Philadelphia: University of Pennsylvania Press, 1980), 111–34.

4. Ibid., 123–24. See Ralph Giesey, "Rules of Inheritance and Strategies of Mobility in Prerevolutionary France," *American Historical Review* 82 (1977): 271–89, for French rules of inheritance and definitions of terms.

5. ADG 3E 19493, #233, Articles de mariage, Daniel Sanfourche de Lamothe and Marie de Sérézac, 16 December 1723. The marriage contract specified, "Ce sont lesdits futurs epoux assossiés en tous les acquets qu'ils fairont pendant et constant leur mariage lesquels seront reversibles aux enfans qui proviendront, avec neanmoins la faculté a chacun des conjoints de disposer de sa portion en faveur de tel des enfans commun que bon luy semblera et au cas qu'il n'y ait d'enfans chacun des futurs epoux sera maitre d'en disposer de sa moitié."

association aux acquêts; my father had valued his property at approximately ninety-two thousand five hundred livres & on that assumption, he gave my eldest sister ten thousand five hundred livres, to Marianne ten thousand francs & to both of them the furnishings of their rooms in Bordeaux, 12 silver place settings, & 12 serving spoons, sheets, towels, etc. To Jules [he left] seven thousand livres in addition to his *titre clérical* of 3000# which he will receive only if he does not have a *bénéfice* with revenues of at least 1200#. To each of you, my dear brothers, thirteen thousand livres, & a pair of engraved silver candlestick holders, and to Alexandre the historical dictionary with its supplements: & for the rest of his property, he appointed Alexis & me [heirs] giving me a *préciput* of three thousand livres. He wanted his bequests to augment or diminish based on the value . . . of his legacy.[6]

The logic behind Daniel's division of his goods is clear. His two eldest sons, who remained in the family home at Rue Neuve, were favored as co-heirs to his worldly possessions. His daughters were awarded money in addition to the furnishings of their rooms, but it was expected that they would remain in the family home, and their inheritance would remain part of the family's resources. Daniel considered Jules provided for once his clerical title was purchased, but set aside a sum of money for him to draw upon if his revenues as priest proved insufficient. The two youngest sons were granted a share of the family fortune as well, but Daniel believed that the expense of their education in Paris reduced their claims to his legacy. Like the patriarchs of Montauban's elite families, Daniel Lamothe tried to provide adequately, if not equally, for all of his children.[7]

Although Daniel favored Delphin and Alexis in the division of property, it would be difficult to interpret this as a scheme to promote the interests of his two eldest sons at the expense of the other children. Provincial noblemen often left the lion's share of their estate to the eldest son, while the cadets were paid in coin to prevent division of the patrimony.[8]

6. Delphin to Victor and Alexandre, 11 March 1763.

7. Margaret H. Darrow, *Revolution in the House: Family, Class, and Inheritance in Southern France, 1775–1825* (Princeton: Princeton University Press, 1989), 98.

8. Robert Forster, *The Nobility of Toulouse in the Eighteenth Century: A Social and Economic Study* (Baltimore: Johns Hopkins University Press, 1960), 120–21. Peasant families sometimes followed a similar arrangement. See Alain Collomp, *La Maison du père: Famille et village en Haute-Provence aux XVIIe et XVIIIe siècles* (Paris: Presses Universitaires de France, 1983); and Emmanuel Le Roy Ladurie, "A System

Wealthy nonnoble families bent on upward mobility also tried to circumvent the more egalitarian rules of *roturier* succession by advantaging one son and preventing excessive partition of the family's fortune.[9]

This did not appear to be Daniel's goal. Rather than marshaling the family's resources to purchase an ennobling office for his eldest son—a common practice among upwardly mobile commoners—he sought to establish all of his sons in respectable professions, sometimes at substantial cost.[10] A suitable position for all male members of the family was more important than assuring a glorious future for the lineage by carefully planning the social ascent of a favored son.[11]

Daniel's children repeatedly asserted that their father had divided his assets with the greatest of benevolence and wisdom. After recounting the provisions of Daniel's will, Delphin noted that "everyone appears quite satisfied, I imagine that it will be the same for you both."[12] However, there was also recognition that the division of property could create envy and resentment within the closest of families, and the exhortations of Victor and Alexandre's siblings in Bordeaux suggest that they feared discontent over Daniel's arrangements.[13] Delphin appealed to their better natures, writing, "I know that I need not recommend to you peace, unity & concord, you are too well born, the sentiments you have demonstrated up to this point are too well placed, & we all have much reason to congratulate ourselves for our amity." At the same time, he reassured his brothers that "although my father is no longer with us, we will do all that we can to

of Customary Law: Family Structures and Inheritance Customs in Sixteenth-Century France," in Robert Forster and Orest Ranum, eds., *Family and Society: Selections from the Annales, E.S.C.*, trans. Elborg Forster and Patricia Ranum (Baltimore: Johns Hopkins University Press, 1976), 75–103.

9. Giesey, "Rules of Inheritance," 271–78.

10. The purchase of venal offices was central to the ambitions of the upwardly mobile bourgeoisie in the eighteenth century. Giesey, "Rules of Inheritance," 281–85; and J. G. C. Blacker, "The Social Ambitions of the Bourgeoisie in Eighteenth Century France, and Their Relation to Family Limitation," *Population Studies* 11 (1957): 52–56. See Robert Forster, *Merchants, Landlords, Magistrates: The Depont Family in Eighteenth-Century France* (Baltimore: Johns Hopkins University Press, 1980) for a case study of one family's rise into the nobility through the careful deployment of resources and the purchase of offices.

11. This is in contrast to the elite of Montauban studied by Margaret H. Darrow. She found that "the primary concern was to preserve the integrity of the patrimony to the lineage." See *Revolution in the House*, 97–98. On the social and professional ambitions of the Lamothe family, see my "Defining État in Eighteenth-Century France: The Lamothe Family of Bordeaux," *Journal of Family History* 17 (Winter 1992): 25–45.

12. Delphin and Alexis to Victor and Alexandre, 11 March 1763.

13. See, for example, Jules to Victor and Alexandre, undated 1763; Marianne to Victor and Alexandre, 7 May 1763.

contribute to the advancement & establishment of both of you."[14] Despite the provisions of Daniel's will, the family would continue to operate financially as a single unit and to fund Victor and Alexandre's education in Paris. The essential thing was that the family remain as close and united as before.[15]

In his study of four wealthy Florentine families, Richard Goldthwaite asserted that "since economic interdependence is one of the strongest ties binding the family together, an examination of the financial relations among members of these families can bring us closer to a definition of the family itself as a social institution."[16] A study of the financial resources of the Lamothe family, their priorities, their goals, and their strategies for managing those resources can tell us a great deal about each member's perception of the meaning of the family, as well as identify his or her role within it. A wide array of legal, financial, and personal documents offers a picture of the family's control of its resources. While they do not give an altogether complete picture of the family's resources, the documents offer clues to the family's wealth at certain key times. All members of the family, especially the male members, had a strong sense of individual possessions or earnings, as each carefully accounted for contributions to the family coffers. At the same time, the family often operated as a single financial unit, with parents, brothers, and sisters sacrificing to advance the good of the others. The strategy chosen by the family was to maximize its resources by promoting the career of each of the brothers and the fortune of the family as a whole. In this sense, the family had "a unity which is more than just genealogical."[17]

The financial relations of the Lamothe family, and their approaches to controlling their resources, are especially useful in understanding the emotional ties of the family. Emotional needs and material interests are always interconnected in the context of family.[18] Never was this more

---

14. Delphin to Victor and Alexandre, 11 March 1763.

15. This emphasis on fraternal harmony was also common among the large extended families of Renaissance Florence. See Francis William Kent, *Household and Lineage in Renaissance Florence: The Family Life of the Capponi, Ginori, and Rucellai* (Princeton: Princeton University Press, 1977), 62.

16. Richard Goldthwaite, *Private Wealth in Renaissance Florence: A Study of Four Families* (Princeton: Princeton University Press, 1968), 234.

17. The phrase is Richard Goldthwaite's. Ibid., 11.

18. See Hans Medick and David Warren Sabean, "Call for Papers: Family and Kinship, Material Interests, and Emotion," *Peasant Studies* 8 (Spring 1979): 139–59; as well as the collection edited by Medick and Sabean, *Interest and Emotion: Essays on the Study of Family and Kinship* (Cambridge: Cambridge University Press, 1984), esp. the introduction and chap. 1, 1–27.

apparent than when Daniel's death and the dictates of his will led his heirs to stress the need for continued union and harmony within the family. Death and marriage were the two life events that clearly illuminated the intersection of emotional and material interests.

Finally, an analysis of the property and other resources of the Lamothe family lends insight to the financial priorities, goals, and investment strategies of an early modern provincial family. This professional family's management of its resources is one clue to understanding the character of the well-to-do eighteenth-century provincial family.

1. Urban and Rural *Propriétaires*

On 21 February 1764, nearly a year after Daniel's death, Delphin de Lamothe appeared before Bordeaux's bureau of the *centième denier* to pay the required tax on the inheritance of his father's Bordeaux property. In his mother's name, he declared that his father had left seven townhouses to his family. They were valued at a total of 74,500 livres, their worth at the time of Daniel's death. All of the houses had been acquired since Daniel's marriage to Marie de Sérézac, and therefore, by the provisions of their *société aux acquêts*, she now owned one-half of the property, and would enjoy usufruct over the rest until her death. On his mother's behalf, Delphin paid the one percent transfer tax.[19]

In general, Daniel purchased townhouses as investments. The exceptions were the three-story family home on Rue Neuve, and the house on Rue Bouquière, purchased in 1757.[20] The house on Rue Bouquière, behind the family home, was to serve in part as a convenient *cabinet* for Alexis's legal work.[21] All of the houses that Daniel owned were located near the family's home, either in their parish of Saint-Michel or in the neighboring parishes of Saint-Pierre or Saint-Colombe, allowing him to keep a close eye on his possessions.

Urban property could be a valuable investment in wealthy Bordeaux.[22] Undoubtedly, Daniel chose to take advantage of this trend. He purchased

19. ADG 2C 474, Record of the *centième denier*, Bureau de Bordeaux, 21 February 1764.
20. ADG 3E 17827, Vente de meuble, 19 August 1737, and ADG 3E 24241, Vente, 3 April 1757.
21. Marie to Victor, 2 April 1757.
22. William Doyle, *The Parlement of Bordeaux and the End of the Old Regime, 1771–1790* (New York: St. Martin's Press, 1974), 106.

some houses in poor condition with the intention of fixing them up to improve their value. The family home at Rue Neuve, purchased for a little more than 11,000 l. in 1737, was valued at 16,000 l. in 1763, "in consideration of its reconstruction," and the house purchased at Rue Gensan for 3,500 l. was valued at 6,000 l. for the same reason.[23] The house at Rue Gensan was sold in 1772 for a price of 8,500 l.[24] However, according to the declaration of the *centième denier* of 1764, some of the other houses had decreased in value "in consideration of [their] extreme decrepitude." One of the houses on Rue Neuve, purchased for 13,000 l. in 1751, was appraised at only 10,000 l., and the house at Rue Bouquière, worth 11,250 l. in 1757, was valued at only 9,000 l. The others were still appraised at their purchase prices. Possibly the family undervalued their property in order to pay a lower tax, although according to Delphin's statement before the bureau, "the value given here . . . is relative to the price of the leases."[25]

However, Daniel did not buy the houses with the intention of fixing them up and reselling them for a quick profit. Rather, in 1763, the six houses were rented out for sums totaling 2,800 l. per year, a return of about 4.5 percent on the purchase prices of 61,250 l. total, or slightly less than the usual 5 percent return on a *rente constituée*. (See Appendix II).[26] Delphin considered this return low, blaming the war with England and the delay in the publication of peace for "the reduction in our house rental rates."[27] The rents paid for the houses diminished considerably in the early 1760s as the family lowered the prices to find renters.[28] It would seem, however, that

23. ADG 2C 474, Centième denier, Bureau de Bordeaux, 21 February 1764. Louis Desgraves also notes that Daniel reconstructed the family house on Rue Neuve the year after he made the purchase. See *Evocations du vieux Bordeaux* (Paris: Les Editions de Minuit, 1960), 214.

24. ADG 3E 20657, Vente, 22 May 1772.

25. ADG 2C 474, Centième denier, Bureau de Bordeaux, 21 February 1764.

26. For each house, Daniel was also responsible for the *cens, lods et ventes* or *rente annuelle et perpetuelle foncière et directe* owed to the seigneur of the property, usually a seminary or other religious house. However, the sum was generally nominal. ADG 3E 21658, Vente, 20 June 1753 and ADG 3E 24241, Vente, 3 April 1757.

27. Delphin to Victor and Alexandre, 7 June 1763. However, Lenard R. Berlanstein notes that a return of 3–5 percent on urban and rural real estate was the norm in eighteenth-century Toulouse. *The Barristers of Toulouse in the Eighteenth Century (1740–1793)* (Baltimore: Johns Hopkins University Press, 1975), 52.

28. Delphin to Alexandre and Victor, 25 September 1761; Marie to Victor, 25 November 1761. This was apparently a problem for many landlords in the early 1760s. Marie wrote to Victor, "Plusieurs maisons de cette rue sont a loüer, celle qui apartenoit autre fois a Mr. Jung et que s'est loüee jadis 1400# vient de se livrer a 800# a un de tes confreres Mr. Doasan." Marie to Victor, 23 February 1762.

the family considered the houses a reliable, if conservative, investment, guaranteed to return a steady income. In 1815, when Victor Lamothe divided the family's property with his nephews, they still owned the house *sur le port*, one house on Rue Neuve, and the houses on Rue Bouquière and Rue du Cerf Volant and had added four houses, two on Rue de Reservoir and two on Rue Fondaudège.[29] Like many prosperous city dwellers, the Lamothes found owning and renting out houses to be a safe and profitable business.[30]

Most of the family's purchases were made using only the funds of the immediate family. The townhouses were all acquired in Daniel Lamothe's name until his death in 1763. At that point, his widow and two eldest sons took over ownership and management of the Bordeaux properties. In 1769, however, Delphin and Alexis joined a group of their friends in order to make a major investment—the purchase of the Duplessy *hôtel* situated on the Jardin-Public, a very prestigious address.

Madame Duplessy was the popular hostess of the most celebrated salon in eighteenth-century Bordeaux—the *salon* Duplessy. Her sumptuous home was the rendezvous of Bordeaux's elite. Delphin and Alexis de Lamothe were also regulars there. But then, in 1769, Madame Duplessy was forced to sell her properties on the Jardin-Public to finance the marriages of her three daughters.[31] The property sold for the sum of 100,000 l. to a consortium of eight men. Besides Alexis and Delphin de Lamothe, the purchasers included Laurent Lalanne, Alexis Dubergier, Guilhaume Duvergier, Pierre Nicolas de Lisleferme, Pierre Cazelet, and Pierre Eloy Doazan, all barristers, and all friends of the Lamothe family.[32]

29. ADG 3E 13205, Acte de partage, 23 June 1815.

30. Most of Bordeaux's *parlementaire* families owned some real estate within the city, and at least one-half of the magistrates rented out urban property. The barristers of Toulouse also often invested in urban property, although less frequently than in rural property and *rentes constituées*. Many of the magistrates of Besançon also invested in urban houses, although the *avocats* and *magistrats subalternes* were much less likely to own several townhouses. Doyle, *The Parlement of Bordeaux*, 106–10; Berlanstein, *The Barristers of Toulouse*, 54; Maurice Gresset, *Gens de justice à Besançon de la conquête par Louis XIV à la Révolution française (1674–1789)* (Paris: Bibliothèque Nationale, 1978), 1:357–58.

31. See A. Grellet-Dumazeau, *La Société bordelaise sous Louis XV et le salon de Mme Duplessy* (Bordeaux and Paris: Feret et Fils and Libraires Associés, 1897), esp. 24 and 342, on the *Hôtel Duplessy* and its subsequent sale.

32. ADG 3E 21579, Contrat de vente, 8 July 1769. Delphin, Alexis, and Nicolas de Lisleferme purchased 3/10 of the property together, but the next day, sold a 1/10 share to Lisleferme's father-in-law, Jean Valeton de Boissière, a Bordelais *négociant*. M. Marc Kirwan, *écuyer*, and M. Simon Pierre Brun, *conseiller du Roy* and *contrôleur ordinaire des Guerres* subsequently bought into the group as well. *Archives historiques du département de la Gironde* (Bordeaux and Paris, 1906), 41:362–70, brings together documents relating to this sale, as well as subsequent negotiations between the purchasers and municipal authorities concerning improved access to the Jardin-Public. The original sales contract of

The Duplessy domain was subsequently sold and auctioned off in bits and pieces, recorded in a series of notarial documents.[33] For the Lamothe brothers, this was an important investment in which financial ties and ties of friendship joined. It was also more speculative than their other real estate purchases in that they sold off the property quite quickly in order to make a rapid profit on their investment, rather than holding on to it over a period of time for a smaller but steady return.

Like most Bordelais notables, the Lamothes did not restrict their property ownership to the city of Bordeaux. The most important piece of country property the family owned was Goulards, located near the small town of Sainte-Foy-la-Grande, east of Bordeaux in the Dordogne. Daniel Lamothe's father, Jean Sanfourche, was a native of Sainte-Foy-la-Grande, and in 1711, Jean Sanfourche's heirs paid the *taille* on the estate of Goulards in the parish of Saint-Avit-du-Moiron.[34] By 1727, the *taille* was established in Daniel Sanfourche de Lamothe's name, marking him as sole owner of Goulards.[35] This property was of sentimental as well as material value to the family. Until the purchase of Muscadet in 1760, the entire family went to Goulards each year in September to bring in the grape harvest, as well as to visit their friends and neighbors in the environs. While visiting Paris in 1755, Alexis wrote longingly to Victor, "Ah! There you all are at Goulards, how is the garden, the paths, those trees, those flowers, is there a lot of fruit?"[36] He later tried to tempt Victor to return home with memories of "our amusements, our pleasures, our active and passive visits, the garden, the pathways, the flower beds, the island, etc." at Goulards.[37] When the family purchased Muscadet in 1760, Alexis noted that despite the commercial value of Muscadet, "Goulards will always conserve the rights of seniority and the prerogatives attached."[38]

Although the family's house at Goulards was probably not sumptuous, Alexis did describe it as a *vaste maison*, and it was comfortable, with five

the Duplessy estate from 1769 is reprinted, as is AM DD 182, Minute informe, 14 August 1770, AM BB, Assemblée des notables, 21 February 1771, and AM BB, Jurade, 14 July 1773.

33. ADG 3E 21700, Licitation, 26 March 1774; 3E 23421, Vente, 25 October 1775; 3E 20584, Vente, 28 November 1775 (two separate contracts); 3E 20585, Vente des emplacements, 14 March 1776; 3E 20586, Licitation, 8 August 1776.

34. Archives municipales de Sainte-Foy, CC 14, Taille, Saint-Avit-du-Moiron, 1711.

35. Archives municipales de Sainte-Foy, CC 32, Taille, Saint-Avit-du-Moiron, 1727, 13. Daniel paid 66 l., 16 s., 1 d. As *avocats*, the Lamothes were not subject to the personal *taille*, but were required to pay it on *terre roturière*. Forster, *The Nobility of Toulouse*, 34.

36. Alexis to Victor, 23 September 1755.

37. Alexis to Victor, 10 October 1762.

38. Alexis to Victor, 2 October 1760.

fireplaces and engravings on the walls.[39] The Lamothes slowly added to
their property in Saint-Avit, purchasing bits and pieces of land eighteen
times between 1728 and 1789, frequently no more than a *journal*, or even
half a *journal* at a time.[40] (See Appendix II). Their lands included forests,
vines, and *métairies* (small farms) and bordered on the Seignal, a stream to
the west of Goulards. Daniel Lamothe paid the *taille* on 53 *journaux*, 15
escats of land in Saint-Avit in 1727, and the *dixième* for 54 *journaux*, 23 *escats*
in 1742.[41] By 1779, the family's property holdings in Saint-Avit had
increased to 61 2/3 *journaux*, and to 63 2/3 *journaux* and 9 *escats* by 1786, or
approximately 51 acres.[42] It is not clear that the Lamothes were participating in full-blown "domain-building," but it appears that they were
attempting to round out their holdings.[43] The Lamothes leased to *métayers*,
or sharecroppers, on their domain land, and when they bought or leased
pieces of land, they sometimes arranged for the original owner to continue
working the land.[44] They hired workers to help bring in the wine harvest
as well.[45]

The family added other valuable properties to their holdings beginning
in 1760. Their largest purchase in the 1760s was the domain of Muscadet,
a noble property lying northeast of Bordeaux in the parish of Bassens in the
Entre-Deux-Mers region of the Gironde. According to the contract of sale
agreed to by Daniel Lamothe and Jeanne Dartigues, the widow of a
marchand boulanger from Libourne, this piece of real estate included a
"house, wine storehouse, vats, and other buildings that are dilapidated and
in very poor condition, garden, vines, plowable lands, and woods" as well

39. Alexis to Victor, 7 October 1761. ADG Série B, Parlement, Répertoire numérique détaillé
provisoire de la Tournelle de Sainte-Foy, Liasse 9, Verbal fait par le Juge dans la maison du Sr. Lamothe,
28 January 1758. Victor Lamothe, as proprietor of Goulards in 1791, was assessed a sumptuary tax
based on the five fireplaces. Archives municipales de Sainte-Foy, G 1 (4), 20. The house believed to
be the Lamothe family home at Goulards is still standing; it is a large, one-story L-shaped brick
building with vineyards close by.
40. One *journal* equals approximately 0.8 acres.
41. Archives municipales de Sainte-Foy, CC 32, 13; and CC 40, 10.
42. Archives municipales de Sainte-Foy, CC 67, 13; and CC 82, 13 bis.
43. See Marc Bloch, *French Rural History: An Essay on its Basic Characteristics*, trans. Janet Sondheimer
(Berkeley and Los Angeles: University of California Press, 1966), 134–36. Bloch focused on the
nobility in his analysis of domain-building.
44. The *capitation* rolls for Saint-Avit-du-Moiron of 1742, 1770, 1772, and 1788, and of Pineuilh for
1742 include *métayers* of Daniel or Delphin and Alexis de Lamothe. Archives municipales de
Sainte-Foy, CC 39, 26 and 40; CC 51, 71 bis; CC 52, 9 and 10; and CC 83, 9. See also ADG 3E 42604,
Engagement de fonds, 9 December 1763.
45. During the grape harvest of 1755, Victor noted that the family had up to 18 *vendangeurs*
working for them. Victor to Alexis, 25 October 1755.

as a *métairie* called de Gauboles situated in the neighboring parish of Ambarès, and pastureland in the *palus* of Monferrant, also in Ambarès. Daniel paid the sum of 28,500 l. for the property.[46] Delphin took possession of Muscadet in his father's name on 22 or 23 August, duly noting the poor condition of the various buildings.[47]

Still, the family was pleased with the potential value of Muscadet. Marie observed to Victor, "The property is of considerable value, but in great need of repair . . . it cost twenty-eight thousand five hundred livres, but well-maintained, it could be worth more than 40,000# in a few years."[48] Delphin was satisfied that Muscadet was conveniently close to Bordeaux, and that it boasted 55 *journaux* of vines and 20 *journaux* of woodland, or 60 acres of valuable land.[49] Muscadet's grape harvest promised to be abundant, and when Daniel purchased Muscadet, their neighbor, the *négociant* M. Corregeolles, agreed to oversee the grape harvest at Muscadet that autumn for a salary of 2,000 l. Daniel was livid when M. Corregeolles reneged on the agreement, leaving him to deal with the burden of the harvest.[50] Despite the family's great attachment to Goulards, they believed that Muscadet would yield greater financial returns.[51] Gradually, they added new properties to round out their landed assets in Bassens and Ambarès.[52]

Furthermore, unlike the *roturier* property of Goulards, Muscadet was *terre*

46. ADG 3E 21673, Vente, 20 August 1760. Demoiselle Dartigues had inherited the property from Maître Charles Louis Robert, *avocat au Parlement*, and was forced to sell it to pay off M. Robert's *légataires*. In the days following the purchase, Daniel made five separate payments before the notary Rauzan to pay off Jeanne Dartigues's debts. ADG 3E 21673, Offre et consignation, 22 August 1760; Quittance, 25 August 1760; Quittance, 29 August 1760; Quittance, 5 September 1760; Quittance, 13 September 1760.

47. ADG 3E 21673, Procuration, 21 August 1760; Delphin to Victor, 21 August 1760.

48. Marie to Victor, 11 August 1760. Delphin noted to Victor at one point that the cost of repairs at Muscadet would easily mount to 12,000 livres. Delphin to Victor, 19 November 1760.

49. Grapes could return an exceptional yield on a relatively small area of land, and a domain of just 55 *journaux* could yield a respectable income. See Robert Forster, "The Noble Wine Producers of the Bordelais in the Eighteenth Century," *Economic History Review* 14 (1961): 22.

50. Alexis to Victor, 28–31 August 1760.

51. Alexis to Victor, 2 October 1760.

52. ADG 2C 593, Contrôle des actes, Bureau d'Ambarès, 4 June 1762 and 6 April 1764; 2C 606, Contrôle des actes, Bureau d'Ambarès, 18 December 1788. However, few proprietors owned estates in a compact block of land, and it is possible that the Lamothes owned a number of widely scattered strips of land in the regions of Sainte-Foy and Bassens. See Doyle, *The Parlement of Bordeaux*, 66–68, and Robert Forster, "Seigneurs and Their Agents," in Albert Cremer, ed., *Vom Ancien Régime zur Französischen Revolution: Forschungen und Perspektiven* (Göttingen: Vanderhoeck and Ruprecht, 1978), 169–87. Bloch's classic *French Rural Society* is still the best discussion of the fragmented and dispersed character of French agricultural holdings. See esp. 35–63.

noble. In 1767, Delphin rendered homage for "the noble house of Muscadet" in his own name as well as that of his brothers and sisters, "children of the late Me. Daniel Lamothe, *avocat en Parlement* and Dame Marie Serezac, *seigneur* of the aforementioned noble house."[53] While neither Delphin de Lamothe nor his siblings would ever hold noble title, it contributed to their prestige to own noble lands.[54]

With his marriage, Delphin became proprietor of another noble property. Marie-Elisabeth de Brulz brought as her dowry the *maison* of Lyde, situated in the parish of Baurech in the Entre-Deux-Mers region.[55] In 1775, Delphin pledged homage in his and his wife's name.[56] Subsequently, he and Elisabeth de Brulz leased out property in the title of *baux à fief.*[57] Not long afterward, in 1778, Delphin de Lamothe requested letters of nobility.[58]

In 1801, after the death of his two older brothers, Victor Lamothe purchased a new property, the country home of Cabanot in the commune of Véline, not far from Goulards.[59] At this point, he enjoyed usufruct over Goulards, but owned no country property of his own. Perhaps he wished to enjoy the status of land ownership in his own name.

The landed holdings of the family as a whole were extensive, totaling a minimum of 138 *journaux*, or a little more than 110 acres for Muscadet and Goulards by the 1780s. Still, it is unclear how profitable they were. The

53. ADG C 2345, Hommage, 11 March 1767, 144.

54. In some cases, the purchase of noble land could prepare the way for the purchase of an ennobling office and legitimate nobility. Forster, *The Nobility of Toulouse,* 26.

55. The property was a donation from her father, François-Marie de Brulz, and her uncle, André-Pierre de Brulz. Her uncle reserved "jouissance" of the house for the remainder of his life. ADG 3E 21696, Contrat de mariage, Delphin de Lamothe and Elisabeth de Brulz, 21 June 1772. It was not uncommon for kin to contribute to marriage contracts. Darrow, *Revolution in the House,* 101.

56. ADG C 2346, Hommage, 22 May 1775, 140.

57. ADG 2C 196, Contrôle des grandes actes, Bureau de Bordeaux, 9 August 1775 and 4 September 1775. The property leased out was in Cenon and Ambarès. The contract registered on 4 September specified that it involved "leur maison noble de Lamothe de Brulz." Although a *bail à fief,* which established fixed returns, was potentially less lucrative than other lease types, it was a feudal tenure, and reflected the prestige of titled property.

58. Pierre Meller, *Essais généalogiques: Familles du bordelais/recueil factice de brochures concernant des familles* (Bordeaux: Feret et Fils, 1897), 29. Meller cites the Archives de Saint-Denis, MM. de Lamothe as his source, but these documents are no longer available. Historian of French law Christian Chêne suggests that "the homage rendered before the *généraux des finances* for the noble house of his spouse Elisabeth de Brulz must have . . . given him the taste" for a noble title. See *L'Enseignement du droit français en pays du droit écrit (1679–1793)* (Geneva: Librairie Droz, 1982), 69.

59. ADG 3E 21754, Vente, 29 Messidor An IX; 3E 34956, Vente, 2 Nivôse An IX. Véline is in the region of the Dordogne, near Bergerac.

family benefited from the produce of Goulards, as well as that from their other properties. Grapes were their major crop. Each year, they made wine which they both drank, and, like other Bordelais wine producers, sold overseas through brokers.[60] The family had long been in the wine business. In 1718, the Community of Sainte-Foy sued Daniel Lamothe for trying to sell his wine in the jurisdiction before the *fête* of Saint-Martin, in violation of the regulations of the Jurade of Sainte-Foy.[61]

Like the rest of Bordeaux's high society, the Lamothes left the city each fall to supervise the *vendange*, or wine harvest.[62] The wine production and the revenues it furnished varied from year to year, but the manufacture and sale of wine could be extremely profitable to Bordelais landowners.[63] However, in 1762, a poor year, the Lamothes sold eight *tonneaux* of white wine in Holland for 609 l., and they produced a few *tonneaux* of red wine that they were unable to sell. According to Delphin, after "the cost of shipping the casks, of cultivation & the harvest," there was no profit to the family whatsoever.[64] In contrast, they had produced eleven and a half *barriques* of wine for sale in 1755.[65] A major factor in Daniel's purchase of Muscadet in 1760 was its potential for abundant and high-quality grape production.[66]

During the late 1750s and 1760s, the wine sales returned little profit to the family, for a variety of reasons. In 1757, Daniel complained to Victor

60. Vine cultivation was the major activity of the magistrates of Bordeaux after their parlementary duties, as it was for most notables in Bordeaux. Doyle, *The Parlement of Bordeaux*, 92. According to historian Camille Jullian, "Le Bordelais, sous Louis XVI, produisait environ 200,000 tonneaux de vin, dont 125,000 étaient chargés pour l'exportation." England and northern Europe, especially Holland, were the primary customers. *Histoire de Bordeaux depuis les origines jusqu'en 1895* (Bordeaux: Feret et Fils, 1895), 533.

61. Archives municipales de Sainte-Foy, HH 17. Procès entre la Communauté de Sainte-Foy et Daniel Sanfourche, Sieur de Lamothe, 1718.

62. Grellet-Dumazeau, *La Société bordelaise*, 191–92; Doyle, *The Parlement of Bordeaux*, 92–93 and 129.

63. Forster, "Noble Wine Producers," 22–25; and Doyle, *The Parlement of Bordeaux*, 86–91. C. E. Labrousse's classic thesis on the global wine situation in France fails to take into account factors such as the quality of wine and the circumstances of each wine producer, and for that reason is less helpful in understanding the situation of the individual wine producer. See *Esquisse du mouvement des prix et des revenus en France aux XVIIIe siècle* (Paris: Librairie Dalloz, 1932), 267–74.

64. Delphin to Victor and Alexandre, 7 June 1763. Operation costs for the cultivation of vineyards were very high. Expenses could mount to one-third to one-half of the gross receipts. Forster, "Noble Wine Producers," 28. See also Doyle, *The Parlement of Bordeaux*, 88–89.

65. Alexis to Victor, 8 November 1755. A *barrique* was a wine receptacle, or *tonneau*, holding approximately two hundred liters.

66. Alexis wrote to Victor in 1760 that they expected the fall wine harvest at Muscadet to be thirty to forty *tonneaux*. Alexis to Victor, 28–31 August 1760.

that the wines of the current year "have rendered very little, all of our wines from Ste. Foy and Bergerac have lost their reputation."[67] In 1763, Alexis decried the fruits of the *vendange*: "The wine harvest is disgusting, the hailstorms damaged everything . . . the wine will be mediocre as a result, and could be absolutely terrible."[68] This was a disappointment to the family considering the excellent quality of their wines in earlier years.[69] In other years the vines produced a sparse harvest.[70] Still, they sometimes fared better than their neighbors: "[Our harvest] is extremely poor; in truth, not as bad as that of the inhabitants of St. Emilion where the best wine storehouses hold only 5 *tonneaux*. We will have 14 of fine [wine] & one of *truillis*."[71]

Further complications arose when they tried to sell their wines abroad.[72] In 1758, Marie wrote to Victor: "The year that you left for Paris, we had 11 casks of wine that we sent to Holland, they were stored somewhere or other until about one or two weeks ago when we were told that we were down to ten, and that after all the necessary deductions we would receive eighteen pistoles and a few livres or sols."[73] With the advent of the Seven Years War, the sale of wine in Holland became more risky.[74] The family

67. Daniel to Victor, 20 April 1757. The wines of the Dordogne could not compete with those of the more prestigious Médoc. Forster, "Noble Wine Producers," 22; and Doyle, *The Parlement of Bordeaux*, 89. Bordeaux's aristocratic producers of wine clustered in the Médoc, the *graves* region, and the *palus* of Ambès. François-Georges Pariset, ed., *Bordeaux au XVIIIe siècle* (Bordeaux: Fédération historique du Sud-Ouest, 1968), 172–73.

68. Alexis to Victor, 27 October 1763. The vulnerability of the vine made it susceptible to weather conditions, especially hailstorms and frost. Forster, "Noble Wine Producers," 23; and Doyle, *The Parlement of Bordeaux*, 88–89.

69. Bibliothèque municipale de Bordeaux (hereafter abbreviated as BM) Ms. 1696 (II), Fonds Lamontagne, Correspondence, 10 October 1753, No. 26.

70. Marianne to Victor, 2 December 1757; Marie to Victor, 28 September 1758. The ten *barriques* of wine produced in 1758 sold for a little more than 40 pistoles, or about 400 livres. Daniel to Victor, 3 February 1759. In an earlier, more abundant year, Daniel Lamothe wrote to his friend M. Lanusse, "Il y a ici deux fois plus de vin que de barriques." AM Fonds Delpit, No. 127, #1, 1748(?).

71. Delphin to Victor, 24 October 1766.

72. Bordeaux wine producers relied heavily on the export of their wines. Jullian, *Histoire de Bordeaux*, 533; Doyle, *The Parlement of Bordeaux*, 89–91. Holland was an especially important trade partner for the Bordelais wine seller, and according to Jean-Pierre Poussou, "les Hollandais dominent l'activité commerciale bordelaise" in the eighteenth century. Jean-Pierre Poussou, *Bordeaux et le Sud-Ouest au XVIIIe siècle: Croissance économique et attraction urbaine* (Paris: Touzot, 1983), 235–36.

73. Marie to Victor, 21 January 1758.

74. Daniel to Victor, 2 December 1758. The war created financial havoc for most of the wine producers and the economy in general in the Bordeaux area, aggravated by the unfavorable weather conditions of the 1760s. ADG 8J 67, Fonds Bigot, Letter to the king, signed by the Parlement of Bordeaux, 1 July 1767; Pariset, *Bordeaux au XVIIIe siècle*, 299–301.

was forced to delay its departure from Goulards in the fall of 1760 because of the British blockade, which prevented them from sending out their wines.[75] By February 1762, they had only managed to sell four *tonneaux* of wine of their fall harvest in Holland.[76] In addition, the expense of the day workers added to their costs that year. Marie complained to Victor: "Our harvests began a few days ago, there have been a lot of intervals of repose, I believe that we will be taking one tomorrow as well, and the day after if the grape pickers don't lower their prices, yesterday and today we paid them 25 or 26 sols."[77]

Wine was not the only commodity that the family produced at Goulards. The food grown in the country was for the family's immediate consumption as well as for sale, and included various grains, livestock, and the produce of their gardens.[78] Like the wine harvest, the abundance and value of these other crops varied from year to year. In 1763, Delphin wrote, "The grain produce, etc. . . . has barely netted us 10 pistolles [*sic*]," and the summer harvest at Muscadet produced far less than hoped for.[79] In 1764, Alexis noted the poor wine and grain harvest and observed, "You see . . . what we have been reduced to, although in truth we must add some vegetables, poultry, herbs, etc., and some other trifles that are only valuable because . . . they save us from having to buy them elsewhere."[80]

The family's wine and crop production may have brought a tidy profit in some years, particularly before and after the Seven Years War, but even with their acquisition of the title of Bourgeois de Bordeaux, it seems likely that their primary pleasure came from drinking the fruit of their lands, and in imitating the noble *parlementaires* of Bordeaux by retiring to the country each fall to bring in the wine harvest.[81] Land in the country and the

75. Delphin to Victor, 19 November 1760.

76. Delphin to Victor, 9 February 1762.

77. Marie to Victor, 30 September 1762.

78. Bordelais magistrates, and French landowners in general, tended to prefer somewhat diversified agriculture, rather than relying on a one-crop economy, even one as valuable as wine. William Doyle, *The Parlement of Bordeaux*, 93–95; Robert Forster, "Obstacles to Agricultural Growth in Eighteenth-Century France," *American Historical Review* 76 (1971): 1603; and *The Nobility of Toulouse*, 39 and 41.

79. Delphin to Victor and Alexandre, 7 June and 19 July 1763. The *métives* at Muscadet were a disappointment in 1764 as well. Delphin to Victor, 4 August 1764.

80. Alexis to Victor, 28–30 September 1764.

81. Daniel wrote to Victor in 1759 that the wine harvests had been much more lucrative in earlier years, and that he had been able to purchase several town houses with the revenues. Daniel to Victor, 3 February 1759. Individuals enjoying the title "Bourgeois de Bordeaux" were allowed to bring their

cultivation of vines were proof of the family's rank as *notable* and essential to their status.[82] Delphin underscored the importance of wine and the grape harvest in the life of the Bordelais when he wrote to his friend François de Lamontagne, "The Bordelais write to each other in the month of October without speaking of wine & the vintage, that would be a phenomenon too surprising for me to want to be the perpetrator."[83]

The financial returns on the Lamothe vineyards improved by the early 1770s. Delphin wrote to Alexis in October 1773 that they had already harvested more than twenty *tonneaux* of wine at Muscadet, and were expecting a total of thirty—"we only need to sell it for a good price." He had not yet made an effort to sell the wine by December, but was instead waiting for a better return. "Other times, in my youth, we hastened to sell the wine as soon as it was ready. But times have changed, we are no longer young." The produce of the vegetable garden at Muscadet was abundant that year as well.[84]

Despite the pleasure they took in the produce of their land, each member of the Lamothe family worked hard during the harvest, and shared the responsibilities. Marianne wrote to Victor during the harvest of 1760 that the family's days consisted of "eat, drink, work, sleep."[85] When the family purchased Muscadet, the three women spent several months there each summer supervising the summer harvest (*métives*). The vintage at both Goulards and Muscadet was a major undertaking. After the fall of 1760, the family separated into two groups each year. Marie and Delphin went to Muscadet to oversee the grape harvest, and the rest of the family went to Goulards, as usual. Each member of the family referred frequently to the intense labors of the harvest season, especially when unforeseen complications created additional tasks.[86]

---

wine into the city free of duty, and had the monopoly of retail sale within the city limits. The privilege became easier to procure after 1720. Doyle, *The Parlement of Bordeaux*, 92; E. Brives Cazes, *Le Parlement de Bordeaux, Bureau de la Grande Police* (Bordeaux: G. Gounouilhou, 1875), 20.

82. See Forster, "Noble Wine Producers," 18–33; and Doyle, *The Parlement of Bordeaux*, 65–101, on the importance of viticulture and land ownership among the nobility of Bordeaux, especially the *parlementaires*. Berlanstein has also noted the prestige attached to landownership by the barristers of Toulouse, asserting, "Landowning was the mark of a *gentilhomme*, and the barrister never felt more like an aristocrat than when he spoke of 'his sharecropper' or when he was addressed as 'maître' at harvest time." See *The Barristers of Toulouse*, 52.

83. BM Ms. 1696 (II), Fonds Lamontagne, Correspondence, 10 October 1753, No. 26.

84. Delphin to Alexis, 24 October 1773; 7 December 1773.

85. Marianne to Victor, 19 October 1760.

86. Marie to Victor, 18 April 1758. See also Delphin to Victor and Alexandre, 10 December 1766.

Still, the properties were well worth the work. The Lamothes enjoyed both the produce of their lands and the status conferred by their position as *seigneurs* at Goulards, at Muscadet, and, in the case of Delphin, at Lyde. While the precise returns on their properties remain hazy, it is clear that they could be an important resource for the family.

2. The Family Fortune: Outlays, *Rentes*, and Revenues

At the time of Daniel's death, his children tried to make an estimate of the family fortune. Delphin wrote to his brothers in Paris that "my father had valued his property at approximately ninety-two thousand five hundred livres," but his mother's possessions were not included in the calculation. Without knowing the value of the goods that Daniel brought to the marriage, it is difficult to ascertain the value of the entire family fortune. We can only estimate that it was close to twice Daniel's share. The value of the family's townhouses was 74,500 l., Muscadet was priced at approximately 28,500 l., and Goulards was probably worth a similar sum, meaning that their real property was worth about 131,500 l. In addition, the capital invested in *rentes* added up to 15,500 l. If we include the value of their *meubles*—furnishings, silver, linens, jewelry, clothing, and books—the family estate very likely climbed close to 180,000 l (see Appendix III). Although not the equivalent of the average Bordelais magistrate, it was a respectable patrimony and superior to the fortune of the average barrister of Toulouse or Besançon.[87] Still, while Daniel Lamothe had amassed a substantial fortune, it was less considerable when shared among seven children.

Real estate was the major investment of the Lamothe family. In this, the Lamothes imitated other professional and bourgeois families in France, and manifested once again their fundamentally conservative nature. The eighteenth-century Frenchman or -woman was most likely to invest in proprietary wealth, that is, land, *rentes*, and offices. These types of invest-

87. Many Bordelais magistrates possessed fortunes close to, or even more than, 1,000,000 l., but most *parlementaire* fortunes lay between 100,000 l. and 400,000 l. Doyle, *The Parlement of Bordeaux*, 55–56. The fortune of the average barrister of Toulouse at the end of the Old Regime lay between 35,000 l. and 40,000 l., while the *avocats* of Besançon generally enjoyed fortunes of 10,000 l. to 60,000 l. Berlanstein, *The Barristers of Toulouse*, 47–79, and Gresset, *Gens de justice*, 1:436–38.

ments provided relatively low returns, but were low risk and very stable.[88] The Lamothes were not interested in taking bold risks to quickly increase their wealth, as were *financiers* and the intrepid wholesale merchants of Bordeaux.[89] At the same time, landownership, investment in townhouses, and the possession of *rentes* secured their rank as notables in Bordeaux. Land, and especially *rentes* and offices, could play a role in the bourgeois family's upwardly mobile strategy.[90] In the case of the Lamothe family, however, it seems that their financial strategy, based primarily on the acquisition of land and houses, was geared more toward providing a comfortable existence for the members of the immediate family and to maintaining their position in Bordelais society than to assuring the upward mobility of unborn children. Bourgeois familial comfort was more important than noble *éclat*.[91]

Unlike the upwardly mobile families described by Ralph Giesey, the Lamothes concentrated their investments in property rather than *rentes constitués* and offices. At the time of Daniel's death, the family was receiving a return of 5 percent on five *rentes*, a yearly total of 707 l., 10 s.[92] Victor and Alexandre invested in *rentes* in the early years of the Revolution, but *rentes* were never the cornerstone of the family's revenues.[93] Furthermore, the only member of the family who purchased an office was the *cadet* Alexandre.

What made up the bulk of the Lamothe family's revenues? In 1762–63, the sum total of the family's revenues per annum, according to Delphin, was about 5,000 l.[94] However, he was vague in delineating the sources of

88. George V. Taylor, "Noncapitalist Wealth and the Origins of the French Revolution," *American Historical Review* 72, no. 2 (1967): 469–96.

89. This cautious nature was not unique to the Lamothes. See Forster, *The Nobility of Toulouse;* and Berlanstein, *The Barristers of Toulouse,* 54–55.

90. Giesey, "Rules of Inheritance," 279–85.

91. This attitude is similar to that of the barristers of Toulouse, for whom "that transcendent notion of family which inspired and compelled sacrifice among the children of aristocrats did not have the same force," and they tried to insure the social standing of each child. Berlanstein, *The Barristers of Toulouse,* 64–65.

92. This return was reduced by the deduction of two or three *vingtièmes* on several of the *rentes*. See Appendix III.

93. Victor purchased a *rente constituée* for 12,000 l. in 1792 for an income of 600 l. per year, and another in 1801 for 1,200 francs, bringing in 60 francs per year. ADG 3E 21737, Constitution de rente, 6 August 1792; and 3E 21754, Constitution de rente, 26 Floréal An IX. Also in 1792, Alexandre Lamothe purchased a *rente* for 8,000 l., with a return of 400 l. per year. 3E 13082, Rente constituée, 2 January 1792.

94. Delphin to Victor, 14 May 1763. This compares to a yearly revenue of 2,500 l. for the average barrister of Toulouse, or 5,000–6,000 l. per annum for the typical Toulousan aristocrat. Most of

income, in particular, the country properties and his and Alexis's professional income. In a rather sharp letter to Victor and Alexandre in July 1763, Delphin outlined some of the family's sources of revenue. (See Appendix III). According to Delphin, the family earned 3,507 l., 10 s. gross on their houses and *rentes*. He eliminated the revenues from the country properties from the discussion, asserting, "I will not talk to you here about the country properties because in years like the present one, the best we can hope for is that [revenues] cover the cost of cultivation." Thus, it seems that the professional fees of Delphin and Alexis contributed a significant amount to the family's income even though Delphin claimed that "the proceeds are unfortunately very slim."[95]

It is possible that Delphin exaggerated the paucity of his and Alexis's earnings to impress upon his brothers the need to spend money wisely, since the professional honoraria that the Lamothes earned in their respective professions certainly played a role in the family accounts. In 1757, Daniel had informed Victor that his continued stay in Paris depended in large part on "the proceeds of my *cabinet*," and warned him that "revenues from . . . my work provided me with resources that necessarily diminish with the weight of my years."[96] Alexis suggested that his father's retirement from the practice of law placed a major strain on the family's finances, and the family eagerly anticipated the day that Victor's medical practice would allow him to earn a salary and "carry a part of the burden that now falls entirely on us."[97]

We can assume that each component of the Lamothe family's revenues— land, houses, *rentes*, and salaries—was essential to maintaining their standard of living. In general, their revenues and the size of the family patrimony allowed them a comfortable, if not lavish, style of living. However, if any of these resources brought a smaller return than expected—or especially when, as Alexis warned in 1761, "nearly all channels that bring us money are blocked or at least obstructed"—the delicate financial balance of the family was threatened.[98]

Bordeaux's *parlementaires* enjoyed a yearly income of between 4,000 and 20,000 l. Berlanstein, *The Barristers of Toulouse*, 47; Forster, *The Nobility of Toulouse*, 119; Doyle, *The Parlement of Bordeaux*, 54.

95. Delphin to Victor and Alexandre, 7 July 1763. Jean Nicolas notes that in Savoy, active barristers earned 2,000–3,000 livres per year. *La Savoie au 18e siècle: Noblesse et bourgeoisie*, 2 vols. (Paris: Maloine, 1978), 1:317.

96. Daniel to Victor, 2 December 1758; 3 February 1759.

97. Alexis to Victor, 10 October 1762.

98. Alexis to Victor, 22 December 1761. Marie also noted in August to Victor and Alexandre, "Les

Like their revenues, the demands on the Lamothe family's resources fluctuated from year to year. Despite the conservative nature of their investments and financial dealings, the variations in the economy, the costs of education and maintenance for Victor and Alexandre, taxes, and new purchases all played a role in determining the family's net income. In a bad year, entreaties of Victor's parents, brothers, and sisters to practice economy held a special urgency. The early 1760s, and especially 1763, the year of Daniel's death, were particularly grim. But the large size of the family meant that the family's resources were always under a certain strain. Marie advised Victor, "You must often think about the fact that there are seven of us, and consequently, you must not be extravagant."[99] Alexis made the same point, observing, "There are seven of us to divide a rather small patrimony."[100] Even in more profitable years, the family was quick to admonish Victor to "watch your time, your health and your purse."

In the 1750s, and 1760s, the major expense the family faced was the cost of educating Victor and Alexandre in Paris.[101] The financial burden on the family increased when Alexandre joined Victor in Paris. Alexis wrote to his two brothers, "Our papa frequently talks with us about the expenditure you require, *mes beaux messieurs* . . . the expenses for one thing or another for you absorb a good half of the revenues."[102] By 1762, the family was providing Victor with 1,100 l. per year to cover his costs, and a similar sum for Alexandre.[103] This expense increased the family's reluctance to allow Victor to continue his medical studies in Paris.[104] With Daniel's death in March 1763, Delphin informed Victor and Alexandre that their stipends would have to be reduced, and warned them, "You see that since you two receive 1,550#, there remains only 1,324# for the five of us . . . if you find it impossible to be satisfied with that which we are

revenues diminüe soit parce que les maisons ne ce loüe pas car nous en aurons bientot trois a loüer, soit même par ce que les danrées ne ce vande pas ou ce vande mal." Marie to Victor and Alexandre, 23 August 1761.

　99. Marie to Victor, 20 April 1757.

　100. Alexis to Victor and Alexandre, 28–31 August 1760.

　101. See Daniel to Victor, 22 November 1757; 20 April 1757; and 22 November 1757; as well as Marie to Victor, 1 December 1756 and 6 January 1759.

　102. Alexis to Victor and Alexandre, 28–31 August 1760.

　103. Alexis to Victor, 23 January 1762.

　104. See Delphin to Victor, 21 August 1762. Despite constant reminders that this stipend was an extraordinary burden on the family's resources, Victor overspent his pension of 1,100 l. by 293 l. in 1762. Delphin to Victor, 9 December 1762.

putting aside for you, it will be necessarily to start using your capital assets," that is, their future inheritance.[105]

Other demands on the family's revenues increased significantly in the 1760s. The purchase of Muscadet, despite its potential, strained the family coffers. In 1761, Delphin wrote, "Muscadet can justly be called expensive, we had to spend 2,000# over the revenues of last year."[106] Outlays increased when they purchased additional land at Muscadet for 1,000 l.[107] Delphin advanced 4,000 l. of his personal funds toward repairs on Muscadet between 1760 and 1763, and was forced to borrow money in order to do so.[108] The other family properties demanded attention as well, and Delphin noted that to renovate the house on Rue Gensan would cost 7,000–8,000 l.[109] In early 1764, Delphin wrote with real concern about the family's financial situation: "For example, we have borrowed or will borrow the 600# that you will receive, not counting the 1,000# that we borrowed last year: we prefer to do so rather than raise [the money] from capital assets that afford us some revenue."[110] It was preferable to borrow money to cover costs rather than to sell off capital, the core of the family fortune, although borrowing was to be kept to a minimum.[111] Like the barristers of Toulouse, the Lamothes were always cautious when incurring financial obligations.[112]

Both Delphin and Alexis complained of the burden of taxes as well. Although as barristers the Lamothes were not subject to a personal *taille*, they were required to pay the *capitation* on themselves and their servants as well as taxes on their properties, both urban and rural.[113] In 1762, Delphin decried "the extraordinary rise in taxes," and Alexis concurred, noting "the increase in taxes, which have doubled in the last few years" because of the

105. Delphin to Victor, 14 May 1763. Victor's new *pension* cost 550 l., and Alexandre's 500 l., so their stipends were reduced to 800 and 750 l. per annum respectively. Delphin to Victor and Alexandre, 7 June 1763.

106. Delphin to Victor and Alexandre, 25 September 1761. See also Marie to Victor, 25 November 1761; and Alexis to Victor, 28–30 September 1764.

107. Delphin to Victor, 10 March 1764.

108. Delphin to Victor and Alexandre, 7 June 1763.

109. Delphin to Victor and Alexandre, 25 September 1761.

110. Delphin to Victor, 10 March 1764.

111. Delphin to Victor and Alexandre, 11 March 1763.

112. Berlanstein, *The Barristers of Toulouse*, 54. Following Daniel's death, the family borrowed 1,000 l. from their relative and financial contact, M. Jauge. Delphin to Victor and Alexandre, 7 June 1763.

113. The Lamothe's tax obligations for the *capitation* can be found in ADG Série C, and their assessments for the *taille* and *dixième* at Sainte-Foy-la-Grande are in the Archives municipales de Sainte-Foy-la-Grande, Série CC. See Appendix IV for table.

fiscal demands of the war.[114] Delphin wrote to Victor and Alexandre in
June 1763 that they had paid 633 l. for the *vingtième de maison* and the
capitation, and Alexis reported that September, "Taxes are going to be
increased, it is believed, and rigorously."[115] In 1764, the cost of the *centième
denier* on the succession of their father's estate was an additional burden.[116]

Although the Lamothe family's investments were conservative, assuring a
steady base income, their net revenues varied from year to year based on
a number of factors. Some years they were forced to borrow money, and
they constantly stressed the need to economize. At the same time, their
standard of living remained well above the majority of Frenchmen and
-women, and their careful management of resources allowed them to
weather the crises of the 1760s in good stead.

3. Family Goals, Roles, and Strategies
in the Management of Resources

The members of the Lamothe family in Bordeaux lived together under the
same roof, and, with some exceptions, their resources were managed in the
interests of the family as a whole. At the same time, Delphin and Alexis
kept careful account of their own contributions to the family coffers when
revenues from the family property and investments were insufficient to
cover the year's expenses. They meticulously recorded the money they
sent to their brothers in the capital, the purchases that Victor or Alexandre
made for them in Paris, and the repayment of those funds. Examination of
the role that each member of the Lamothe family played in the administration of the family's wealth, the strategies that lay behind their financial

114. Delphin to Victor, 9 February 1762; Alexis to Victor, 10 October 1762. The heavy costs of
the Seven Years War brought about several tax increases, including a second *vingtième* in 1756, a *don
gratuit* from the cities of France in 1759, and a third *vingtième* and a doubling or tripling of the *capitation*
in 1760. The end of the war in 1763 brought some relief, with the abolition of the third *vingtième* and
double *capitation*, but taxes remained high due to the staggering debts incurred by the royal
government during the war. Dale Van Kley, *The Jansenists and the Expulsion of the Jesuits from France,
1757–1765* (New Haven: Yale University Press, 1975), 164–65 and 206, and Michel Antoine, *Louis XV*
(Paris: Fayard, 1989), 790–94.
115. Delphin to Victor and Alexandre, 7 June 1763; Alexis to Victor and Alexandre, 6 September
1763.
116. Delphin to Victor, 10 March 1764.

decisions, and their method of handling resources illuminates family relations and patterns of authority within the family.

Until his death in 1763, Daniel directed the resources of his large family, although he occasionally delegated authority.[117] But with the death of the family patriarch, the structure of authority and decision making within the family concerning financial matters changed greatly. Daniel's widow, Marie de Sérézac, played a new and important role in controlling the family's finances. Legally, French widows enjoyed much greater control over the management of their resources than did wives, who were required to submit to their husbands' financial decisions.[118] Her marriage contract with Daniel de Lamothe gave her possession outright of one-half of the *acquêts* of their marriage.[119] However, Marie de Sérézac was around sixty-five years old at the time of her husband's death and willing to delegate many of her fiscal responsibilities to her two elder sons.[120] She seemed willing to defer to her elder sons in most cases, especially since the family as a whole was forced to rely on Delphin and Alexis's income from the practice of law in the tight years following Daniel's death.[121] Still, Marie de Sérézac continued to act on her own behalf in many instances, and signed a number of contracts relating to joint property alongside her sons.[122] She also saw to it that one-half of Muscadet, their most costly

117. See, for example, ADG 3E 21673, Procuration, 21 August 1760; 3E 21676, Procuration, 12 April 1762.

118. Darrow argues that elite widows generally gained some independence, and lived quite comfortably, in *Revolution in the House*, 116. However, Julie Hardwick found among the widows of notaries in Nantes that "widows often found it difficult in daily practice to take advantage of the autonomy their legal position promised," and argues that patriarchal cultural practices effectively circumscribed their enhanced legal rights. See "Widowhood and Patriarchy in Seventeenth Century France," *Journal of Social History* 26 (Fall 1992): 133. Adrienne Rogers also outlines the legal and cultural restrictions placed on widows in "Women and the Law," in Samia I. Spencer, ed., *French Women and the Age of Enlightenment* (Bloomington: Indiana University Press, 1984), 38–39.

119. ADG 3E 19493, #233, Articles de mariage, Daniel Sanfourche de Lamothe and Marie de Sérézac, 16 December 1723.

120. See, for example, ADG 2C 165, Contrôle des grandes actes, Bureau de Bordeaux, 18 April 1763; 2C 474, Centième denier, Bureau de Bordeaux, 21 February 1764.

121. Hardwick found that generational timing often determined whether some widows took a more active role in the management of their affairs. The widowed mothers of minors were more likely to handle business as the household head, while the mothers of adult children often transferred management to sons, or even sons-in-law. See "Widowhood and Patriarchy," 141.

122. ADG 2C 593, Contrôle des actes, Bureau d'Ambarès, Vente, 24 March 1764; 2C 166, Contrôle des grandes actes, Bureau de Bordeaux, Reconnoissance, 23 July 1763; 3E 21025, Achat, 11 December 1764; 2C 3843, Centième denier, Bureau de Sainte-Foy, 21 December 1768; 3E 20657, Vente, 22 May 1772.

acquêt, was registered in her name after Daniel's death.[123] Despite her affection for and trust in her sons, Daniel's widow was careful to protect her own interests. When Delphin prepared his marriage contract with Elisabeth de Brulz in 1772, his mother played an active role in establishing the conditions of their marriage. She gave her permission to the marriage, agreeing to house and feed her son and his wife, their children, and their servants. At the same time, a clause was inserted, stipulating, "In case of incompatibility on the part of one or the other party, the aforementioned *dame* [Marie de Sérézac] will leave to her son the possession of the property inherited by him through the decease of the late Sieur de Lamothe, his father, and the brothers and sisters who have predeceased him, reserving, however, to the aforementioned *dame* the property in which she retains ownership or usufruct, to make whatever arrangements with her other children she deems appropriate."[124] Marie de Sérézac possibly feared the destabilizing impact of the introduction of Delphin's wife into the household. As the widow and mother of lawyers, she understood the need to protect her own interests.[125]

A telling sign of Marie de Sérézac's enhanced role in the management of the family's finances was the attitude of her children. In a letter, Delphin chided his brothers in Paris: "As for the rest, I am pleased to inform you that when you speak of your plans, you should be more careful than you have been in the past to include my dear mother. Thanks be to God, she continues to manage her own affairs, and we do nothing without consulting her."[126] This admonition suggests two things. First, despite Marie de Sérézac's control of her own goods, Victor and Alexandre recognized that Delphin and Alexis were the primary decision makers concerning the family's finances and the management of their property. At the same time,

123. ADG 2C 1795, Mutations des immeubles de toutes manieres, Table alphabétique, Bureau of Cenon-Carbon Blanc, 9 April 1765, 53 bis.

124. ADG 3E 21696, Contrat de mariage, Delphin de Lamothe and Elisabeth de Brulz, 21 June 1772.

125. This arrangement was similar to contracts drawn up by peasants when the household head made the decision to transfer property to a son. In regions where the stem family was part of the developmental cycle of a household, legal contracts specifying both the rights of the parents and the children were customary procedure, effecting the transfer of property between parents and heir. The reservations in the contract were often the parents' only guarantee of future support. According to Lutz Berkner, "The fact that the peasants invariably chose to include the details of their rights in the contract suggests a common-sense awareness of the frailty of such agreements without any legal guarantees." See "The Stem Family and the Developmental Cycle of the Peasant Household: An Eighteenth-Century Austrian Example," *American Historical Review* 77 (April 1972): 402.

126. Delphin to Victor and Alexandre, 10 March 1764.

it implies that Delphin and Alexis were eager to assure their mother that they and the rest of her children were taking into account her desires and concerns relating to the family finances.

Ultimately, Delphin and Alexis, as co-heirs to their father's fortune, exercised the greatest control over the family's finances following the death of their father, and even earlier.[127] Daniel bequeathed a great deal of power to his two eldest sons in the disposition of his goods, as the will specified that Delphin and Alexis had the power to pay the heirs "in property or cash."[128] Like their father, they were determined to manage their resources so as to bring the greatest benefits to the family as a whole. This included providing Victor with a good education so that he would be able to establish a profitable medical practice, and it meant helping Alexandre to buy his costly venal office at the Conseil du roi.[129] While frequently chiding Victor for his high expenses in the capital, his brothers were also generous in sending him small presents of their own money to pay for certain expenses, or even to go sightseeing.[130] They determined the size of Victor and Alexandre's pensions after Daniel's death. They sent them money to finance their trips to Bordeaux.[131] But their generosity had definite limits.[132] Alexis and Delphin's control over the family's coffers and, consequently, authority over their brothers in Paris was most dramatically illustrated when they insisted that Victor return to Bordeaux in 1766, and he complied.

The two sisters, Marie and Marianne, exercised little control over the major financial decisions of the family. They were consulted, however, on

127. When Victor overspent his stipend by nearly 300 l. in 1762, he turned to his brothers for assistance in breaking the news to his father. Alexis to Victor, 1 January 1763. It was not unusual in early modern Europe for fathers and adult sons to increasingly share responsibility for management of the household. See Kent, *Household and Lineage in Renaissance Florence*, 56–58.

128. It was not until 18 February 1772 that the family chose to register Daniel's last will and testament, which suggests that until 1772, the year of Delphin's marriage, the provisions spelled out in the will were perhaps not so important. The entry in Bordeaux's *contrôle des actes* reads in its entirety, "Testament olographe de M.M. Daniel Lamothe avocat au parlement par lequel il institue Mrs. Simon-Antoine Delphin aîné et Alexis [ ] Lamothe ses fils et legue a M. Jules Lamothe pretre, a Dlle Marie Lamothe fille aîné, a Dlle Marie Anne Lamothe [ ] et aux Mrs. Victor et Alexandre Lamothe tous ses enfans ses sommes que les deux heriteres generaux ont le pouvoir de leur paient en fonds ou argent en date du 26 aout 1762." ADG 2C 189, Contrôle des grandes actes, Bureau de Bordeaux, 18 February 1772, 85.

129. In a letter to Victor, Alexandre asserted that it would cost 50,000–60,000 livres to purchase the office of *avocat aux conseils* in Paris. Alexandre to Victor, 18 February 1761.

130. Delphin to Victor, 6 May 1757; 3 January 1758; 9 January 1759.

131. Delphin to Victor and Alexandre, 6 August 1765.

132. Alexis to Victor, 28 October 1762.

certain financial matters, especially those relating to the management of the household. Their father and brothers relied upon them to help economize and to persuade their brothers in Paris to spend money wisely. Both Marianne and Marie emphasized their "taste for thrift," which they tried to impart to Victor and Alexandre.[133]

In only one instance did a major dispute arise over the management of the family's money. Shortly after Daniel's death, Jules raised objections to several loans at interest that his father had made and persuaded his mother and sisters that the family was obliged to refund the money, because of the evil of usury. Delphin and Alexis were clearly irritated by Jules's misgivings, but they wanted to avoid the problems that his objections "could give rise to in the family." Delphin requested that Victor search out support from the Sorbonne or *petit Carmes* supporting their position that "one can, in [good] conscience, draw an honest interest from a sum that one loans to a person who is not obliged by necessity to borrow it." The issue of usury was very much alive for families of the eighteenth century, and Delphin and Alexis felt obliged to persuade their mother and sisters to support their point of view by searching out the opinions of sympathetic ecclesiastics.[134] This suggests that Marie de Sérézac and her daughters claimed the right to intervene in the family's financial arrangements. Furthermore, Delphin and Alexis respected the opinions of the women of the family enough to try to win them over rather than assert their authority. On the other hand, they were sufficiently convinced of the correctness of their own views and the need to protect the financial underpinnings of their family that they were unwilling to submit to the dictates of Jules's "scruples."

Daniel, Delphin, and Alexis's revenues from their law practice went in part to pay for Victor and Alexandre's education. Professional training was a financial investment even more important than real estate, for not only did the family's fortune depend on the professional revenues of the men, but an agreeable livelihood was also considered essential to one's happiness, and to one's masculine identity.[135] Consequently, the entire family

---

133. See, for example, Marianne to Victor, 20 April 1757; Marie to Victor, 10 January 1758.

134. Delphin and Alexis to Victor, undated 1764. Delphin asked that Victor not mention the contents of the letter to his brother, suggesting that he suspected that the very pious Alexandre might side with Jules, his mother, and his sisters. Robert Forster's study of the Depont family of La Rochelle indicates that the problem of usury was still important to Catholic families of the eighteenth century. Forster, *Merchants, Landlords, Magistrates*, 23–24.

135. Alexis to Victor, 14 October 1755. In general, well-to-do fathers tried to provide their

pooled resources to educate the male members of the family and, in the case of Alexandre, to pay for his office at the Conseil du roi—despite Alexis's and Delphin's concerns about the price.[136] When informing Victor that he could stay to continue his education in Paris, Delphin wrote, "[Our father] is willing to pay for the expenses that are necessary for you & if the condition of our little fortune does not change due to some unforeseen circumstance, these expenses will not even be drawn on your future inheritance."[137]

But they expected gratitude for these sacrifices. Shortly after Daniel's death, Delphin was extremely offended when Victor wrote to him, suggesting that he and Alexis were keeping their law revenues to themselves.[138] Delphin's response was pointed:

> It is far from the case that we have received a *multiplicité de bons honoraires* & even less so that they are *for us alone* [emphasis his] since in truth, we have merged them with those of the household (not without hoping for a return . . . we are keeping an account so as to recuperate [our investment] at a more opportune time), since as I have told you, I have advanced nearly 4,000# for Muscadet, & beyond that which I have borrowed, Alexis has also advanced a considerable amount to our household. The 20 pistoles that we are sending to Victor today come from him, in short his little purse is our resource for our small immediate needs.[139]

Delphin and Alexis stressed that Victor and Alexandre's pensions would be even smaller "without the small revenue from our *cabinets* which contributes each year to either the payment of your allowances, or the upkeep of the house, or the repairs at Muscadet."[140]

The fate of the sisters, on the other hand, did not seem to worry their

children with sufficient capital to insure a suitable standard of living, but they also planned for their sons to have careers. Darrow, *Revolution in the House*, 103. Bernard Groethuysen argues that work, or professional activity, was central to the identity of the bourgeois male in the eighteenth century in *The Bourgeois: Catholicism Versus Capitalism in Eighteenth-Century France*, trans. Mary Ilford (New York: Barrie & Rockliff the Cresset P., 1968), 161.

136. Alexis to Victor, 29 June 1764.
137. Delphin to Victor, 31 March 1759.
138. See note penned by Victor at the bottom of a letter from Delphin written 14 May 1763.
139. Delphin to Victor and Alexandre, 7 June 1763.
140. Alexis to Victor, 28–30 September 1764.

parents or brothers. There was no concerted effort to place them in a "suitable" position, either through marriage or a religious vocation. The expense of a dowry would have probably created havoc in the family's finances, making it more desirable to keep Marie and Marianne living in the family household.[141] Furthermore, the sisters did not receive an education on par with their highly trained brothers. They must have received some schooling, for their writing ability was far superior to their mother's who, according to Marianne, could "barely write."[142] Still, in contrast to Delphin and Alexis's easily composed missives, it was a struggle for Marie or Marianne to write a letter. Marie made this clear when she scolded Victor for complaining that the family did not write frequently enough: "Don't you know that my brothers are very busy, and that our correspondence falls on two poor souls who do not regard [writing] a letter as a minor affair."[143] She and Marianne apologized frequently for their mistakes in spelling and the lack of grace in their writing styles.[144]

It does not appear that their parents or brothers had to force Marie or Marianne into spinsterhood. Family discipline and close ties insured their willingness to sacrifice themselves for the good of the family, that is, their brothers. In short, the sisters had internalized a strong ethic of self-sacrifice to the advantage of their brothers. While reminding Victor and Alexandre of the need to economize in Paris, Marie frequently vowed her willingness to sacrifice on their behalf, and that "no one in the world

141. Dowries were a major expense for an elite family desirous of maintaining social status. Still, that neither Lamothe daughter married was unusual, for even in the well-disciplined families of the Toulousan nobility and the Montauban elite, at least one daughter usually married, and among the barristers of Toulouse, the majority of daughters married and were generously dowered. Forster, *The Nobility of Toulouse*, 125–36; Darrow, *Revolution in the House*, 105–10; Berlanstein, *The Barristers of Toulouse*, 65.

142. Marianne to Victor, 29 June 1764. The few letters that Marie de Sérézac penned to her sons were in large, childish handwriting, full of spelling errors, and manifestly a great effort for her. See, for example, her letter to Victor written on 1 March 1757. In the eighteenth century, most upper- and middle-class women received their early education at home, and were sent to the convents of teaching orders around the age of ten or twelve for further education. Samia I. Spencer, "Women and Education," in *French Women in the Age of Enlightenment*, 85–87. But this education was much narrower than that of their brothers, and indicated their inferior status in the family. Margaret R. Hunt, *The Middling Sort: Commerce, Gender, and the Family in England, 1680–1780* (Berkeley and Los Angeles: University of California Press, 1996), 80–84.

143. Marie to Victor, 11 August 1760.

144. See, for example, Marie to Victor, 28 May 1757; 6 January 1759; 24 August 1759; Marianne to Victor, 24 March 1761. Despite advances in female literacy in the eighteenth century, women were still poorly trained in the skills of writing and spelling, and the quality of their formal education was unimpressive. Even the letters of the well-known author Mme. de Graffigny were full of spelling errors. Spencer, "Women and Education," 83–94.

desires your advancement and your well-being more than I do."[145] In return, the sisters were assured of the affection of their brothers and parents.[146]

Joint management of the family resources became more complicated with the marriage of Delphin. Presumably at this time, or following the death of their mother, Marie de Sérézac, in 1773, the Lamothe brothers decided to make a more definitive division of the family's property.[147] By the marriage contract of Delphin and Elisabeth de Brulz, Marie de Sérézac had instituted Delphin as heir to one-third of her property, *meubles et immeubles*, plus 1,000 l., with the remaining two-thirds presumably to be divided among the three younger sons.[148] Marie and Marianne died before 1772, the year of Delphin's marriage, and the division was thus not complicated by their claims. The brothers may have paid Alexandre, the youngest, his portion around this time, because a later official *partage* noted that he had received his legacy.[149] Thus, Delphin, Alexis and Victor, along with Delphin's offspring, were left to share the remaining family wealth. The precise divisions in the family property made in the early 1770s were not recorded. However, Delphin apparently became master of Muscadet around this time, while Alexis took possession of Goulards.

There had been earlier indications that the division of real property would fall along these lines. Alexis had always expressed greater affection for Goulards than did Delphin, who seemed a bit bored with life in the country.[150] Muscadet was much closer to Bordeaux, which allowed Delphin to go back and forth between the city and the grape harvest at Muscadet. From 1761 on, Delphin took charge of the vintage at Muscadet while Alexis occupied himself with the wine harvest at Goulards. By the early 1770s, all purchases of property at Saint-Avit were made exclusively

---

145. Marie to Victor, 2 April 1757.

146. For an analysis of Marie and Marianne's decision to remain single, see my "A Choice Not to Wed? Unmarried Women in Eighteenth-Century France," *Journal of Social History* 29 (Summer 1996): 884–94. Hunt demonstrates how families could effectively use love to ensure self-sacrificing behavior on the part of daughters in *The Middling Sort*, 81–82.

147. The entry of the marriage contract into the *contrôle des actes* of Bordeaux notes that both Delphin and Elisabeth de Brulz were bringing to the marriage fortunes worth 46,000 l., which suggests that Delphin's share of the family's property had been calculated by this time. ADG 2C 190, Contrôle des grandes actes, 30 June 1772.

148. ADG 3E 21696, Contrat de mariage, Delphin de Lamothe and Elisabeth de Brulz, 21 June 1772.

149. ADG 3E 13205, Partage, 23 June 1815. The document does not specify, however, when Alexandre received his portion.

150. BM Ms. 1696, Fonds Lamontagne, Correspondence, November 1746, No. 3. See Lamothe Family Letters, passim, for Alexis's deep affection for Goulards.

in Alexis's name.[151] In his will, Alexis confirmed that "the domain of Goulards came into my possession in our division of the family property, being an inherited property to which we have always been extremely attached."[152] Following Delphin's death, the domain of Muscadet went to his eldest son, despite Delphin's failure to write a will or to specify in his marriage contract that Muscadet was exclusively his property.[153]

Alexis, Victor, Delphin, and his wife continued to live together and to invest their money by common consent, while Alexandre's residence in Paris and the payment of his share of the family inheritance removed him from joint financial decisions. Strong evidence of the continued intertwining of the family's resources can be found in the complicated *acte de partage* agreed to by Victor, Alexandre, and Delphin's two surviving children, François-Marie-Jean-Delphin and Dugravier de Lamothe in 1815:

> The three brothers . . . Lamothe *aîné*, Alexis and Victor lived together and from the fruits of their work and their industry, they purchased and built two houses on Rue Fondaudège . . . and two other houses on Rue du Reservoir . . . in addition, they reconstructed a house on Rue Neuve . . . for which they used the funds from the legacy of their common father and mother . . . After the death of the eldest M. Lamothe, MM. Alexis & Victor Lamothe continued to live together and also rebuilt a house on Rue Bouquière . . . for which they used the funds from the legacy of their common father and mother.[154]

151. The *taille* for the years 1779 and 1786 was established in the name of both Alexis and Simon (Delphin) Lamothe, despite Delphin's death in 1781, probably a bureaucratic oversight. See Archives municipales de Sainte-Foy, CC 67, 13; and CC 82, 13 bis.

152. ADG 3E 21732, Testament, Alexis Lamothe, opened on 25 March 1790.

153. A *contrat de vente*, ADG 3E 28078, 29 August 1821, notes François-Marie-Delphin-Jean Lamothe *aîné* as living in the commune of Bassens, "sur son domaine de Muscadet." Another *contrat de vente*, registered in the *Actes civiles publics de Bordeaux* in 1819, lists François Lamothe as *maire* of Bassens. ADG, Administration de l'enregistrement et des domaines: Hypothèques. Registre de formalité. Transcriptions des actes translatifs de propriété d'immeuble, Direction de Bordeaux, vol. 305, 12 October 1819, 58. The *partage* of 1815 included the domaine of Muscadet as part of the *lot* of François Lamothe and specified that Delphin died *ab-intestat*. ADG 3E 13205, Partage, 23 June 1815. The marriage contract of Delphin and Elisabeth de Brulz did specify that Delphin was the "fils de defunt Sr. Daniel de Lamothe, Seigneur de La maison noble de Muscadet en Montferrand," which was perhaps a way of asserting Delphin's claim to this property. ADG 3E 21696, Contrat de mariage, Delphin de Lamothe and Elisabeth de Brulz, 21 June 1772.

154. ADG 3E 13205, Partage, 23 June 1815.

Delphin's interest in the family's joint property passed to his sons at the time of his death.

Delphin's marriage to Elisabeth de Brulz was a good one from a material standpoint. In 1783, the property of Lyde, part of her dowry, was valued at 60,000 l., a very respectable sum.[155] As a result of Delphin and Elisabeth's numerous holdings, their sons were well provided for after Delphin's death in 1781 and that of their mother in 1812.[156] In addition, Alexis and Victor, both childless bachelors, chose to treat their nephews as sons, naming them as heirs to their possessions. Through their investments and financial management, the three (and later two) brothers maintained, and apparently increased, the value of their father's legacy.[157]

Alexis and Victor were the only children of the Lamothe family who wrote wills, curious in a family of lawyers. Alexis wrote and sealed his last will and testament in September 1786, three years before his death in November 1789. In establishing his nephews as his universal heirs, Alexis explained: "In addition [to my nephews], I have two brothers, to whom I am equally very attached, but who will excuse me if, in the distribution of my property, I show some preference to my nephews. In a sense, this is a kind of compensation which became necessary because of what they lost." Alexis did not neglect his two surviving brothers, however. To Alexandre, he bequeathed the sum of 4,000 l. and a *rente viagère* of 180 l. on a capital of 2,000 l., along with a number of personal items. Victor was to inherit all of Alexis's "furniture and possessions neither given nor bequeathed," and his share of two tickets from the royal lottery, which he and Victor had purchased together. He also requested that Victor take charge of his estate and pay his debts, for Victor was awarded usufruct of all Alexis's property and guardianship over his nephews until they reached the age of twenty-five. At this time, they would be given rights to one-half of their inheritance, and Victor would continue to enjoy usufruct over the rest of the property until his death. Alexis was confident that Victor would manage his possessions well and to his nephews' benefit: "I assume that the

155. ADG 3E 15033, Contrat de mariage, René de La Faye and Elisabeth de Brulz, 28 June 1783.

156. The division of Elisabeth de Brulz's property following her death was complicated considerably by her second marriage to René, Vicomte de la Faye. See ADG 3E 13203, Partage, 18 March 1813; and 3E 15033, Contrat de Mariage, René de La Faye and Elisabeth de Brulz, 28 June 1783.

157. When Alexis died in 1790, his share of one-third of the town property was worth about 48,833 l., and Goulards was valued at 35,000 l. This means that the town property in its totality was worth approximately 146,500 l. in 1790, as compared with its value of 74,500 l. in 1763. ADG 2C 490, Centième denier, Bureau de Bordeaux, 19 April 1790; and 2C 3855, Centième denier, Bureau de Sainte-Foy, 1 May 1790.

intention of my brother, based on what he has said to me many times, is to conserve [my property] . . . in its totality for my nephews," and he was reassured by Victor's "paternal feelings for them."

Alexis felt a strong family duty to provide for his nephews, who had been deprived of a father at a young age, but he also felt obliged to insure that his brothers would continue to live comfortably. In his will, Alexis expressed some concern that the nephews might not show the proper gratitude, or might even try to challenge his and Victor's previous management of their property. He assured his nephews that "my brother and I have done our best to manage and administer their property and revenues with a rare generosity that was controlled by our tender affection for the children, and by the memory of their father; and [we] took such care for their persons that each year we used our own property and revenues to their advantage, because their own were not sufficient; this will be easy for them to ascertain through examination of the accounts and records that we have maintained." However, Alexis warned them if any were "ungrateful and unjust enough to complain, conduct research, or cause problems for my brother concerning this matter," he would revoke the provisions of his will, reducing the portion of the ungrateful nephew to only five sols, the minimum required by customary law, and Victor would be instituted as universal heir.[158]

Alexis's testament attests to the conflation of sentimental and financial ties in the Lamothe family. Trust and affection were essential components of the family life and facilitated the joint management of their assets. At the same time, Alexis was not willing to assume that the sentimental attachment of his young nephews would be a sufficient guarantee, and he took legal measures to assure Victor's future in the case of ungratefulness or cupidity on the part of his nephews.

However, in planning the provisions of his will, Alexis did not anticipate one major event. He had assumed that his brother Alexandre would remain a barrister at the Conseil du roi in Paris. However, the Revolution in 1789 left Alexandre without a profession, since his office at the *conseil* was abolished in 1790.[159] He returned to Bordeaux and Victor opened the family home to his brother. Alexandre stayed in Bordeaux for a time, but

---

158. ADG 3E 21732, Testament, Alexis de Lamothe, opened 25 March 1790.

159. The French legal profession was entirely overhauled in 1789–90. Michael P. Fitzsimmons, *The Parisian Order of Barristers and the French Revolution* (Cambridge: Harvard University Press, 1987), 33–89.

left for Goulards as the events of the Terror began to unfold.[160] Local historian Jules Delpit wrote with some drama: "Like so many others, whose talents were inferior to his, the former *avocat au conseil* could have easily made for himself a new life among these ruins; but with a heart full of bitterness, he preferred to follow the precept of the wise, and vowed go into retirement. Alexandre de Lamothe shut himself up in his château at Goulards."[161]

The Revolution ruined the fortune of Alexandre Lamothe. Living in Paris, provided with his profession and portion, he had been excluded from the joint investments of his brothers in Bordeaux. With the abolition of his profession in 1790, he lost his main source of income. Although Victor surely provided his brother with all his basic needs at Goulards, Alexandre's possessions were comparatively meager upon his death in 1819. He left only a library of 499 books valued at 524.50 francs and a *rente* of 100 francs per year based on a capital of 2,000 francs.[162]

In contrast, Victor's fortunes were not so adversely affected by the Revolution. He continued to practice medicine without apparent interruption. He paid heavy taxes to the municipal governments of Bordeaux and Sainte-Foy during the 1790s, often under protest, and these levies indicate that he still enjoyed a high level of prosperity.[163] His property was not confiscated by the revolutionary government. He was sufficiently wealthy

160. Alexandre may have experienced some difficulty with the municipal government under the Terror. In the *Repertoire des rejections*, maintained by the Sections for Year II, it was noted that Alexandre Lamothe, "homme de loi" "n'a presque pas paru a la section." AM I 59, Sections. Section No. 8, Michel Montagne aux Feuillants, #66: Repertoire des rejections: Frimaire-Nivôse An II, 13 Nivôse.

161. Jules Delpit, *Notes biographiques sur les Messieurs de Lamothe* (Bordeaux: Balarac Jeune, 1846), 8. The *acte de partage* of 1815 specified that Alexandre would receive usufruct of Goulards for the rest of his life in the case that Victor predeceased him. ADG 3E 13205, Partage, 23 June 1815.

162. ADG Q 31/d 5, Registre de recette: Déclaration des mutations par décès, Bureau de Sainte-Foy, 4 March 1820, No. 65.

163. On 26 December 1792, the Jurade of Sainte-Foy-la-Grande refused to reduce the charges on Victor Lamothe's property, noting, "Toutes les propriétés de la municipalité . . . sont également trop chargées." See Jean Valette and Jean Cavignac, eds., *Les Jurades de Sainte-Foy-la-Grande*, 2 vols. (Bordeaux: Association pour l'édition des Jurades de Sainte-Foy-la-Grande, 1980–83). Délibérations du Conseil Général de la commune de Sainte-Foy, 1792, 1:60. In Year IV, Victor was required to make a *contribution foncière* of 810 l., 16s, 3d, a sum that was agreed upon after he received a *modération* from the municipal government of Bordeaux. ADG 11 L 15. Under the Directory, he sought a reduction in his contribution to the *emprunt forcé* on the grounds that he had turned over several pieces of property to his nephews, but he was still required to pay 787.41 francs. ADG 3L 241, Arrondissement du Centre, Dec. du C. Victor Lamothe. Taxé. The document is undated, but we can assume that it was around 1797, since this is the year that Victor and his nephews informally divided their property. See ADG 3E 13205, Partage, 23 June 1815. Victor also paid a substantial *contribution foncière* in Year V. ADG 3L 241.

to purchase from his eldest nephew his half-interest in the domain of Goulards in 1821 for 12,000 francs. This meant that Victor now owned the property in partnership with his other nephew, the physician Dugravier, whom Victor treated as a son and medical partner.[164] When Victor died in 1823, his share of the Bordeaux property was worth 70,500 francs, and his property at Goulards was valued at 18,000 francs.[165] In addition, he had purchased the property of Cabanot in the commune of Véline for 10,000 francs in 1801.[166] Victor died a well-off man, and his two surviving nephews and heirs, François and Dugravier, were the beneficiaries.[167]

The administration of the Lamothe family's wealth illuminates several important aspects of their familial life, their priorities, and their goals. Fiscal prudence was the watchword as they invested predominately in land and houses, foregoing large financial returns for the security and status of real estate. They were willing to stretch their resources to purchase *immeubles* and to finance the education of Victor and Alexandre, but they always exercised caution, borrowing only when necessary and avoiding dissipation of the family's capital. This caution reveals a certain amount of anxiety in a family whose revenues fluctuated from year to year and who could not rely upon noble title to protect them in case of shortfall. Fiscal prudence and thrift were ways of managing this insecurity and maintaining family status.[168] This generally conservative approach to financial management suggests that the Lamothes were more desirous of maintaining their *rang* in society than in attempting rapid upward mobility through risky ventures or promoting the career of one favored son. Rather, they sought to administer their capital so that an *honnête* way of life could be sustained for each son. This approach to life did not rule out individual

164. ADG 3E 28078, Contrat de vente, 29 August 1821. Dugravier and his brother François had agreed to share the "nue propriété" of Goulards during the lifetime of their uncle, who enjoyed usufruct over Goulards until his death. ADG 3E 13205, Partage, 23 June 1815. Victor shared a home and medical practice in Bordeaux with Dugravier, as well as ownership of two houses on Rue Fondaudège.

165. ADG 3Q 2509, Registre des recettes: Déclarations des mutations par décès, Bureau de Bordeaux, 2 October 1823, No. 330; Q 31/d 5: Registre de recette: Déclaration des mutations par décès, Bureau de Sainte-Foy, 7 October 1823.

166. ADG 3E 21754, Contrat de vente, 29 Messidor An IX; 3E 34956, Contrat de vente, 2 Nivôse An IX.

167. The following year, Dugravier contracted a very favorable marriage to the daughter of a former nobleman. ADG 3E 26675, Contrat de mariage, Dugravier de Lamothe and Marguérite-Coraly de Pineau, 28 November 1824.

168. In *The Middling Sort*, Hunt suggests that the virtues of the English middle classes—rigorous morality and fiscal prudence—were a response to their hard-won but insecure status in the face of an unstable marketplace.

ambition. Delphin married well and tried to advance a claim to noble title. For a time, Victor sought a prestigious career as a Parisian physician. However, the family did not show a desire to sacrifice for a more brilliant future for their descendants, as did the upwardly mobile bourgeois families described by Ralph Giesey and Natalie Zemon Davis.[169]

Despite the financial difficulties of the 1760s, the Lamothe family's administration of resources was quite successful. Each son enjoyed a solid profession, at least until the Revolution cut short Alexandre's career in Paris. The family managed to retain and add to its property as a unit, even though in some cases ownership was delegated to individual members. The trust and affection of the family members, combined with a healthy dose of prudence, was key to their success. Each male of the family carefully recorded his own contributions to the family coffers and each member asserted legal title to his or her properties, but at the same time, all worked for the good of the family as a whole. When at times they omitted taking legal precautions, the family members respected these understood arrangements. Alexis and Victor treated their nephews as their own children following the death of Delphin, and made sure that his sons received legal title to Muscadet and to Delphin's share in the town property. Not only did Victor take in his brother Alexandre when the Revolution ended his career, but he successfully navigated the tides of revolution and brought the family's patrimony through intact to the benefit of his nephews. For the Lamothe family, bonds of property and affection were mutually reinforcing.

169. Giesey, "Rules of Inheritance," 81–85, and Natalie Zemon Davis, "Ghosts, Kin, and Progeny: Some Features of Family Life in Early Modern France," *Daedalus* 106 (1977): 87–92.

The Wider Circle

Kin and Friends

The Lamothes valued their kin.[1] However, the conjugal family—the immediate family of Daniel Lamothe, Marie de Sérézac, and their seven children—was the essential family unit. The Lamothes seldom used the word *famille* to mean anything other than the immediate family.[2] When

1. The role of the wider family circle in early modern Europe has been explored by a number of historians and sociologists in a variety of contexts. Examples of the abundant literature include Miranda Chaytor, "Household and Kinship: Ryton in the Late Sixteenth and Early Seventeenth Centuries," *History Workshop Journal*, no. 10 (Autumn 1980): 25–51; Jean-Louis Flandrin, *Families in Former Times: Kinship, Household, and Sexuality in Early Modern France*, trans. Richard Southern (Cambridge: Cambridge University Press, 1979); Julie Hardwick, *The Practice of Patriarchy: Gender and the Politics of Household Authority in Early Modern France* (University Park: Penn State Press, 1998); Francis William Kent, *Household and Lineage in Renaissance Florence: The Family Life of the Capponi, Ginori, and Rucellai* (Princeton: Princeton University Press, 1977); Christiane Klapisch-Zuber, *Women, Family, and Ritual in Renaissance Italy*, trans. Lydia Cochrane (Chicago: University of Chicago Press, 1985); Alan MacFarlane, *The Family Life of Ralph Josselin, a Seventeenth-Century Clergyman: An Essay in Historical Anthropology* (Cambridge: Cambridge University Press, 1970); Miriam Slater, *Family Life in the Seventeenth Century: The Verneys of Claydon House* (London: Routledge and Kegan Paul, 1984). Collections of essays such as Hans Medick and David Warren Sabean, eds., *Interest and Emotion: Essays in the Study of Family and Kinship* (Cambridge: Cambridge University Press, 1984); Robert Wheaton and Tamara K. Hareven, eds., *Family and Sexuality in French History* (Philadelphia: University of Pennsylvania Press, 1980); and Robert Forster and Orest Ranum, eds., *Family and Society: Selections from the Annales, E.S.C.*, trans. Elborg Forster and Patricia Ranum (Baltimore: Johns Hopkins University Press, 1976) deal with a variety of approaches to the study of kin relations.
2. The historical meaning and inclusiveness of terms such as "family" and "household" have been

Alexis wrote to Victor, "Return . . . to the bosom of your family," he referred only to his parents and siblings.[3] First loyalties were to the nuclear family. Daniel underscored this when he wrote to Victor, "We do not doubt that our relatives [are] filled with affection for you . . . but you must give us preference."[4] The immediate family came first.[5]

At the same time, the Lamothes enjoyed close relations with relatives in both the Guyenne and Paris, and a wide social circle in Bordeaux and Sainte-Foy. The Lamothes were part of a vast network of relatives, friends, and acquaintances whom they visited, assisted, and solicited for help. A series of vertical and horizontal bonds linked them to kin across a large area of southern and western France. Their connections stretched from Bordeaux to Castillon and Sainte-Foy and all the way four hundred miles north to Paris.

All members of the family carefully cultivated ties to relatives, friends, and subordinates. Letters to Victor often included regards to *nos chers parents* in Paris and listed friends and relatives who wished to send their compliments. Victor's siblings included news of friends and relations and asked for information about the kinfolk in Paris. On social occasions, friends and relatives habitually toasted Victor's health in his absence.[6] While these standard greetings suggest a conventional formulation, they were also a concrete means of reinforcing the bonds of consanguinity and amity.

The Lamothes led an active social life, both in Bordeaux and Sainte-Foy.

---

widely debated. See Flandrin, *Families in Former Times*, 4–9; Peter Laslett, "Introduction: The History of the Family" in Laslett and Richard Wall, eds., *Household and Family in Past Time* (Cambridge: Cambridge University Press, 1972), 1–89; Michael Mitterauer and Reinhard Sieder, *The European Family: Patriarchy to Partnership from the Middle Ages to the Present*, trans. Karla Oosterveen and Manfred Hörzinger (Chicago: University of Chicago Press, 1982), 5–10; Robert Wheaton, "Introduction: Recent Trends in the Historical Study of the French Family," 3–26, and "Affinity and Descent in Seventeenth-Century Bordeaux," 115, in Wheaton and Hareven, *Family and Sexuality*.

3. Lamothe Family Letters, Alexis to Victor, 10 October 1762.

4. Daniel to Victor, 24 July 1758.

5. This is reinforced by the fact that Daniel, Alexis, and Victor made bequests only to members of the immediate family, and in the case of Alexis and Victor, to their nephews, whom they considered their sons. See Delphin to Victor and Alexandre, 11 March 1763; ADG 3E 21732, Testament, Alexis de Lamothe, opened 25 March 1790; ADG 3Q 2509, Registre des recettes: Déclaration des mutations par décès, Bureau de Bordeaux, 2 October 1823, No. 330; ADG Q 31/d 5, Registre de recette: Déclaration des mutations par décès, Bureau de Sainte-Foy, 7 October 1823. Natalie Zemon Davis found that many families above the level of the very poor were beginning to develop a new sense of their boundaries in the sixteenth and seventeenth centuries, with interests of the immediate family becoming dominant. See "Ghosts, Kin, and Progeny: Some Features of Family Life in Early Modern France," *Daedalus* 106 (1977): 100.

6. See, for example, Marie to Victor, 20 April 1757; Marianne to Victor, 6 February 1758; Delphin to Victor, 20 May 1758.

However, both friends and relatives provided more than social diversion. Robert Wheaton argues that in seventeenth-century Bordeaux, close kin served as "a self-conscious group available to demonstrate solidarity and to affirm collectively its social identity."[7] The same was true of the Lamothe's circle of kin and friends. They were a professionally, geographically, and socially linked group, providing companionship and mutual support. It was also important that friends and relations be *useful*. Social superiors, equals, and inferiors could all be tapped to provide favors. Patronage and the mutual exchange of favors was a way of life, and the Lamothes knew how to successfully tap their wide social network.[8]

1. Ties of Blood and Friendship

The Lamothes recognized the need to foster ties with their relatives and friends, both close and distant. Few individuals could succeed socially or professionally without the strong support of not only the immediate family, but also the wider circle of uncles, aunts, and cousins.[9]

Individuals nurtured these kin connections in a number of ways. Relatives were invited to participate in key life events, such as baptism and marriage. They were often asked to serve as godparents, a role that reinforced ties of blood and affection.[10] Delphin de Lamothe's godparents were Simon Gorin, his father's cousin, and Delphine Filhol, his great-grandmother.[11] Simon de Lamothe and Marie de Lamothe were the

7. Wheaton, "Affinity and Descent in Bordeaux," 117.

8. For a sociological analysis of the structure and function of interpersonal relations and social networks, see Jeremy Boissevain, *Friends of Friends: Networks, Manipulators, and Coalitions* (Oxford: Blackwell, 1974).

9. Gayle K. Brunelle's study of the New World merchants of Rouen documents the vital necessity of kin connections for social mobility, and the importance of practical services rendered by kin. *The New World Merchants of Rouen, 1559–1630* (Kirksville, Miss.: Sixteenth Century Journal Publishers, 1991), 71–82. Also see Margaret H. Darrow, *Revolution in the House: Family, Class, and Inheritance in Southern France, 1775–1825* (Princeton: Princeton University Press, 1989), 101–4, and passim; Davis, "Ghosts, Kin, and Progeny," 100–105; Flandrin, *Families in Former Times*, 19–49; and Hardwick, *The Practice of Patriarchy*, chap. 7.

10. Wheaton found that in seventeenth-century Bordeaux about one-half of all godparents were related to their godchildren. See "Affinity and Descent in Bordeaux," 117. Flandrin and Darrow also note the coincidence of spiritual and consanguineous kinship in *Families in Former Times*, 30; and *Revolution in the House*, 102–3.

11. Pierre Meller, *Essais généalogiques: Familles du bordelais/recueil factice de brochures concernant des familles* (Bordeaux: Feret et Fils, 1897), 28.

godparents of Marie, born in 1733.[12] Alexis and Marie acted as godparents to their brother Alexandre.[13] Marie was asked to serve as *marraine* to her young Sérézac cousin, and Alexis de Lamothe was later godfather to Delphin's son, his nephew, Alexis-Ange-Antoine.[14] Daniel and his wife, and later Delphin, reinforced these bonds of kinship by giving their children the names of relatives. Simon-Antoine-Delphin probably took his names from his father's cousin, Simon Gorin; his mother's cousin, Anthoyne Vanderbet; and his maternal great-grandmother, Delphine Filhol. He later gave the name Delphin to his first-born son. Alexis and Alexis-Alexandre were likely named for their mother's brother, Alexis de Sérézac. Rose-Marguerite, who died in infancy, was named for her aunt, Marie de Sérézac's sister. This use of names served to create ties between different generations of Lamothes and Sérézacs.[15]

Daniel Lamothe and Marie de Sérézac's marriage contract reveals the importance of kin connections as well. The articles of marriage stated that Daniel Sanfourche, Sieur de Lamothe, had undertaken the proceedings "with the advice and consent of Sr. Etienne Jauge, former infantry captain and Me. Simon Gorin, royal notary and attorney in the locality of Ste. Foy, his germane cousins." Marie de Sérézac signed the contract with the advice and "authority" of her mother; her grandmother, Delphine Filhol; her maternal grandfather, Sieur Descombes; her aunt, Marie Meynard; her brother Alexis and sister Rose; and her germane cousins, the priest Anthoyne Vanderbet and Marie de Sérézac, as well as other "relatives and friends."[16] Delphin and Elisabeth de Brulz's marriage contract reveals the same reliance on kin for advice and support.[17] Delphin's marriage created a new series of affinal ties to the de Brulz family, as well as to Elisabeth's cousins, the Boudins and the Bacalans.[18]

12. Archives municipales de Sainte-Foy, GG 26, Registre de Saint-Avit-du-Moiron, 257.

13. Meller, *Essais généalogiques*, 27.

14. Marianne to Victor, 19 October 1758; ADG 3E 21732, Testament, Alexis de Lamothe, opened 25 March 1790.

15. Christiane Klapisch-Zuber explores the connections between kinship and name-giving in the Florentine context in "The Name 'Remade': The Transmission of Given Names in Florence in the Fourteenth and Fifteenth Centuries," in *Women, Family, and Ritual*, 283–309.

16. ADG 3E 19493, #233, Articles de mariage, Daniel Sanfourche de Lamothe and Marie de Sérézac, 16 December 1723.

17. Kin consent to marriage was commonplace in many regions of France in the early modern era. See Hardwick, *The Practice of Patriarchy*, 162–64; Wheaton, "Affinity and Descent in Bordeaux," 126–27.

18. ADG 3E 21696, Contrat de mariage, Delphin de Lamothe and Elisabeth de Brulz, 21 June 1772.

Baptismal certificates and contracts of marriage establish the presence of relatives at these meaningful life events.[19] However, the letters of the Lamothe family provide further verification of the importance attached to kin ties in everyday life. For example, the annual trip to Sainte-Foy for the *vendange* provided an opportunity to nurture ties with the Sérézac relatives in the region of Castillon.[20] *La voye ordinaire*, or *la route ordinaire*, as Marie called it, was a journey of about four days as they used the necessary trip to Goulards to fulfil familial obligations.[21]

Once they arrived at Sainte-Foy, the Lamothes renewed ties with relatives. Marie visited les Baratons, near Goulards, to walk in the garden with her "dear cousin Jaufumat."[22] The *demoiselles* Lajonie were often guests at Goulards, and the Lamothes made frequent trips to visit these cousins as well.[23] Alexandre appreciated the charms of his cousin Mlle. Lamothe, and these Lamothes were often guests at Goulards, as were the Jauges and Gorins.[24]

The Lamothes and their kin were quick to open their homes to each other. On their journeys from Paris to Goulards, Alexandre and Victor spent the night with their cousin St. Martin Chanceaulme in Bergerac, who also stayed with the Lamothes in Bordeaux from time to time.[25] The Pipaud cousins of Saint-Emilion visited the family on occasion, both in Bordeaux and Sainte-Foy.[26] M. Girardot, the brother of their formidable cousin Madame Cotin of Paris, stayed with them when returning to Paris from Lisbon, and the curé of Gardegan, Marie de Sérézac's cousin, stayed

19. For an analysis of the various meanings in a seventeenth-century marriage contract, see Orest Ranum and Louis d'Adhémar de Panat, "Vers une histoire de l'esthétique sociale: Le Contrat de mariage du comte de Grignan et de Marie-Angélique du Puy du Fou et de Champagne," in Wolfgang Leiner and Pierre Ronzeaud, eds., *Correspondances: Mélanges offerts à Roger Duchêne* (Tübingen and Aix-en-Provence: Gunter Narr and Publications de l'Université de Provence, 1991), 355–63.
20. Marie to Victor, 13 September 1757; 28 September 1758; Alexis to Victor, 28–30 September 1764.
21. Marie to Victor, 13 September 1757; 7 September 1762.
22. Marie to Victor, 28 September 1758.
23. For example, Alexis to Victor, 9 October 1757; 30 November 1757.
24. Marie to Victor, 20 October 1757; 28 September 1758; 7 October 1758; Alexandre to Victor, 17 November 1757; Marianne to Victor, 2 December 1758.
25. Alexandre and Alexis to Victor, 3 October 1765; Marianne to Victor, 24 January 1757. Alexis and Delphin also stayed with him on occasion while attending to business in Bergerac. Delphin to Victor, 2 November 1757.
26. Delphin to Victor, 2 November 1757; 31 August 1765. The Pipauds were related to the Sérézacs by marriage. See ADG 3E 19493, #233, Articles de mariage, Daniel Sanfourche de Lamothe and Marie de Sérézac, 16 December 1723.

with them for ten days in 1758.[27] When Marie, the eldest Lamothe daughter, took ill, she spent three months with her Sérézac uncle and aunt in Belvès in hopes that the fresh country air would speed her convalescence.[28] The Lamothes returned the favor shortly thereafter when their cousin from Belvès, the young Sérézac, came to Bordeaux to attend school.[29]

Kin often provided practical assistance to each other.[30] Jules's uncle in Belvès helped him to procure his position as *archiprêtre* in nearby Saint-Magne and accompanied him to take possession of his new *bénéfice*.[31] When the Lamothe's country home of Goulards was burglarized in 1758, cousin Jean Gorin assisted Delphin with the investigation of the house and with the legal complaint. He agreed to serve as Delphin's *procureur* in any future legal action and attended the testimony of witnesses to the crime.[32] M. Cotin loaned furniture to Victor when he moved into an unfurnished room in Paris, and M. Linotte later provided Alexandre with a bed to use.[33] Alexis's godmother, Madame Lagardelle, left him one hundred *écus* in her will to thank him, in Alexis's words, "for all the care I took concerning her affairs."[34] Daniel Lamothe provided a louis d'or annually to a Benedictine aunt living in a convent in Sens.[35]

Although historians have found that individuals often preferred to use

27. Delphin to Victor, 6 and 20 May 1758. Daniel de Lamothe and Marie de Sérézac's marriage contract identifies Monsieur Me. Anthoyne Vanderbet, the bride's "cousin germain" as the "pretre et curé de la parroisse de St. Martin de Gardegan." ADG 3E 19493, #233, Articles de mariage, Daniel Sanfourche de Lamothe and Marie de Sérézac, 16 December 1723.

28. Marie to Victor, 1 July 1764; 18 August 1764.

29. Marie to Victor, 6 December 1764. See also Sérézac *fils* to Victor and Alexandre, 19 February 1765; Alexis to Victor, undated 1765; Marie to Victor and Alexandre, 30 July and 20 August 1765.

30. The prevalence of kin assistance has been documented in a number of cultures. For example, Conrad M. Arensberg and Solon T. Kimball found an obligation of mutual kin assistance among the peasant farmers of Ireland. *Family and Community in Ireland* (Cambridge: Harvard University Press, 1940), 70–78. Tamara K. Hareven, *Family Time and Industrial Time: The Relationship Between Family and Work in a New England Industrial Community* (Cambridge: Cambridge University Press, 1982), 85–119, also documents patterns of mutual assistance among kin. Michael Anderson in *Family Structure in Lancashire* (Cambridge: Cambridge University Press, 1971), 136–61, argues that kin were the major source of assistance for the Lancashire working class.

31. Marie to Victor and Alexandre, 12 January 1765; Delphin to Victor and Alexandre, 23 April 1765.

32. ADG, Série B, Parlement, Répertoire numérique détaillé provisoire de la Tournelle de Sainte-Foy, Liasse 9, 28–30 January 1758.

33. Alexis to Victor, 3 February 1759; Alexandre to Victor, 18 February 1761.

34. Alexis to Victor, 2 March 1762.

35. Marianne to Victor, 6 February 1758; Alexis to Victor, 4 May 1758; Delphin to Victor, 9 January 1759; 30 January 1762.

friends and acquaintances rather than kin for loans, the Lamothes turned to their relatives for short-term loans and other transactions.[36] M. Cotin, a Parisian relation, advanced money to Victor while he was studying in Paris.[37] They occasionally drew *lettres de change* on other relatives in Paris.[38] Their cousin, the *négociant* M. Jauge, helped the Lamothes with their finances and to negotiate their wine sales. He also loaned them 1,000 livres in 1763, the difficult year of their father's death.[39]

The Lamothes stayed informed of all news concerning their relatives, through letters as well as the visits of friends and kin. Pregnancies, marriages, and illnesses were major topics of interest.[40] Correspondence kept them well informed on the activities of their cousins in Paris.[41]

However, while the bonds linking the Lamothes to their kin were close, so were ties between the Lamothes and their friends. The vast network that linked the Lamothes to their relatives also encompassed their circle of friends.[42] Certain close friends, such as the Rigauds de Grandefon, "who love us like brothers," were nearly as important as kin.[43]

36. Although Brunelle notes that merchants of Rouen provided and requested a number of loan services for and from their kin—they served as guarantors and procurators, as well as investment partners—she does not mention examples of kin making loans to each other. *New World Merchants of Rouen*, 72–73. Hardwick found in her study of Nantais notaries that although kin frequently cosigned loans for each other, only about 10 percent of loans in which notarial families were either borrowers or lenders were made entirely between kin. See *The Practice of Patriarchy*, 183–85.

37. Daniel to Victor, 20 April 1757; 22 November 1757; 10 January 1758; 2 December 1758; Marie to Victor, 24 August 1759.

38. Delphin to Victor, 17 March 1764.

39. Delphin to Victor, 19 December 1758; 7 June 1763; Alexis to Victor, 25 November 1761; 7 September 1762. AM Fonds Delpit, No. 127, Letter from Delphin de Lamothe addressed to Monsieur Jauge, négociant aux Chartrons, 1770s(?).

40. Delphin to Victor, 6 May 1758; 9 December 1762; Marianne to Victor, 19 October 1758; 29 October 1760; Marie to Victor, 6 January 1759; 24 August 1759.

41. See, for example, Alexis to Victor, 9 October 1757; Delphin to Victor, 9 January 1759.

42. Randolph Trumbach found that for aristocratic England, "friendship was the larger institution under which kinship was subsumed," although the English did consider their affection for relatives "natural." *The Rise of the Egalitarian Family: Aristocratic Kinship and Domestic Relations in Eighteenth-Century England* (New York: Academic Press, 1978), 66.

43. Alexis to Victor, 13 November 1764. It should be noted, however, that it is difficult to differentiate between the close friends and the actual relations of the Lamothe family, especially in the context of Sainte-Foy. Because the residents of Sainte-Foy intermarried—for example, Rigaud de Grandefon with Papus, Turcaud, and Rossane; Lajonie with Mestre, Gaussen, and Jaufumat; and Jauge with Rigaud du Marchet and Gaussen—it seems that nearly all of the families were interrelated to a certain degree. The archivist at Sainte-Foy-la-Grande, Mlle. Guesnon, provided me with the family trees of many of the families of the Sainte-Foy region, most of whom are mentioned in the Lamothe Family Letters. See Archives municipales de Sainte-Foy, Séries GG and E. Historians have noted the high instance of endogamy in French villages. See Maurice Aymard, "Friends and Neighbors," in

The Lamothe family made their friends in a number of venues. Professional contacts often became close friends. The names Laloubie, Maignol, Lamontagne, Dubergier, Lanusse, Lisleferme, and Boudin, among a number of others, all of which appear in the family letters, were also listed in the *Tableau de MM. les avocats* of the Parlement of Bordeaux.[44] Messieurs Caze, Doazan, Brichaud, and Deslandes were family friends from the medical profession.[45] Even in Sainte-Foy, the Lamothes often maintained especially close ties with friends and relatives from the legal or medical professions. Etienne de Lajonie was a lawyer, as was Etienne Jauge.[46] Several members of the Mestre family were barristers, as was the local *conventionnaire*, Pierre-Anselme Garrau.[47] One of the Gaussens was a physician who stayed in touch with Victor through the grim years of revolution.[48]

But the Lamothes also found friends of other professions among their neighbors. The Corregeolles, neighbors on Rue Neuve in Bordeaux, worked in commerce, and André-Daniel Laffon de Ladebat, Victor and Delphin's colleague from the Academy of Bordeaux, also came from a family of *négociants*.[49] At Sainte-Foy, proximity and longstanding social and marital ties were the foundations of friendship, as the Lamothes enjoyed warm social relations with neighbors from a variety of walks of life. The Lamothes were equally close to the noble family of Rigaud de Grandefon; to the *sieur* Papus, son of the *secrétaire du roy*; to the curés of Saint-Avit and Sainte-Foy; and to their cousins, the notary and *procureur* Simon Gorin and the *bourgeois* Jean Gorin.[50]

Philippe Ariès and Georges Duby, gen. eds., *A History of Private Life*, trans. Arthur Goldhammer (Cambridge: Harvard University Press, Belknap Press, 1989), vol. 3: *The Passions of the Renaissance*, ed. Roger Chartier, 452–53.

44. ADG 6E 13, Compagnie des avocats, Tableaux.

45. Lamothe Family Letters, passim.

46. Archives municipales de Sainte-Foy, GG 69; GG 55, 35.

47. See "Hommage à nos concitoyens, Mestre, Jay, Garrau, députés aux assemblées révolutionnaires: Exposition des Archives municipales du 17 au 31 juillet 1989," a pamphlet for the bicentennial exhibition in Sainte-Foy-la-Grande, which outlines the legal backgrounds of Mestre and Garrau, whose families were closely linked to the Lamothes.

48. See ADG 8J 692, Fonds Bigot, Letter from Victor Lamothe to M. Gaussen, 24 Floréal An XIII.

49. In the notarial *étude* of Maître Rauzan are a number of documents for Corregeolles, *père et fils*, *négociants*, living at Rue Neuve in Bordeaux. See, for example, ADG 3E 21676, 13 February and 24 July 1762. For Laffon de Ladebat's roots in commerce, see Paul Butel, *Les Dynasties bordelaises de Colbert à Chaban* (Paris: Perrin, 1991), 153–54.

50. ADG C 2719, the *capitation* for the Election d'Agen, lists both Rigaud de Grandefon and Papus as paying the *capitation noblesse*. For information on Jean Gorin, see Jean Corriger, *Au fil des eaux . . . Au*

The vintage season at Sainte-Foy was a time of sociability for the Lamothes, their neighbors, and their relatives.[51] Marie observed, "We lead a wild life here, always making merry, always out and about."[52] Victor described a party that illustrates vividly the gaiety of the social season at Sainte-Foy: "Some people eat, the others drink, we laugh, we joke, we do silly things; we take walks, arm in arm . . . we dance, we play the guitar (I should mention that it's the instrument *à la mode* now), we play backgammon, we run about, we play the fool . . . I believe that we would have passed that night not sleeping, but rather laughing, singing and amusing ourselves."[53] Even the visits of the abbé of Sainte-Foy contributed to the merriment, as he performed his comedy routine at the dinner table.[54] Alexandre noted on one occasion that "the multitude of visits that we must make & receive" made it difficult to find time for other obligations.[55]

As time passed, however, the mood at Sainte-Foy changed. Already in 1757, Marianne told Victor that the harvest time was not the same without him there.[56] In 1762, as the economic climate harshened, the merry parties and dinners with their neighbors at Sainte-Foy nearly ceased. Alexis noted that "the destitution is making nearly everyone sad and sedentary, we rarely see M. Rigaud, we seldom see M. Lajonie or our Curé, M. Bricheau came to supper one time. The Grandefon family is in mourning . . . in short, you would scarcely recognize this place."[57] Daniel Lamothe's death in 1763, and the deaths of other friends, as well as the obligation on the part of Delphin and Marie to go to Muscadet for the grape harvest after 1760 further eroded the festivity of the vintage season.[58] In 1764, Marianne complained to Victor that life at Goulards had greatly changed: "The parties are no longer so frequent, and we no longer

fil des siècles: Mon village du grand coeur, Sainte-Foy-la-Grande. 700 ans de souvenirs (Groupe Girondin des Etudes Locales, 1974), 101.

51. The majority of the Lamothe's friends in the area made Sainte-Foy their principal residence, unlike the Lamothes, who came only for the vintage season. Jean Corriger, *Au fils des eaux*, 109.

52. Marie to Victor, 7 October 1758.

53. Victor to Alexis, 25 October 1755.

54. Delphin to Victor, 20 October 1757.

55. Alexandre to Victor, 17 November 1757. See also Victor to Alexis, 1–5 October 1755; Marie to Victor, 1 December 1756; 20 October 1757; Marianne to Victor, 9 October 1757; Alexis to Victor, 30 November 1757.

56. Marianne to Victor, 9 October 1757.

57. Alexis to Victor, 10 October 1762.

58. Alexis to Victor, 27 October 1763.

see as many people as before, and we don't even have fun with those we see, rather they worry and annoy us."[59]

During happier times, it had often been difficult for the Lamothes to leave the social whirl of Sainte-Foy and their many friends there, and equally difficult for their neighbors to see them go.[60] The Lamothe family letters paint the *voisinage* of Sainte-Foy as a large family, a place of amusement and cheer with beloved friends. Many of these social ties lasted through the years of revolution, and Victor retained the property of Goulards until his death in 1823, possibly in tribute to these happier times.[61]

Bordeaux's social life had its attractions as well. Gatherings with friends were full of gaiety, and even the pious Marie and Marianne greatly enjoyed luncheons and *soirées* with their closest friends, although they rejected balls and more public social events.[62] Meals were a particularly sociable time for the Lamothes and their circle.[63] The frequency with which they ate at the homes of others and invited friends to sup suggests a home in which the door was always open. The "family meal" had not yet become a private and closed ritual.

Among their wide circle of friends, many of the individuals mentioned in the letters were probably no more than agreeable acquaintances. But both the Lamothe brothers and sisters enjoyed more intimate friendships with a select number of persons. While the entire family shared a friendship with the Laloubie family, the Laloubie daughters were particularly close to Marie and Marianne.[64] When they were separated, they

59. Marianne to Victor, 17 October 1764.

60. Marie to Victor, 10 December 1757; Delphin to Victor, 17 December 1757; Alexis to Victor, 22 December 1761.

61. In Year VI, Victor Lamothe acted as *procureur constitué* on behalf of Suzanne Rigaud de Grandefon, the daughter of their close friend M. Rigaud de Grandefon. ADG 3E 21748, Opposition, 27 Germinal An VI. In a letter to Citoyen Mestre of Sainte-Foy, written by Citoyen Meinicken in Year II, Meinicken mentioned "notre ami commun le Cit. Lamothe," and sent his regards to "les Citoyens Lamothe," presumably Victor and his nephews. ADG 8J 694, Fonds Bigot, Letter to Citoyen Mestre, Homme de loi, 21 Floréal An II.

62. Marie to Victor, 20 April 1757; 28 May 1757; 20 June 1757; 21 January 1758; 23 February 1762; Marianne to Victor, 6 February 1758; 2 February 1761.

63. See, for example, Delphin and Alexis to Victor, 4 July 1757; Alexis to Victor, 9 October 1757; 9 May 1758; Delphin to Victor, 2 November 1757; 17 March 1764; 12 January 1765; Delphin to Alexis, 14 September 1773; Marie to Victor, 20 October 1757; 21 January 1758; 22 August 1758; 24 March 1760; 23 February 1762; Marianne to Victor, 6 February 1758; Victor to Alexis, 31 July 1773.

64. See, for example, Marie to Victor, 17 March 1758; 23 August 1761; 23 February 1762; 30 September 1762; 30 July 1765; Marianne to Victor, 2 February 1761.

stayed in touch through letters.[65] According to Marie, "I believe that there is more amity between us than there is in many families."[66]

Alexis, and especially Delphin, were very attached to François de Lamontagne, a companion of Delphin's from the collège. Lamontagne was a conseiller au parlement, perpetual secretary of the Academy of Bordeaux, and a celebrated local savant. These interests guaranteed him much in common with the culturally refined Lamothe sons. Delphin and Alexis's letters to Lamontagne, which employed the familiar "tu," reveal an ardent friendship, full of protestations of affection as well as teasing jocularity.[67] The familiar tone of the letters suggest an easy and close relationship.[68] Delphin's letters scolded Lamontagne for not writing more: "Come now, throw off that indolence that is so harmful to us, wake up, speak to me, write to me, say nothing if you wish. Your 'nothings' are always agreeable."[69]

In their letters, Delphin and Lamontagne shared observations about art, books, politics, and the affectations of polite society.[70] It appears that Delphin admired, and was perhaps a bit jealous of, Lamontagne's energy and social success: "Lamontagne here, Lamontagne there; a comet, a song, a promenade, these extravagances, & always Lamontagne!"[71] However, their close relationship endured. All of the Lamothe family members who visited Paris searched for books and brochures for Lamontagne to add to his impressive collection.[72] This was despite the fact that Lamontagne was notorious for his laxity in paying his debts, and Victor was often forced to foot the bill for Lamontagne's expenses, sometimes for months at a time.[73]

65. Marie to Victor, 7 October 1758; 25 November 1761; 18 August 1764.

66. Marie to Victor, 21 January 1758.

67. A number of letters written to François de Lamontagne by Delphin and Alexis de Lamothe are located in the Fonds Lamontagne of the Bibliothèque municipale de Bordeaux, Ms. 1696 (II), Correspondence.

68. See, for example, BM Ms. 1696 (II), Fonds Lamontagne, Correspondence, 10 October 1753, No. 26; 2 August 1755, No. 55; and 18 November 1755, No. 60.

69. BM Ms. 1696 (II), Fonds Lamontagne, Correspondence, November 1746, No. 11.

70. For example, BM Ms. 1696 (II), Fonds Lamontagne, Correspondence, 10 November 1746, No. 10.

71. BM Ms. 1696 (II), Fonds Lamontagne, Correspondence, 10 October 1753, No. 26.

72. BM Ms. 1696 (II), Fonds Lamontagne, Correspondence, and Lamothe Family Letters, passim. Lamontagne was well known for his magnificent library. See Paul Courteault, "Notice sur François de Lamontaigne," in François de Lamontaigne, Chronique bordelaise de François de Lamontaigne, (Bordeaux: Imprimerie Delmas, Chapons, Gounouilhou, 1926), XXV.

73. Alexis to Victor, 17 July 1761; 7 August 1762; 7 September 1762; 26 September 1762; 1 January 1763; 8 February 1763; Delphin to Victor and Alexandre, 7 June 1763; 19 July 1763; 29 June 1764.

The Lamothe's circle of kin and friends, both in Bordeaux and the countryside, offered assistance, companionship, and affection. But their social circle extended beyond the confines of Bordeaux and the surrounding area. Even in Paris, Victor and Alexandre found *chers parents* to take them under their wing and to introduce them to life in the capital.

2. The Relatives in Paris

The cousins in Paris were particularly useful when Victor and Alexandre pursued their studies there. Although geographic mobility could strain the bonds of kinship, the Lamothes carefully maintained their ties to their cousins in the capital.[74] Delphin and Alexis had strengthened their friendship with their Parisian kinfolk during their visits to Paris in 1754 and 1755, and they subsequently encouraged their brothers to take advantage of their amity.[75] Their precise social status is unclear, but the *bon ton* of their gatherings, and their splendid apartments at Place Vendôme and Rue de Richelieu, suggest wealth.[76] The cousins invited Daniel's sons to dine, and the Cotins hosted them at their country estate at Ivry.

When Victor first arrived in Paris, Delphin informed him, "You should limit your visits, at least for quite a while, to family members." His medical studies would keep him too busy for other social activities. However, even "among the family, you must choose the people who will be most profitable to you." Delphin proceeded to specify which relatives Victor should embrace, and which he should keep at arm's length. The Carons, he observed, "are certainly very good relatives" and extremely affectionate, "but since they are not well educated, & that being said, between us, they are a bit gossipy, and even scandalmongers, you have to watch yourself with them." Mr. Linotte, the *conseiller* at the Conseil souverain of the duc de Bouillon, "is another relative whom you can visit from time to time, he is a clever man, of good advice, & has a hardworking and serious son who is about your age, and who could be a suitable companion." Of the Cotins,

74. See Wheaton, "Affinity and Descent in Bordeaux," 116.

75. See Lamothe Family Letters, letters from Alexis, 1755; and BM Ms. 1696 (II), Fonds Lamontagne, Correspondence, 7 July 1754, No. 37.

76. Lamothe Family Letters, Alexandre to Victor, 8 August 1760; 10 November 1760; and passim. The splendor of the Cotin's country home at Ivry also suggests wealth. See Victor to Jules, 26 May 1758.

Delphin warned, "Only visit M. Cotin on rare occasions . . . he's a clever man, of good judgment & good advice, but as you have seen, he is buried in his *cabinet*, as is his son; you will only find his wife." Of the wife, he noted, "It is true that her spirit, her heart, & her character are accomplished; but those qualities that make her company agreeable will cost you time that you could more usefully spend elsewhere." Mlle. Langadie could offer him good advice, and Madame Girardot was a nice person, but "her husband is not the most intelligent man in the world." Finally, Delphin advised Victor that he could go visit Madame Tassin and her daughter, Madame Sarrau, "on important holidays," but warned that "you will understand for yourself that the atmosphere at their house is not suitable at all for a young student who wants to save money."[77]

Despite their protestations of affection and messages for "our dear relatives," the Lamothes betrayed an ambivalent attitude toward their relatives in Paris. Victor's parents and siblings were pleased that the relatives appeared to be attached to him, and Alexis advised Victor to watch them carefully to learn how to conduct himself in polite society.[78] On the other hand, Alexandre noted that the Caron daughters were a bit *libertines* in their conversation and he found the mother "interfering and nosy and gossipy," while Alexis criticized Madame Tassin as "the most insipid little woman."[79] The entire family believed that the Cotins were social climbers, *parvenus*, and they disapproved of their "haughtiness" and their efforts to *se debourgeoiser*.[80]

On occasion, tensions arose between Victor and his family and the Parisian clan. The first serious instance of discord concerned the *poule dinde* that Victor's family sent to him each year. It was mailed to him in care of his relatives, and apparently Mesdames Tassin and Sarrau decided to eat it themselves. The family was shocked by their conduct, but uncertain how to react. Marianne advised Victor not to make a fuss; "it's not worth the trouble."[81] Daniel finally took the matter in hand, writing a letter to Madame Tassin, as recounted by Delphin to Victor, "full of affection, compliments, and politeness, but where he adroitly conveyed to her how

77. Delphin to Victor, 17 December 1756.

78. Delphin to Victor, 30 April 1757; 20 October 1757; Alexis to Victor, 30 November 1757; 22 December 1761.

79. Alexandre to Victor, 9 July 1760; 8 August 1760; Alexis to Victor, undated 1757.

80. Alexandre to Victor, 8 August 1760. See also 10 November 1760; and Alexis to Victor, 22 December 1761; undated 1762.

81. Marianne to Victor, 6 February 1758.

surprised we were at the way she behaved toward you: my father did not tell her that he had heard about it from you, but rather, he pretended to have learned indirectly that you had complained of her lack of concern for you, fearing to have brought it upon yourself due to some shortcoming on your part of which you are unaware."[82] By this complex circumlocution, Daniel conveyed his displeasure that the cousins had cheated Victor out of his New Year's treat, but still managed to keep peace in the family.

Despite elaborate declarations of affection on the part of the Parisian relatives, some of them, it appears, did not always treat Victor with respect. Perhaps they considered the young and earnest cousin from Bordeaux a little boring and not up to Parisian standards. Madame Cotin, in particular, seemed to condescend to, and even snub, Victor on occasion, despite her earlier "obliging attentions" to him.[83] Alexis expressed anger at her indifference to Victor, but admitted that "it makes me worry that you did not really know how to keep yourself in her good graces, not because of your morals or character, but maybe because of your manner and deportment you may have picked up from other people you see frequently, and who have a certain ill-bred and rustic air."[84] Despite these indignities, Alexis urged Victor to continue his relations with Madame Cotin: "I am upset . . . that you have resolved to me to never see Madame Cotin again, except on important occasions, even if she writes to you . . . this seems a bit extreme to me, because basically, while you do not enjoy being with the woman, she could be useful to you sooner or later, as well as her husband."[85]

Victor and Alexandre were also forced to confront jealousies and disputes between different branches of the Paris family. The Cotins resented the amount of time that Victor spent at the home of the Carons and accused him of wasting time better spent studying.[86] When the young Madame Cotin and her mother-in-law quarreled, Alexis urged Victor not to take sides in the disagreement. However, "it would still be better to take the side of the father and mother, as they are the strongest and since you can expect the most assistance from them."[87]

82. Delphin to Victor, 18 February 1758.
83. Delphin to Victor, 2 November 1757.
84. Alexis to Victor, 9 March 1759. See also Alexandre to Victor, 8 August 1760.
85. Alexis to Victor, undated 1762.
86. Alexandre to Victor, 8 August 1760. On another occasion, Madame Cotin complained that Victor was neglecting them, and did not visit frequently enough. Marie to Victor, 8 May 1759.
87. Alexis to Victor, 9 October 1757.

Victor, Alexandre, and the rest of the Lamothe family maintained their ties to the relatives in Paris, despite their ambivalence about the goodwill of certain members of the extended family in the capital. Ultimately, some of the tensions in Victor and Alexandre's relations with them may have arisen from two conflicting cultures—that of the provinces, more open, friendly, and sincere, and that of Paris, which seemed more duplicitous, more superficial, and more focused on the trappings of wealth and power. While the Cotins and the Carons found their young cousin from the provinces gauche and unrefined, Victor, more used to the open and exuberant company of Bordeaux and Sainte-Foy, considered them shallow and frivolous social-climbers. Still, Paris seduced Victor despite these reservations, for he wished to settle in Paris and take part permanently in the "excellent society" he found there.

3. Relations with Women

When the Lamothe sons spoke of the "excellent society in Paris," it was especially the company of the women they enjoyed. Although very discreet on matters of sex in their letters, the Lamothe sons appreciated the company of women. Their social lives at Bordeaux and especially Sainte-Foy during the vintage allowed them to mingle freely with women of their social class. Alexis evidently knew how to charm the ladies, and gave Victor advice on how to cultivate the fairer sex.[88] Delphin sometimes discussed women in his letters to Lamontagne. During his *séjour* in Paris in 1754, he wrote to his friend, "Meanwhile, you should admire the strength of my affection for you, I am in charming company; stretched out on a bed of laurels [*lit de garou*] between 2 very pleasant ladies, a young German & a very pretty Parisian . . . *eh bien*, I slipped away from my place to come write to you."[89] Despite the somewhat puritanical tone of the family letters at times, it does not seem that Daniel Lamothe's sons led a monkish existence.

The Lamothe men had definite ideas on the qualities that they appreciated in the opposite sex. *Esprit*, *douceur*, and *complaisance* were the qualities

88. See Alexis to Victor, undated 1757; 9 March 1759.

89. BM Ms. 1696 (II), Fonds Lamontagne, Correspondence, 4 July 1754, No. 37. See also November 1746, No. 11.

that the Lamothe brothers mentioned most often when admiring the
women of their social circle.[90] Nevertheless, they did not hesitate to
associate with women of a different class as well. Alexis offered no censure
when Victor requested information about two ballet dancers of questionable reputation from Montpellier and, indeed, expressed some admiration
of their charms:

> Now you would like for me to tell you about the Dlles Bous-
> carel . . . I have known of them for nearly two years, an acquain-
> tance that everyone can acknowledge, and that one comes by
> going to the theater, where they dance as extras in the ballets; they
> have a reputation, not the kind that, according to the common
> proverb, is worth more than a belt of gold, but a *reputation d'état* that
> even gives them a certain fame. They are protected by *M. le maréchal*
> [of Richelieu] . . . they have spirit, discretion, and are a bit
> *méchantes;* in one word, they are P. . . . [*putains* (whores)] of good
> breeding.[91]

When Alexis later made the acquaintance of the Bouscarel sisters, he noted
that "they carry out with much decency the most indecent of professions,"
and enjoyed his rendezvous with them.[92]

Alexis had close, and perhaps affective, relationships with several
women of his own social standing. During his stay in Paris in 1755, he met
a young woman, Mademoiselle Houssemaine, whom he praised highly: "I
knew her during that short time, I had the pleasure of seeing in her a lively
spirit, vivaciousness, complaisance, a charming sweetness, in one word, all
the proper talents to create admirers; along with that, a figure which is not
displeasing, that which we call *un petit air chien* which is extremely
appetizing; of all the people that I knew in Paris, she is the one that I would
most like to see again."[93] She gave him the nickname of *petit outil* (little
tool), and he referred to her jokingly as *ma marraine*.[94] Victor met Mlle.
Houssemaine in Paris as well, and Alexis subsequently mentioned her in
his letters with affection, and some sexual longing.[95] Alexis continued his

90. See, for example, Alexandre to Victor, 17 November 1757.
91. Alexis to Victor, 17 February 1761.
92. Alexis to Victor, 9 May 1761.
93. Alexis to Victor, 26 June 1759.
94. Alexis to Victor, 9 March 1759.
95. See in particular Alexis to Victor, 26 June 1759.

somewhat ribald comments concerning Mlle. Houssemaine after she became Madame du Pars: "So she has cleared that step so difficult for so many young ladies who groan beneath the oppressive weight of virginity . . . I have always retained a memory of her that I dare call tender, despite her new position; it was her gaiety, her sweetness, her vivacity, her kindness, even . . . I would certainly have taken great care to give her a gown for her wedding night [*chemise de noces*] . . . I will say nothing more about it, her new condition is saved, I would profane it if I continued with all the ideas that come to mind."[96]

Another young woman, a Mademoiselle Victoire Vignes, caught Alexis's fancy for a time as well. The beautiful and amiable daughter of a wealthy Bordelais *négociant*, her unexpected collapse and death in the middle of the street created a sensation in Bordeaux.[97] Possibly Alexis had a romantic relationship with her. Certainly, he was very moved by her sudden death: "Last year I often had the pleasure of seeing a young woman whom I wanted you to meet this winter, Mlle. Victoire Vignes, pretty, kindly, amiable, lively, everyone watched her when she appeared on the *promenade*, she engaged the hearts of nearly everyone she met as well, everywhere she went. *Eh! bien*, she is dead, and in a nearly tragic manner last Holy Thursday . . . I do not need to, and I would be almost embarrassed to tell you how much I regretted her, I would never have believed it before."[98] Victor's correspondence with Alexis in 1773 revealed that the two of them continued to seek out the company of attractive women, despite their committed bachelorhood.[99]

At the same time, Alexis demonstrated a jaded view of women in general and the married state in particular. In his last will and testament signed on 3 September 1786, he wrote: "By God's grace, I did not marry: circumstances were opposed to it in my youth, and as I grew older, [and] I was more in control of my own satisfaction, I congratulated myself for having no real inclination for the state of matrimony. The experiences of others that I saw (without speaking ill of it) sufficed to put me off the idea. The bitterness and the many vexations of the married state are rarely compensated by the sweetness and the pleasure that it brings: luckily not everyone

96. Alexis to Victor, 28 October 1762.

97. BM Ms. 1461, "Journal," edited by Jules Delpit, 3 April 1760, 49.

98. Alexis to Victor, 19 May 1760.

99. See, for example, Victor to Alexis, 18 August, 28 August, 26 September, 3 October, and 7 December 1773.

feels the same way."[100] He expressed his distaste of marriage even more forcefully in a letter to Victor: "If you only knew how much misery accompanies marriage! The enormous expenses it exposes you to, the time that the care of a household, a wife, children, steals from you, you would not think about it without turning pale."[101]

Alexis's negative attitude seems curious, especially in light of the successful marriages of his parents and brother, although he was exposed to the less happy marriages of relatives in Paris and served as lawyer in a particularly messy separation suit in 1761.[102] Alexis may also have had a falling out with his sister-in-law, which could have embittered him toward women. He and Elisabeth de Brulz had been very friendly during the years of her marriage to Delphin, and she and her children continued to share the home of her brothers-in-law on Rue Neuve in the two years following her husband's death.

However, something apparently went wrong in their relationship prior to her marriage to René, vicomte de la Faye, in 1783. In his will, Alexis wrote movingly of the death of his eldest brother, and the great loss experienced by Delphin's children and family, "which has become much greater due to subsequent events . . . which I will not recount here." Possibly he was referring to a dispute with his sister-in-law, perhaps concerning the division of the family patrimony when she left the Lamothe household to join that of her new husband. Alexis addressed his nephews specifically concerning this matter in his will: "During the approximately two and a half years that their mother stayed with us before she remarried, she enjoyed all of her own revenues, as was her right, as well as those of her husband, our brother . . . those revenues, which nearly all passed through our hands, were used entirely either for the maintenance, the cultivation, or the restoration of property, or for food, upkeep, or other expenses relative to the maintenance either of the mother or the children."[103] This strong assertion suggests that Elisabeth had questioned Alexis and Victor's control of the family's assets at the time of her departure, leading to bitterness between them.[104]

100. ADG 3E 21732, Testament, Alexis de Lamothe, opened 25 March 1790.

101. Alexis to Victor, 22 December 1761.

102. Alexandre to Victor, 10 November 1760; Delphin to Victor, undated 1758. BM Ms. 1461, "Journal," May 1761, 98.

103. ADG 3E 21732, Testament, Alexis de Lamothe, opened 25 March 1790.

104. Conflicts between widows and their deceased husband's kin were common in early modern Europe, especially when money, property, or children were involved. These problems multiplied if the widow chose to remarry. See Julie Hardwick, "Widowhood and Patriarchy in Seventeenth Century France," *Journal of Social History* 26 (Fall 1992): 133–48; Adrienne Rogers, "Women and the Law," in

The break between Elisabeth and her brothers-in-law did not affect Victor and Alexis's relationship with their nephews. They seem to have treated them like their own children following the death of Delphin, and Delphin's surviving children were made heirs to Alexis and Victor's entire fortunes.[105] In addition, Victor and Dugravier de Lamothe, Delphin's youngest son, shared a home and practiced medicine together in Bordeaux until Victor's death in 1823. Family affection won out over other disputes.

In sum, romantic relationships were secondary to family and friends for members of the Lamothe family. However, the sons still sought out friendships with women, for they, like men, could ultimately serve as useful contacts—which, for the Lamothes, was a vital requirement in a friend.

4. *Rendre Service*: The Obligations of Friends and Kin

Utilité was an essential quality in both friends and relations. The ability to render service was a key component of personal relationships. Although the Lamothes demonstrated true affection for their friends, an element of calculation always played a role in relationships.[106] Acquaintances were scrutinized for their potential usefulness as social contacts, for professional connections, or for their ability to do favors. In return, the Lamothes were always aware of their reciprocal obligation to provide services to others.[107]

Often these services rendered were simple and concrete. Alexis made some loans to the Mademoiselles Lajonie, noting that "they are certainly

Samia I. Spencer, ed., *French Women and the Age of Enlightenment* (Bloomington: Indiana University Press, 1984), 39–40; and, in the Florentine context, Christiane Klapisch-Zuber, "The 'Cruel Mother': Maternity, Widowhood, and Dowry in Florence in the Fourteenth and Fifteenth Centuries," in *Women, Family, and Ritual*, 117–131.

105. Jules Delpit, *Notes biographiques sur les Messieurs de Lamothe* (Bordeaux: Balarac Jeune, 1846), 23; ADG 3E 21732, Testament, Alexis de Lamothe, opened 25 March 1790; ADG 3Q 2509, Registre des recettes: Déclaration des mutations par décès, Bureau de Bordeaux, 2 October 1823, No. 330; ADG Q 31/d 5, Registre des recettes: Déclaration des mutations par décès, Bureau de Sainte-Foy, 7 October 1823.

106. Although perhaps not so calculating as that of the patrons, brokers, and clients described by Sharon Kettering in her study of seventeenth-century networks of patronage. *Patrons, Brokers, and Clients in Seventeenth-Century France* (New York: Oxford University Press, 1986).

107. As Maurice Aymard writes, "Calculated friendships . . . confirmed and reinforced kinship and marriage ties, translating them into practical terms, reciprocal obligations extending over two or three generations. Hence people sought to replenish and accumulate this essential capital of friendship." See "Friends and Neighbors," 453.

solvent, and it is a pleasure to be their creditor."[108] Nicolas de Lisleferme, a close family friend, asked if Alexandre would serve as his *procureur* for a contract that he wished to record in Paris, and Alexis observed, "I imagine that he will gladly do this favor for one of our best friends."[109] As the family contact in Paris, Victor was often asked to locate and purchase items for friends and relatives, in addition to his constant tasks on behalf of the immediate family.[110] In exchange, friends and neighbors offered to carry letters and packages to Victor in Paris from his parents and siblings, thus saving the cost of postage, and returned home with parcels for the family.[111] Small favors like these created a series of reciprocal obligations that served to strengthen the bonds of friendship.

More often, the Lamothes initiated and nurtured contacts with relatives and acquaintances in order to improve their *crédit*, that is, to stretch their circle of contacts, their social network, to individuals who could provide an introduction, advice, a good word—in other words, individuals who could open social and professional doors that might otherwise remain closed.[112] These less tangible services were even more important than concrete favors, as an individual's status was heavily dependent upon his or her connections and influence.

Patronage was essential to career advancement, as it is today, and the Lamothes sought the advice of relatives, friends, and associates to help Victor and Alexandre with their career decisions. Friends such as Drs. Castetz, Deslandes, and Caze passed on educational and career advice to the medical student Victor, and M. Leberthon, *premier président* at the Parlement of Bordeaux, made recommendations to Daniel concerning Alexandre's professional plans.[113] M. Linotte's assistance to Alexandre when beginning his legal career in Paris was appreciated.[114]

108. Alexis to Victor, 9 October 1757.

109. Alexis to Victor, 12 July 1765.

110. Delphin to Victor, 23 June 1758; 23 June 1759; 30 June 1759; 27 July 1762; 23 April 1765; 11 May 1765; 13 November 1766; Alexis to Victor, 26 October 1766.

111. Alexandre to Victor, 20 April 1757; Marie to Victor, 16 March 1759; Delphin to Victor, 31 March 1759; 14 April 1759; 23 June 1759; 9 February 1762; 12 July 1765; Alexis to Victor, 7 October 1761.

112. Jeremy Boissevain stresses the importance of this "reservoir of social relations" from which one "recruits support to counter his rivals and mobilizes support to attain his goals" in *Friends of Friends*, 27.

113. Alexandre to Victor, 17 January 1757; Delphin to Victor, 26 March 1757; 30 January 1762; 6 July 1762; Alexis to Victor, 12 May 1766; undated 1766; 1 July 1766.

114. Alexandre to Victor, 1 September 1759; 27 April 1760. See Chapters 4 and 5 below.

The assistance of friends and acquaintances was crucial to both professional and personal advancement, for one's professional life could not be separated from one's social standing. The Lamothes recognized the importance of cultivating their contacts. They utilized their friends as a means of introduction to potentially useful individuals, and fostered ties with the protégés of their friends. These friends of friends created an interlinking chain of contacts in the family's social network. Of the abbé Labadie, who wished to be introduced to Victor, Delphin observed, "He is a good friend of the household of M. Laloubie, that is sufficient for us to take an interest in him."[115] Letters of introduction and recommendation were essential tools in this complicated social network, and Delphin and Alexis frequently called upon their friends to provide assistance to Victor and Alexandre.[116] At times, these efforts came to naught. Delphin tried to put Victor in touch with a M. Fournier through his son-in-law, M. Pichard, Delphin's colleague from the Parlement of Bordeaux, but later noted, "The letter for M. de Pichard did not accomplish much, it was not our fault, nor was it yours."[117]

Because it was so difficult for a young, unknown man from the provinces to establish himself in Paris, Victor needed to make use of a wide variety of social contacts.[118] The relatives were his most crucial point of contact, and even distant kin were solicited. Victor was urged to pursue the good graces of Madame Larrard, a distant relative who was possibly unaware of their connection: "This woman could definitely obtain opportunities & assistance for you if she so desires."[119] At the same time, Victor should exercise caution and discretion in his pursuit of assistance. Alexis counseled him to watch himself "vis-à-vis Mde de Larrard . . . you must not *expend* [*user*] this patronage, by that I mean you must not ask for it at every opportunity, but rather save it for important occasions."[120]

Victor's brothers prodded him to widen his social circle. The larger one's circle of friends and acquaintances, the more potential benefit. The cultivation of social superiors could be particularly advantageous. Alexis advised him: "I believe that a clever man must obtain the friendship and familiarity of several persons of a certain status, who have certain connec-

115. Delphin to Victor, 20 March 1764.
116. For example, Delphin to Victor, 7 April 1760; Alexis to Victor, 26 February 1765.
117. Alexis to Victor, 22 December 1761; Delphin to Victor, 6 July and 26 September 1762.
118. Alexis to Victor and Alexandre, 29 June 1764.
119. Delphin to Victor, 26 December 1761; 30 January 1762.
120. Alexis to Victor, undated 1762.

tions and practices, who associate with a certain type of society, [who have] the ways and means to help you become known, and accordingly it seems to me that it would certainly be helpful to seek out the company of M. *le président* Sorbier as well as Madame de Larrard, M. Boutin when he is in Paris, M. *le duc* (son of M. le maréchal) of Duras, with whom we even have a relationship to renew."[121] But individuals of a less exalted social status could be equally valuable. Alexis suggested that Victor and Alexandre make the acquaintance of the abbé Lafon, an admirable young man who could be an exemplary and useful friend, and urged Victor to keep up his association with the abbé Blondet in Paris.[122] M. le Moine, one of the directors of the Compagnie des Indes, was also touted as a potentially useful acquaintance, and Alexis thought that it would be a good idea for Victor and Alexandre to establish ties with the brother of their good friend M. Dessieux.[123] Still, when seeking new acquaintances, one should not neglect old contacts.[124] For example, Alexis advised that Victor look after M. Hosty, one of his patients, "from whom I see you can expect many advantages," perhaps even an introduction to M. le maréchal de Richelieu, the powerful governor of the province of Guyenne.[125]

Realizing that the surest way to secure both patronage and influence for themselves was to be recognized as useful contacts, the Lamothes were quick to volunteer their aid to others.[126] As residents of Paris, Victor and Alexandre could be particularly helpful to friends from Bordeaux visiting the capital, and their brothers counseled them to welcome and offer their services to voyagers from their *patrie*.[127] They also sought information for friends and acquaintances from home. The family's friend, M. Nelle, asked Victor to check on the conduct of a young man in Paris on behalf of his mother.[128] While in Montpellier, Victor received a request on behalf of Alexis's friend Gourhan to locate a shady character named Baccare, who had cheated him out of nine months' room and board.[129]

121. Alexis to Victor, 23 March 1765.
122. Alexis to Victor, 5 March 1763; 29 June 1764; 28–30 September 1764; Delphin to Victor, 6 May 1757; to Alexandre, 12 April 1763.
123. Delphin to Victor and Alexandre, 25 June 1765; Alexis to Victor, 6 August 1765.
124. Alexis to Victor, 26 February 1765.
125. Alexis to Victor, 21 January 1764.
126. See, for example, Alexis to Victor, 21 January 1764.
127. Alexis to Victor, 20 April 1757; 3 January 1758; 26 February 1765; Delphin to Victor, 20 October 1757; 12 July 1765; 24 October 1766.
128. M. Nelle to Victor, 13 June 1766.
129. Alexis to Victor, 14 April 1760; 19 May 1760.

The Lamothe's relations of patronage and service with their social inferiors serve as an interesting commentary on society's vertical bonds and on the deeply ingrained ethic of mutual exchange in eighteenth-century France. The Lamothes recognized their obligations to their social inferiors, and Delphin carefully outlined the gifts (*étrennes*) that Victor should give the servants of his Parisian friends and relatives during the Christmas season.[130] The family took a paternalistic interest in their servants and the villagers at Goulards. As a good *seigneur*, Delphin received visits from his peasants during his trips to Goulards, and offered legal advice to a peasant woman living near Goulards when her husband was imprisoned for theft.[131] Daniel asked Victor and Alexandre to assist "Bernard Goulard whom we can fairly claim to patronize" in procuring a better position in the *brigade* at Sainte-Foy.[132] They also helped to establish in Paris the cobbler son of their servant Jeanneton, and later looked into his proposed marriage to a fruit seller to determine whether the young woman was actually pregnant and whether it would be an advantageous marriage.[133] This paternalistic assistance was by no means uncommon in early modern France.[134]

However, even social inferiors could be useful in return at times. The son of M. St. André, a clockmaker of Bordeaux, carried to Victor and Alexandre in Paris a letter of introduction from their brother. Alexis noted that the young man's family

> has been strongly attached to us for a long time and is even under obligation to us concerning some small matters, which they clearly recognize. The son . . . wished to be given the means of making your acquaintance. We believed that we should seize the occasion with alacrity. As you are determined to spend some time in that immense city, it is always good to know a person of our *patrie*,

130. Delphin to Victor, 17 December 1757.

131. Marianne to Victor, 6 February 1758; ADG Série B, Parlement, Répertoire numérique détaillée provisoire de la Tournelle de Sainte Foy, Liasse 9. Audition de Toinette Busseuilh, 2 March 1758. This same woman, Antoinette Busseuilh, was later found guilty of taking part in the robbery at Goulards in 1758 and sentenced to be hanged.

132. Daniel to Victor and Alexandre, 16 March 1762.

133. Alexis to Victor and Alexandre, 4 September 1764; Marie to Victor and Alexandre, 22 July 1766; Delphin to Victor, 5 August 1766. Delphin expressed no surprise or shock at the purported condition of the young fruit vendor, simply a desire to settle the affair.

134. See Jonathan Dewald, *Pont-St-Pierre, 1398–1789: Lordship, Community, and Capitalism in Early Modern France* (Berkeley and Los Angeles: University of California Press, 1987), 204–5.

established in Paris in a respectable *état*, someone steady and hardworking, and especially when that person has a relationship with our family . . . you will see . . . for yourself the advantages that you will be able to derive from this acquaintance.[135]

No potentially useful ties were to be neglected.

While they recognized their obligation, and indeed the utility of assisting even social inferiors, the Lamothes were conscious of both the character and social status of those they admitted into their social network, and the appropriate level of *politesse* and assistance to be offered. They hesitated to enter into an exchange of favors with individuals whose character they questioned.[136] On one occasion, Alexis scolded Victor for showing insufficient discrimination in his social patronage:

Permit me . . . to make a small observation that all the family has made, it is that you are perhaps a bit too prodigious with your praise for the people you recommend to us, [praise] that does not always hold true in reality . . . to which I must add that you do not always sufficiently indicate the sort of person that it is, so that in some cases we have made a bigger fuss for them than they really merit. For example, last year, based on what you had told us about that Spanish physician or surgeon and his wife, we thought that they were people of consequence, your eagerness even that my brother or I go to meet them at the boat . . . can you imagine our surprise to see, in truth a good man, but quite plump, a bit coarse, and a little woman who appeared quite disconcerted to see our table, which is not imposing? We had done our best to welcome them, and we had expected the physician or surgeon of the King of Spain, for if I am not mistaken, that was his title [but] he was a man of little consequence, you know it yourself.[137]

Social obligations were carefully calibrated to the social standing of the individual.

This careful web of favors and duties created certain expectations in the

135. Alexis to Victor and Alexandre, 29 June 1764.
136. See, for example, Delphin to Victor, 16 July 1763.
137. Alexis to Victor, 27 March 1762.

conduct of friends. The Lamothes considered themselves good and reliable friends, and they expected the same of others. On occasion, they were disappointed in the conduct of formerly close companions. Delphin was peeved when MM. Lisleferme and Jaure failed to respond promptly to his letters.[138] The entire family was outraged when their neighbor M. Corregeolles reneged on his promise to help bring in the harvest at Muscadet in 1760, and this led to harsh words and bad feelings between the two families.[139] Daniel's death in 1763 led the whole family to reassess whom they could consider their true friends:

> Bricheau . . . (between us) is a bit unrefined, he has not given us a sign of life since we suffered our loss, and came but one time (quite late) on an afternoon visit. And M. de Brugière seems to think quite little of our friendship, since we have neither seen him nor had news of him since we arrived at Goulards, although he had written to us at Bordeaux. Those are people who will do anything for you [*qui vous mettroient dans Leur chemise*] when they have need of you, but whom you cannot depend upon . . . but it is quite a different story for those whom I mentioned to you just a bit ago, especially MM. Lajonie, Grandefon, and Rigaud, the house of Bellevüe is also still completely devoted to us. Those are our real friends, of the heart.[140]

Although the exchange of favors played a key role in friendship, crass calculation could not be the basis of *amitié*. Most of all, the Lamothes valued their friends of the heart.

The immediate family held precedence in both the hearts and minds of the Lamothes, but their *parents et amis* played an important role as well. Kin, friends, and other contacts provided both companionship and a safety net for individuals venturing beyond the confines of the immediate family. While material interest and the hope for future services certainly played a role in the selection of friends, the Lamothes more often stressed sentiment and affection and did not see utility and emotion as mutually

---

138. Delphin to Victor, undated 1758.
139. Alexis to Victor, 28–31 August 1760.
140. Alexis to Victor, 27 October 1763. See also 27 November 1763.

exclusive. Professional, economic, and class ties could further solidify networks, creating a consciousness of solidarity among members of the professional class. Both sociability and reciprocal obligations reinforced ties of kinship and affection that were so important to the Lamothes and their social group.

PART II

Identity Through Profession

The next two chapters will explore the professional culture, ambitions, and identity of the lawyer and the doctor in eighteenth-century France. In the case of the Lamothe family, a mix of traditional and modern values is evident. Respectability, reputation, and family solidarity were important to them, as were the more professional notions of specialized education, expertise, constant application, and service to the public. They believed in advancement through personal merit and in the importance of making a name for oneself through hard work and application, but they also held more traditional views, emphasizing the importance of patronage, social standing, and family connections. To a large extent, the masculine and class identity of the Lamothe males was closely tied to both their career choices and to their dedication to their professions. While the law careers of Delphin, Alexis, Alexandre, and Daniel ended in the eighteenth century, Victor's career in medicine spanned the Revolution, into the nineteenth century, allowing us to examine shifts and changes in the practice and perceptions of the physician, as well as of professions more generally, during this critical period.

The Professional Man and the World of Law

In 1777, Maître Albert Camus, *avocat au parlement* in Paris and royal censor, presented his flattering portrait of the barrister:

> A man of substance, capable of advising & defending his fellow citizens . . . I would want a barrister to speak & write like an orator, as well as think & reason like a jurisconsult; but . . . the quality of man of substance is always the primary attribute. The importance of the affairs that one deposits in confidence into the hands of the barrister; the confidence that he must merit; the certitude that he must inspire in those addressing him, that they will always be faithfully advised, never cheated, much less betrayed, requires that he combine qualities of the heart with those of the spirit. A scrupulous probity, a decency always maintained because it is but the result of principles deeply engraved in his soul, these are the essential qualities.[1]

Daniel Lamothe and his barrister sons would have appreciated this idealized image of their profession. They considered themselves men of

---

1. Albert Camus, *Lettres sur la profession d'avocat, sur les etudes relatives à cette profession, & sur la maniere de l'exercer; avec un catalogue raisonné de livres de droit qu'il est le plus utile d'acquérir & de connoître* (Paris: Chez Méquignon, 1777), 5–6.

probity and talent, well suited to their chosen career. They considered themselves professionals, not just because of the independence, statutory security, and privilege associated with their position, but also because of their specialized knowledge of the laws of France.[2]

The barrister occupied an important position in Old Regime France. He held first rank within the Third Estate and enjoyed a number of civil and social advantages.[3] Lawyers played an important role in both provincial and national cultural life, and the leading figures in government and administration in the seventeenth and eighteenth centuries were drawn from the legal milieu.[4] Both the socially mobile and those who wished to maintain their rank urged their sons to enter the field of law.[5]

The lawyer holds a peculiar position in eighteenth-century French history. Although the legal profession is conservative by nature, for judges and lawyers are dedicated to upholding the law and the status quo, many historians have argued that French barristers, frustrated by obstacles to social mobility, and eager to promote changes in the legal system, were

2. Michael Fitzsimmons argues that the crystallization of professionalism began quite early among French barristers, and that in the early eighteenth century, barristers attached to a parlement enjoyed all the attributes associated with a "profession." *The Parisian Order of Barristers and the French Revolution* (Cambridge: Harvard University Press, 1987), 8. Jan Goldstein also notes that law had long been considered a "profession", possibly since medieval times. "Foucault Among the Sociologists: The 'Disciplines' and the History of the Professions," *History and Theory* 23 (June 1984): 174–75.

3. Baron Francis Delbèke, *L'Action politique et social des avocats au XVIIIe siècle* (Louvain and Paris: Librairie Universitaire, 1927), 109–10 and 114–15; Maurice Gresset, *Gens de justice à Besançon de la conquête par Louis XIV à la Révolution française (1674–1789)*, 2 vols. (Paris: Bibliothèque Nationale, 1978), 1:68; Lenard R. Berlanstein, *The Barristers of Toulouse in the Eighteenth Century (1740–1793)* (Baltimore: Johns Hopkins University Press, 1975), 28; Fitzsimmons, *The Parisian Order of Barristers*, 9; M. Antoine-Gaspar Boucher d'Argis, *Règles pour former un avocat, tirée des plus celebres auteurs, anciens et modernes* (Paris: Chez Durand, 1778), 191.

4. David A. Bell's *Lawyers and Citizens: The Making of a Political Elite in Old Regime France* (New York: Oxford University Press, 1994) analyzes the growing political and cultural influence of barristers over the course of the eighteenth century. See also L. W. B. Brockliss, *French Higher Education in the Seventeenth and Eighteenth Centuries: A Cultural History* (Oxford: Oxford University Press, 1987), 7–8; Sarah Maza, *Private Lives and Public Affairs: The Causes Célèbres of Prerevolutionary France* (Berkeley and Los Angeles: University of California Press, 1993), 86–97. William Bouwsma notes that many men destined for fame in other connections first studied law. "Lawyers and Early Modern Culture," *American Historical Review* 78 (1973): 306–7.

5. At the same time, the *barreau* was careful to exclude those of "vile" background, and economic and social barriers generally limited recruitment to those of respectable background. Lenard R. Berlanstein, "Lawyers in Pre-Revolutionary France," in Wilfrid Prest, ed., *Lawyers in Early Modern France and America* (New York: Holmes and Meier, 1981), 168–69; and *The Barristers of Toulouse*, 32–35; Delbèke, *L'Action politique*, 112–14; Richard Kagan, "Law Students and Legal Careers in Eighteenth-Century France," *Past and Present* No. 68 (August 1975): 56–58.

prominent among the leaders in the French Revolution.[6] Perhaps their intimate knowledge of law and the legal system made them more sensitive to rampant inequalities and injustices. True, a number of radical revolutionaries, most notably Robespierre, were *avocats* by profession. However, social studies of barristers in Toulouse and Paris have modified these conclusions. Most lawyers were socially and politically quite conservative, loyal to their professional association, the Ordre des avocats, and conscious of the dignity of their profession. They were often willing to consider and even promote gradual legal reform within the system and were active in the early phases of the Revolution, but they were appalled by the excesses of the Terror and reluctant to work within the "reformed" legal system.[7]

Delphin de Lamothe died in 1781, followed by his brother Alexis in November 1789, just as dramatic changes were taking place in France. We do not know how they would have reacted to the upheaval created by revolution. While their choice of reading material and personal papers reveal men open to the Enlightenment and legal reform, there is also much that suggests a fundamental conservatism, and reluctance to overturn a system that privileged them.

Like most of their contemporaries, they would have deplored the devaluation of their *compagnie* and profession brought about by revolutionary changes.[8] The degree to which Daniel Lamothe and his barrister sons identified with their profession and took pride in their status is obvious in their social and professional ties to other members of the legal profession; in their dedication to their work and their prolific production of published and unpublished works dealing with the law; and the manner in which legal views and discussion permeated their everyday lives. They saw their profession as different from an ordinary *métier*, because of the professional

6. Alfred Cobban, *The Social Interpretation of the French Revolution* (Cambridge: Cambridge University Press, 1964); Colin Lucas, "Nobles, Bourgeois, and the Origins of the French Revolution," *Past and Present*, no. 60 (August 1973): 84–126.

7. See Fitzsimmons, *The Parisian Order of Barristers*, and Berlanstein, *The Barristers of Toulouse*. Sarah Maza arrives at a similar conclusion about eighteenth-century barristers in *Private Lives and Public Affairs*, 86–97. David Bell, however, argues that the political engagement of barristers in the latter half of the eighteenth century (especially after the Maupeou reforms of France's parlements) made many of them willing to support the more radical changes of the Revolution. But the Parisian barristers studied by Bell were undoubtedly more radical than their provincial counterparts. Bell, *Lawyers and Citizens*, chapters 5 and 6.

8. See Fitzsimmons, *The Parisian Order of Barristers*, esp. 65–110.

expertise that the practice of law required, the social status it conferred, and the possibility of serving the public good.

1. The Barrister of the Parlement of Bordeaux

The citizens of Bordeaux took pride in the sovereign court of parlement located in their city, one of only twelve parlements in France. The Parlement of Bordeaux was a supreme court of appeal for a jurisdiction of more than two million souls, the third oldest and fourth largest in France. While customary laws of the various regions played an important role in jurisprudence, Roman law, or *droit écrit*, was considered the common law of the land.[9] The magistrates of parlement were men of great prestige and wealth, the social and political leaders of the city.

Directly below the *parlementaires* in status were the barristers or *avocats au parlement*. The bar was in theory open to any man of merit, but it was expected that the barrister be "an *honnête homme* and a man of substance."[10] The *avocats au parlement*, or the *barreau de Bordeaux*, formed an elite group because of their ties to this sovereign court, which placed them far above other lawyers in prestige.[11] The orders of barristers of parlement, whether in Paris or other provincial towns, were not considered official *corps*, or corporations, under the Old Regime, but rather "an association of individuals freely united in a common discipline for the practice of their profession."[12] In a letter to the municipal authorities in 1788, the *barreau de*

9. Alan Watson, *Roman Law and Comparative Law* (Athens: University of Georgia Press, 1991), 151. Also see Jonathan Dewald, *The Formation of a Provincial Nobility: The Magistrates of the Parlement of Rouen, 1499–1610* (Princeton: Princeton University Press, 1980), 37–38, for an analysis of the interplay of Roman and customary law in early modern France. On the structure, function, and operations of the Parlement of Bordeaux, see *Almanach historique de la province de Guienne*, pour l'Année commune 1778 (Bordeaux, 1778), 114–20; and William Doyle, *The Parlement of Bordeaux and the End of the Old Regime, 1771–1790* (New York: St. Martin's Press, 1974), 6–8.

10. Berlanstein, *The Barristers of Toulouse*, 32; see also Gustave Saulnier de la Pinelais, *Le Barreau du Parlement de Bretagne, 1553–1790* (Paris and Rennes: J. Plihon and L. Hervé, 1896), 191–92; André Damien, *Les Avocats du temps passé: Essai sur la vie quotidienne des avocats au cours des âges* (André Damien, 1973), 30; Boucher d'Argis, *Règles pour former un avocat*, 2–3.

11. This was true in all cities possessing a parlement. See Saulnier de la Pinelais, *Le Barreau du Parlement de Bretagne*, xvi; Berlanstein, *The Barristers of Toulouse*, 17–18; Fitzsimmons, *The Parisian Order of Barristers*, 8–9; M. Paul Péquignot, *Le Barreau de Bordeaux au XVIIIe siècle* (Bordeaux, 1903), 8.

12. Fitzsimmons, *The Parisian Order of Barristers*, 3.

Bordeaux asserted that "the barristers neither form nor claim to form a *corps*," but in practice, the bar usually acted as a disciplined corporate body.[13]

The lawyer practicing at the Parlement of Bordeaux was expected to possess extensive legal knowledge, including that of feudal law, canon law, civil and customary law, and Roman law. The jurisdiction of the Parlement of Bordeaux alone included eleven *coutumes*, each unique to a particular region.[14] All members of the Order of Barristers were listed on the *Tableau des avocats* in order of admission. It was essential that a lawyer be registered on the *tableau*, controlled by the Order, if he wished to practice before the parlement.[15] The barristers of the Parlement of Bordeaux pleaded at the Palais de l'Ombrière, wearing a black robe and wig. Costume and ritual were an essential aspect of the prestige of the barrister, down to the gloved left hand.[16]

Although for the most part the barristers enjoyed good relations with the parlement, with whom their fortunes were so closely linked, they were also careful to maintain their honor and independence vis-à-vis the parlement. Periodically, conflicts arose that impeded operation of the court, in most cases because the barristers believed that the parlement had injured their honor by overstepping its bounds and by trying to interfere in the internal affairs of the order, usually in matters of discipline. The barristers of Bordeaux had a very clear sense of the need for professional independence and self-regulation of their company.[17]

13. Fitzsimmons, *The Parisian Order of Barristers*, 3; ADG 4L 375, "Requisition d'adresser à Messieurs les Maire, Lieutenant-de-Maire et Jurats, Gouverneurs de la même ville," 1788. David Bell sees the "corporatism," or corporate nature, of the Order of Barristers in Paris as ambiguous, because of their professional independence and lack of venal offices. Bell, *Lawyers and Citizens*, 16 and 50–53. For a more general discussion of corporations in *ancien régime* France, see Emile Coornaert, *Les Corporations en France avant 1789*, 3d ed. (Paris: Gallimard, 1941).

14. M. Léon Cosme, *Aperçu sur le barreau de Bordeaux depuis ses origines jusqu'à vers 1830* (Bordeaux: Feret et Fils, 1886), 13, 19–20.

15. See ADG 6E 13, *tableaux* of 1752, 1754, and 1762; Boucher d'Argis, *Règles pour former un avocat*, 112–13. Control of the *tableau* was an important right, for it gave the order control over the legal practice of *avocats* and professional independence. Fitzsimmons, *The Parisian Order of Barristers*, 7.

16. Péquigont, *Le Barreau de Bordeaux*, 14–15; Damien, *Les Avocats du temps passé*, 78–82; Boucher d'Argis, *Règles pour former un avocat*, 136–37. The barrister traditionally left his right hand ungloved so that he could leaf through papers more easily.

17. For the details of some of these conflicts, and the parlement's relationship with the *barreau* more generally, see BM Ms. 1696 (VI), Fonds Lamontagne, "Notes et pièces diverses relative à l'histoire du Parlement de Bordeaux depuis son origine," No. 105, "Mémoire pour les avocats du Parlement de Bordeaux qu'ils ont l'honneur de présenter M. le premier président et M. le procureur général"; BM Ms. 1709, "Recueil des plaidoyers et mémoires," "Mémoire apologetic pour le barreau de Bordeaux, 1774," 423–54; A. Grellet-Dumazeau, *La Société bordelaise sous Louis XV et le salon de Mme Duplessy* (Bordeaux and

The barristers at the Parlement of Bordeaux held an envied position in the city. In choosing to become members of the Order of Barristers of Bordeaux, the Lamothes joined an elite group. William Bouwsma has suggested that "lawyers were often peculiarly conscious of themselves as an international community of professional men that transcended political and confessional boundaries and was held together by common goals and ideals, common problems and a common intellectual culture."[18] This may have been more the case in Renaissance Italy, or perhaps in the larger capitals of Europe,[19] but for the Lamothes, the profession of *avocat* was of more parochial interest, a profession that joined them first and foremost to their order, to their social class, and to the parlement of their city of Bordeaux.

2. Professional Formation, Identity, and Status

Law was the profession of choice among the Lamothes and became a family tradition. Daniel Lamothe, son of a *substitut du procureur du roi*, joined the bar in 1705, the first member of his family to do so. He was followed by three of his sons.[20]

Delphin de Lamothe's preparatory education followed a traditional path. He was sent to the Jesuit-run Collège de la Madeleine at the age of ten, and eventually went on to the Collège municipal de Guyenne, where he earned his *maître-ès-arts* at the age of fourteen. Soon afterward, he began

Paris: Feret et Fils and Libraires Associés, 1897), 392. Paul Péquigont concludes that, despite some conflicts, "les rapports sont plus cordiaux en général." *Le Barreau de Bordeaux au XVIIIe siècle*, 17–18. Other *barreaux* enjoyed similar relations with their parlement. Saulnier de la Pinelais, *Le Barreau du Parlement de Bretagne*, xvi–xvii and 269; Berlanstein, *The Barristers of Toulouse*, 139–41. However, Sarah Maza suggests that, despite the frequent displays of political solidarity between magistrates and lawyers, clear tensions existed and, in some cases, led to open conflict between the two groups, due to the animosity that some lawyers felt over the closed nature of the magistracy to which they aspired. See *Private Lives and Public Affairs*, 93–97. David Bell also notes the tensions, as well as the solidarities, between barristers and magistrates in *Lawyers and Citizens*, passim.

18. Bouwsma, "Lawyers and Early Modern Culture," 317.

19. In *Lawyers and Citizens*, David Bell makes this case for the lawyers of Paris, arguing that barristers came to see themselves as spokesmen for a broader "public opinion," one that transcended narrow corporate interests.

20. In the eighteenth century, a majority of law students were the sons of men involved in the legal profession. Kagan, "Law Students," 58. David Bell writes of the "dynasties" of barristers in *Lawyers and Citizens*, 28–30.

his studies in law, probably at the University of Bordeaux, and received the
licence three years later. In 1744, at the age of nineteen, he joined the
Parlement of Bordeaux.[21]

Many jurists scoffed at legal education in eighteenth-century France.
Like medical education, it was faulted for its emphasis on theory over
practice, a criticism leveled by the law students themselves as well as by a
growing number of jurisconsults and government ministers. In general,
the curriculum focused on Roman and canon law and neglected practical
applications. In addition, academic standards at many universities were lax
to nonexistent, a constant embarrassment to the legal profession.[22] To
compensate for this perceived lack of diligence on the part of the
universities, the orders of barristers in French cities generally required a
probationary period during which the new lawyer attended sessions of
parlement and filled the gaps in his legal education.[23] Thus, it was not until
two years after his acceptance at the bar that Delphin made his first plea
before the parlement, after a period of further study and observation.[24] His
brother Alexis followed him to the bar in 1747.

Unlike some law students, the Lamothes took their professional training
very seriously. Daniel directed his elder sons in an organized plan of study
for their law exams.[25] As a young lawyer, Delphin helped to organize
several *conférences* on various points of law, including the "Conférence du
droit romain avec le droit français sur le Code."[26] These *conférences*, or

21. See Christian Chêne, "Simon Antoine Delphin de Lamothe: Portrait d'un professeur bordelais
du XVIIIe siècle," in Gérard Aubiu, ed., *Etudes offertes à Pierre Jaubert: Liber Amicorum* (Bordeaux: Presses
Universitaires de Bordeaux, 1992), 134–35, on Delphin's education. Most students of law attended the
law faculty in their region. Since 1679, eighteen had been officially the youngest age at which a
student could begin the study of law at a university, which indicates that Delphin received a *dispense
d'âge.* Kagan, "Law Students," 43 and 48; Edmond Faurie, *Eloge des frères Lamothe, avocats au Parlement de
Bordeaux* (Bordeaux: Emile Crugy, 1850), 7–8.
22. Kagan, "Law Students," 40–42; Brockliss, *French Higher Education,* 277–82. Francis Delbèke
argues that this indictment of eighteenth-century legal education is too harsh, although he agrees that
certain universities were notoriously lax. *L'Action politique,* 1–3 and 59–61. David Bell recounts the
notorious case of the future revolutionary Brissot, who, like many others, purchased his law degree in
Reims. *Lawyers and Citizens,* 34.
23. The duration of the stage varied from city to city, but legal commentators of the eighteenth
century emphasized its importance. Fitzsimmons, *The Parisian Order of Barristers,* 5–6; Delbèke, *L'Action
politique,* 69–74; Camus, *Lettres sur la profession d'avocat,* 33–36 and 87; Boucher d'Argis, *Règles pour former
un avocat,* 128–29. See Bell, *Lawyers and Citizens,* 34–35, on the professional formation of barristers
aspiring to the Order of Barristers of Paris.
24. Faurie, *Eloge des frères Lamothe,* 8.
25. Lamothe Family Letters, Delphin to Victor, 18 October 1760.
26. AM Ms. 684, Fonds Meller, vol. 1; Pierre Meller, *Essais généalogiques: Familles du bordelais/recueil*

seminars, were gatherings of young barristers under the guidance of an older jurist, during which they would research, compare, and argue certain points and systems of law.[27] But despite their careful preparation, both Delphin and Alexis acknowledged that they found their early years of law practice trying, due to "the difficulties that always appear in trying to apply theory to practice."[28] Their frequent exegeses of ordinances and their father's substantial unpublished works on customary and civil law represent an interest in continued study.

The Lamothes were well aware of the privileges and distinctions due the barrister and commented frequently on the various advantages and signs of respect they enjoyed.[29] They also appreciated the particular honors they received. The whole family took satisfaction in the election of Delphin and Alexis as syndics to the Compagnie des avocats, a position of great honor to the barrister.[30] Each year, on the eve of the festival of Saint Yves, patron saint of barristers and attorneys, Bordeaux's Order of Barristers and the parlement chose two lawyers, one junior and one senior, to serve as syndics for the year. The syndic held a position similar to that of the *bâtonnier* in the Parlement of Paris and other parlements, and along with the *doyen*, had the responsibility of representing and governing the order for that year.[31]

Delphin served twice as syndic of his *ordre*, in junior capacity in 1757, and as senior syndic in 1773. Alexis was also chosen in 1759.[32] The family

---

factice de brochures concernant des familles (Bordeaux: Feret et Fils, 1897), 28. Delphin and his colleagues compiled an enormous two-volume record of their *conférence* on the Code. See BM Ms. 1572, "Conférence du droit romain avec le droit français sur le Code (de la bibliothèque Lamothe)." Delphin later instructed his brother Victor on the best way to prepare a *conférence* for young *médecins*. Delphin to Victor, 25 September 1761.

27. Camus recommended these *conférences* for the professional formation of the young *avocat* in *Lettres sur la profession d'avocat*, 47–50; Bell, *Lawyers and Citizens*, 34.

28. Delphin and Alexis to Victor, 21 August 1762.

29. See, for example, Delphin to Victor, 2 November 1757; Delphin to Victor and Alexandre, 11 March 1763; Alexis to Victor, 21 January 1764. On the legal and other privileges due the barrister, see Delbèke, *L'Action politique*, 109–12; and Boucher d'Argis, *Règles pour former un avocat*, 198–99.

30. The family's papers include a *mémoire* on the honor of the position of syndic. E. C. Richardson Collection, Library of Congress, Manuscripts Division, Container #2, Folder #2, "Manuscripts and Pamphlets in French, Many relating to Law and Medicine."

31. Henri Chauvot, *Le Barreau de Bordeaux de 1775 à 1815* (Paris: Auguste Durand, 1856), 11; *Almanach de Guienne*, 1778, 133; Fitzsimmons, *The Parisian Order of Barristers*, 13. The *doyen* was the longest registered living member of the *barreau* and a position that Daniel Lamothe held at the time of his death.

32. Faurie, *Eloge des frères Lamothe*, 5 and 12; Alexandre Nicolaï, *Histoire de l'organisation judiciaire à Bordeaux et en Guyenne et du barreau de Bordeaux du XIIIe au XIXe siècle* (Bordeaux: Gounouilhou, 1892), 105.

was extremely proud of the honor. Upon Delphin's election, Marie wrote to Victor: "It is with pleasure that I tell you about the new honor that my brother received yesterday, he was chosen *sindic* [*sic*] of the young barristers, apparently to the great pleasure of the *compagnie*."[33] Two years later, Marianne reminded Victor to send congratulations to Alexis upon his election as syndic.[34] The brothers believed that their position entitled them to a certain amount of deference. When the Lamothe's friend M. Lisleferme, who was in Paris, failed to respond to a letter, Delphin complained good-humoredly, although with some pique, "He is strangely deceiving himself if he believes that the syndic of the barristers of the Parlement of Bordeaux and his little brother have more leisure time than an indolent resident of the fortunate banks of the Seine."[35]

Never was the family's elevated perception of the status of barrister more evident than during the crisis that attended Alexandre's choice of profession. In the eighteenth century, parental influence played a major role in an individual's choice of profession as parents sought to place their children in a fitting *état*. The two oldest Lamothe sons were happy to pursue a career in law, and Daniel was willing to allow his next two sons to choose the acceptable alternatives of the priesthood and medicine. He wanted his youngest son, however, to become a lawyer as well, despite Alexandre's obvious reservations. In a letter to Alexis in 1755, Alexandre wrote, "I must now think about a lifelong profession [*état de vie*], I must tell you that I am having a very hard time deciding between commerce and the law. On the one hand, it seems to me that I would benefit much more from a career in commerce . . . but on the other hand, I see that my dear father and my dear mother would prefer that I become a barrister." There was, however, as he pointed out, the problem of "the little inclination that I have for that profession."[36] Delphin, glancing over Alexandre's letter, expressed surprise: "I had thought . . . that he had a desire to be a barrister, & I see that on the contrary, he is leaning toward commerce." He also observed with some impatience "the passion for the law that my dear father & my dear mother have, undoubtedly they imagine that it is the most wonderful profession in the world." Delphin was more willing than his father to consider another *métier* for his younger brother.[37]

33. Marie to Victor, 28 May 1757.
34. Marianne to Victor, 26 May 1759.
35. Delphin to Victor, undated 1758.
36. Alexandre to Alexis, 23 August 1755.
37. Delphin to Alexis, 23 August 1755 and undated 1755.

In the end, the pressure of his father and his own change of heart persuaded Alexandre to study law after all, although he suggested that "the idea of being three [brothers] in the same Parlement did not please me." But Daniel had the solution. "My dear father has resolved that I should study law, but with the intention of becoming a barrister at the *conseil* in Paris," and perhaps one day an embassy secretary. This idea pleased Alexandre, who declared, "As you see, my *état* is fixed & decided."[38]

Alexandre arrived in Paris in May 1760 and was placed with Me. Marais, an attorney, or *procureur, au Châtelet,* who was to teach Alexandre the skills necessary to his career at the Conseil du roi.[39] After about a year, however, Alexandre suggested purchasing an office at the Châtelet, the central criminal and civil court in Paris, and becoming an attorney himself. The expense and insecurity of a position with the royal government, either as embassy secretary or *avocat au conseil,* worried him, as did the need for a protector. Alexandre feared the "loss of honor and virtue" in such a position, and believed that an attorneyship would offer greater independence.[40]

Alexandre's plan sent shock waves through the family. Their reaction proves that for the lawyer, professional identity was a matter of social status, and not just of identification with the legal profession. The position of attorney was socially and professionally inferior to that of barrister, and the sons of barristers did not become attorneys. The role of the attorney was to handle the more mechanical, procedural aspects of the legal process. According to seventeenth-century jurisconsultant Ferrière, the profession of barrister was "noble and independent," while that of attorney was "vile, abject and *dérogeante.*"[41] The attorney did not exercise a "liberal" profession as did the barrister, but rather, purchased his office. Despite his lower status, the attorney could often earn as much or more than the barrister. Alexandre, defending the purchase of an office as *procureur au Châtelet* at a cost of 20,000 livres, asserted that he could easily earn

38. Alexandre to Victor, 17 January 1757. For an analysis of Alexandre's choice of profession, see Christine Adams, "Defining *État* in Eighteenth-Century France: The Lamothe Family of Bordeaux," *Journal of Family History* 17 (Winter 1992): 29–31.

39. Alexandre to Victor, 27 April and 27 May 1760. Apprenticeship as clerk to an attorney was one means of meeting the requirement for a legal education, although a difficult one, since the clerk continued his legal studies while maintaining a heavy workload. The prospective *avocat* received a practical education in legal procedure in addition to his own studies. Fitzsimmons, *The Parisian Order of Barristers,* 5; Camus, *Lettres sur la profession d'avocat,* 35–36. See also Bell, *Lawyers and Citizens,* 34–35.

40. Alexandre to Victor, 18 February 1761.

41. Quoted in Gresset, *Gens de justice,* 1:68–69.

12,000–15,000 livres per year.[42] If true, this was considerably more than the average salary of the *avocat*. Furthermore, the *procureur au parlement* held a strategic position, particularly in the allocation of cases among the barristers.[43] This was a frustrating dependence for the barrister, who often felt obliged to defer to the attorney, a man he considered his social and professional inferior. Delphin acknowledged this tension between attorney and barrister when he wrote to Victor and Alexandre lamenting his and Alexis's relatively low earnings as lawyers, "whether due to scorn for our talents (between us, I can definitely say that we cannot believe this), or primarily because we have never, as have many others, tried to curry favor with the attorneys [*fait . . . une cour basse & servile aux procureurs*]."[44]

Strongly aware of the distinction between barrister and attorney, Delphin expressed dismay at Alexandre's plans: "I will not hide from you that we are a little surprised that Alexandre shows so little [ambition] in his choice . . . to be an attorney at the Châtelet, we had thought that he could aspire to other positions."[45] His sister Marie expressed in even stronger terms the disapproval of the family toward Alexandre's choice of profession: "Our father and mother . . . are opposed to the profession that Alexandre has proposed to pursue only because it does not appear suitable to them . . . this *état*, no matter what you say about it, seems to them to be less gracious, and lower [*plus bas*] than that of barrister."[46]

The family eventually triumphed, for Alexandre was persuaded to abandon his plans. While Delphin asserted that "we will never force him into a profession that is repugnant to him," he suggested strongly that Alexandre use the family's contacts to procure a position as secretary in a government bureau, a position that would compromise neither "his conscience nor his morals."[47] Alexandre made a different choice that met with the approval of his family, and became an *avocat* at the Conseil du roi in

---

42. Alexandre to Victor, 18 February 1761.

43. For a discussion of the status and professional functions of the *procureur*, see Berlanstein, *The Barristers of Toulouse*, 5–6, 10, and 20; and "Lawyers in Pre-Revolutionary France," 165–67; Bell, *Lawyers and Citizens*, 38–40 and 61–62; Saulnier de la Pinelais, *Le Barreau du Parlement de Bretagne*, 153; Fitzsimmons, *The Parisian Order of Barristers*, 2–3; Damien, *Les Avocats du temps passé*, 32–33; and Isser Woloch, "The Fall and Resurrection of the Civil Bar, 1789–1820s," *French Historical Studies* 15 (Fall 1987): 242.

44. Delphin to Victor and Alexandre, 7 June 1763. Resentment toward attorneys on the part of barristers was widespread. Berlanstein, *The Barristers of Toulouse*, 20.

45. Delphin to Victor and Alexandre, 13 June 1761.

46. Marie to Victor, 23 August 1761.

47. Delphin to Victor, 26 December 1761; 30 January 1762.

1770. He held this position until 1790, when all venal offices were abolished by the revolutionary government.[48]

Their positions as barristers before the parlement secured a respected reputation, social status, and civic honors for the Lamothes practicing law in Bordeaux. Alexis expressed satisfaction that "the name of Lamothe is well known at Bordeaux . . . we are known as men of substance, respectable people."[49] Daniel Lamothe was one of the oldest and most successful members of the bar. As *sous-doyen* and later *doyen*, he sometimes held gatherings of the Order of Barristers at his home to deliberate on matters.[50] He was known as a premier barrister at the Parlement of Bordeaux during the first half of the eighteenth century and, after his death, was praised as "the ornament and oracle" of the Bordeaux bar.[51]

However, Daniel's sons obtained many more marks of distinction for the family in positions of professional and civic leadership. In addition to serving as syndic, Delphin was elected member of the prestigious Academy of Bordeaux, and acted as secretary of the newer Academy of Painting, Sculpture, and Architecture. He also served the city government on the Assembly of *Cent-Trente* in 1767, and as member of the Assembly of Notables, a position to which he was first elected in November 1772.[52] In 1780, Alexis was chosen to serve as *jurat*, highest official of the city government.[53] The most important recognition of Delphin's status and skills as lawyer came when he was chosen to replace Joseph de Bacalan as professor in French law at the University of Bordeaux.

The field of law was known as one in which a man could advance through hard work and merit. However, a good family background and

---

48. Delphin to Victor and Alexandre, 6 July 1762; 21 January 1764; Alexis to Victor, 29 June 1764. Jules Delpit, *Notes biographiques sur les Messieurs de Lamothe* (Bordeaux: Balarac Jeune, 1846), 8. The *avocats au conseil* formed an order, and enjoyed a monopoly over the right to plead before all sections of the Conseil du roi, the *commissions du conseil* and the *requêtes de l'hôtel*. See Michel Antoine, *Le Conseil du roi sous le règne de Louis XV* (Geneva: Libraire Droz, 1970), 244–47.

49. Alexis to Victor, 12 May 1766.

50. See, for example, BM Ms. 1461, "Journal," edited by Jules Delpit, 8 January 1762, 141.

51. These words are taken from an attestation by the *doyens* and syndics of the *barreau de Bordeaux* of 21 March 1775, quoted in Delpit, *Notes biographiques*, 6; Péquigont, *Le Barreau de Bordeaux*, 12.

52. *Archives municipales de Bordeaux*, vol. 6: *Inventaire sommaire des registres de la Jurade*, Dast le Vacher de Boisville, ed. (Bordeaux, 1896), 1:461 and 484; *Almanach de Guienne*, 1778, 181.

53. *Archives municipales de Bordeaux*, vol. 13: *Inventaire sommaire des registres de la Jurade*, Xavier Védère, ed., (Bordeaux, 1947), 8:390. On the institutions of Bordeaux's municipal government, see François-Georges Pariset, ed., *Bordeaux aux XVIIIe siècle* (Bordeaux: Fédération historique du Sud-Ouest, 1968), 50–61.

connections made the path to success easier for a young lawyer.[54] Daniel's reputation as a skilled lawyer eased the way for his sons, who nonetheless achieved a reputation for merit on their own. But patronage and connections also helped them in achieving their goals. Daniel and his elder sons consulted M. Leberthon, the influential *premier président* of the Parlement of Bordeaux, on Alexandre's career decisions.[55] M. Linotte, *conseiller* at the Conseil souverain of the duc de Bouillon in Paris and family relation, agreed to take Alexandre under his wing in Paris.[56] As Alexandre prepared to commence his career in Paris, Alexis urged him to make use of professional contacts and to seek out a mentor.[57] Delphin was introduced into the Parlement of Bordeaux under the auspices of two distinguished barristers, Messieurs Pelet and Brochon.[58]

Personal contacts were crucial to Delphin in obtaining his position as professor at the University of Bordeaux as well. The position of *professeur royal en droit français* at French law universities had been created by Louis XIV in 1679 as part of a reform edict to improve the practical education of law students (see section 3 below). Unlike other professors in law at the university, the professor in French law was not required to be a *docteur agrégé*, but rather, an experienced barrister.[59] Delphin, as a barrister who "enjoyed a certain renown," at least in the locality of Bordeaux, was eminently qualified for the position.[60] However, his contacts were undoubtedly of equal importance. Prior to Delphin, Joseph de Bacalan, a member of the Parlement of Bordeaux, held the professorial position, as did his son, Isaac de Bacalan. In 1771, Bacalan *père* was called upon to serve as *président* in the Maupeou Parlement. He obtained certain favors for his acquiescence, among them the right to name his successor at the university. He chose Delphin de Lamothe.[61] The Bacalans were friends of

<hr/>

54. Delbèke, *L'Action politique,* 112–13; Berlanstein, "Lawyers in Pre-Revolutionary France," 169; Maza, *Private Lives and Public Affairs,* 87–88.

55. Alexandre to Victor, 17 January 1757; Delphin to Victor and Alexandre, 6 July 1762.

56. Delphin to Victor, 24 August 1759; Alexandre to Victor, 27 May 1760. It also seems likely that M. Linotte, who served as consultant to the Bouillon family in Paris, helped Daniel Lamothe obtain his prestigious position as *conseiller* to the duc de Bouillon for his affairs in the Guyenne. See Archives nationales R², Papiers Bouillon, 75 and 87.

57. Alexis to Victor and Alexandre, 20 March 1764.

58. Delpit, *Notes biographiques,* 13; Faurie, *Eloge des frères Lamothe,* 8.

59. Christian Chêne, *L'Enseignement du droit français en pays du droit écrit (1679–1793)* (Geneva: Libraire Droz, 1982), 45.

60. Ibid., 31.

61. Maurice Campagne, *Histoire des Bacalan du XVe au XXe siècle* (Bergerac: Imprimerie générale du Sud-Ouest, 1905), 209–13; Chêne, *L'Enseignement du droit français,* 35–36.

the Lamothe family whom Delphin and Alexis mentioned in letters to Victor.[62] They also shared family ties. The Bacalans were connected by marriage to the family of Delphin's wife, Marie-Elisabeth de Brulz.[63] When Delphin married Mademoiselle de Brulz in 1772, Bacalan was one of the signatories to the marriage contract.[64]

Delphin de Lamothe's appointment to the chair in French law, a prestigious position, reflected his status in the community as well as his knowledge and erudition.[65] In their day-to-day life, Delphin and Alexis sought friends as learned as themselves, and most often from the legal world. Social and professional ties led to a frequent exchange of legal favors, which may strike the modern reader as unprofessional. In 1751, Delphin wrote a short note to his friend François de Lamontagne, a *conseiller au parlement*, asking him to intervene in a legal affair: "The woman Ferrié who is bringing you this letter, my dear friend, is a poor woman of respectable family. She is involved in a case at the Tournelle, which may be judged tomorrow, against her nephews who have not treated her with the respect she deserves . . . I count sufficiently on your friendship to [know that you will] render this woman the justice due her, she was referred to me by a close relative whom I can refuse nothing, and it is he who asked me to write you this letter."[66] Even when requesting a professional legal service, the Lamothes spoke the language of favors and patronage. When his mother, Marie de Sérézac, was involved in a legal proceeding in 1751, Delphin wrote to M. Richon, the *procureur* at Libourne, asking him to "do us the pleasure of attending to the legal process that my dear mother will be involved in tomorrow at your seneschal's court against M. Trapaud . . . we beg of you to act with exactitude concerning the time limits. The confidence that our relatives from St. Emilion have in you is our firm guarantee that you will give this affair your attention."[67] Daniel used his contacts to pass information and request favors as well, addressing one private letter to M. Meymac, the *juge royal* at Sainte-Foy.[68]

62. Alexis to Victor, 26 February 1765; Delphin to Victor, 23 March 1765.

63. Campagne, *Histoire des Bacalan*, 199.

64. ADG 3E 21696, Contrat de mariage, Delphin de Lamothe and Marie-Elisabeth de Brulz, 21 June 1772.

65. See A. Curzon, "L'Enseignement du droit français dans les universités en France au XVIIIe siècle," *Nouvelle revue historique de droit français et étranger* 43 (1919): 209–69 and 305–64, on the prestige associated with the position of *professeur royale en droit français*.

66. BM Ms. 1696 (II), Fonds Lamontagne, Correspondence, 19 March 1751, No. 17.

67. ADG 8J 692, Fonds Bigot, Lamothe dossier, Letter to M. Richon, 29 December 1751, No. 1.

68. E. C. Richardson Collection, Container #2, Folder #2, "Manuscripts in English and French, Many Relating to Law and Medicine," undated letter.

While preparing their legal manuscripts, Daniel and his sons requested information on *arrêts* and other points of law from their friends in the legal profession.[69] In turn, colleagues asked the Lamothes for professional favors as well, and the latter often handled legal matters for their friends.[70] The documents suggest a network of mutual professional and personal exchanges among the barristers and other legal professionals of Bordeaux and the Guyenne.

A legal culture permeated the everyday life of the Lamothe family, and not only because they surrounded themselves with friends in their chosen profession.[71] They read voraciously on legal matters, as evidenced by their constant requests to Victor for law books, legal pamphlets, and *arrêts*. They assiduously kept abreast of legal affairs concerning the Parlement of Paris, the Parlement of Bordeaux, and current *procès* of interest, such as the Calas affair and the expulsion of the Jesuits from France (see Chapter 7 below). They took a particular interest in the legal proceedings of friends and neighbors.[72] In addition, Lamothe *père* and *fils* frequently used their legal skills to resolve problems, and their intimate knowledge of the law undoubtedly lessened the complexities of daily life. When the family's country home, Goulards, was robbed, Delphin went to Sainte-Foy to begin legal proceedings, attending to the necessary paperwork and depositions.[73] Both Daniel and Alexis wrote their own wills.[74] Before consenting to a series of *baux à fief*, or perpetual leaseholds, on his wife's property

---

69. Messieurs Raynal, Destoup, and Laborie are among those who provided responses to inquiries. See E. C. Richardson Collection, Container #7, Folders #1–3 and Container #8, Folder #1, "MS. Dictionary of Civil Law(?)."

70. See, for example, E. C. Richardson Collection, Container #2, Folder #2, "Manuscripts in English and French, many relating to Law and Medicine," undated letter; ADG 3E 26582, Certificat, Delphin de Lamothe for Leberthon, 9 April 1765; ADG 2C 478, Centième denier, Bureau de Bordeaux, declaration by Alexis de Lamothe for M. de Rigaud de Grandefon, 26 March 1775; ADG 2C 479, declaration by Delphin de Lamothe for the succession of Jeanne-Angélique de Brulz, 3 July 1776; ADG 3E 17578, Procuration et vente, Delphin de Lamothe for Roy, 3 August 1764.

71. David Bell also notes a specific "legal culture" that molded the professional identity of the barrister in *Lawyers and Citizens*, 35–36.

72. References to the *procès* of friends can be found throughout the family letters, but see in particular Alexis to Victor, 20 April 1757; Delphin and Marie to Victor, 18 February 1758; and Delphin to Alexis, 18 August and 30 September 1773.

73. ADG, Série B, Parlement, Répertoire numérique détaillé provisoire de la Tournelle de Sainte-Foy, Liasse 9, depositions of 28, 29, and 30 January 1758; Jules to Victor, 28 January 1758; and Delphin to Victor, 6 February 1758.

74. ADG 3E 21732, Testament of Alexis de Lamothe, opened 25 March 1790; ADG 2C 189, Contrôle des grandes actes, Bureau de Bordeaux, Registration of the Testament of Daniel Lamothe, 18 February 1772; Delphin to Victor and Alexandre, 11 March 1763.

in 1775, Delphin, an expert on feudal law, examined previous *baux* issued by the de Brulz family.[75]

Their positions as *avocats au parlement* brought the Lamothes recognition in Bordeaux. However, for the Lamothes the profession of barrister was more than a label entitling them to a position of stature in the community. It also entailed an obligation to work hard and to bring honor to the family and to their order through continuous application and professional expertise. They believed in the work ethic and considered it essential to their identity as professionals and men.

3. Work Ethic and Public Service

In 1755, Delphin de Lamothe wrote to his brother Alexis, "Many things are necessary for success in this profession: health, taste for work, & what work! Hard work, continuous work, engrossing work, luck."[76] Eighteenth-century handbooks for barristers emphasized that law was a burdensome and laborious profession, one that brought honor and not fortune to those who exercised it with diligence.[77] The work ethic of the dedicated professional was internalized by the Lamothe brothers, having been instilled by their diligent father, and was coupled with the need to work hard even for a modest remuneration.[78] Constantly occupied with their work, or on the run to the *palais* for sessions of parlement, they dedicated themselves to their profession. They had internalized what would later be called a "bourgeois work ethic," which drove them to excel in their chosen profession.[79]

What was the work of the eighteenth-century lawyer? Of course, the *avocat au parlement* could plead cases before that tribunal, a performance that required great skill and eloquence. But the barrister also served as consult-

75. ADG 2E 467, Extraits de baux à cens, issued by Messire Pierre de Brulz; ADG 2C 196, Contrôle des grandes actes, Bureau de Bordeaux, Record of six *baux à fief* by Delphin de Lamothe and Elisabeth de Brulz, dated 5 August, 29 August, and 4 September 1775.

76. Delphin to Alexis, undated 1755.

77. Camus, *Lettres sur la profession d'avocat*, 5; Boucher d'Argis, *Règles pour former un avocat*, 55–56.

78. Berlanstein, "Lawyers in Pre-Revolutionary France," 168.

79. Robert A. Nye argues that already in the eighteenth century, the French bourgeoisie sought honorability through their work and believed that diligence in a chosen profession could insure honor and social standing. *Masculinity and Male Codes of Honor in Modern France* (New York: Oxford University Press, 1993), 42.

ant, as arbiter, and prepared briefs and opinions for his client. Pleading was the most admired professional function of the barrister, for it allowed him to display publicly his eloquence, learning, and erudition. Written briefs and printed procedures permitted the less theatrically gifted barrister to demonstrate his rhetorical skill and command of law on paper. Consultants, who advised clients and colleagues as well as magistrates, helped to interpret the law and create precedents. Arbitration was a final important function, for it allowed individuals to settle private disputes without a public airing of differences.[80]

The Lamothes, father and sons, exercised a variety of professional functions. Delphin in particular was known for his eloquence, an essential skill of the successful pleader.[81] His first plea, made two years after his entry into the *barreau*, reportedly received "much applause."[82] On one occasion, Marianne wrote to Victor concerning the trial of M. Chanceaulme, "our dear relative," a case that her brothers were handling. She expressed great admiration for their oratory skills: "Their pleading gained the admiration of all the listeners; their eloquence, their mental feats [*tours d'esprit*], the force of good law; they used all means to defend a cause that they believe right."[83] While Delphin and Alexis's frequent trips to the *palais* suggest they were attending to plead before the parlement, it is not clear how often the Lamothes made oral arguments there.[84] The number of barristers who pleaded before parlement frequently was low. A career as pleader, which required a strong and sonorous voice, ended early for many lawyers, who turned to the less physically demanding careers of consulting and arbitration as they grew older.[85] By the 1750s, Daniel had given up pleading, and devoted himself to consulting and composing *mémoires*.[86]

The Lamothes were active and esteemed for their talents in various areas of legal practice. Daniel Lamothe's consulting work was influential in helping to interpret and clarify law in the Guyenne. L. F. de Salviat relied

80. On the work of the lawyer, see Camus, *Lettres sur la profession d'avocat*, 144–58; Boucher d'Argis, *Règles pour former un avocat*, 128; and Berlanstein, *The Barristers of Toulouse*, 7–10.

81. BM Ms. 1234, Archives de l'Académie de peinture, sculpture et architecture civile et navale de Bordeaux, 13 March 1790, 601.

82. Faurie, *Eloge des frères Lamothe*, 8.

83. Marianne to Victor, 24 January 1757.

84. Lamothe Family Letters, passim.

85. Berlanstein, *The Barristers of Toulouse*, 13–23; Gresset, *Gens de justice*, 1:97–99.

86. Archives nationales R[2] 87, Papiers Bouillon, Letters of 9 December 1752 and 17 August 1753, signed by Me. Molinié, procureur to the duc de Bouillon.

heavily on Daniel's consultations in his analysis of the jurisprudence of the
Parlement of Bordeaux, citing a variety of Daniel's opinions. Concerning
one point on the intricacies of exemption from the *dîme*, Salviat noted that
since Daniel's "wisdom is acknowledged by the whole parlement, and since
he draws his conclusions according to incontestable principles, I doubt not
that he will carry all the votes if the occasion presents itself."[87] Daniel was
well versed in feudal and private-property law, preparing consultations
concerning a variety of legal issues.[88] His opinions reveal extensive
knowledge of the customary law of the region, as well as a deeply
ingrained conservatism in his interpretation of law, typical of Old Regime
lawyers.

Some of the most prestigious families of the province and of France
retained Daniel Lamothe as legal consultant, including the Bouillons and
the Duras.[89] Although serving as consultant to rich religious houses or
prominent landowning families could form a lucrative practice, it does not
seem that Daniel Lamothe's consulting work for the noble families of the
Guyenne was especially rewarding financially.[90] As *gages* for his position as
consultant to the duc de Bouillon, Daniel received 100 livres per year, and
10 livres for his clerk, a nominal sum.[91] Daniel took on this position
because of the prestige associated with the title of *conseiller* to an important
noble family, which also offered important professional contacts. He
hoped to pass that prestige on to his sons. Upon accepting the position in
February 1752, he wrote, "I hope that among my two children who have
embraced the same profession [as I] there will be one who will prove
himself worthy to follow me in this position."[92]

However, in view of this small honorarium, Daniel strictly limited the

87. L. F. de Salviat, *La Jurisprudence du Parlement de Bordeaux, avec un recueil de questions importantes agitées en cette cour & les arrêts qui les ont décidées . . .* , 2 vols. (Paris and Limoges: Arthus Bertrand and J.-B. Bargeas, 1824), 1:85–86, 335–40, 338, and 453; 2:189, 276–77, 410, and 530. Jonathan Dewald notes the importance of lawyers in the interpretation of law for magistrates. *Formation of a Provincial Nobility*, 33.

88. See, for example, AM Fonds Delpit, No. 127, Legal document signed by Daniel Lamothe, 21 May 1757; ADG 8J 692, Fonds Bigot, Lamothe Family Dossier, No. 3, Lamothe fils avocat, Son consulte retrait lignager, pour Jean Dumand contre Jean Perier, Goulards, 19 November 1751; No. 4, Lamothe, avocat à Bordeaux, consultation pour Jean Baptiste Betuleau, Bordeaux, 5 March 1739. The *mémoire* from No. 3 was clearly signed by Daniel Lamothe, and not by one of his sons, despite the indication on the document.

89. Delpit, *Notes biographiques*, 5.

90. Berlanstein, "Lawyers in Pre-Revolutionary France," 168; Maza, *Private Lives and Public Affairs*, 89.

91. AM Ms. 293, "Extraits et analyses par J. Delpit de quelque manuscrits de la Bibliothèque et des Archives nationales," 276. Copied from the Archives du royaume, Papiers Bouillon, Boite No. 35.

92. AM Ms. 293, "Extraits et analyses," 276; and quoted in Delpit, *Notes biographiques*, 6.

work that he was willing to do for the duc de Bouillon. He declined to follow the practice of the duke's previous legal consultants, who had provided *mémoires* for court cases free of charge, collecting an additional fee only if the case were decided in the duke's favor. Daniel considered the 100 livres "uniquely for the consultations he gives during the course of the year and . . . moreover, the documents that he prepares must be paid for as soon as he delivers them, without waiting for the outcome of the legal action." The quality of his work and the call for his services permitted him to set these conditions, which he explained by citing the high demands on his resources and time. The duke's attorney noted: "I am convinced that the examination of the slightest detail can occupy M. Lamothe for several days, the works that flow from his pen are excellent, and therefore expensive. He has said that he must use his time fruitfully having a large family to support." Daniel eventually declined to provide oral or written services for the various legal proceedings of the duke and limited himself strictly to consultations. Despite these conditions, the duc de Bouillon continued to make use of Daniel's services.[93]

Delphin and Alexis also accepted positions as counselors to important families and institutions in the Guyenne. Alexis took over his father's position as consultant to the family of Bouillon. Delphin was personal counsel to several of the "most important families" of the region, as well as to the clergy of Bordeaux.[94] Alexis may also have served as retainer to the municipal government of Sainte-Foy-la-Grande, where his knowledge of feudal and customary law would have been an asset.[95] These retainer positions guaranteed them a certain minimum income, and the opportunity to pursue their personal intellectual work. Although Delphin and Alexis were constantly busy and their work was respected, we cannot assume that their remuneration was generous. Because barristers received "honoraria" rather than fees, and few documents remain that indicate the average income of lawyers, we have little direct indication of the salary of barristers. The evidence available suggests that for most, a career as barrister was not lucrative.[96] Furthermore, the brothers suggested that the

93. Archives nationales, R² 87, Papiers Bouillon, Letters of 9 December 1752, 10 April, and 17 August 1753, and 13 May 1755.

94. Meller, *Essais généalogiques*, 26 and 28.

95. On 26 February 1782, Alexis prepared a *mémoire* concerning an *arrêt* of the Conseil d'Etat of 15 November 1781 which attributed to the king the *murs et fossés* of the cities of the generality of Bordeaux. Archives municipales de Sainte-Foy, DD 1, "Mémoire pour la communauté de Ste. Foy," 44.

96. Berlanstein, *The Barristers of Toulouse*, 26; and "Lawyers in Pre-Revolutionary France," 21–23;

revenues of their law practice were not high; according to Delphin, "these proceeds are unfortunately very slim."[97] Delphin's income as a professor, which he received directly from his students, was probably of little consequence as well.[98] Professors of French law were unable to support themselves solely through their course fees.[99] The Lamothe family's private fortune and investments were essential to their maintaining their status as provincial notables.

The wide range of issues that the Lamothes considered indicates the breadth of their legal expertise and the efficacy of their education and personal research. They were called upon at times to help clarify certain points of law for the Parlement of Bordeaux through attestations.[100] Salviat defines these *attestations* as legal opinions agreed upon and certified by the *avocats au parlement* of Bordeaux in assembly. Because they were always based upon a series of *arrêts* and agreed to by the entire Order of Barristers, attestations of the barristers of the Parlement of Bordeaux were treated with great respect, and considered legally binding in most cases.[101]

Due to the major constraints placed upon the accused's right to legal representation under the French legal system, lawyers were seldom prominently involved in criminal cases, except as commentators on some of the most celebrated cases, such as the Calas and Sirven affairs.[102] But while the majority of cases defended or prosecuted by eighteenth-century lawyers probably concerned land and feudal rights, the Lamothes also took on cases of a more private nature. In 1761, Alexis pleaded for M. Dussault St. Laurent, *écuyer* and former *jurat*, who wanted a separation from his wife, the

---

Damiens, *Les Avocats du temps passé*, 138–39. However, as Sarah Maza notes, few barristers suffered dire poverty either. *Private Lives and Public Affairs*, 89.

97. Delphin to Victor and Alexandre, 7 June 1763.

98. In a letter to Alexis from 1773, Delphin wrote that he had "six écoutants" for his course. Delphin to Alexis, 7 December 1773.

99. Chêne, *L'Enseignement du droit français*, 89–97; Curzon, "L'Enseignement du droit français," 227–28; Agnès Daffos, "L'Enseignement supérieur à la fin de l'Ancien Régime: Exemple de la Faculté de droit de l'Université de Bordeaux" (D.E.A., Bordeaux, 1988–89), 21–29.

100. See, for example, AM B 6/15, "Consultation des avocats de Bordeaux, rédigée en forme d'attestation, pour justifier de la jurisprudence du Parlement de Bordeaux, sur les questions qui y sont traitées," 234–40. Signed by Romain de Seze, with Peyraud, Lagrange, Duvergier, and Lamothe listed as participating in the deliberations.

101. The equivalent for the Parlement of Paris was an *acte de notoriété*. Salviat, *La Jurisprudence du Parlement de Bordeaux*, 1:108; also see Péquigont, *Le Barreau de Bordeaux au XVIIIe siècle*, 18–19.

102. Agénor Bardoux, *Les Légistes: Leur influence sur la société française* (Paris: G. Baillière et Cie., 1877), 182; Berlanstein, *The Barristers of Toulouse*, 102; Delbèke, *L'Action politique*, 137–45; Maza, *Private Lives and Public Affairs*, passim.

former Mademoiselle Forell, "who had for her dowry only her lovely figure." Madame Dussault had allegedly carried on an affair with the notorious Maréchal de Richelieu until her unhappy husband discovered her passionate love letters to the governor of the province. Alexis's plea resulted in an eighteen-month confinement in a convent for Madame Dussault before the separation took place.[103] Perhaps his participation in cases such as this one contributed to Alexis's cynical view of women and marriage.

The Lamothes offered their expertise through arbitration of legal problems as well. Arbitration lawyers had a reputation for probity, and their decisions were respected.[104] In his position as consultant to the clergy of Bordeaux, Delphin joined his colleagues, Roberel de Climens, professor of law at the University of Bordeaux, and M. Peyraud, to arbitrate a settlement to a conflict between the curé, the syndics, the *grands ouvriers*, and other *bénéficiers* of the Church of Saint-Michel in 1777, a task that required delicacy, skill, and compromise.[105] Arbitration was a common way in which to resolve differences between parties, and Alexis also assisted in settling legal disputes in this manner.[106]

Related to arbitration was resolution of potential legal conflicts between family and friends. In a society heavily dependent upon personal relations, much legal advice was likely issued through letters and personal conversations, especially when one was dealing with family problems. In June 1788, Alexis wrote to his friend and relative Madame Jauge concerning a financial quarrel between M. Fumouse *fils* and M. Dupuy, brothers-in-law, pertaining to a debt of nearly 19,000 livres contracted by M. Fumouse *père* in 1783. Alexis proposed a solution that he considered "the simplest and most appropriate to calm these arguments about to take shape between two brothers-in-law." He warned Madame Jauge that if the matter were not settled privately that it could lead to public unpleasantness, and ended with a personal plea to Madame Jauge to use her influence as mother-in-

103. BM Ms. 1461, "Journal" edited by Delpit, May 1761, 98. Madame Dussault left the convent of the Order of Saint Benoît without authorization on 3 August 1765. ADG 3E 17580, Inventaire des effets de Mad. Dussault de St. Laurent, 30 September 1765.

104. Berlanstein, *The Barristers of Toulouse*, 9; Camus, *Lettres sur la profession d'avocat*, 157–58.

105. ADG G 2306, Folio 51, "Compromis avec les bénéficiers, confiant à Peyraud, Lamothe aîné et Roborel, avocats, le soin de régler arbitralement le litige," 16 March 1777; ADG G 1675, "Règlement rédigé par Payraud, Lamothe et Roborel de Climens, arbitres, pour mettre fin aux contestations entre les bénéficiers, les ouvriers et le curé," 14 July 1777.

106. AM Fonds Delpit, No. 127, Legal document signed at Bordeaux, 12 March 1764, by Despiaux, Lagrange, and Alexis de Lamothe.

law to persuade M. Dupuy to accept the settlement and maintain peace in the family.[107] Alexis had earlier interceded in another legal affair involving the Jauge family.[108] A trusted family lawyer and friend could undoubtedly be useful in quietly settling intrafamilial disputes.

Law was a career for Daniel, Alexis, and Delphin de Lamothe, their means of earning a living. However, their profession was a calling as well. Each clearly felt an affinity for the practice of law, and all three found intellectual stimulation in their work. How else to explain the prodigious amount of personal work by both the brothers and their father, culminating in the publication of the *Coutumes du ressort du Parlement de Guienne* in 1768 and 1769, and the *Coutumes et statuts de la ville de Bergerac* in 1779?[109]

Daniel left an enormous body of unpublished research dealing with the law, a collection that would serve Delphin and Alexis in producing their published work on customary law.[110] His sons made use of his papers when editing their books on the *coutume* of Bordeaux, and noted in the foreword to the book, "Our success would have been much more difficult without the substantial aid that we found in the manuscripts of a father who devoted his days to study."[111]

In preparation for editing the *Coutumes de Guienne*, as well as in his work as a university professor, Delphin also annotated and analyzed various ordinances and laws that formed the basis of French law in the eighteenth century.[112] He and Alexis used their extensive historical knowledge to

107. AM Fonds Delpit, No. 127, Letter to Madame Jauge from Alexis de Lamothe, 24 June 1788.

108. ADG 8J 694, Fonds Bigot, Letter to Monsieur Mestre, avocat en Parlement à Sainte Foy from M. Jauge, 27 September 1784.

109. The full citations for these works are *Coutumes du ressort du Parlement de Guienne, avec un commentaire pour l'intelligence du texte: & les arrests rendus en interprétations; par deux avocats au même Parlement*, 2 vols. (Bordeaux: Chez les Frères Labottière, 1768–69); and *Coutumes et statuts de la ville de Bergerac, traduits de latin en français par M. Etienne Trelier, conseiller du roi en la cour de Parlement de Bordeaux, et Chambre de l'édit de Guienne, commenté par MM. de Lamothe, avocats au Parlement de Bordeaux* (Bergerac: J.-B. Puynesge, 1779).

110. Delpit, *Notes biographiques*, 7. See also the four-volume manuscript in the E. C. Richardson Collection, a "dictionary" of legal terminology, which appears to have been compiled over a lengthy period of time and in a variety of handwriting, some those of the Lamothes, others possibly belonging to their law clerks. Based on a number of sources, this manuscript contains references to various points of law, and would have been useful to the brothers in the composition of their book. E. C. Richardson Collection, Container #7, Folders #1–3, and Container #8, Folder #1, "MS. Dictionary of Civil Law."

111. *Coutumes de Guienne* 1:vi.

112. See BM Ms. 365, "Ordonnance de Louis XIV avec des notes de Delphin de Lamothe"; BM Ms. 1573, "Ordonnances de Louis XV—provient de la bibliothèque Lamothe"; and Lamothe Family Papers, Library of Congress, Manuscripts Division, Folder #6, "Explication de L'Ordonnance civile, 1667." The Ordinances of 1667 and 1670 were fundamental to French law, for they regulated procedure for French criminal and civil law. Albert Camus emphasized the importance of studying in

refine and expand their analysis of law, as well as their understanding of
the law, to explain historical transformations in society. Beginning in the
sixteenth century, French jurists rose to the forefront of historical research,
using a new historical method to explain the evolution of the law and its
practice in various societies, both Roman and customary. According to
these "historicist" jurists, as they are labeled by George Huppert, law was
a product of history and laws changed constantly, reflecting the needs of
society, a view challenging any notion of universal "natural laws."[113]
Delphin stressed in particular the importance of understanding the societal
context of laws. In a foreword to his analysis of the Ordonnance civile of
1667, he argued, "It does not suffice to know the laws & the principles of
law, if one is unaware of the ways in which they are used to uphold
justice."[114]

The Lamothe brothers' emphasis on methodical historical research and
the need to go back and examine the original sources in order to
understand the evolution and the intent of customary law is most evident
in their *Coutumes du ressort du Parlement de Guienne.*[115] In the introduction to
their book, Delphin and Alexis decried the neglect of customary law by
jurists and historians, who believed that customary law "is of a quality so
inferior to Roman Law that it is not worthy . . . of comparison."[116] In
this *pays du droit écrit*, where Roman law was still so important, little had
been done on the evolution of Bordelais customary law since the sixteenth
century, when the first official text appeared. But the work of the Lamothe
brothers was the first integral edition of both the *anciennes* and *nouvelles
coutumes*, bringing up to date various decisions of the parlement. The
objective of their work was to bring to life the customary usages, showing
the progression of commentaries on the Bordelais law and comparing them
to those of the great French jurists such as Dumoulin, Pothier, and
Loysel.[117]

depth all French ordinances when preparing for a career in law. Camus, *Lettres sur la profession d'avocat,*
84–85.

113. George Huppert, *The Idea of Perfect History: Historical Erudition and Historical Philosophy in
Renaissance France* (Urbana: University of Illinois Press, 1970), esp. 151–69. See also Donald R. Kelley,
Foundations of Modern Historical Scholarship: Language, Law, and History in the French Renaissance (New York:
Columbia University Press, 1970) for an overview of the role of jurists in the study of history.

114. Lamothe Family Papers, Folder #6, "Explication de L'Ordonnance civile, 1667."

115. See Faurie, *Eloge des frères Lamothe,* 14.

116. *Coutumes de Guienne* 1:ii.

117. See Gérard D. Guyon, "Les Textes de la coutume de Bordeaux de leurs éditions," *Revue française*

Delphin and Alexis's commentary on the *coutume* has been widely praised by nineteenth- and twentieth-century jurists.[118] The resulting work demonstrated the breadth of their juridical and historical, as well as linguistic, knowledge, for the old customary law was written in Gascon, the patois of the Guyenne.[119] The first volume of the commentary contains the body of customary law, while the second includes *arrêts* interpreting the text of the *coutume*, juridical discussion of various points, and numerous corrections. Clearly, the brothers had a lawyerly interest in the text of the law and its application.[120] But in the foreword, they emphasized the importance of historical and linguistic commentary in order to "lay out or facilitate an understanding of the Law" in its historical context.[121]

In contrast to the recognition by later jurists of the excellence and the usefulness of this edition of the *coutume*, it was not a great success when it was first published. Pierre Bernadau, a contemporary of the brothers, wrote many years later that "the work was underrated during the life of the authors," but that "now, its merit is universally recognized."[122] Another writer blamed "that century of coteries and prejudices" for their book's lack of success.[123] The brothers responded to criticism in the introduction to the second volume of their work, which appeared the following year. The disapproval and lack of support for their first volume had struck a nerve, and they pointed out that if their commentaries were not as detailed as some of their critics would have liked, "we did not claim to write for

d'histoire du livre 47 (April-May-June 1978): 399–414, esp. 411–14, on the importance of the Lamothe brothers' work in the publication and analysis of customary law.

118. See, for example, Nicolaï, *Histoire de l'organisation judiciaire*, 88. In addition, their text provides one of the few remaining guides to the *Livre des coutumes* of Bordeaux, a manuscript record of the customary law of Bordeaux, composed by order of the municipal government around 1700, and which was in very poor condition by the nineteenth century. Henri Barckhausen, the prolific Bordelais *jurisconsulte*, relied heavily on the Lamothe brothers' commentary for his *Livres des coutumes publié avec des variantes et des notes*, from the *Archives municipales de Bordeaux*, vol. 5 (Bordeaux: G. Gounouilhou, 1890).

119. Their contemporary the abbé Baurein relied on the philological expertise of the Lamothe brothers in his celebrated *Variétés bordeloises*, written between 1784 and 1786, especially for the evolution of place names. See Abbé Baurein, *Variétés bordeloises ou Essai historique et critique sur la topographie ancienne et moderne du diocèse de Bordeaux* (Bordeaux: Feret et Fils, 1876), esp. vol. 2 book 3, 40 and 129, and book 4, 295.

120. Chêne, *L'Enseignement du droit français*, 193–94.

121. *Coutumes de Guienne* 1:iv and vii.

122. Pierre Bernadau, *Annales politiques, littéraires et statistiques de Bordeaux* (Bordeaux: Moreau, 1803), 208.

123. Faurie, *Eloge des frères Lamothe*, 16.

beginners, nor to write an elementary book."[124] They ended the *avertisse-ment* to the second volume with a plea to their colleagues "and to those who have the common good & gain at heart to give us assistance, to help us, especially with their advice & their salutary criticism: it is the only way to support and encourage the Authors in the career they have undertaken only because of their love for the public good, & to hearten their steps that can only be slow on barren and uncultivated soil, & across the brambles & the thorns on which they are obliged to walk."[125] Delphin and Alexis, who believed that their commentary on the *coutume* performed an important public service by providing an analysis of the complex laws of the Guyenne, resented the lack of appreciation for their dedicated work.

The criticism of their book stalled their long-term project permanently. Delphin and Alexis had originally intended to edit all eleven customary law codes in the jurisdiction of the Parlement of Guyenne. Their first two volumes comprised only the *coutume* of Bordeaux. However, the only subsequent edition they published was that of the customary law of Bergerac in 1779, based on Etienne Trelier's text of 1627. It appeared two years before Delphin's death.[126]

Delphin's work ethic, not unmixed with a sense of public service, and his extensive examination of the law prepared him for his work as professor in French law at the University of Bordeaux. Although personal and profes- sional connections, as well as a reputation for erudition and learning, helped him to obtain the position, he showed a strong commitment to his work as professor.

The position of *professeur royal en droit français* at French universities was created to fill a lacuna in French legal education. Prior to the creation of this position in 1679, law students in Bordeaux were instructed solely in canon and civil law, with the heaviest emphasis on Roman law. Classes were taught in Latin. Thus, students had little or no exposure to living law, in other words, laws that were in the process of being created through custom, ordinance, or *arrêts* of parlement. The introduction of a professor of French law, who taught his courses in French, was an attempt to introduce practical education into the system.[127] Even in Bordeaux, where

---

124. *Coutumes de Guienne* 2:x.

125. *Coutumes de Guienne* 2:xii.

126. Chêne, *L'Enseignement du droit français*, 193–95.

127. On the introduction of the position of *professeur royal en droit français* into the university system, see Curzon, "L'Enseignement du droit français," and Jean Portemer, "La Politique royale de

Roman law practices predominated, an increasing number of royal edicts and ordinances of national application superseded civil law, reducing the value of concentrated study of Roman law.[128] The introduction of courses in French law was an attempt to show students how the law was applied, instead of focusing solely on the theory behind the law.[129]

What was included in the teaching of French law? A course in it would generally include the study of royal ordinances, edicts, declarations, *arrêts*, the jurisprudence of *arrêts*, and customary law and its particular usages, as opposed to Roman or canon law. Thus, French law was a combination of two things: universally applicable laws, or the *maximes du droit français*, and regional (customary) laws.[130] Delphin, with his careful analyses of the ordinances of Louis XIV and Louis XV, along with his lifelong study of customary law, was uniquely qualified to teach courses in French law. Local historian Jules Delpit praised Delphin as a skillful teacher of law who presented the material with order and clarity, emphasizing customary and statutory law.[131] And unlike many professors of law, he was a diligent instructor and dedicated to his students.[132]

The professor in French law placed greatest emphasis on the teaching of private law. Many of the philosophes, especially Diderot, and even well-known jurists such as Boucher d'Argis, leveled criticism at the law faculties for their neglect of the study of natural law, the rights of persons,

---

l'enseignement du droit en France au XVIIIe siècle: Ses survivances dans le régime modern," *Revue d'histoire des facultés de droit et de la science juridique*, no. 7 (1988): 15–43. For a discussion in the context of the University of Bordeaux, see Chêne, *L'Enseignement du droit français*, 2–3; and Daffos, "L'Enseignement supérieur," 11–18.

128. Brockliss, *French Higher Education*, 280. However, law professors continued to insist upon the importance of extensive knowledge of Roman law.

129. Daffos, "L'Enseignement supérieur," 35–40.

130. Chêne covers in detail the various aspects of "droit français" as taught in French universities in the eighteenth century in *L'Enseignement du droit français*, 200–252.

131. Delpit, *Notes biographiques*, 19–20. According to Christian Chêne, Delpit is our sole source today concerning Delphin de Lamothe's courses, because of the lack of surviving manuscripts. A nineteenth-century Bordelais historian, Delpit had access to many Lamothe family documents, as well as university archives, that are no longer available. Chêne, *L'Enseignement du droit français*, 175.

132. Daffos, "L'Enseignement supérieur," 30; Chêne, *L'Enseignement du droit français*, 321; Faurie, *Eloge des frères Lamothe*, 16. As the position of royal professor in French law was not highly remunerative, most professors continued with outside activities, sometimes at the expense of their students. The king attempted to remedy this situation by improving the financial position of the *professeur en droit français* at the University of Bordeaux in 1738, but it continued to be a problem. See "Déclaration par Louis XV, portant réglement pour la chaire de professeur de droit français en L'Université de Bordeaux, du Janvier 1738," published in H. Barckhausen, ed., *Statuts et réglements de l'ancienne université de Bordeaux (1441–1793)*, (Libourne and Bordeaux: Georges Bouchon, 1886), 117–19.

and public law.[133] The law schools did not include the philosophy of natural law in their curricula, but courses in public law were created at a number of universities, the first at Besançon in 1745, despite resistance to the idea among more conservative professors of law. Delphin, "more open than many of his colleagues to new ideas," expressed interest in the idea of teaching public law, perhaps intrigued by the close connection between public law and the political history of France.[134] In January 1775, he wrote to Hue de Miromesnil, royal keeper of the seals, and requested that a chair in public law be created at the University of Bordeaux, a position that he, of course, hoped to fill. Miromesnil responded on 5 February 1775 that he considered it an excellent idea, but that there was no money to finance the innovation.[135] Perhaps Delphin coveted the status attached to an additional university position, but his efforts also suggest a real desire to improve the curriculum of the law school.

Despite their interest in other cultural pursuits and refinements, legal work was the primary focus of the three Lamothe lawyers at the *barreau de Bordeaux*, betraying the professional's work ethic and belief in the importance of professional expertise and productiveness. The brothers also saw certain endeavors as useful to the public. Sustained work and application, along with utility, were essential aspects of their professional and, indeed, their personal identities.

4. Political Views and Justice in the Age of Enlightenment

The French barrister, because of his study of the foundations of law, the legal system, and political society, was exposed to many important aspects of political discussion, including legitimacy, authority, the role of the church and state, and various concepts of law and justice. This education was not a neutral one, for the student of law was given "a series of definite answers to key national political and social questions concerning status,

133. Portemer, "La Politique royale," 28.
134. The article in the *Encyclopédie* written by Boucher d'Argis defines public law as "celui qui est établi pour l'utilité commune des peuples considéré comme corps politique." Quoted in Daffos, "L'Enseignement supérieur," 59.
135. Portemer, "La Politique royale," 28–38; Delpit, *Notes biographiques*, 20.

property and royal power," which conformed to the political principles of Old Regime France.[136] French jurists had traditionally provided most of the accepted commentary on political thought, firmly grounded in established law and providing fundamental support to the monarchy and traditional views of state and royal authority.[137] At the same time, lawyers played a prominent role in the formation of modern culture, as members of an articulate and socially respectable class. The Lamothe brothers were lawyers, educated in a tradition steeped in the authority of the king and the state, but they were also men of the Enlightenment, exposed to new currents of thought, which they eagerly sampled. How did these twin trends affect their political and legal views, including their ideas on justice, reform, and the political system?

The *barreau de Bordeaux*, as a whole, was influenced by the legal and cultural trends of the eighteenth century.[138] For example, under the influence of the philosophes, pleading changed completely in character and "the barrister progressively extended the circle of his activity and his influence; he ceased to limit himself exclusively to the discussion of private interests in order to grapple with the study and the discussion of the public interest; he attacked the law itself when he found it unjust; in short, he prepared for the advent of political eloquence."[139] Undoubtedly, the Lamothe brothers were affected by these philosophical and political currents.[140]

Throughout his life, Delphin de Lamothe expressed a deep and abiding interest in legal reform and codification of laws, one of the primary goals of the philosophes.[141] Some of his more radical ideas were exposed in his

136. Brockliss, *French Higher Education*, 320.
137. See William F. Church, "The Decline of the French Jurists as Political Theorists, 1660–1789," *French Historical Studies* 5 (Spring 1967): 1–40.
138. This was true throughout France. As Sarah Maza notes, many of the leading barristers read a wide variety of books, including the philosophes, and promoted religious toleration and enlightened reform. See *Private Lives and Public Affairs*, 91.
139. P. La Violette, *La Plaidoirie devant la critique littéraire* (Bordeaux, 1900), 321–22. Roger Chartier notes the impact of lawyers on public opinion through control of juridical and political language in the years leading up to the French Revolution, culminating in their crucial role in the preparation of the *cahiers* in 1788–89. *The Cultural Origins of the French Revolution*, trans. Lydia G. Cochrane (Durham: Duke University Press, 1991), 172–77. Maza's *Private Lives and Public Affairs* also focuses on the importance of barristers in shaping public opinion in the second half of the eighteenth century.
140. David Bell traces the growing political engagement of barristers in the second half of the eighteenth century, as well as their more aggressive attitude toward legal and political reform and a dedication to a more abstract ideal of justice in *Lawyers and Citizens*, 174–89.
141. Voltaire in particular sought greater unity in the French system of law. Bardoux, *Les Légistes*, 199.

letters to M. Formey, historiographer of the Royal Academy of Berlin in 1749, when Delphin was a young man of twenty-four. Delphin initiated the correspondence to discuss Frederick II's project to reform justice in Prussia. He opened with an attack on the formalities of legal procedure, calling for a more "enlightened" method:

> I believe that it would be easy to dispense with barristers and attorneys, especially if legal procedure no longer involved cumbersome formalities that, nearly always, muddle the decisions in the proceedings, and render them so formidable; enlightened judges could use their wisdom [lumières] to supplement anything that a timid or crude party might forget to say in his defense; and since he [the judge] would himself be the advocate both for and against, he would have no need to be on his guard against two dangerous adversaries and all their artificial resource.[142]

These views suggest a rather naive belief in the benevolence and impartiality of judges, particularly in light of Delphin's comment in the same letter on the danger of corruption of judges, in which he cited the cozy relations between the magistrates of the Parlement of Bordeaux and merchants who helped them to sell their wines.[143] In a later letter, he modified his earlier position, noting, "Judges are men like all others."[144] At a still later date, in the foreword to his commentary on the Civil Ordinance of 1667, Delphin totally rejected his earlier views. Legal procedure, in his words "can be left neither to the fancy of the pleader, nor to the discretion of the judge; the cupidity and the bad faith of the former would each day create a new labyrinth in which chicanery would close off all just solutions; and the judges, following in the instruction and judgments of affairs only the course of their fancy, would soon degenerate into despots even though they might have the best intentions in the world."[145] Edmond Faurie attributes Delphin's change of heart to "his more mature spirit, instructed by experience," but it is also possible that as an estab-

---

142. Juin-Mai 1749.—Lettres de Simon-Delphin de Lamothe à M. Formey, historiographe de l'Académie royale des sciences de Berlin, sur le projet du roi de Prusse pour la réformation de la justice. Published in *Archives historique du département de la Gironde*, vol. 32 (Paris and Bordeaux, 1898). Letter of June 1749, 247. Only portions of the correspondence are published.

143. Faurie, *Eloge des frères Lamothe*, 9.

144. Quoted in Faurie, *Eloge des frères Lamothe*, 11.

145. Lamothe Family Papers, Folder #6, "Explication de L'Ordonnance civile, 1667."

lished member of the bar, he had a greater interest in defending the practices of his profession.[146]

The Lamothe brothers' views on criminal law reveal the impact of the Enlightenment in several instances. For example, Delphin and Alexis strongly questioned the severity with which the crime of *vol domestique* (thievery by servants) was treated under the law.[147] Delphin also deplored the excesses of torture in his commentary on the Criminal Ordinance of 1670, calling for the abolition of Title XIX of the law. He argued that torture was a practice "as cruel in its practice as it is uncertain in its results!"[148] Delphin was possibly influenced by Beccaria's *Dei delitti e delle pene* and, more likely, by Dupaty, the *avocat-général* at the Parlement of Bordeaux who opposed torture and supported reform of criminal law.[149] His views on torture carried over into his university courses in criminal law where he criticized many of the penal code's excesses.[150]

Despite his obvious discomfort with the use of torture, Delphin's views on this sensitive matter were not unequivocal. In 1777, the council in Geneva, in the name of the Société economique de Berne, offered a prize of fifty louis for a comprehensive criminal code. Delphin's eagerness to take on this task reveals his deep interest in legal reform, but surprisingly, his plan included the use of torture in some limited cases. Perhaps in conservative fashion, he believed that his plan would be more acceptable if it contained these harsh measures. Still, it is curious that in an era when torture was quickly losing legal and moral justification, he was willing to support it, at least partially and in particular instances.[151] At the same time, in a letter enclosed with his work, Delphin deplored the severity of the penal system, suggesting that rewarding good behavior and virtuous people could be more effective.[152]

Delphin's proposals concerning reform of the criminal code were not his first venture into the area of legal codification, an important topic in eighteenth-century France. Both philosophes and the state sought a means

146. Faurie, *Eloge des frères Lamothe*, 17.

147. See *Coutumes et statuts de la ville de Bergerac*, 11, quoted in Chêne, *L'Enseignement du droit français*, 171. Servants convicted of theft could be sentenced to death. Cissie Fairchilds, *Domestic Enemies: Servants and Their Masters in Old Regime France* (Baltimore: Johns Hopkins University Press, 1984), 72.

148. Faurie, *Eloge des frères Lamothe*, 17; Nicolaï, *Histoire de l'organisation judiciaire*, 88–89.

149. Chauvot, *Le Barreau de Bordeaux*, 21.

150. Péquigont, *Le Barreau de Bordeaux au XVIIIe siècle*, 38.

151. Toward the end of the eighteenth century, jurists were increasingly disgusted by torture. Bardoux, *Les Légistes*, 238; Berlanstein, *The Barristers of Toulouse*, 104.

152. Faurie, *Eloge des Frères Lamothe*, 18–19.

of unifying the legal system of France and of superseding the hundreds of customary laws and overlapping jurisdictions.[153] From 1774, Delphin was interested in reformation of the Code rural, or agricultural laws, specifically to assist the poor of the countryside. His code included provisions for tax exemptions for large families, fixed hours of work, assistance to disabled peasants, and the reduction of corvées. In an effort to bring his work to the attention of the central government, Delphin sent his project to three successive contrôleurs-généraux between 1775 and 1778: Turgot, Necker, and Bertin. In late 1778, M. Parent fils, agricultural minister to M. Bertin, wrote to Delphin, requesting a copy of his project, which he had heard "contained some very useful propositions." M. Bertin's career as minister was short, and Delphin's project on the Code rural was lost in government red tape.[154] But his efforts were prescient. Agricultural reform remained a complex problem for France, even following the Revolution, which failed to standardize rural legislation.[155]

Both Delphin and Alexis were deeply influenced by the political ideas of their compatriot Montesquieu. Delphin composed an alphabetized list of the main legal and political ideas discussed in Montesquieu's work, copying some of the most liberal ideas, citing the volume and page in the text, and sometimes adding his own commentary. Under "Slavery," Delphin approvingly noted Montesquieu's "excellent refutation of all the reasons given by jurisconsults to justify it . . . in Chapter V, the author employs clever and pointed irony to prove our injustice in enslaving the Negroes."[156] Delphin's belief that legal and political systems must be adapted to the needs of a specific nation and culture reveals the impact of Montesquieu's philosophy. At the same time, like those of Montesquieu,

153. George Hubrecht notes that Delphin "s'est tout particulièrement intéréssé au mouvement en faveur des codifications qui se manifestait partout en cette seconde moitié du XVIIIe siècle." "Remerciment de reception de Mr. Hubrecht," séance du 15 février 1966, in Actes de l'Académie nationale des sciences, belles-lettres et arts de Bordeaux, 4e Série, 1966 (Bordeaux, 1967), 21:42. For further discussion of the interest in codification of laws in the eighteenth century, see Bardoux, Les Légistes, 189–90; and Church, "The Decline of French Jurists," 25–26.

154. The text of Delphin's correspondence with the successive ministries is in Delpit, Notes biographiques, 21–22; Faurie, Eloge des frères Lamothe, 19, provides the details of his law reforms cited here. No traces of Delphin's rural reform project exist today.

155. As late as 1819, six separate legal codes, including the Law of 6 October 1791, directed rural jurisprudence, and the minister of the interior sought assistance from various experts in establishing a new Code rural. See Archives nationales F[10] 288 for a series of letters and pamphlets relating to these efforts to establish a uniform rural code.

156. E. C. Richardson Collection, Container #2, Folder #2, "Manuscripts in English and French, many relating to Medicine and Law."

Delphin's views suggested the acceptance of a universal natural law, since he believed that certain legal traditions were timeless and that a higher equity or justice could override national and particularist considerations.[157] He wrote to M. Formey: "A while ago, we read with infinite satisfaction the first part of the translation of your *Code Frédéric;* we recognized in that work the true principles of laws perfectly developed; we saw the laws that so many nations have adopted reappear with both their original wisdom and modifications suitable to the times, mores, religion . . . Justice has no country, or rather, it is naturalized everywhere, and one must regard a good law, whether it comes to us from the Indies or the Hottentots, as laid down by our own lawmakers."[158]

Delphin criticized certain aspects of the French political system in his correspondence with M. Formey as well. Concerning venal offices, he wrote with Voltairian irony: "I see here with amazement that the venality of offices is unknown among you. What! positions and honors are given on the basis of merit? A Frenchman would never believe it, and will think that you are speaking of something that exists in Plato's republic or in the kingdom of Mentor."[159] He also suggested his displeasure with the system of censorship prevalent in France when M. Formey invited him to publish their correspondence in a literary journal. Delphin objected that "the frankness and the liberty with which we can discuss a thousand different things would be incompatible with the inhibitions that constrict Frenchmen; our letters would be ruthlessly truncated, changed, disfigured, according to the fancy of the *Mercurio-graphe* [of the *Mercure de France*]."[160]

It is difficult to ascertain the views of the Lamothe brothers on certain emotional political issues of the late eighteenth century, such as the competing claims to sovereignty of the parlement and the king, which reached a full-blown crisis with the institution of the Maupeou Parlement in 1771.[161] Bordeaux's barristers tended to support the parlement, but there was no sympathetic strike by the bar, and most lawyers continued to

157. For a synthetic discussion and analysis of Montesquieu's political philosophy, see Melvin Richter, *The Political Theory of Montesquieu* (Cambridge: Cambridge University Press, 1977).
158. Formey Correspondence, *Archives historiques,* Letter of 27 May 1751, 252.
159. Ibid., Letter of 1 July 1749, 248.
160. Ibid., Letter of 8 June 1750, 251.
161. For the background of events leading to the Maupeou crisis, see Durand Echverria, *The Maupeou Revolution: A Study in the History of Libertarianism in France, 1770–1774* (Baton Rouge: Louisiana State University Press, 1985), 1–34. Doyle, *The Parlement of Bordeaux,* 144–76, deals with the reforms in the context of the Bordeaux Parlement.

practice before the new parlement.[162] Delphin and Alexis's close friend François de Lamontagne served as *conseiller* in the Maupeou Parlement.[163] Delphin's position as professor in French law was confirmed under Maupeou, suggesting his willingness to cooperate with the new order. However, on 8 September 1771, the day following the institution of the Maupeou reforms, Alexis and Delphin wrote and signed a secret declaration, which reads in its entirety:

> We, the undersigned, Simon-Antoine-Delphin and Alexis de Lamothe, *avocats au parlement*, fundamentally free, and as Frenchmen and barristers, considering the actions that are being put into effect against our Order, so as to force them to take actions that they reject, fearing that more violent [means] will be employed, [we] declare that the liberty of our profession and that of our will [*volonté*] does not comport with any commitments that we might be forced to make, whether to continue or to cease the functions of our *état*: this is why we protest in advance against these steps or any other that would be involuntary, and against any consequences that may be the result. [We] declare that the expression of these sentiments, engraved in our hearts, were dictated to us by our consciences, our honor, our ardent zeal, and our inviolable attachment to the service of the King, for which we are ready to make any sacrifices that our duties may permit.
>
> Lamothe   A. de Lamothe
> Protesting as above   Protesting in conformity[164]

This statement provides a clear statement of Delphin and Alexis's understanding of both their profession and its obligations. They proudly asserted the independence of their profession and their unwillingness to be forced into actions contrary to their rights and duties, either by Maupeou or the former magistrates of the Parlement of Bordeaux. Like many other French, Delphin and Alexis were undoubtedly torn by conflicting emotions concerning Maupeou's actions, as the desire to see legal reform

162. Doyle, *The Parlement of Bordeaux*, 147–48. The situation was quite different in Paris. Bell, *Lawyers and Citizens*, 138–48.

163. Grellet-Dumazeau, *La Société bordelaise*, 335; Paul Courteault, "Notice sur François de Lamontaigne," in François de Lamontaigne, *Chronique bordelaise de François de Lamontaigne, conseiller au Parlement* (Bordeaux: Imprimeries Delmas, Chapons, Gounouilhou, 1926), xvi–xvii.

164. AM Ms. 519, Fonds Delpit, No. 5. Also published in the *Archives historiques de la Gironde* 1:133.

warred with their indignation over this blow to the dignity of the parlement to which their *compagnie* was so closely linked.

In their work on the Coutume de Bordeaux, the Lamothe brothers acknowledged the impact of the new humanitarian ideas of the Enlightenment on their analysis of law. They believed that the Enlightenment had significantly changed old standards for reviewing the laws of the kingdom, as the new ideas brought an exactness and a precision that had not previously existed in law.[165] They would have agreed with jurist Agénor Bardoux on the close relationship between legislation and the "philosophical movement of an era."[166]

The Lamothes tried to fit the idealized image of the eighteenth-century lawyer presented by commentators such as Camus and d'Argis. They were well educated, dedicated to their profession and their order, and imbued with a strong work ethic. They were convinced of the elevated purpose and public worth of their calling. In short, they were professionals. Their secret declaration in the wake of the Maupeou reforms demonstrated their own professional creed, emphasizing their professional calling, their honor, and their independence. However, their professional identity went beyond these more traditional attributes of the barrister. As Colin Jones has suggested, members of the legal profession, like others, were in the process of redefining what it meant to be a professional in the second half of the eighteenth century, adopting notions of what Jones calls civic professionalism, incorporating ideas of justice, public utility, and good citizenship.[167] Following this trend, the Lamothes showed commitment to the new public-service credo of the professional. They saw their books on the customary law of the Guyenne as a service to the public, and Delphin's dedication to his work as professor indicated a strong desire to both serve his students and improve the quality of legal education. They were committed to the ideals of justice and good law.

Alexis, and especially Delphin, as Enlightened men, accepted the new ideas of their century concerning law, justice, and administrative reform, questioning the legal process, the severity of the penal system, and the

165. *Coutumes de Guienne* 1:vi.

166. Bardoux, *Les Légistes*, 181.

167. Colin Jones, "Bourgeois Revolution Revivified: 1789 and Social Change," in Colin Lucas, ed., *Rewriting the French Revolution* (Oxford: Oxford University Press, 1991), 95–109. David Bell's focus on the political activism of barristers and their claims to speak for the "public" by the 1770s and 1780s is also useful in this context. *Lawyers and Citizens*, esp. chap 5.

irregularity of the legal structure in general and condemning censorship, venality, and corruption in France. At the same time, nothing in their works suggests a radical desire to overthrow the Old Regime political or legal system, or any real challenges to basic assumptions of the authority of the state and the king. Like most barristers in France, the Lamothes mixed traditional standards and authorities with new humanitarian concerns and avoided boldness in their political views.[168] It is highly unlikely that a professor in French law, appointed by the king, held or expressed ideas that were truly subversive or that marked a straightforward rejection of monarchical principles. Delphin and Alexis's secret declaration of 1771 stressed their commitment to *le service du roi* as well as to their profession. The Lamothe brothers were first and foremost lawyers, loyal to their *compagnie* and steeped in a traditional professional education that preserved their conservative instincts. While critical of certain aspects of the legal system, they would have been reluctant to disband a system that they knew so well and that so privileged them. Still, as Sarah Maza points out, "The fact that many, perhaps most, barristers eventually turned against the Revolution should not blind us to the crucial role played by members of the legal profession in shaping the public discourse of prerevolutionary France."[169]

The Revolution that came to France after the deaths of Delphin and Alexis de Lamothe overturned the system of law and the orderly society they had known. Although certain lawyers supported the upheaval and even exercised leadership throughout the years of revolution, most barristers bitterly resented the denigration of their profession and their order. Both in the provinces and Paris, the majority of *avocats* opposed or withdrew from the new legal and political structure.[170] Many of these were men who had been reform minded prior to the Revolution. In 1791, five professors of the law faculty of Bordeaux were denounced at the Club

168. Maza, *Private Lives and Public Affairs*, 91–92; Berlanstein, *The Barristers of Toulouse*, 109 and 115.

169. Maza, *Private Lives and Public Affairs*, 97. David Bell, in his analysis of the Parisian Order of Barristers, argues that the political activism of lawyers, especially in the second half of the eighteenth century, contained within it a dynamism that eventually led to the decline and collapse of their profession, culminating in the abolition of their order on 2 September 1790. See chap. 6 of *Lawyers and Citizens*. However, even Bell acknowledges that in the end, most barristers turned against the Revolution. See 193.

170. See Berlanstein, *The Barristers of Toulouse*, 148–82; and Fitzsimmons, *The Parisian Order of Barristers*, 56–153, for the reaction of members of the *barreaux* during and immediately following the Revolution. Woloch, "The Fall and Resurrection of the Civil Bar," 241–62, also details the changes in the civil bar during and following the Revolution.

des amis de la constitution for insufficient commitment to the revolutionary cause.[171] Would Delphin and Alexis also have been denounced? When
Alexandre Lamothe lost his position as *avocat au conseil* in Paris, he returned
to Bordeaux and never practiced law again. Victor Lamothe, a doctor
whose medical skills remained in high demand, survived the Revolution
with greater success than his brother in the legal profession.

---

171. R. Brouillard, "Les Professeurs de droit et la Révolution," *Revue historique de Bordeaux et du
département de la Gironde* 4 (1911): 56.

5

The Professional Identity of the Physician

In 1755, Delphin wrote to his brother Alexis, "As for Victor, I believe that he truly intends to take up medicine . . . he does not appear far from donning the gown of Rabelais."[1] From an early age, Victor Lamothe wished to study medicine, and his family was eager to support his inclination. While this field encompassed a broad range of practitioners, including surgeons, apothecaries, midwives, bonesetters, empirics, and any number of charlatans, the physician in the eighteenth century held a respectable position in bourgeois society. Physicians were part of the educated professional elite and played an important role in the social and cultural life of urban France.[2] The expense of degrees and admission to the medical associations, *collèges*, and corporations, as well as the required *maître-ès-arts* in philosophy and knowledge of Greek, Latin, and rhetoric, limited recruitment mostly to the comfortable middle and upper classes. Like barristers, respected physicians in provincial towns were ranked as *nobles hommes*, which accorded them privileges such as exemption from certain taxes and impositions.[3] Medicine was largely a profession for the well established, rather than an opportunity for the upwardly mobile.

1. Lamothe Family Letters, Delphin to Alexis, undated 1755.
2. L. W. B. Brockliss, *French Higher Education in the Seventeenth and Eighteenth Centuries: A Cultural History* (Oxford: Oxford University Press, 1987), 1–9.
3. Matthew Ramsey, *Professional and Popular Medicine in France, 1770–1830: The Social World of Medical Practice* (New York: Cambridge University Press, 1988), 54–55; A. Corlieu, *L'Ancienne Faculté de médecine de Paris* (Paris: V. Adrien DeLaHaye, 1877), 17.

Still, the eighteenth century was a time of flux in the medical profession, both in perception and practice, a process that was accelerated by revolution in 1789.[4] The university-trained physician had traditionally been considered superior in education and social status to all other medical practitioners, including surgeons, who carried the stigma of working with their hands. While physicians remained the elite of the medical profession throughout the century, advances in professional formation and the practice of surgery conferred new status upon surgeons.[5] This was also a time of debate over the nature of medical practice, health, and culture as physicians and surgeons, imbued with enlightened notions of public service, tried to ameliorate the health and sanitary conditions of the public. Royal administrators, in an effort to improve the public health, granted letters patent to the Royal Society of Medicine in 1778.[6] However, the Revolution brought about the greatest changes in the practice of medicine. The revolutionary government abolished the privileged monopoly position held by the *collèges*, or corporations, of physicians in many cities, and it questioned the physician's claims to expertise. At the same time, the years of war following the outbreak of revolution in France called for rapid improvement and creativity in the treatment of injured soldiers by physicians and surgeons.[7]

Victor Lamothe's career, which lasted from 1768 through 1823, spanned this period of turmoil and change. Although he adapted to the strictures and language of the revolutionary government after 1789 and continued his medical practice in Bordeaux, his values and views on the practice of medicine changed little during his fifty-six-year career. The title of *médecin*

4. For a recent overview, see Laurence Brockliss and Colin Jones's excellent book, *The Medical World of Early Modern France* (Oxford: Clarendon Press, 1997).

5. See Toby Gelfand, *Professionalizing Modern Medicine: Paris Surgeons and Medical Science and Institutions in the Eighteenth Century* (Westport, Conn.: Greenwood Press, 1980), 149–71.

6. Caroline Hannaway's doctoral dissertation is the most complete work on the Société royale de médecine and its public health function. "Medicine, Public Welfare, and the State in Eighteenth-Century France: The Société royale de médecine of Paris (1776–1793)," 2 vols. (Ph.D. diss., Johns Hopkins University, 1974). See also Terence D. Murphy, "The French Medical Profession's Perception of Its Social Function Between 1776 and 1830," *Medical History* 23 (1979): 259–60.

7. Murphy, "French Medical Profession," 262–64; David M. Vess, *Medical Revolution in France, 1789–1796* (Gainesville: University Presses of Florida, 1975); Dora Weiner, "French Doctors Face War, 1792–1815," in Charles K. Warner, ed., *From the Ancien Régime to the Popular Front: Essays in the History of Modern France in Honor of Shepard B. Clough* (New York: Columbia University Press, 1969), 51–73.

was an essential component of Victor's personal and professional identity, and he valued the status and respect associated with the name. It has been argued that officially accredited medical practitioners of the eighteenth century had little claim to the title of "professional" founded on a specialized knowledge base, despite the complicated theoretical discourse of these physicians, and that the effectiveness of the eighteenth-century *médecin* was not necessarily greater than that of the "charlatans" and empirics scorned by university-trained doctors.[8] But Victor took pride in his education and his knowledge of science. His devotion to the principles of observation and experience reflects the ethos of the eighteenth-century surgeon more than the outlook of the stereotypical physician, who was often accused of valuing theory over practice.[9]

At the same time, Victor emphasized the service aspect of his profession and his obligation to serve the public good.[10] While rhetoric about compassion for the sick and exemplary lives was commonplace in the eulogies of eighteenth-century physicians, a preoccupation with the public good was evident in the career choices and professional activities of Victor Lamothe.[11] His personal pride and identity as a physician required a code of professional behavior emphasizing specialized knowledge, practical skill, and public service.

---

8. Gelfand, *Professionalizing Modern Medicine*, 191; Jan Goldstein, "Foucault Among the Sociologists: The 'Disciplines' and the History of the Professions," *History and Theory* 23 (June 1984): 184–85; François Lebrun, *Se soigner autrefois: Médecins, saints et sorciers aux 17e et 18e siècles* (Paris: Temps Actuels, 1983), 183–85; Jean-Pierre Goubert, "The Art of Healing: Learned Medicine and Popular Medicine in the France of 1790," in Robert Forster and Orest Ranum, eds., *Medicine and Society in France: Selections from the Annales*, trans. Elborg Forster and Patricia Ranum (Baltimore: Johns Hopkins University Press, 1980), 1–23. George Weisz argues that the professionalization of medicine did not take place until the nineteenth century in "The Politics of Medical Professionalization in France, 1845–1848," *Journal of Social History* 12 (Fall 1978): 3–30.

9. Gelfand, *Professionalizing Modern Medicine*, 10–11; Vess, *Medical Revolution in France*, 10. However, Laurence Brockliss has argued that medical students and physicians under the *ancien régime* had begun to place increasing emphasis on practical education in the eighteenth century, and that many physicians received an excellent practical education in addition to a theoretical one. "L'Enseignement médical et la Révolution: Essai de revaluation," *Histoire de l'éducation*, no. 42 (May 1989): 79–110.

10. For a discussion of the characteristics of a profession, including that of "service ideal" or orientation, and ethical attributes, see Goldstein, "Foucault among the Sociologists," 174–75; and Eliot Freidson, *Profession of Medicine: A Study of the Sociology of Applied Knowledge* (New York: Dodd, Mead, 1970), esp. 71–84.

11. Daniel Roche, "Talent, Reason and Sacrifice: The Physician During the Enlightenment," in Forster and Ranum, *Medicine and Society in France*, 66–88.

1. Calling and Education

It was obvious to the rest of his family by 1755 that Victor Lamothe's professional and intellectual interests pointed toward a career in medicine, but young Victor was not sure that it was the best choice. Alexis, sensing Victor's hesitation, encouraged him to reflect on the career that would best suit him: "Look at you now, uncertain as to what course to take, undecided as to whether it should be medicine or another *état*; it is primarily your feelings that you must consider . . . you must think about it and examine yourself."[12] Choice of profession was a serious matter, one that required long reflection and self-examination.

Victor did not deny the attraction that the field of medicine held for him, but asserted that other factors led him to question the wisdom of a career in medicine: "It seems from your last letter, my very dear brother, that you find no *état* that suits me better than medicine; but have you thought about all the obstacles that present themselves in that profession? There are several that appear serious enough to turn me away from medicine altogether."[13] The first of these obstacles was the cynical attitude of the public regarding the physician: "First of all, no matter what attraction or taste I have for medicine, at this time the public is disgusted [by this profession]. This truly noble and useful science has never been, I believe, more despised . . . in general, it seems that doctors, far from being esteemed, are held in contempt." Victor was obviously influenced by the ridiculous figure of the physician caricatured in the plays of Molière.[14] Many individuals, and not just the credulous poor, placed greater faith in the cures of the local empiric or bonesetter than in the learned physician, despite his superior social standing.[15] While acknowledging that the public often judged things superficially, Victor argued: "When one is in the position to choose a profession, one must make a choice that is not only honorable, and estimable, but also honored and esteemed. Unfortunately, the medical profession is neither."

But the opinion of the public was not his only worry. Victor also expressed concern at the length of time and strenuous effort required for

12. Alexis to Victor, 23 September 1755.

13. This and the following references are from the Lamothe Family Letters, Victor to Alexis, 1–5 October 1755.

14. Brockliss and Jones, *The Medical World of Early Modern France*, 336–44.

15. Ramsey, *Professional and Popular Medicine*, 281–95; Jean-Pierre Goubert, "The Art of Healing," 18–19; and *Malades et médecins en Bretagne, 1770–1790* (Paris and Rennes: C. Klincksieck, 1974), 233–40.

the study of medicine: "In order to accomplish anything early in life, one must study constantly. Do you enjoy *belles-lettres?* In choosing this profession, we must renounce them completely, and not expect any time to take an interest in them, for one moment, one instant of slackening, one book that does not concern medicine serves only to lead us astray . . . Consider for just one moment, I ask you, how I could [do this], with my delicate health and when the slightest exertion causes me such stress." The program of study for the intending physician was quite rigorous in the best universities.[16]

The expense of studies was another major concern, especially taking into consideration his father's advanced age: "If my dear father were to leave us before I had finished my studies, I would find it very difficult financially to continue, for [medical studies] cost 1,000 livres per year in Montpellier."

A final consideration for Victor was of a more personal nature. He feared that the practice of medicine could be dangerous to his moral virtue: "One does not think about this in our society, one counsels a young man to go into medicine without examining the religious obstacles that exist . . . Do you believe that one can easily be saved in this profession? The different books that one is obliged to read, all the maladies that one must treat, the persons of the opposite sex [*personnes du sexe*] . . . Are these not more obstacles to our salvation? All is exposed, nothing is hidden from a physician, even the most seductive objects, who can delude himself into thinking that he could resist?" But it was not only the tempting subject matter that presented a danger for the prospective physician. Victor asserted that medical students in particular appeared to be "very debauched" and irreligious. It was widely believed that physicians lacked piety, and they were frequently condemned for their religious skepticism and "libertinage."[17] The reputation of medical students was such, accord-

16. After three or four years of study, and a series of exams, which varied by school, the *philiatre* received the *baccalauréat* and became a *bachelier en médecine*. The faculty of medicine in Paris required four years of study for a student to receive the *baccalauréat*, while three years of study was the norm at provincial universities. At Montpellier, the *baccalauréat* was followed by two series of exams for the *licence*, and the *doctorat* was obtained after six more exams. Most students needed eight years to obtain the doctorate in Paris (ten years for the degree *docteur-régent*), but significantly less time at provincial *facultés*. The actual length of time depended upon the more or less stringent requirements of the school. Charles Coury, *L'Enseignement de la médecine en France des origines à nos jours* (Paris: Expansion Scientifique Française, 1968), 51–52; René Taton, ed., *Enseignement et diffusion des sciences en France aux XVIIIe siècle* (Paris: Hermann, 1964), 177; Ramsey, *Professional and Popular Medicine*, 50.

17. René Pintard, *Le Libertinage érudit dans la première moitié du XVIIe siècle* (Paris: Boivin et Cie., 1943),

ing to Victor, that "they are avoided like the plague" and that "a young student is received in respectable homes only after thorough research concerning his conduct."

Despite these reservations, there was no other career choice that pleased Victor more. He feared that if he did not go into medicine, he would regret it. Alexis offered the necessary encouragement. While agreeing that one must reflect carefully before choosing a profession, he gently urged Victor not to create unnecessary, and perhaps imaginary, obstacles.[18] Alexis acknowledged that many people were contemptuous of the medical profession, because so many physicians were full of a "foolish *amour-propre*" and self-importance that they exposed themselves to ridicule. This, however would not be a problem for Victor, who was "too sensible and reasonable to allow himself such ridiculous impulses."

According to Alexis, another reason that the public held many doctors in low esteem was that physicians were too often ignorant in the practice of their profession. Once again, this should not concern Victor:

> Do you believe that if a young doctor, against whom there could not be a bit of prejudice, that is, who, like you, had pious and religious parents, and whose conduct was correct, if that doctor had done his studies at Montpellier with assiduity, if upon his return he continued to study, and he only associated with good company, if he were only heard to hold competent and judicious opinions whether concerning his profession or any other subject . . . the dominant prejudice against members of the [medical] profession would change in this case to a title of recommendation for him.

By being a model doctor, Victor could avoid the poor opinion held of many physicians and, indeed, could turn it to his advantage by demonstrating his superior work habits.

Alexis also dealt with Victor's fears about the long years of difficult

79–82. François Millepierres discusses the life of the medical student, noting, "Les étudiants en médecine étaient plutôt turbulents." See *La Vie quotidienne des médecins au temps de Molière* (Paris: Hachette, 1964), 14–16. Despite Victor's fears, university students in general were much more disciplined and better behaved by the eighteenth century. Brockliss, *French Higher Education*, 103.

18. This and the following references are from the Lamothe Family Letters, Alexis to Victor, 14 October 1755.

study facing the intending physician. Moderation in work habits was the best choice for the medical student. Victor would not be obliged to place his health in danger through constant study. "Regular, assiduous, and seasoned study habits carried out with intelligence" would be sufficient to learn his material, and more beneficial than "an excess of immoderate application." Victor was well pleased with Alexis's "good advice," and was convinced by Alexis's reasoning to pursue his career in medicine.[19]

Victor spoke to Alexis of his intention to study medicine at Montpellier. He eventually received his *baccalauréat, licence,* and *doctorat* at the Montpellier school of medicine in 1760. However, he first spent nearly four years studying medicine in Paris.[20] It was common practice for medical students to study in Paris, but then to get their degree at a cheaper provincial university. Montpellier, as the most prestigious medical school in France after Paris, was an attractive second choice.[21] It was the oldest medical school in France, and had long sought to rival the Paris school of medicine, leading to frequent quarrels between the two schools.[22] Diplomas from the *facultés* of Paris and Montpellier conferred upon the student the right to practice medicine anywhere in France—most faculties only granted the right to practice in their environs.[23]

The family supported Victor's decision to study in Paris, but they did not intend for him to stay for long. Living in Paris was far more expensive

19. Victor to Alexis, 25 October 1755. The rest of the letter from 14 October 1755 is missing, so we do not know Alexis's response on the matter of finances and on the question of Victor's salvation.
20. There are several errors concerning the education of Victor Lamothe in the various *éloges* and short biographies of his life. None mentions that he studied in Paris from November 1756 through the autumn of 1759. However, the family letters verify that he studied in Paris before receiving his medical degrees in Montpellier, then returned to Paris in 1761. See Charles Dubreuilh, *Eloge académique de Victor de Lamothe,* (Bordeaux: Emile Crugy, 1869), 6–7; and M. Capelle, "Notice sur M. le Docteur Lamothe," delivered May 1824, *Actes de l'Académie nationale des sciences, belles-lettres et arts de Bordeaux* 1819:106. Perhaps this gap in his biographies is explained by the fact that he took private courses, or classes through the Collège royal and Collège de Navarre, during this first stay in Paris rather than registering at the Paris faculty. Private and specialized courses were popular even among Parisian students registered at the *faculté.* See Brockliss, "L'Enseignement médical," 89; and Taton, *Enseignement et diffusion des sciences,* 182, 190, 223, and 261–341.
21. Ramsey, *Professional and Popular Medicine in France,* 51; Lebrun, *Se soigner autrefois,* 34. A letter from Alexis to Victor suggests that in the provinces, it was considered even more desirable to have a degree from Montpellier than from Paris. Alexis to Victor, 22 January 1759. In 1760, six of the seventeen *médecins* of the Collège des médecins of Bordeaux had received their degrees from Montpellier. *Almanach historique de la province de Guienne* (Bordeaux, 1760), 363.
22. Coury, *L'Enseignement de la médecine,* 19–29; Brockliss, *French Higher Education,* 18 and 427–29.
23. Lebrun, *Se soigner autrefois,* 27–29. However, in towns boasting a medical corporation or *collège,* it was normally necessary to become an *agrégé* in order to practice in the town and its surrounding area. Ramsey, *Professional and Popular Medicine in France,* 40.

than in the provinces, as were registration costs at the faculty.[24] Nevertheless, Victor enjoyed studying and living in Paris, and he convinced his family that it was of benefit to his future career to continue his studies there.

In 1758, a year and a half after Victor arrived in Paris, Delphin wrote that his father had agreed to allow Victor to stay in Paris for another two to three years, or for as long as it would take him to become a "skilled physician."[25] But he injected a word of warning into his letters to Victor. While he agreed that Victor could take useful medical classes in the capital, he felt that it was not the best place for Victor to establish a medical practice. Despite their many relatives in Paris, Victor would always be a stranger there. Furthermore: "There are undoubtedly more opportunities [in Paris] than in Bordeaux, but there are also many more individuals chasing after the same positions, so that in either place you will always need a little bit of what is vulgarly called *luck* [*bonheur*]: therefore, you should not yet fix your sights on establishing yourself in Paris . . . a plan to stay in Paris may not be suitable, it has been said for a long time, except for those people who are very rich or very poor, those of mediocre fortune are less successful there."[26] The family was ambivalent about Victor's desire to stay in Paris beyond the three years originally agreed upon. Delphin suggested a compromise that could eventually allow Victor to return to Paris: "Don't you believe that it would perhaps be more advisable for your advancement, after having spent three years in Paris to go spend one year in Montpellier in order to receive your doctorate there . . . then to return to Paris to improve [your skills], & to find a physician to follow on his hospital rounds, etc. Would you not even be in more of a position to profit from the circumstances advantageous to your fortune which could present themselves in Paris having already been received as physician, even by a faculty *étrangère*."[27]

24. Charles Coury, "The Teaching of Medicine in France from the Beginning of the Seventeenth Century," in C. D. O'Malley, ed., *The History of Medical Education* (Berkeley and Los Angeles: University of California Press, 1970), 129–30; and *L'Enseignement de la médecine*, 48–49; Paul Delaunay, *Le Monde médical parisien au dix-huitième siècle* (Paris: Jules Rousset, 1906), 7. Matthew Ramsey notes that the cost of a medical education in Paris could mount to 8,000–10,000 livres, while the cost was generally less than half that amount in the provinces. Ramsey, *Professional and Popular Medicine*, 51.

25. Delphin to Victor, 7 July 1758. Daniel confirmed this in a subsequent letter. Daniel to Victor, 24 July 1758.

26. Delphin to Victor, 7 July 1758.

27. Delphin to Victor, 19 December 1758. Alexis supported this plan, as eventually did Victor's parents. Alexis to Victor, 22 January 1759; Delphin to Victor, 31 March 1759.

Victor's advancement in his chosen profession was a major concern for both him and his family, and they constantly counseled him on the best way to achieve his goals. Belief in hard work and application, the ethic of the dedicated professional, was the underpinning of these letters. Shortly after Victor's arrival in Paris, Delphin wrote to him: "I have seen with particular pleasure the ardor with which you seem to devote yourself to the study of medicine, the wise precautions that you have resolved to take so that the company of people less dedicated than yourself does not divert you from your application."[28] Delphin offered Victor practical advice on study techniques, and his father, Daniel, advised Victor to curtail other activities to leave more time for medicine and to apply himself to the observations of his professors.[29]

The family was pleased with Victor's assiduous study habits, his application to his work, and his conduct in general.[30] But they also worried lest he work too hard. Victor's elder sister, Marie, wrote, "I exhort you to never work too hard, and to calculate your work by your strength [*mesurer ton travail a tes forces*]."[31] Delphin concurred: "We all approve of your zeal & your application to succeed in the laborious & arduous profession you have chosen, but you must act prudently & especially consult your temperament & your health." Victor could profit "less in studying a great deal than in working prudently & systematically."[32]

The priest Jules, as well as Victor's sisters, expressed greater concern over the potential dangers to Victor's moral character in the profession he had chosen. They urged him to maintain his religious practices and serious lifestyle regardless of any temptations, and to avoid the irreligious habits of other physicians. Jules wrote to Victor: "I exhort you to always conserve your [religious] practices . . . especially be careful concerning the company with which you associate and avoid the shoals that you should fear . . . you must be extremely discreet and extremely cautious when reading certain books which can only be very harmful to you."[33] His sister Marie was equally concerned that his behavior as medical student remain pious and exemplary: "You know that physicians are reproached, and

28. Delphin to Victor, 17 December 1756.
29. Delphin to Victor, 18 October 1760; Daniel to Victor, 22 November 1757 and undated 1761.
30. Alexandre to Victor, 17 May 1757; AM Fonds Delpit, No. 127, Letter from Daniel to Victor, 26 October 1760.
31. Marie to Victor, 17 March 1758.
32. Delphin to Victor, 7 July 1758.
33. Jules to Victor, 2 July 1757.

justly, I believe, for not being very religious. Make a lie of this prejudice against them, I beg of you . . . that these bad examples may only serve to revive your zeal and your fervor, pray to God to preserve you from the contagion."[34] They were determined that Victor's entry into the medical profession should not lead him away from his religious faith.

In addition to general advice on study habits and morality, Victor's brothers and father counseled him on the best courses to take and subject matter to study, as well as books to read.[35] They often consulted friends of the family concerning Victor's plans. Immediately upon his arrival in Paris, Delphin suggested that Victor spend time on physics, "one of the good foundations of medicine," and that he try to attend the experiments of the abbé Nollet at the Collège de Navarre, as well as continue his Greek studies at the Collège royal.[36] Delphin warned Victor that when reading medical works, he should remember that:

> most of these works . . . were written with the appearance of order that accustoms the mind to believe that nature conforms to the same simplicity, but fundamentally, [nature] mocks all the forms, the categories, the limits that one claims to place on it, it is a question of learning to know [these manifestations], to observe them, & to follow them, it is the fruit of experience alone & one would not know how to acquire it to the necessary degree without reading & without deep meditation concerning the great observers, especially the Ancients, and it is with this knowledge that you can hope to gain some profit in the hospitals.

Unlike many who believed that the theories of Hippocrates and Galen sufficed for the physician, Delphin, influenced by the ideals of the Enlightenment, suggested that Victor should add practical training to his repertoire.[37] Both he and Alexis urged Victor to spend time working in the

34. Marie to Victor, 2 April 1757.

35. For the core curriculum and range of courses offered the eighteenth-century medical student, see Brockliss, *French Higher Education*, 391–440; Coury, *L'Enseignement de la médecine*, 69–79; Corlieu, *L'Ancienne Faculté de médecine*, 18–19; Taton, *Enseignement et diffusion des sciences*, 177–86.

36. Delphin to Victor, 17 December 1756. It was common for medical students at the *faculté* in Paris to supplement their curriculum by attending lectures at the Collège royal and the Jardin du roi. Lebrun, *Se soigner autrefois*, 34; Delaunay, *Le Monde médicale*, 16; Ramsey, *Professional and Popular Medicine*, 47. See Taton, *Enseignement et diffusion des sciences*, 261–341, for the professors and courses available at the Collège and the Jardin.

37. Colin Jones notes that "Enlightenment medicine prized the idea of the clinic and urged its

Parisian hospitals, both to gain experience and to make a name for himself.[38]

Victor also believed in the importance of practical experience in a hospital setting, and informed his family of his intention to follow a parish or hospital doctor in his practice.[39] Despite the traditionally theoretical education of physicians, medical students and doctors of the eighteenth century had begun to take notice of the superior practical education of surgeons, including hospital training and clinical teaching, and efforts were made to incorporate these reforms into the medical school curriculum.[40] Physicians also began to respect the skills of surgeons and to recognize the need for some surgical training themselves.[41] Against the wishes of his father and brothers, Victor frequently expressed interest in acquiring surgical skills, and especially childbirth techniques.[42] Delphin argued, "As for surgical operations, it is necessary to understand them, even to have practiced them up to a certain point, but you should not intend to become as skillful [in surgery] as the masters of the art themselves."[43] As Victor continued to press, noting that it would be to his financial advantage to study surgery in more depth, Delphin responded: "This field of medicine which you would like to study this winter, & which you regard as lucrative; it is, very, in fact, but at Bordeaux it is hardly practiced except by surgeons . . . as with childbirth, I doubt that one

---

practitioners to haunt the bedside." See *The Charitable Imperative: Hospitals and Nursing in Ancien Régime and Revolutionary France* (New York: Routledge, 1989), 16.

38. Delphin to Victor, 7 July 1758; 30 January 1762; 6 July 1762; Alexis to Victor, 21 August 1762.

39. Victor to Delphin, 7 August 1760.

40. Brockliss, "L'Enseignement médical," 92–93; Jones, *The Charitable Imperative*, 16.

41. Gelfand, *Professionalizing Modern Medicine*, 131–45 and 149–56; Brockliss, *French Higher Education*, 394. The practical orientation of studies occurred earlier at Montpellier than at other universities. Coury, "The Teaching of Medicine in France," 131. Brockliss notes, however, that much of the practical education of physicians remained largely outside the university curriculum, in the hospitals and private courses. See "L'Enseignement médical," 91–96.

42. Despite the prejudices against males' attending women in childbirth, surgeons, and eventually physicians, were increasingly called upon to assist at difficult deliveries in the eighteenth century. Mireille Laget, "Childbirth in Seventeenth- and Eighteenth-Century France: Obstetrical Practices and Collective Attitudes," in Forster and Ranum, eds., *Medicine and Society*, 137–76, esp. 157–58. Colin Jones points to a "craze" for medical "fads," including male *accoucheurs* in Paris in the second half of the eighteenth century. See "Bourgeois Revolution Revivified: 1789 and Social Change," in Colin Lucas, ed., *Rewriting the French Revolution* (Oxford: Clarendon Press, 1991), 105. See Jacques Gélis, *History of Childbirth: Fertility, Pregnancy, and Birth in Early Modern Europe*, trans. Rosemary Morris (Cambridge: Polity Press, 1991) on the history of childbirth and the roles of midwives and physicians.

43. Delphin to Victor, 7 July 1758.

would willingly see a physician exercise [this craft]."[44] On the subject of *accouchement*, Delphin reiterated their father's views:

> Concerning this subject, he does not exactly approve, any more than do we, your desire to practice childbirth, he does not believe that it is exactly the concern of a physician . . . it is not that he does not believe that it would not be desirable, even necessary, that you know everything about the illnesses of pregnant women . . . but he believes that you should stop there, & that you should study that field of surgery as well as the others only in order to be able to help someone in case of an emergency . . . reflect especially on the fact that all that you see practiced in Paris is not equally possible in the provinces. It is necessary to respect certain prejudices. In short, I do not believe that one would look favorably upon a physician who publicly assisted at the birth of infants here.[45]

The letter contained a not too subtle reminder that the techniques Victor saw practiced in Paris would not necessarily benefit him when he returned to Bordeaux.

Both his father and brothers emphasized frequently that Victor should not spread himself too thin. In early 1757, Delphin approved Victor's decision to drop his private course in chemistry with M. Rouelle in order to concentrate on physics with the celebrated Abbé Nollet. Delphin noted that, according to their friend Dr. Castets, "you will get more out of 3 months with that professor than you would have in 2 years without his help."[46] That fall, Daniel expressed concern that Victor was taking on more than he could handle: "I fear that you take on too many projects at the same time. You must go to the public schools . . . which takes up a part of your time, you are learning Greek, and you are starting a class in botany, another in chemistry, and you intend to take another in anatomy, there you have four things that must occupy you at the same time, which appears to me to be beyond the ordinary forces of a young man."[47]

44. Delphin to Victor, 19 November 1760.
45. Delphin to Victor, 13 June 1761.
46. Delphin to Victor, 26 March 1757. Abbé Nollet was an important popularizer of science in the eighteenth century, and his lecture series on physics was perhaps the most popular ever given on the Continent. See Margaret C. Jacob, *The Cultural Meaning of the Scientific Revolution* (New York: Alfred A. Knopf, 1988), 200–201.
47. Daniel to Victor, 22 November 1757.

The family was intimately involved in Victor's career strategies, and tried to direct his decisions. His sisters assured him that they and the rest of the family looked only to his professional success, and Delphin concurred, "My father & my mother have sought only that which might contribute to your greatest advancement."[48] However, they had differing ideas on the best way to fulfill his professional ambitions, and constantly debated his choices. Most important was the discussion of a longer stay in Paris for Victor, or even the possibility that he might choose to establish himself there permanently.

At least in part because of family pressure, Victor went to Montpellier in March 1760 and proceeded with his qualifying examinations. He was awarded the *baccalauréat* in the summer of 1760.[49] In quick succession, he received his *licence* that fall, followed by his *doctorat* on 29 November 1760.[50]

Victor spent the winter of 1761 in Montpellier in order to take an anatomy course.[51] But he soon returned to Paris, and it was obvious to his family that he wished to set up practice there permanently, because of a combination of personal ambition and attraction to the brilliant capital. For a young man who wished to make a name for himself as a doctor, Paris was clearly the location of choice.[52] For a time, it seemed that the family would acquiesce, perhaps hoping to see a family member established as a powerful physician in the capital. However, as Alexis pointed out to Victor, returning to the provinces would also have its advantages, and he suggested that Victor was creating unnecessary difficulties in order to avoid returning to practice medicine in Bordeaux.[53]

Victor seemed most unhappy with the prospect of a two-year *noviciat* in the provinces, a disagreeable prospect for a young man now accustomed to the more exciting lifestyle of Paris.[54] But although Victor was loathe to acknowledge it, the prospect of setting up practice in Paris was equally if

48. Delphin to Victor, 31 March 1759.

49. Victor to Delphin, undated 1760; Alexis to Victor, 19 May 1760; Alexandre to Victor, 9 July 1760.

50. Victor to Alexis, 7 August 1760; Victor to Jules, 30 December 1760.

51. Victor to Alexis, 7 August 1760; Marie to Victor, 27 November 1760.

52. The practice of medicine in Paris could be highly lucrative. Ramsey, *Professional and Popular Medicine*, 56.

53. Alexis to Victor, 22 December 1761.

54. To be accepted into Bordeaux's Collège des médecins, the physician's corporation, the young physician was required serve a two-year probationary period "dans quelque lieu du ressort du Parlement." G. Péry, *Histoire de la Faculté de médecine de Bordeaux et de l'enseignement médical dans cette ville,*

not more daunting. The Faculty of Medicine of the University of Paris controlled the practice of medicine in the city, and Victor would have need of powerful patronage, resources and luck to work in the capital.[55]

This did not discourage Victor from trying to persuade his clearly skeptical family that he should stay in Paris. Delphin warned Victor that he would need a stable position in order to stay. It was very expensive to keep him in Paris, especially now that Alexandre was there as well, studying law: "Certainly, no one desires your advancement & your well-being more than we, but it must also be in line with your position in life [*il faut qu'il s'accorde aussi avec La position dans La quelle on se trouve*]."[56] Delphin suggested that Victor seek a position as physician to a noble family in exchange for board while he completed his studies.[57] But little came of Victor's efforts to enter into a noble household as physician.[58]

As long as it appeared that Victor had a chance of obtaining a suitable position in Paris, the family had been willing to tolerate his long absence and the considerable expense of his studies. But as this started to seem less likely, his family began to pressure him to return and practice medicine in Bordeaux: "We imagined, without wanting to decide it entirely, that this would suffice to acquire the necessary knowledge in order to prepare you to exercise your profession in the provinces. This last word will make you tremble, *come back to the provinces!* Yes, my dear friend, and is that a terrible challenge? To return to your *patrie*, to the bosom of your family."[59] Victor's stay in Paris had become too expensive, a constant theme of the family's letters to him.

Alexis found a potential *noviciat* for Victor in the village of Langon, near Bazas, where he could serve under the tutelage of Langon's elderly and

1441–1888 (Paris and Bordeaux: Conseil général des Facultés de Bordeaux, 1888), 4. Alexis alluded frequently to this *noviciat*. See, for example, Alexis to Victor, 5 March 1763.

55. The Faculté de médecine of Paris was the most powerful medical corporation in France, exercising strict monopolistic control over most aspects of access to medical practice in the capital. Hannaway, "Medicine, Public Welfare, and the State," 19; Lebrun, *Se soigner autrefois*, 33; Coury, *L'Enseignement de la médecine*, 21–26; Vess, *Medical Revolution in France*, 17.

56. Delphin to Victor, 21 August 1762.

57. Delphin to Victor, 6 July 1762. One of the best ways for a physician to build a practice was to find a position as *médecin* to a noble family. Vess, *Medical Revolution in France*, 15. In addition, physicians attached to the service of members of the royal family were allowed to practice medicine in any part of France, most notably Paris, without belonging to the local *corps*, a common practice of physicians with a degree from Montpellier. Hannaway, "Medicine, Public Welfare, and the State," 26.

58. Alexis to Victor, 26 September 1762.

59. Alexis to Victor, 10 October 1762.

experienced physician for the required two-year period, but Victor's imminent return home was delayed by the death of his father in 1763.[60] Alexandre requested that Victor stay in Paris to console him in his time of grief. Victor proposed once again that he obtain a doctorate from the faculty in Paris and stay there to practice. Delphin cited the expense of such a step, which would be unnecessary if Victor returned to practice in Bordeaux. He sympathized with Victor's reluctance to return to the provinces and Alexandre's desire to keep Victor in Paris, but questioned the wisdom of a longer stay in a letter to Alexandre: "He is afraid, if he comes home, of being obliged to go vegetate in some little town, with people who neither know nor understand, nor appreciate nor even less reward true merit, that is very true, but in order to be able to work in Paris, where talent is a much greater & more useful recommendation . . . I always come back to the objection that I have made [in the past], it is necessary to have the right to work there, since Victor surely does not intend to work clandestinely, something that is suitable only for empirics."[61]

The family continued to pressure Victor about his choice, but with the death of Daniel, the authority figure, they were clearly reluctant to order him back to Bordeaux, preferring that he arrive at the decision himself. Abbé Jules suggested that "it is time to return to the provinces and to think about something solid," but the family regretfully realized that he still wished to stay in Paris.[62] Alexis suggested that Victor procure an introduction to M. le maréchal Richelieu, governor of the province of Guyenne, and that he make use of their relatives and acquaintances in Paris to find a position.[63] Delphin was further encouraged regarding Victor's career potential after speaking to the family's friend, Dr. Caze of Bordeaux, who assured him that a doctor in Paris could easily earn 8,000–10,000 livres per year. "What a difference between [Paris] and this region, where . . . all the physicians together earn barely 60,000 livres, and that might even be saying too much."[64] In apparent preparation for a career in Paris, Victor received his *bachelier* at the Faculty of Paris on 14 April 1764. His family sent 600 livres to cover the cost of the degree.[65]

60. Alexis to Victor, 5 March 1763; Delphin to Me. Marais, 7 March 1763.
61. Delphin to Alexandre, 12 April 1763.
62. Jules to Victor, 17 September 1763; Delphin to Victor and Alexandre, 16 July 1763.
63. Alexis to Victor, 29 June 1764.
64. Delphin to Victor, 23 March 1765.
65. Delphin to Victor, 10 March 1764; 17 March 1764. G. Sous, *Notice historique de la Société de*

But Delphin and Alexis soon began to express serious doubts once again. To practice medicine in Paris, Victor would need the title of *docteur régent* at the Faculty of Medicine, an expensive proposition.[66] For the degree of doctorate in Paris, the cost could easily mount to 6,000 livres, which roughly equalled a year's revenues for the entire Lamothe family.[67] Alexis pointed this out to Victor, adding that the cost of his stay in Paris would be another 3,000 to 4,000 livres, all before he would be in a position to earn a living, and he enlisted the authority of the family's friend Dr. Caze to help persuade Victor that it would be best to return to Bordeaux.

Dr. Caze acknowledged that while the profession of medicine was "more attractive, more brilliant, more lucrative, more agreeable in Paris," than in Bordeaux, it was hard for a young man to find success there, especially a young man of Victor's character, because "success is more difficult there, whether because of the obstacles and the rivalries of the competitors, of whom there is an enormous number, or because it is necessary that one appear to be bombastic or a charlatan, to have much confidence or temerity . . . I have realized that M. your brother does not fit that first description."[68] Alexis admitted that the rest of the family as well as many of their friends had entertained these same doubts about Victor's chances of success in Paris: "It is the opinion of Mr. Caze and Doazan, of Barbeguière whom I mention only because he is one of many and of Lislefeme and Alexandre even, who being with us during the holidays, told us that he believes that you are too timid, too suspicious, in short, *trop honnete homme* [sic]. The opposite qualities are the principle instruments for persons of your *état* in Paris."[69] As an unknown and timid young man with no powerful protectors, Victor in reality had little possibility of great success in Paris. Bordeaux, however, needed doctors, and Dr. Caze suggested that Victor had an excellent chance of obtaining a position as physician at the hospital Saint-André, which would give him

---

médecine et de chirurgie de Bordeaux (Paris and Bordeaux, 1895), 63; Capelle, "Notice sur M. le Docteur Lamothe," 106. The *Eloge académique* by Dr. Charles Dubreuilh incorrectly asserts that Victor was received as doctor by the Faculty of Medicine in Paris in 1764. *Eloge académique*, 10.

66. Capelle, "Notice sur M. le Docteur Lamothe," 106.

67. According to an account by Michel Bermengham from 1754, the cost of exams in Paris, from *bachelier* to *médecin*, was 5,615 livres, or 6,000 livres in round numbers. A. Corlieu, cited by Delaunay in *Le Monde médical parisien*, 7.

68. Alexis to Victor, 12 May 1766.

69. Alexis to Victor, undated 1766.

the opportunity to become well known and to make contacts.[70] In addition, Dr. Caze, who held a chair as professor in medicine at the University of Bordeaux, offered to direct the *survivance* of that chair to Victor if possible. As a final piece of bait, Alexis informed Victor that it might no longer be necessary for him to serve a two-year probationary period in the provinces in order to gain acceptance to the Collége des médecins in Bordeaux, "provided that you have a certificate [verifying] that you worked with a hospital or an experienced physician during that time period," and a letter from the vice-chancellor of the University of Paris supporting his candidature. In short, Alexis was proposing to Victor a respectable career in Bordeaux, compared to the uncertainty and expense of a longer stay in Paris.[71]

It was hard for Victor to give up his dream of a brilliant career in Paris, but his family was no longer willing to accept his arguments. Alexis told him shortly that they all believed that the real reason he wished to stay "is fundamentally because of your excessive attachment to Paris," especially since his opportunities for a successful career now looked much better in Bordeaux than in Paris.[72] Finally, the family wanted Victor to return home. Apart from the expense of his stay in Paris, they missed him, and wanted him to return to the bosom of his family, to his *patrie*. In the end, it was probably this argument that convinced Victor to renounce his plan to stay in Paris and to return to Bordeaux in December 1766.

2. Professional Activities, Professional Attitudes

Upon returning to Bordeaux, Victor charted a careful course in order to obtain quick acceptance into his professional milieu. All physicians practicing within the city of Bordeaux were required to belong to the Collège des médecins.[73] The *collège* acted as a *corps*, and physicians were taxed as

70. Physicians considered it an honor, and sometimes a charitable obligation, to hold a position as consultant to a hospital, although they generally devoted little time to these duties. Gelfand, *Professionalizing Modern Medicine*, 101; Jones, *The Charitable Imperative*, 12–14.

71. Alexis to Victor, 12 May 1766; undated 1766; 1 July 1766; Delphin to Victor, 13 November 1766; 10 December 1766.

72. Alexis to Victor, undated 1766; 1 July 1766.

73. The *collège* numbered roughly twenty members—seventeen in 1760 when the first *Almanach de Guienne* was published, and twenty-one in 1788. *Almanach de Guienne*, 1760, 363; and 1788, 229–30.

members of the company.[74] The *collège*, in theory, accepted only physicians who were already doctors in medicine and who had practiced
medicine for the two-year probationary period in an area under the
jurisdiction of the Parlement of Guyenne. A candidate was required to be
a practicing Catholic, with "irreproachable morals." Requirements for
admittance were quite rigorous, as the candidate underwent six qualifying
exams in the space of two years, the first and last taking place at the *hôtel
de ville*, in the presence of the mayor, the *jurats*, and other members of the
public.[75]

As his brothers had promised, Victor was not obliged to fulfill the
requirement of the two-year *noviciat* in the countryside. The register of the
Collège des médecins for 6 September 1766 recorded:

> Lamothe, native of Bordeaux, doctor in medicine of Montpellier
> for six years, *bachelier* of Paris for two years, asked the Chancellor to
> exempt him from the two years of practice necessary in order to
> come forward [as a candidate] for the *agrégation*, the Chancellor
> sent the petition to the Collège des médecins to request their
> opinion. The *Collège*, seeing the qualifications of Lamothe, deter-
> mined that he could dispense with the two years of practice in the
> neighboring towns of Bordeaux, if he had certificates showing that
> he had practiced in Paris or its hospitals.[76]

Victor's hard work in Paris, as well as cultivation of family friends within
the Collège des médecins, had paid off. He was still required to undergo
several examinations, and defended two theses before the *collège*, before he
was accepted as member on 20 June 1767. He took the oath on 2 January

74. ADG 6E 71, Compagnie des médecins. See Hannaway, "Medicine, Public Welfare, and the
State," 8–14; and Matthew Ramsey, "The Politics of Professional Monopoly in the Nineteenth
Century: The French Model and Its Rivals," in Gerald Geison, ed., *Professions and the French State,
1700–1900* (Philadelphia: University of Pennsylvania Press, 1984), 225–305, esp. 232–37, for a
discussion of the corporate outlook of *médecins* in the eighteenth century. Although the *collèges* in the
various towns sometimes had limited teaching functions, their primary role was to control professional
privileges, and to look out for the interests of their members. Ramsey, *Professional and Popular Medicine*,
39. Jan Goldstein, *Console and Classify: The French Psychiatric Profession in the Nineteenth Century* (New York:
Cambridge University Press, 1987), 15–20, also discusses the corporate model of medicine under the
ancien régime.

75. Unlike in Paris, where the *faculté* constituted the corporation of *médecins*, in Bordeaux, the
Faculté de médecine, affiliated with the University of Bordeaux, and the Collège des médecins, which
controlled the exercise of medicine in Bordeaux, were two distinct entities, and usually enemies. Péry,
Histoire de la Faculté de médecine, 4 and 138.

76. Péry, *Histoire de la Faculté de médecine*, 62.

1768.[77] Victor became an active and respected member of the *collège*, elected to represent the *corps* as syndic almost continuously throughout the 1780s.[78] Like the other physicians, he took part in the required religious activities of the *collège*, participating in the vespers and other masses.[79]

While Victor was never appointed to the chair at the university dangled by M. Caze, he did obtain a coveted position as one of the four physicians at the Hôpital Saint-André, Bordeaux's largest and most important hospital for the sick, in 1769.[80] This gave Victor a certain amount of visibility and allowed him to serve with other respected doctors of Bordeaux such as MM. Boniol, Barbeguière, and Betbéder.[81] Victor held this position at Saint-André for about ten years and, according to his biographer, tried unsuccessfully to introduce a number of reforms into the hospital.[82] In the early 1770s, he took on another position that he would hold for more than fifty years—that of physician at the Hôpital des enfants trouvés et de la manufacture.[83]

Victor came to the foundling hospital at a time of change. Since April 1714, the Hôpital Saint-Louis, in the center of town, had accepted and cared for foundlings until they were old enough to work. Older children and indigent adults were housed at the Hôpital de la manufacture, primarily a workhouse, founded on the outskirts of the city in 1619. In December 1772, letters patent granted by Louis XV united the two hospitals at the site of the Hôpital de la manufacture. The hospital retained only one physician, as well as one surgeon, but was known for being relatively spacious and well equipped.[84] Bordeaux's German visitor, Ma-

77. Capelle, "Notice sur M. le Docteur Lamothe," 107; Dubreuilh, *Eloge académique*, 11; Pery, *Histoire de la Faculté de médecine*, 62. *Quaestiones medicae, an irruptioni lactis in cerebrum, mammarum sectio? Utrum rachitidi lac maternum mediatur? et Assertiones duodecim*, by Victor Lamothe, was published in 1767 by F. Séjourné. See Louis Desgraves, *Les Livres imprimés à Bordeaux au XVIIIe siècle (1701–1789)* (Geneva: Droz, 1975), 82. In 1768, Victor paid the company 108 livres for the cost of his second exam, and again for his third exam. ADG 6E 71, Compagnie des médecins.

78. Pery, *Histoire de la Faculté de médecine*, 65–71.

79. ADG 6E 71, Compagnie des médecins.

80. For a discussion of the St. André Hospital in the eighteenth century, see Philippe Loupès, "L'Hôpital Saint-André de Bordeaux au XVIIIe siècle," *Revue historique de Bordeaux et du département de la Gironde*, 21 (1972): 79–111. Saint-André was a *hôtel-Dieu*, devoted to caring for the sick. For an overview of the hospital system in eighteenth-century France, see Muriel Joerger, "The Structure of the Hospital System in France in the Ancien Régime," in Forster and Ranum, eds., *Medicine and Society in France*, 104–36; and Jones, *The Charitable Imperative*, 1–28 and 31–86.

81. *Almanach de Guienne*, 1778, 96; Loupès, "L'Hôpital Saint-André," 95.

82. Dubreuilh, *Eloge académique*, 12–13.

83. It is not clear when Victor was appointed to the Hôpital des enfants trouvés, as the various sources give conflicting accounts, but it was sometime between 1770 and 1772.

84. In 1779, the residence housed 492 inhabitants, a number that would nearly double before the

dame de la Roche, spoke well of the establishment in 1785.[85] But conditions for the inhabitants of the foundling hospital were far from ideal. As in many hospitals and orphanages in eighteenth-century France, mortality was high, disease was rampant, and there was the constant problem of finding wet nurses for the children in the hospital.[86]

In addition to his consultations at the foundling hospice and private practice of medicine, Victor was involved in other professional activities, most visibly as an associate at the Academy of Science of Bordeaux, where he participated in a number of scientific and medically related investigations (see Chapter 6, section 1 below). He composed scientific essays as well, one of which was published in the *Journal de physique* in 1773.[87] Victor also was a member of other professional organizations, including the newly created Royal Society of Medicine in Paris, as well as that of Montpellier.[88] He demonstrated a keen interest in meteorology, and published his observations in the *Journal de Guienne* from 1778 through 1792.[89] Throughout the eighteenth century, doctors were interested in quantifying the relationship between rainfall, weather patterns and patterns of sickness, especially epidemics and epizootics. The Royal Society of Medicine collected meteorological information from corresponding physicians all over France between 1776 and 1792 in order to chart trends and determine possible connections. Perhaps Victor's interest in meteorology was related to this project.[90]

---

end of 1789. According to Dr. Fernand Durodié, there were 899 *pensionnaires* at the hospital in 1789. *Les Médecins et les hôpitaux du vieux Bordeaux* (Bordeaux: A. Destout, 1924), 95–132; ADG E 22, Hôpital registres antérieurs à 1790: Hôpital général de la manufacture, Registre de déliberation du 12 mars 1775–22 aout 1784, 17 January 1779.

85. Meaudre de Lapouyade, *Impressions d'une allemande à Bordeaux en 1785* (Bordeaux: G. Gounouilhou, 1911), 20–21.

86. While historians have traditionally deplored the high mortality rates in ancien régime hospitals, Colin Jones has challenged this belief. The provincial *hôtels-Dieux*, which catered primarily to itinerant and migrant workers, enjoyed relatively low mortality rates. However, mortality was quite high at the *hôpitaux-généraux*, which accepted the elderly and the incurably ill, and the foundling hospices, due to the fragile health of these children. Jones, *The Charitable Imperative*, 9–12, and 48–86.

87. Dubreuilh, *Eloge académique*, 17.

88. *Etrennes bordelaises, ou Calendrier raisonné du Palais* (Bordeaux: Jean Chappuis, 1790), 164. See Hannaway, "Medicine, Public Welfare and the State" on the *Société royale de médecine* of Paris. Murphy, "The French Medical Profession," 259–62, gives a brief introduction to the function of the society.

89. Dubreuilh, *Eloge académique*, 17; Camille Jullian, *Histoire de Bordeaux depuis les origines jusqu'en 1895* (Bordeaux: Feret et Fils, 1895), 582.

90. See Murphy, "The French Medical Profession," 261; and Hannaway, "Medicine, Public Welfare, and the State," 156–61.

Victor Lamothe's various positions and affiliations with respected professional organizations indicate his ability to conform to the strictures of the profession of medicine in Old Regime Bordeaux. As revolution brought social and political changes in 1789, Victor demonstrated an ability to adjust and adapt.[91] As long as the Collège des médecins remained intact, Victor continued to actively participate in its deliberations. He took part in the *collège's* examination of M. Capelle, an aspiring physician, at the *hôtel de ville* in June 1790. He represented his medical corporation before the *corps municipal* in August 1790, pleading for a continuation of its special privileges in recognition of the charitable work of physicians in assisting the poor. The promise by the city government to consider this request, despite the decrees of the National Assembly, attests to the local esteem in which Victor Lamothe and his colleagues were held.[92]

Despite the growing Jacobin distrust of physicians and others belonging to exclusive professional groups and "privileged" corporations, Victor and the other *médecins* continued to enjoy cordial and cooperative relations with the city until 1793.[93] This continued even after the fall of the constitutional monarchy, indicating once again Victor's ability to adapt and conform. The decree of 15 September 1793 abolished all *collèges* and *facultés* in France, including those of medicine, and the tight control of members of the *collège* over the certification of doctors ended. The Jacobins brought sweeping changes to the practice of medicine as regulation of the field collapsed, and the titles of *médecin* and *chirurgien* were replaced by that of *officier de santé*. "Medical liberty" became the rallying cry, as regular certification and instruction of practitioners ended, not to be restored until

91. See Alan Forrest, *Society and Politics in Revolutionary Bordeaux* (New York: Oxford University Press, 1975), for an overview of Bordeaux's volatile municipal government from the early stages of the Revolution through the Terror.

92. "Délibérations du Corps municipal": Archives municipales, Période révolutionnaire, Art. 86 and Art. 87, in Ariste Ducaunnès-Duval, ed., *Inventaire sommaire des Archives municipales de la ville de Bordeaux. Période révolutionnaire (1789–An VIII).* (Bordeaux: Emile Crugy, 1896), 1:61–62 and 93.

93. The municipal government requested that Victor help scrutinize the fitness of candidates for the post of *chirurgien-majeur* of the battalion of Bordeaux in 1792 and attend the public exams and the distribution of prizes for Madame Coutanceau's midwifery students in 1791 and 1792. "Délibérations du Conseil général": Art. D. 99; "Registre de correspondance de la municipalité": Art. D. 139, and Art. D. 140, in Ariste Ducaunnès-Duval, *Inventaire sommaire* (Bordeaux, 1910), 2:10, 259, and 268. Madame Coutanceau's *école d'accouchement* was founded in 1782 for the training of midwives in the Guyenne. Vicomte de Pelleport, *Etudes municipales sur la charité bordelaise* (Paris and Bordeaux: Librairie Académique and P. Chaumas, 1869), 1:28–29.

1795.[94] Changes in the medical profession continued after the end of the Terror and the creation of the more conservative Directory. In Bordeaux, a centralized *commission administrative* was placed in charge of the *hospices civiles de Bordeaux*.[95]

The Revolution also brought about changes in the administration of the Hôpital des enfants trouvés. In July of 1793, the Sisters of Charity were replaced by *citoyennes servantes de la maison*, because the Sisters refused to take the oath to the Civil Constitution of the Clergy. At the same meeting, the Municipal Council also tried to institute a new and more enlightened attitude toward the unfortunate foundlings, proclaiming with Jacobin rhetorical flourish that "the children abandoned in the hospitals, stigmatized until this day by unjust prejudice, rejected from the bosom of society solely because of their birth, today are counted among and identical with the citizens and called upon like them to pay the same debt to their country."[96] Four years later, on 20 October 1797, under the Directory, the administration of the hospital was reorganized, and the name was changed. It was known now by the more politically correct Hospice des enfants de la patrie.[97] These efforts at reform were at least partially in response to the appalling conditions at the hospice. The registers of the Administrative Commission trace constant problems of high mortality, indifferent wet nurses who neglected their charges, lack of money, and unhealthy living conditions.[98] The commission tried to

94. G. Péry, *Les Ancêtres des la Société de médecine & de chirurgie de Bordeaux: Essai historique sur la Société clinique de santé et la Société philanthropique de santé (1796–1798)*, (Bordeaux, 1889), 1. For a discussion of the radical changes in the medical profession in France during the early stages of the Revolution, see Ramsey, "The Politics of Professional Monopoly," 235–36 and *Professional and Popular Medicine*, 71–77. Gelfand, *Professionalizing Modern Medicine*, esp. 156–88, looks at the changes in light of unification of the field of medicine, and Brockliss, "L'Enseignement médical," examines the changes in the education of doctors. Vess, *Medical Revolution in France*, is primarily concerned with changes in military medicine prompted by Revolution and war.

95. The Registers of the Commission administrative des hospices civiles de Bordeaux make up part of the Dépôt des hôpitaux de Bordeaux and are being classified as part of Série X. The Registers for the "Affaires générales" of the hospices begin in Year V of the Revolution (1797), so there is no direct record of the commission during the years of the Terror and immediately following the Terror. I thank Jean-Pierre Bériac for introducing me to these archives.

96. Quoted in Eugène Mabille, *De la condition des enfants trouvés au XVIIIe siècle dans la généralité de Bordeaux* (Bordeaux: Y. Cadoret, 1909), 141–42; see also ADG Dépôt des hôpitaux de Bordeaux, Register 169, 16 Vendémiaire An III. The revolutionary government was sensitive to the stigma of the word "bastard," and tried to formulate a more humane policy toward illegitimate children. James Traer, *Marriage and the Family in Eighteenth-Century France* (Ithaca: Cornell University Press, 1980), 154–57.

97. Mabille, *De la condition des enfants trouvés*, 143.

98. For example, ADG Dépôt des hôpitaux de Bordeaux, Register 1, 26 Prairial An V, 137. Over

combat these problems, apparently with little success.⁹⁹ The food crisis throughout France during these years, aggravated by war and requisitions, undoubtedly made it more difficult to care for these children.

Part of the reorganization effort by the Administrative Commission under the Directory included the decision to again name a physician to the Hospice des enfants de la patrie.¹⁰⁰ At a meeting in March 1797, the Administrative Commission recorded:

> considering that it has only been a short while since this [position of] *officier de santé* was abolished; that perhaps this lack of aid has contributed to the extraordinary mortality in newborn infants that the commission noticed during this time period . . . Considering that whatever talents the surgeons *officiers de santé* who are required to care for the infants of the hospice may have, *they cannot be sufficiently extensive to replace those of a physician whose [skills] are absolutely necessary in many cases* [emphasis mine] . . . considering that for a long time, the Citizen La Motte, was connected to this hospice in that quality, & that there was only praise for his zeal . . . The commission named him *médecin* of the Hospice des enfants de la patrie, and asked Citizen Betbeder to inform him of his nomination & to find out if he will accept the position.¹⁰¹

Despite the efforts of the revolutionary government to break the monopoly of the medical profession over the exercise of medicine, by 1797 the commissioners on the board of the civil hospices placed greater faith in an experienced doctor, known for his long service and zeal, than in an *officier de santé* who might have received inadequate training, or no training at all, in medicine. While Matthew Ramsey has written of the "medical anarchy" and anticorporate legislation that encouraged unqualified practitioners prior to the law of Ventôse Year XI (1803) reorganizing the medical profession, it seems likely that most individuals stayed with

---

a two-month period, 175 nursing children died at the hospice, a figure blamed partially on the "nourrices découragées par defaut de payements." The commission seldom had sufficient funds to pay their wet nurses. Register 4, 28 Prairial An VIII, 107; Register 6, 6 Frimaire An X, 35.

99. Mabille, *De la condition des enfants trouvés*, 145.

100. Because medical registers for the early revolutionary years in Bordeaux were not available, no information exists on Victor's relationship with the hospice until 1797.

101. ADG Dépôt des hôpitaux de Bordeaux, Register 1, 16 Ventôse An V, 79.

doctors, surgeons, or indeed empirics that they trusted.[102] Victor accepted the unpaid position at the hospice, and the commission lauded his "zeal" and "unselfish concern [*désintéressement*] for the poor."[103] Little had changed in Victor's work, attitude, or relationship with the municipal government despite seven years of revolution.

The workload at the Hospice des enfants de la patrie was such that Victor soon petitioned the commission for an adjunct.[104] At the same time, he continued to take on additional responsibilities as he accepted a position on the Vaccination Committee, and took an unpaid post as physician at the Hospice de la maternité.[105]

After thirty years of unremunerated service at the Hospice des enfants de la patrie, and three at the Maternity Hospice, Victor presented another petition to the commission requesting payment for his efforts. His petition carefully maintained the Old Regime language of the professional, who received *honoraires* for service, rather than a salary. The commission acknowledged that he was "the only physician in the service of these hospices who does not receive a salary" and that "the remote location of the Hospice of the *Enfans de la patrie* and the care he is obliged to give there render his service laborious," which justified his request. He was granted the nominal sum of six hundred francs per year.[106]

By 1813, Victor, a venerable doctor of seventy-seven, was able to use his position of respect and authority to obtain for his nephew Dugravier de Lamothe a position as adjunct at the Hospice des enfants abandonnés, formerly Hospice des enfants de la patrie.[107] Dugravier's career was closely linked with that of his uncle, for they shared a house and medical practice. Dugravier's position was unpaid, but it allowed him to claim the paid position of physician at the hospice upon the death of his uncle in 1823.[108] Dugravier took on more of his uncle's responsibilities as Victor grew

102. See Ramsey, "The Politics of Professional Monopoly," 235–38, and *Professional and Popular Medicine*, 74–77.

103. ADG Dépôt des hôpitaux de Bordeaux, Register 1, 26 Ventôse An V, 85.

104. ADG Dépôt des hôpitaux de Bordeaux, Register 2, 6 Germinal An VII, 196. There is no follow-up on Victor's request in the registers.

105. ADG Dépôt des hôpitaux de Bordeaux, Register 5, 12 Messidor An IX, 108–9; Edouard Feret, *Statistique de la Gironde: Biographie* (Bordeaux and Paris: Feret et Fils and G. Masson/Emile Lechevalier, 1889), 3:369.

106. ADG Dépôt des hôpitaux de Bordeaux, Register 10, 6 Pluviôse An XII, 91; and 27 Pluviôse An XII, 102.

107. ADG Dépôt des hôpitaux de Bordeaux, Register 17, 26 May 1812, 32. Dugravier did not receive an official certificate confirming this position until 1816. Register 20, 26 August 1816, 133.

108. ADG Dépôt des hôpitaux de Bordeaux, Register 27, 26 April 1823, 87; 6 May 1823, 93. Another adjunct physician joined the hospice in 1819. Ibid., Table 73, 6 November 1819.

older.[109] Victor's good relations with his medical colleagues and patients and the respect that they had for him cleared the path for his nephew.

Victor's relations with his colleagues and his identification with other physicians and men of science contributed to his own professional identity. The respected social and professional position of Victor's family eased the way for him, especially as Delphin and Alexis, as well as his father Daniel, frequently sought the advice of family friends in medicine, such as Dr. Caze, on Victor's behalf. Victor carefully maintained and cultivated these ties with the medical community after his return to Bordeaux. His precocious election to the Academy of Bordeaux allowed him to sustain these contacts, as more than half of the associates of the academy were men of medicine.[110]

Victor sought out other physicians as social companions.[111] In addition, he shared ideas on maladies and treatments with other doctors in letters that carefully emphasized friendly as well as professional ties: "Moreover, please excuse my frankness, which I permit myself only with a colleague & a friend."[112] While still in school in Paris, he freely offered medical advice to family, friends, and acquaintances, frequently asking about their welfare and the efficacy of the remedies he suggested.[113] Once a doctor, he continued to tend solicitously to the health of his patients, many of whom were also family friends.[114] By all indications, Victor had a thriving medical practice.

Was this practice also financially lucrative? The fortune of physicians varied greatly, both under the Old Regime and following the Revolution.[115]

109. ADG Dépôt des hôpitaux de Bordeaux, Register 24, 20 December 1820, 177–78; Register 25, 7 June 1821, 108.

110. Daniel Roche, "Milieux académiques provinciaux et sociétés des lumières: Trois académies provinciales au 18e siècle: Bordeaux, Dijon, Châlons-sur-Marne," in François Furet, ed., *Livre et société du XVIIIe siècle* (Paris and The Hague: Mouton et Cie., 1965), 1:127. Also see Chapter 6, section 1 below.

111. See, for example, Victor to Alexis, 1773, passim; AM Fonds Delpit, No. 127, Letter from Victor to Alexis, 7 August 1773.

112. ADG 8J 692, Fonds Bigot, Dossier on the Lamothe Family: Letter from Victor Lamothe to Monsieur Gaussen, Docteur en Médecine à Sainte-Foy, 24 Floréal An XIII. See also Victor's correspondence with the doctor Montbalon, administrator of the Bibliothèque de Bordeaux, concerning his donation of books to the library. Lamothe Family Letters, Montbalon to Victor, Letters from 1820 to 1823.

113. See, for example, Victor to Jules, 27 February 1760; Victor to Alexis, 7 August 1760; Delphin to Victor, 21 August 1760; Marianne to Victor, 6 February 1765; Marie to Victor, 29 April 1766.

114. Victor to Alexis, 18 August 1773; 24 October 1773; 5 December 1773; 7 December 1773.

115. During the eighteenth century, many physicians, especially those in urban areas, were able to live quite well on the income of their practices, although earnings varied widely. Matthew Ramsey points out that the financial situation of many physicians became more difficult in the early 1800s as they adjusted to more competition. Theodore Zeldin concurs that it was often difficult for the doctor

Much of Victor's work was charitable. His service to the poor of the parishes of Saint-Eloi and Sainte-Croix in Bordeaux, like his service to the hospices until 1804, was presumably unpaid.[116] However, his hospital positions gave him visibility and prestige among the wealthier families of Bordeaux. His friend Dr. Capelle proclaimed after Victor's death that Victor "constantly enjoyed the medical confidence of a certain number of the most highly regarded families of our city."[117] Although we have no direct evidence of Victor's fortune or salary, which undoubtedly varied from year to year, we can assume that his inheritance from his brother Alexis, as well as his practice, allowed him to maintain a comfortable lifestyle. He died leaving property in ownership and usufruct worth 70,500 francs in Bordeaux, as well as the property of Goulards in Sainte-Foy-la-Grande and Cabanot in the commune of Vélines.[118]

Victor's ability to keep his position and good reputation through successive governments suggests a capacity to adapt and conform, as well as medical skill. But his behavior implies a certain nostalgia for the days of the Old Regime, for the exclusivity of the Collège des médecins, and the intellectual stimulation of such organizations as the Academy of Bordeaux and the Royal Society of Medicine. As the Terror passed, and life became more normal in Bordeaux, Victor played an active role in founding several professional organizations, including the Société d'histoire naturelle in 1797 (heir to the Academy of Bordeaux), and the Société de médecine de Bordeaux in 1798.[119] The new Society of Medicine was devoted to "public utility" and "the art of healing," as well as "the progress of science," terms familiar to Victor when he had participated in the Academy of Bordeaux.

---

without private resources to live well, but notes that the political and social influence of doctors increased during the nineteenth century. Ramsey, *Professional and Popular Medicine*, 56 and 110–15; Zeldin, *France, 1848–1945: Ambition and Love* (New York: Oxford University Press, 1979), 23 and 32–33.

116. Pierre Meller, *Essais généalogiques: Familles du bordelais/recueil factice de brochures concernant des familles* (Bordeaux: Feret et Fils, 1897), 27.

117. Capelle, "Notice sur M. le Docteur Lamothe," 110.

118. ADG 3 Q 2509, Registre des recettes: Déclaration des mutations par décès, Bureau de Bordeaux, 2 October 1823; Q 31/d 5, Registre de recette: Déclaration des mutations par décès, Bureau de Sainte-Foy, 7 October 1823.

119. Dubreuilh, *Eloge académique*, 16–17; Capelle, "Notice sur M. le docteur Lamothe," 109–10. The Directory Constitution of the Year III allowed the formation of professional societies with a scientific purpose. Ramsey, *Professional and Popular Medicine*, 106. Like the earlier Academy of Science of Bordeaux, the Society of Natural History included a large number of physicians. Pery, *Les Ancêtres de la Société de médecine*, 3.

The society was also dedicated to eliminating charlatans, treating epidemics, and destroying ignorance and superstition about science and medicine, ideals reminiscent of the Enlightenment.[120] Victor officially became a member of the new society on 30 June 1798, and was one of the physicians named to draft its new regulations. He served as archivist in 1803 and president in 1799 and 1806.[121]

The society was respected in Bordeaux, enjoying a close relationship with the municipal government, which asked the society to investigate and pass judgment on a number of issues related to public health in Bordeaux and its environs, including public hygiene, the sanitary conditions of the soldiers, and the new practice of vaccination, issues of major interest in early nineteenth-century France.[122] The society worked closely with the government, and encouraged active policing of the population, advocating the creation of a bureau of health to promote sanitary conditions and combat epidemics. Members corresponded with the prefect concerning other matters of public health.[123] The society also fought what it perceived as charlatanism, forbidding its members to issue medical certificates that would allow nonqualified individuals to practice medicine.[124] And in response to requests by the city government, the Society of Medicine issued reports on a number of issues of concern to the local authorities. Victor served on the commissions that authored most of these reports.[125]

120. The Society of Medicine of Bordeaux was the result of the union of two organizations formed in 1796; the Société de clinique and the Société philanthropique de santé. The two societies, sharing similar membership and goals, were joined on 6 June 1798. Pery, *Les Ancêtres de la Société de médecine;* and Sous, *Notice historique de la Société de médecine.*

121. Sous, *Notice historique de la Société de médecine,* 63; Dubreuilh, *Eloge académique,* 15–16.

122. Sous, *Notice historique de la Société de médecine,* 5–7.

123. ADG 5M 48, Letter addressed to the Prefect from the Société de médecine de Bordeaux, 30 Floréal An X; 5M 75, Letter addressed to the Prefect from the Société de médecine de Bordeaux, 28 Frimaire An IX; 5M 112, "Mémoire sur la maladie qui a régné à Bordeaux," 6 January 1806. The *société,* which became the Société royale de médecine de Bordeaux after 1814, continued its close relations with the royal government after the fall of Napoleon. See, for example, ADG 5M 112, Rapport de la Commission nommé par la Société royale de médecine de Bordeaux, en sa séance du 27 Janvier 1817; and 5M 120, Letter addressed to the mayor of the City of Bordeaux, 16 September 1817.

124. Sous, *Notice historique de la Société de médecine,* 10.

125. Société de médecine, *Mémoire de la Société de médecine de Bordeaux sur les moyens qu'on doit employer pour guérir l'asphyxie des noyés* (Bordeaux: Chez Racle, 1807); *Opinion de la Société de médecine de Bordeaux sur l'étendue et le placement des divers hospices de cette ville* (Bordeaux: Chez Lawalle Jeune, 1810); *Instruction sur les champignons vénéneux du département de la Gironde, et sur les moyens de remédier leurs pernicieux effets* (Bordeaux: Chez Racle, 1814). See also M. J.-M. Caillau, *Notice des travaux de la Société de médecine de Bordeaux depuis sa dernière séance publique* (Bordeaux: Lawalle Jeune, 1810).

Victor's medical philosophy seems to have been in line with that of most doctors of his time. He believed in the efficacy of bleeding, but in moderation, preferring to let nature play the greatest role in the healing process.[126] He believed that purgation was still of value, and he promoted the therapeutic effects of mineral waters.[127] His career suggests belief in traditional medical treatments and cautious interest in new approaches. In short, nothing in Victor Lamothe's letters nor in his academic and scientific writings indicates a doctor of great creativity and originality or a man far ahead of his time. Not even Victor's fulsome eulogists tried to claim that he was in the forefront of medical discoveries. Rather, his friend Dr. Capelle pointed approvingly to Victor's conservative side, stressing that Victor never aspired to be a "physician *à la mode*, because he knew that in order to be one, knowledge and skill were much less necessary than boastfulness, intrigue, and charlatanism." Victor experimented with new methods of treatment "with a circumspect curiosity," valuing progress in his field, but never with a blind faith in "so-called inventors."[128] Victor's virtues as a doctor were those of the cautious, dependable, and charitable practitioner. He was a solid bourgeois professional.

3. The Ethic of Public Service

One aspect of Victor Lamothe's medical ethic illuminates both his beliefs and the course he pursued in his career. The ethic of service, of public utility, played a major role in his concerns and activities. While the theme of selflessness and charitable work was a common one in eulogies of doctors, Victor's work with the foundlings and other poor of Bordeaux, his role in the propagation of the smallpox vaccine, and his support for the Society for Maternal Charity of Bordeaux all indicate that for him, the obligation of the physician to serve the public was more than just an ideal.[129]

126. Victor to Alexis, 31 July 1773.

127. Victor to Jules, 27 February 1760; Delphin to Victor, 21 August 1760; Victor to Alexis, 31 July 1773.

128. Capelle, "Notice sur M. le Docteur Lamothe," 111–12.

129. See Roche, "Talent, Reason, and Sacrifice," 82–84; Brockliss and Jones, *The Medical World of Early Modern France*, 474–76. Colin Jones argues that by the second half of the eighteenth century, many physicians "tried to transcend the corporative petty-mindedness for which they were famous,

In his *éloge* of Victor Lamothe in 1869, Dr. Charles Dubreuilh proclaimed that "the benevolence of Lamothe was exercised not only on behalf of particular individuals; it was offered to . . . all institutions useful to the unfortunate."[130] The enlightened physician, while knowledgeable and wise, was also a man of compassion, a man devoted to the public good through projects for the public welfare and service to the poor. The lessons that Victor learned during his medical education and his participation in Old Regime organizations shaped his ideas on public welfare and public hygiene. Following the Revolution, he helped to put these ideas into practice as the medical profession worked closely with the state to police public hygiene and the behavior of the poor.

Historians have argued that the medicalization of French society, the escalating intervention of the state into private matters with increased "tutelage" of the family, and the alliance of medicine and the state took place primarily in the nineteenth century.[131] However, the activist state, promoting a more rational and hygienic society, had its roots in Old Regime "Enlightened Absolutism."[132] Educated physicians had long been at the forefront of efforts to wipe out "superstition" and "incredulity" among the populace through the promotion of science and rationality. The Royal Society of Medicine, really an agency of the state, tried to set new guidelines for French medical control of epidemics and epizootics by "exploit[ing] the administrative bureaucracy of the government to the full," thus preparing the ground for the *police médicale* of the nineteenth century.[133] Still, despite the dark view Michel Foucault and his followers have taken of the intrusion of the national government into the lives of the

---

and to stress the public benefits of medical professionalism." See "Bourgeois Revolution Revivified," 100.

130. Dubreuilh, *Eloge académique*, 28.

131. See esp. Michel Foucault, *The Birth of the Clinic: An Archaeology of Medical Perception*, trans. A. M. Sheridan Smith (New York: Pantheon Books, 1973); and Jacques Donzelot, *The Policing of Families*, trans. Robert Hurley (New York: Pantheon Books, 1979). Evelyn Ackerman raises objections to the Foucault-Donzelot schema, disputing the periodization and noting that "Whig history in reverse," the increasing domination of the state and the bourgeoisie, is not an all-encompassing guide to medical history. See *Health Care in the Parisian Countryside, 1800–1914* (New Brunswick: Rutgers University Press, 1990), 8.

132. Jan Goldstein also pinpoints the origins of this alliance between medicine and the state, and efforts toward a rationalized state policy on epidemics and hygiene to the eighteenth century. "'Moral Contagion': A Professional Ideology of Medicine and Psychiatry in Eighteenth- and Nineteenth-Century France," in Geison, *Professions and the French State*, 181–222, esp. 195–201.

133. Hannaway, "Medicine, Public Welfare, and the State," 1–6; Murphy, "The French Medical Profession," 259–60.

poor, surely individuals such as Victor Lamothe often acted with a true sense of benevolence and a desire to improve society, and not just to impose their values on a reluctant populace.

One of Victor's first experiences in working with the state to promote the public welfare was his experiment on behalf of the Academy of Bordeaux in 1783 to test the use of artificial milk in feeding newborn infants at the Hôpital des enfants trouvés, where Victor served as physician.[134] Victor's position as physician at the foundling hospice also led to his prominent role in the promotion of smallpox vaccination in Bordeaux and the Gironde, in imperial France's greatest experiment in public health control. Smallpox was one of the deadliest diseases in early modern Europe. The fight to stop it began in the early eighteenth century with the discovery of inoculation, the insertion of material from a pustule of a person with smallpox into a healthy person.[135] But the celebrated Edward Jenner did not publish his case histories on smallpox vaccination until 1798.[136] It soon superseded inoculation, owing to its greater safety and effectiveness.[137] The procedure was introduced into France in late 1799 and soon had the firm support of the state.[138]

In 1801, M. Deseze, *officier de santé* at Saint-André, wrote a letter asking for the support of the Commission administrative des hospices to promote

134. BM Ms. 1696 (XXVIII), Fonds Lamontagne, passim, correspondence between François de Lamontagne, *secrétaire perpetuel* of the Academy of Bordeaux and Dupré de St. Maur, intendant of the Guyenne; BM Ms. 828 (XCIII), Archives de l'Académie de Bordeaux, Journal maintained by M. de Ladebat, 20 July–17 August 1783, Nos. 19–23. See Chapter 6, section 1 below, for a discussion of this experiment.

135. Pierre Darmon, *La Longue Traque de la variole: Les Pionniers de la médecine préventive* (Paris: Librairie Académique Perrin, 1986), 82–86; Sir Arthur Salusbury MacNalty, "The Prevention of Smallpox: From Edward Jenner to Monckton Copeman," *Medical History* 12 (January 1968): 4. For the most complete account of the history of inoculation, see Genevieve Miller, *The Adoption of Inoculation for Smallpox in England and France* (Philadelphia: University of Pennsylvania Press, 1957), esp. 180–240, for the introduction of inoculation in France. See also Gelfand, *Professionalizing Modern Medicine*, 11; Emil F. Frey, "Early Eighteenth-Century French Medicine: Setting the Stage for Revolution," *Clio Medica* 17 (May 1982): 10.

136. He made his discovery when investigating the reason why milkmaids who had been infected with cowpox did not get smallpox. In 1796, Jenner tried his first vaccination, using a pustule from the hand of a milkmaid who had been infected with cowpox. MacNalty, "The Prevention of Smallpox," 8; Darmon, *La Longue Traque*, 157.

137. Two of the best books on the spread of vaccination, its successes, and resistance to the procedure in France and the rest of Europe are Darmon, *La Longue Traque*, and Yves-Marie Bercé, *Le Chaudron et la lancette: Croyances populaires et médecine préventive (1798–1830)* (Paris: Presses de la Renaissance, 1984).

138. Darmon, *La Longue Traque*, 177–82. Evelyn Ackerman details the strong official support and campaign to promote vaccination in *Health Care*, 67–76.

vaccination in Bordeaux. He suggested that the Society of Medicine sponsor a program to vaccinate a group of children at the Hospice des enfants de la patrie to demonstrate the safety and efficacy of smallpox vaccination.[139] The Commission provisionally approved M. Deseze's proposal, contingent upon the permission of higher authorities, and authorized the creation of a vaccination committee.[140]

The *officiers de santé* of Bordeaux met soon afterward in order to elect a vaccination committee to carry out the experiment. The committee, consisting of five physicians and two surgeons, included Victor Lamothe, who, in a mark of respect, was named president of the committee by his fellow doctors.[141] As an "enlightened" physician, Victor was a strong supporter of vaccination, an "ardent propagator," according to Bordelais historian Pierre Meller.[142] Even as a young medical student, he had expressed a positive interest in inoculation while in Paris in the early 1760s as philosophes and the Parisian medical community debated its merits.[143]

The vaccination of foundlings was successful, as the procedure protected the children from smallpox and none of them suffered ill effects.[144] Following this success, the Administrative Commission promoted vaccination widely through *circulaires* and correspondence with the communes of the Gironde and neighboring departments.[145] A *dépôt* for the conservation of vaccine material for the Gironde and neighboring departments was established at the foundling hospice, and Victor Lamothe, physician of the hospice, was named *conservateur*, or *dépositaire, du vaccin* and head vaccinator.[146]

139. Michel Foucault has noted that the poor were often used in medical experimentation to the benefit of bourgeois society. *The Birth of the Clinic*, 85.

140. ADG Dépôt des hôpitaux de Bordeaux, Register 5, 15 Pluviôse An IX, 41. The prefect of the Gironde gave his approval for an experiment on twenty children by the Committee of Seven through a letter read before the commission on 6 Messidor An IX (106).

141. ADG Dépôt des hôpitaux de Bordeaux, Register 5, 21 Messidor An IX, 108–9 and 17 Messidor An IX, 111–12.

142. Meller, *Essais généalogiques*, 27.

143. Delphin to Victor, 16 July 1762. See Miller, *Adoption of Inoculation*, 229–40, on the controversy over inoculation during these years.

144. ADG Dépôt des hôpitaux de Bordeaux, Register 6, 6 Frimaire An X, 35.

145. ADG 5M 129, *Circulaire* issued by the Société de vaccine du département de la Gironde, Bordeaux, 4 Prairial An XII, addressed to the "médecins, chirurgiens and officiers de santé du département." See also Dépôt des hôpitaux de Bordeaux, Register 13, 27 April–7 December 1807; Register 15, 8 September 1807, 31.

146. ADG Dépôt des hôpitaux de Bordeaux, Register 15, 15 September 1810, 198; Meller, *Essais généalogiques*, 27; Capelle, "Notice sur M. le docteur Lamothe," 112. The Comité central de vaccine at Bordeaux had questioned whether the Hospice des enfants trouvés was the best place to establish the

As the official administrator of the vaccine material, Victor gave a speech at a meeting of the Central Committee of the Society for Vaccination of the Gironde in 1812, which outlined his views on the value of vaccination. He lamented the persistent obstacles to the propagation of vaccination, particularly "the prejudice, so difficult to vanquish in many rural communes, against this most beneficial practice."[147] He noted approvingly the harsh official measures that had been taken to encourage "fathers & mothers reluctant to have their children vaccinated," such as exclusion from school and the refusal of charitable assistance. He praised the efforts of a number of enlightened doctors and other individuals who had worked to promote vaccination in Bordeaux and the countryside, including Madame Coutanceau, instructor at the *école d'accouchement*, who educated her students concerning its benefits.[148]

Victor was well known and respected for his personal efforts to promote vaccination. From 1800 until his death in 1823, he devoted one day each week to vaccinating the children of Bordeaux free of charge.[149] He was one of the most active vaccinators in Bordeaux and the Gironde in 1812, vaccinating 492 individuals out of a total of 1534 vaccinated in Bordeaux that year.[150] Victor worked with his nephew Dugravier de Lamothe, who was also a zealous promoter of vaccination. The *Etat numérique* for 1815 recorded that the Lamothes, uncle and nephew, had vaccinated 655 individuals, out of a total of 887 in Bordeaux that year.[151]

dépôt, considering the location of the hospice, as well as the fear of contamination that the good citizens of Bordeaux would have if taking the vaccine from a resident at the Hospice des enfants trouvés, "le fruit du Libertinage." ADG 5M 129, Letter from the Comité central de vaccine to the prefect, 10 May 1810.

147. The rural population in general remained reluctant to submit to vaccination. Ackerman, *Health Care*, 72.

148. ADG 5M 129, Société de vaccine du département de la Gironde, Comité central. Rapport fait par Victor Lamothe, médecin de l'Hospice des enfans abandonnés & de celui de la maternité, conservateur du dépôt de vaccin, etc., 25 July 1812. Both the Baron Gary, prefect of the Gironde, and the comte Lynch, mayor of Bordeaux, were present at the meeting. For background information on Mme. Coutanceau, the adopted niece of celebrated royal midwife Mme. du Coudray, see Nina Rattner Gelbart, "The Monarchy's Midwife Who Left No Memoirs," *French Historical Studies* 19 (Fall 1996): 997–1023.

149. Dubreuilh, *Eloge académique*, 22. Evelyn Ackerman points out that the vaccination campaign owed much to the devotion of isolated individuals personally responsible for large numbers of vaccinations. *Health Care*, 72–73.

150. ADG 5M 129, Etat numérique des vaccinations faites à Bordeaux en 1812.

151. ADG 5M 132, Etat numérique des vaccinations faites à Bordeaux en 1815, signed 1816. A series of Etats numériques des vaccinations can be found in Série 5M 132–33 at the Archives départementales de la Gironde. For each year until his death in 1823, Victor Lamothe, along with his

Victor and his nephew promoted vaccination in other ways. They served as commissioners to investigate an outbreak of smallpox in 1821 in the Gironde that led individuals opposed to vaccination to claim that the vaccine was ineffective and dangerous.[152] Victor's work in support of vaccination was recognized by the royal government shortly before his death when he was awarded a prize of five hundred francs by the Minister of the Interior in recognition of "the individuals who have vaccinated the largest number of people, and who have most contributed to the propagation of vaccination" for the year 1820.[153]

Victor's role as chief vaccinator of Bordeaux and as physician at the foundling hospice placed him in daily contact with children, and his biographers lauded his affection for them.[154] His interest in the welfare of children, especially poor children, was a clear factor in his decision to accept the position at the Maternity Hospice in 1799. Since his university days, Victor had indicated an interest in childbirth, to the dismay of his father and brothers.[155] As a doctor, he expressed a profound admiration for the bravery of women in labor. Caring for his sister-in-law after the birth of his nephew, he wrote to Alexis: "Ah! what a terrible thing it is to give birth! To spend 6 or 7 hours in a bed of misery, suffering the most intense pain . . . one need be a witness but once to this spectacle to feel for women all the reverence they deserve. I have been at these touching scenes several times, but it still always tears my heart."[156] Victor had sufficient knowledge of the techniques of childbirth to participate in examining Madame Coutanceau's midwifery students for their certificates from the Bordelais *école d'accouchement*.[157]

---

nephew, was one of the most active vaccinators in Bordeaux, usually vaccinating several hundred more individuals than had the other doctors and surgeons. In 1822, they vaccinated more than one thousand individuals.

152. ADG 5M 127, *Rapport fait à la Société royale de médecine de Bordeaux au nom d'une Commission chargée de faire des recherches sur les prétendues petites véroles survenues chez des individus qui avaient eu la vraie vaccine* (Bordeaux, 1822).

153. ADG 5M 127, Ministère de l'Intérieur, *Rapport présenté à son excellence le Ministre de l'Intérieur, par le Comité central de vaccine, sur les vaccinations pratiquées en France pendant l'année 1820* (Paris, 1823). Prizes for diligent vaccinators were first established in 1809. Ackerman, *Health Care*, 70.

154. Dubreuilh, *Éloge académique*, 14.

155. Delphin to Victor, 13 June 1761.

156. Victor to Alexis, 14 October 1773.

157. "Registre de correspondance de la municipalité": Art. D. 139, and Art. D. 140, in Ducaunnès-Duval, *Inventaire sommaire* 2:259 and 268. The *école pratique d'accouchement* was established at the Hospice de la maternité on 17 Brumaire An XI. ADG Dépôt des hôpitaux de Bordeaux, Register 31, 27 April 1807, 50–51.

This concern for poor women and their children was put to a more practical use when Victor helped to found Bordeaux's Société de charité maternelle.[158] The society received official support in 1805 when the Administrative Commission for the Hospices agreed to support the foundation of the organization through a subscription of one thousand francs, expressing admiration for its mission to assist poor mothers during the crucial period of childbirth and nursing, which would in turn diminish the burden on the city of abandoned infants.[159]

What precisely was the philosophy and the mode of operation of the Society for Maternal Charity? The bylaws of the society set out its goals: "This Society has the goal of reducing the enormous mortality that exists among the newborn infants of the indigent classes; to prevent the abandonment of the fruit of a legitimate union, as they so often are, in the foundling hospice; to improve the condition in life and the morals of their mothers." The society proposed to offer help through the first crucial year of a child's life, providing the indigent mothers with a layette, the costs of childbirth, an allowance to help support the mother and child, and the financial means for the mother to have her child vaccinated.

The society implemented a highly interventionist program to preserve poor families and promote good morals among the poor of Bordeaux. Only legally married mothers could receive the assistance of the society. Inspectors visited the homes of poor women to determine who most needed assistance and to assure the good morals and character of the women receiving aid. The mothers receiving assistance were required to nurse their children themselves. The society continued to survey the efforts of the mother to care for her child during the first year after childbirth.[160]

158. Delpit, *Notes biographiques*, 10.

159. ADG Dépôt des hôpitaux de Bordeaux, Register 11, 19 Germinal An XIII, 122–23. See Pelleport, *Etudes municipales*, 7–23, on the founding and history of the *Société de charité maternelle*.

160. The *fonds* of the *Société de charité maternelle* at the Archives départementales de la Gironde are located under 3X 16–18, 4J 710, and 4J 727. Once again, I would like to thank M. Jean-Pierre Bériac for directing me to these documents. The most complete run of *Comptes rendus des opérations de la Société de charité maternelle de Bordeaux* is at the Bibliothèque municipale de Bordeaux, D 11096. The goals and methods of the society can be found in ADG 3x 18, *Règlement de la Société de charité maternelle de Bordeaux* (Bordeaux, 1810). Each woman assisted by the society received approximately 100 francs in total assistance. For a history of Bordeaux's Society for Maternal Charity, see Annie Flacassier, "La Société de charité maternelle de Bordeaux de 1805 à 1815," *105e Congrès, Comité d'histoire de la Sécurité sociale* (Caen: n.p., 1980), 33–58; and Christine Adams, "Constructing Mothers and Families: The Society for Maternal Charity of Bordeaux, 1805–1860," *French Historical Studies* 22 (Winter 1999): 65–86.

The ties of the society with the government illustrate a new and tighter relationship between central authorities and local charities. Whereas prior to the Revolution charitable distributions had been primarily in the hands of the church, the imperial government, following on the activist revolutionary government, was willing to take a leading role in the allocation of charity to promote social goals. The Society for Maternal Charity was originally established as a local organization, dependent upon local contributions and subscriptions, but it soon became linked with the imperial government. By a decree of the emperor Napoleon issued 5 May 1810, a Société impériale de charité maternelle was created and placed under the protection of the empress. This imperial society was to be funded by a bequest of five hundred thousand francs granted by the emperor, as well as annual subscriptions of five hundred francs and other charitable gifts. The Bordelais society was incorporated into the national organization.[161]

The society worked hard to maintain its ties to the central and local government, communicating frequently with the prefect of the Gironde, as well as with Cardinal Fesch, head of the Central Committee of the imperial society. When the Bourbon regime replaced Napoleon, the society adjusted, shifting its homage from the beneficent empress to its new patroness, the duchess of Angoulême.[162] The imperial society was dissolved, and the Society for Maternal Charity of Bordeaux nominally achieved an independent existence once again in 1815.[163]

Victor Lamothe played an active role in the operations of the Society for Maternal Charity. As a founding member, he helped to formulate the interventionist philosophy of the society. He served as vice-president for six years, until the honorary positions of the society were turned over to women. He made regular financial contributions to the society, and offered free medical assistance to women requiring aid.[164] Victor and the other physicians of the Society for Maternal Charity used the organization

161. ADG 3X 18, 5 mai 1810; Décret impérial, au Palais d'Anvers, arrêté par le Prefet de la Gironde, Baron de l'Empire, Gary, le 5 juillet 1810; Letters of 7 December 1810 and 15 December 1810; Letter of 31 August 1811 presenting the regulations of the Société de charité maternelle.
162. ADG 3X 18, Letter of 7 February 1816; BM D 11096, *Compte rendu des opérations de la Société de charité maternelle de Bordeaux* (Bordeaux, 1814), 4–5.
163. ADG 3X 18, *Règlement de la Société de charité maternelle de Bordeaux* (Bordeaux, 1815). For a fuller discussion of this period, see Christine Adams, "The Provinces Versus Paris? The Case of the Société de charité maternelle of Bordeaux, 1805–1820," *Proceedings of the Western Society for French History* 23 (Fall 1996): 418–30.
164. See BM D 11096, *Comptes rendus des opérations.*

to promote related concerns; for example, the administrative council of the society required indigent mothers to vaccinate their children.[165] Victor's participation in the society, like his vaccination work, was for him a means of fulfilling his sense of service to humanity and promoting his vision of an enlightened society.

When Victor Lamothe died on 24 April 1823, the Administrative Commission for the Hospices of Bordeaux expressed its regrets, praising his fifty-three years of service to the Hospice des enfants trouvés.[166] Although Victor had lived through a great many changes, both in the practice of medicine and in society in general, his philosophy, his perception of his profession, and his sense of obligation as a physician appear to have changed little from the time of his medical education in Paris and Montpellier in the 1750s and 1760s.

He was first and foremost a professional, a man of medicine and learning, dedicated to the belief that science would bring progress to humanity. Despite Victor's initial concerns and doubts about entering the field of medicine, he enjoyed his *métier* and took pride in his professional status. His preference would have been to remain in Paris to practice medicine, but he adjusted well to his career in Bordeaux, relying heavily on the support of family and friends. They were undoubtedly correct in arguing that he would be more successful in Bordeaux than in the capital.

Victor's sense of public service was also developed during his early years as a physician, as both the Academy of Bordeaux and the Royal Society of Medicine stressed the ideal of public welfare. Victor put these ideals into practice through membership in the Society for Maternal Charity and his active championship of the benefits of vaccination. The postrevolutionary government supported a more interventionist enforcement of "public welfare" than was common under the Old Regime, and Victor was willing to work toward his goals in close cooperation with the municipal and central government. Certainly a sense of professional duty, or even "the charitable imperative," pushed him to "fulfil the duties of his *état*,"[167] but Victor seems to have had a genuine sympathy for the poor and a desire to

---

165. ADG 3X 18, Letter of 9 May 1818.

166. ADG Dépôt des hôpitaux de Bordeaux, Register 27, 26 April 1823, 87; 6 May 1823, 93.

167. Dubreuilh, *Eloge académique*, 27. See Jones, *The Charitable Imperative*, 1–22, on "the charitable imperative."

help them. Possibly the respect of the public, as well as the gratitude of the poor he served, kept him safe during the worst months of the Terror.[168]

The values and professional identity of Victor Lamothe parallelled those of other physicians of the late eighteenth and early nineteenth century and reflect the slowly changing image of the *honnête homme*, the respectable urban professional. Honoré de Balzac's nineteenth-century country doctor was not so far removed from the physician of the Enlightenment.

168. Dubreuilh, *Eloge académique*, 15.

PART III

Identity Through Cultural Activities

These final two chapters will explore the multifaceted cultural activities of the Lamothe brothers. These practices played an important role in the construction of their masculine social identities and in representing their status and rank as provincial professionals. Chapter 6 is a study of the institutional bases of the Enlightenment in action. The two academies of Bordeaux—the Académie royale des belles-lettres, sciences et arts and the Académie de peinture, sculpture et architecture civile et navale—were both devoted, at least in theory, to the ideals of public service, usefulness, and the common good. By taking part in the academies, Victor and Delphin hoped to serve the public and to enhance the reputation of their city. Through participation in the academies, the Lamothe brothers reinforced their civic identity and their sense of personal worth. At the same time, as with their other cultural pursuits, they sought to increase their status and dignity through the title of *académicien*. The academician was, by definition, an *honnête homme*, the epitome of the kind of man that the Lamothe brothers strove to be.

Chapter 7 will examine the broad spectrum of intellectual pursuits that Delphin, Alexis, and Victor enjoyed. They associated with Bordeaux's salon society and participated in other informal intellectual and social gatherings. They read extensively, the books of their professions, as well as literature that contributed to their personal cultivation. They were collectors and creators of culture as well, including poetry and prose, some high-minded, some doggerel. Most importantly, they were familiar with the intellectual trends of the eighteenth-century Enlightenment—political, scientific, and social. The Lamothe brothers read the philosophes extensively, and were patently influenced by the spirit of the *siècle des lumières*. They provide a striking example of the extent to which Enlightenment philosophy penetrated and perhaps influenced the provincial professional classes in the eighteenth century.

Civic Pride and Public Service

The Academies of Bordeaux

While the Lamothe brothers pursued a wide variety of informal cultural activities, they also took part in the structured and state-sanctioned world of the academies. The late seventeenth and early eighteenth centuries marked an important transitional period in western European perspectives on science, history, literature, and art as a belief in rationality and empiricism, in the application of science and technology, and in the possibility of human improvement became more widespread.[1] The explosion of printing, the spread of literacy, and the growth of socially open associations such as the freemasons all played a part in the changing mentality, but also essential was the academy. This "multiplier" of new ideas brought

---

1. Many books have been written on the philosophy of the Enlightenment, and I will not go into detail on the many aspects of it here. Among the classic works on the Enlightenment are Ernst Cassirer, *The Philosophy of the Enlightenment*, trans. Fritz C. A. Koelln and James P. Pettegrove (Boston: Beacon Press, 1955); Peter Gay, *The Enlightenment: An Interpretation*, 2 vols. (New York: Alfred A. Knopf, 1967–69); and Daniel Mornet, *Les Origines intellectuelles de la Révolution française, 1715–1787* (Paris: A. Colin, 1933). More recent works include Keith Michael Baker, *Inventing the French Revolution: Essays on French Political Culture in the Eighteenth Century* (Cambridge: Cambridge University Press, 1990); Keith Michael Baker, ed., *The French Revolution and the Creation of Modern Political Culture*, 4 vols. (Oxford: Pergamon Press, 1987); Jack R. Censer, ed., *The French Revolution and Intellectual History* (Chicago: Dorsey Press, 1989); Roger Chartier, *The Cultural Origins of the French Revolution*, trans. Lydia G. Cochrane (Durham: Duke University Press, 1991); Dena Goodman, *The Republic of Letters: A Cultural History of the French Enlightenment* (Ithaca: Cornell University Press, 1994); and Daniel Roche, *Les Republicains des lettres: Gens de culture et lumières au XVIIIe siècle* (Paris: Fayard, 1988).

a certain discipline and authority to the formulation of ideas and new advances in the sciences, *belles-lettres*, and the arts.[2] Unlike more ephemeral *sociétés savantes*, the academies left a solid documentation, for they were officially recognized, and generally kept careful records of their activities.

The first academy of France was the Académie française in 1635, which served as inspiration for a number of provincial academies.[3] Peter Gay has labeled the age of Enlightenment the "age of academies," with "academies of medicine, of agriculture, of literature, each with its prizes, its journals, and its well-attended meetings. In academies and outside them . . . intelligence . . . devoted itself to practical results; it kept in touch with scientists and contributed to technological refinements."[4] The academies, with their lectures, scientific experiments, public libraries, reading rooms, and private classes filled, in part, the intellectual void left by the conservative, even moribund, French universities of the eighteenth century.[5] The academies also played an important role in the creation of the "civil public sphere," in which new ideas were discussed and debated.[6]

What exactly was an academy in eighteenth-century France? Like the salon, the club, and the café, the academy was dedicated to the ideals of "good company" and "good conversation." However, unlike these less formal groupings, it was an official institution, and demanded a certain social dignity of its members. Moreover, the academy emphasized the

2. Pierre Chaunu, *La Civilisation de l'Europe des lumières*, (Paris: Flammarion, 1982), 179; Roger Chartier, *The Cultural Uses of Print in Early Modern France*, trans. Lydia G. Cochrane (Princeton: Princeton University Press, 1987); Robert Darnton, "Reading, Writing, and Publishing in Eighteenth-Century France: A Case Study in the Sociology of Literature," *Daedalus* (December 1970): 214–56; François Furet and Jacques Ozouf, *Reading and Writing: Literacy in France from Calvin to Jules Ferry* (Cambridge: Cambridge University Press, 1982); Ran Halévi, *Les Loges maçonniques dans la France d'Ancien Régime* (Paris: A. Colin, 1984); and Daniel Roche, "Milieux académiques provinciaux et sociétés des lumières," in François Furet, ed., *Livre et société dans la France du XVIIIe siècle*, 2 vols. (Paris and The Hague: Mouton & Cie., 1965–70), 1:99.

3. Roland Mousnier, *The Institutions of France under the Absolute Monarchy, 1598–1789*, trans. Brian Pearce (Chicago: University of Chicago Press, 1979), 456–57.

4. Gay, *The Enlightenment*, 2:9–10. Roger Hahn's *The Anatomy of a Scientific Institution: The Paris Academy of Sciences, 1666–1803* (Berkeley and Los Angeles: University of California Press, 1971) traces the political, social, and technological impetus behind the creation of the Royal Academy of Sciences.

5. See Mornet, *Les Origines intellectuelles*, 304–5.

6. Jürgen Habermas, *The Structural Transformation of the Public Sphere: An Inquiry into a Category of Bourgeois Society*, trans. Thomas Burger and Frederick Lawrence (Cambridge: MIT Press, 1989), 33–34. However, Daniel Roche notes that the discussion of politics was traditionally excluded from the academies, in favor of emphasis on the ideology of public and monarchical service in "Académies et politique au siècle des lumières: Les Enjeux pratiques de l'immortalité," in Baker, *The French Revolution and the Creation of Modern Political Culture*, 1:332.

importance of learning, and members used the forum both to instruct and to be instructed.[7]

Thus, the academy fulfilled two important functions: that of sociability and that of education and the propagation of new ideas, especially "useful ideas." Although the second function has traditionally been emphasized at the expense of the first, the sociability aspect of the academy is important, for members were recruited from the same social milieu and were often friends. The academy provided a meeting ground for men of education and letters, a place for learned discussion as well as formal addresses, for diffusion of thought through social contact.[8]

While the first academies were begun in Paris, the provinces were not far behind.[9] The provincial French were as eager as their Parisian counterparts to partake in the spread of new ideas, to be on the cutting edge of scientific experiments, to enlighten their fellow citizens and to enhance their sense of utility by effecting public improvements. In the provinces, the academies assumed the additional task of supporting regional intellectual activities, thus fanning local pride and patriotism.[10]

Provincial academies sought to recruit cultivated, well-educated men, men of substance and status who would lend both their good names and intellectual gifts to the academy. As officially sanctioned organizations whose members formed an elite in French society, albeit one of talent as well as rank, provincial academies did not openly advocate materialism, atheism, or egalitarian principles.[11] Academies were increasingly open to new ideas, and, from the mid-eighteenth century, as Voltaire, d'Alembert, and Buffon became members of the Académie française, the more radical beliefs of the philosophes involving public utility came to gain greater recognition.[12] Nevertheless, the fundamental social elitism of the acad-

7. Pierre Barrière, *L'Académie de Bordeaux: Centre de culture internationale au XVIIIe siècle* (Bordeaux and Paris: Editions Bière, 1951).

8. Barrière, *L'Académie de Bordeaux*, 6. Maurice Agulhon stresses the social aspect in the formation of academies, circles, and clubs in *Le Cercle dans la France bourgeoise, 1810–1848* (Paris: A. Colin, 1977), 7–14.

9. Mornet, *Les Origines intellectuelles*, 298–99.

10. The most comprehensive work on the provincial academies is Daniel Roche, *Le Siècle des lumières en province: Académies et académiciens provinciaux, 1680–1789*, 2 vols. (Paris and The Hague: Mouton, 1978).

11. Roche, "Encyclopédistes et académiciens: Essai sur la diffusion sociale des lumières," in Furet, *Livre et société*, 2:80 and 86–87, and "Académies et politique au siècle des lumières," 334–35; and Mornet, *Les Origines intellectuelles*, 145–47.

12. Hahn, *Anatomy of a Scientific Institution*, 116–18; Gay, *The Enlightenment*, 2:80–83; and Mornet, *Les Origines intellectuelles*, 150–51 and 298–305.

emies was never disputed. Popular perception of the academies as another "privileged corporation" contributed to their closing by the revolutionary government in 1793 as an obstacle to civil equality and to the unity of the nation.[13]

The provincial academies could not compete with Paris in prestige, but they fulfilled a specific intellectual and local role. The goals of the Royal Society of Metz parallelled those of most provincial academies: "We aspire more to utility than *éclat*, to the progress of public wisdom and general reason than the glory of letters; we propose to clarify the objectives of public utility rather than embellishing and enlivening obvious truths."[14] For all their rhetoric of *éclat* and *gloire*, the academies saw their primary function as a utilitarian contribution to the public good and the promotion of civic pride.[15]

Bordeaux, as the self-proclaimed "second city of France," was host to a large number of intellectual societies and associations. However, there were only two academies—the Académie royale des belles-lettres, sciences et arts de Bordeaux, and the Académie de peinture, sculpture et architecture civile et navale. The Lamothe brothers were ideal candidates for election to the academies of Bordeaux, as men with a wide variety of talents and interests and imbued with the ideas of the Enlightenment. They were eager to participate in the academies, share the work, and contribute to the common good. During the sixteenth and seventeenth centuries, lawyers and doctors were often discouraged by the mores of society from pursuing activities that would keep them from concentrating on their professional endeavors. By the eighteenth century, however, a wider world beckoned, and rising status required acquiring the attributes of responsibility and cultivation. Professionals sought a more ambitious cultural role.[16] Victor and Delphin de Lamothe fit the mold of the new

13. Hahn, *Anatomy of a Scientific Institution*, esp. 126–58 and 226–51.

14. Quoted in Mornet, *Les Origines intellectuelles*, 302.

15. Roche traces the importance of the academy in the urban cultural and civic sphere in *Le Siècle des lumières*, 75–135.

16. Many historians have examined the new cultural awareness of this social class in the eighteenth century. Norbert Elias, in *The Civilizing Process: The History of Manners*, trans. Edmund Jephcott (New York: Urizen Books, 1978), 35–50, argues that the French bourgeoisie of the eighteenth century had a new consciousness of themselves as "bearers of civilization." Barristers of Toulouse were members of both the prestigious Academy of Floral Games and the Academy of Sciences. See Lenard R. Berlanstein, *The Barristers of Toulouse in the Eighteenth Century (1740–1793)* (Baltimore: Johns Hopkins University Press, 1975), 94–96. At the same time, doctors joined the academies in large numbers and formed their own learned societies devoted to public service and the spread of new ideas on public health, meteorology, and sanitary conditions. Caroline Hannaway, "Medicine, Public Welfare, and the State in Eighteenth-Century France: The Société royale de médecine of Paris (1776–1793)," 2 vols.

professional man. Each participated in the academies of Bordeaux, and each left his mark. Their participation illustrates the structure and function of the provincial academy, as well as the role of the provincial academician.

1. The Academy of *Belles-Lettres*, Sciences, and Arts of Bordeaux

The Académie royale des belles-lettres, sciences et arts de Bordeaux, or the Academy of Bordeaux, originated in 1707 as an amateur musical group. The musical assemblies gave way to discussion groups for other topics, and eventually, part of the group broke away to form a society devoted to the study of the arts and sciences. This new group sought the protection of the duc de la Force, governor of the Guyenne, who helped to obtain letters patent in 1712. At the inaugural assembly, Director Antoine de Gascq, a magistrate of the parlement, dedicated his opening speech to the utility of the sciences.[17] Thus from the beginning, the Academy of Bordeaux was directed to the support and study of science.

In one sense, this new academy in Bordeaux was a manifestation of a national, even international, movement, an expanded spirit of intellectual inquiry and the exchange of new ideas in the form of societies and academies. The scientific orientation of the Academy of Bordeaux placed it on the cutting edge of utilitarian progress.[18] At the same time, the academy was a source of provincial patriotism, an organization that allowed the Bordelais to assert their dignity and commitment to the spread of the ideals of the Enlightenment.[19]

Early in its existence, the academy, which attracted the social and intellectual elite of Bordeaux, took steps to seek protection and guarantee

---

(Ph.D. diss., Johns Hopkins University, 1974). Robert Darnton has documented the intellectual and cultural role of the many doctors and lawyers who contributed to Panckouke's *Encyclopédie Méthodique. The Business of Enlightenment: A Publishing History of the* Encyclopédie, *1775–1780* (Cambridge: Harvard University Press, Belknap Press, 1979), 437–46. See Roche, *Le Siècle des lumières*, 185–255 for an analysis of the socioprofessional composition of the provincial academies.

17. Jean de Feytaud, "L'Académie de Bordeaux sous l'Ancien Régime," *Revue historique de Bordeaux et du département de la Gironde* 23 (1974): 72–74.

18. Barrière, *L'Académie de Bordeaux*, 12–13; Gay, *The Enlightenment*, 2:126–28.

19. Barrière, *L'Académie de Bordeaux*, 35–36, and François-Georges Pariset, ed., *Bordeaux au XVIIIe siècle*, (Bordeaux: Fédération historique du Sud-Ouest, 1968), 81.

its continuation. The first official protector, the duc de la Force, was key in the obtention of letters patent. He was succeeded as protector by equally powerful governors of the Guyenne and high noblemen: the comte de Morville, the cardinal de Polignac, the duc de Richelieu, and the prince de Beauvau. The patronage of these powerful noblemen gave the academy a certain luster, but had some practical advantages as well.[20] The House of La Force funded a physics prize, a gold medal worth 300 livres, beginning in 1714.[21] However, this reliance on the governors of the Guyenne as patrons rather than the city magistrates created some head-aches for the academy. Bordeaux was controlled by six *jurats* who made up the municipal council, as well as the royal administrator, the intendant. The intendant played a key role in the region, especially when this was a skillful and powerful administrator such as the Marquis de Tourny.[22] This presented problems for the academy when the goals and interests of the intendant conflicted with those of the academy, most notably when the location of the Hôtel de Bel, the official lodging of the academy, disrupted the intendant and city magistrates' plans for urban renewal.[23]

The Hôtel de Bel, a gift from one of the academy's earliest members, Jean-Jacques Bel, was an imposing building, decorated by the academy to display its brilliant connections and high-minded interests.[24] A German visitor to Bordeaux in 1785 was impressed by the main rooms of the academy, which displayed portraits of Newton, Gassendi, and Galileo, as well as of Louis XIV, the duc de la Force, Montesquieu, and Bel himself.[25] The academy also housed an extensive library, a boon to the city. Bel's thousands of volumes, which he left to the academy—along with his *hôtel*—on the condition that they be made available to the public, brought the academy library into existence in May 1740. It was expanded through

20. Barrière, *L'Académie de Bordeaux*, 30. On the role of patronage in provincial academies, see Roche, *Le Siècle des lumières*, 118–20; and David S. Lux, *Patronage and Royal Science in Seventeenth-Century France: The Académie de physique in Caen* (Ithaca: Cornell University Press, 1989).

21. Pariset, *Bordeaux au XVIIIe siècle*, 95.

22. On the municipal political life of Bordeaux, see Pariset, *Bordeaux au XVIIIe siècle*, 9–28; and Alan Forrest, *Society and Politics in Revolutionary Bordeaux* (New York: Oxford University Press, 1975), 22–23.

23. Feytaud, "L'Académie de Bordeaux," 80; and Barrière, *L'Académie de Bordeaux*, 25–27. Montes-quieu, the academy's most illustrious member, championed the claims of the Bordeaux academy in Paris and at Versailles. See Robert Shackleton, *Montesquieu: A Critical Biography* (New York: Oxford University Press, 1961), 213–17.

24. P. Bernadau, *Annales politiques, littéraires et statistiques de Bordeaux* (Bordeaux: Moreau, 1803), 131–32. The academy held its first official meeting there in February 1739.

25. Meaudre de Lapouyade, *Impressions d'une allemande à Bordeaux en 1785* (Bordeaux: G. Gounouilhou, 1911), 24.

the donations of other academicians, and on the eve of the Revolution, the library contained 10,370 works in 19,819 volumes. These would serve as the core of the Bibliothèque municipale following the Revolution.[26] Victor Lamothe later followed the example of these earlier academicians, donating many of his own books to the Municipal Library in 1820.[27]

The Academy of Bordeaux attracted the elite of Bordelais society. The most illustrious member of the academy was Montesquieu, the "glory and the pride of the Academy."[28] He was one of the most effective propagators of the academy's interests—certainly more useful than the official protectors of the academy, even if his attendance record was somewhat spotty.[29] Delphin de Lamothe paid homage to Montesquieu in his reception speech in 1777, declaring, "Montesquieu, you live still, you light the way for us, you warm us, may the Academy live as long as your name and your work.[30] The *éloge* of Montesquieu was the subject of the academy's *concours* from 1782 to 1789, but no entry was considered deserving of the prize.[31] Apparently, no eulogy could do the great philosophe justice.

Less famous, but perhaps more important to the academy, was Montesquieu's nephew and close friend of the Lamothe brothers, François de Lamontagne. Unlike Montesquieu, whose intellectual achievements are legendary, Lamontagne was more celebrated in the academy's history for his administrative skills than for his literary skills. He was the individual most essential to the management of the Academy of Bordeaux and the preservation of its history during the second half of the eighteenth century. When the Revolution led to the closing of all academies in 1793,

26. Contributors included Jean Barbot, François de Lamontagne, and Nicolas Beaujon. BM Ms. 1460, "Journal," edited by Jules Delpit, 26 May 1751, 12; Paul Courteault, "Notice sur François de Lamontaigne," introduction to François de Lamontaigne, *Chronique bordelaise de François de Lamontaigne, conseiller au Parlement* (Bordeaux: Imprimeries Delmas, Chapons, Gounouilhou, 1926), XXV; Pariset, *Bordeaux au XVIIIe siècle*, 99–100. For a listing of the library's holdings, see BM Ms. 834, "Catalogue alphabétique des livres de la bibliothèque de l'Académie."

27. Lamothe Family Letters, December 1820–March 1823.

28. Barrière, *L'Académie de Bordeaux*, 51.

29. "Discours de M. Paul Courteault, président de l'Académie," in *Actes de l'Académie nationale des sciences, belles-lettres et arts de Bordeaux* (4e Série, 1er année, 1913), 69; Barrière, *L'Académie de Bordeaux*, 51–63. See Shackleton, *Montesquieu*, passim, for further discussion of Montesquieu's participation in the Academy of Bordeaux.

30. AM Fonds Delpit, No. 127, #3, "Compliments de Reception à l'Académie des sciences le 16 fevrier 1777, par Lamothe p.e.d.f."

31. *Programme de l'Académie royale des belles-lettres, sciences et arts de Bordeaux* du 25 août 1771 au 25 août 1790; and Barrière, *L'Académie de Bordeaux*, 63.

Lamontagne personally saved the registers of the academy along with much of the archives.[32]

Lamontagne, *conseiller au parlement* and a contemporary of Delphin de Lamothe, was unanimously elected member of the academy in April 1752 at the age of only twenty-seven. He served as its director in his first year.[33] In July 1755, he was elected perpetual secretary, a position he held until its abolition in 1793, nearly forty years later.[34] Lamontagne followed Jean Barbot, who had previously served as secretary of the academy. Barbot was a loyal and active member, but notorious for his negligence and laziness as secretary.[35] In contrast, Lamontagne is recognized as the most scrupulous of the academy's secretaries.[36] The extensive correspondence in the archives of the Academy of Bordeaux demonstrates the extent of his personal involvement in various administrative activities.[37] François de Lamontagne embodied the provincial academician and *honnête homme*: a well-educated man of many interests straddling the arts and sciences, with a wide circle of friends and acquaintances, an indefatigable collector of documents and texts and greatly concerned with the history and the renown of his city and province—a real patriot. One did not have to be a Montesquieu to be an academician. Lamontagne personifies the ideal provincial academician—a dedicated "workhorse" who carried out the *travaux* of the academy. In any case, he comes closer to the typical Bordelais academician than does the philosophe of La Brède.

Although the provincial academies were in theory dedicated to the ideal of equality among enlightened men of merit—already an elite group—

32. Ministre de l'Education Nationale, *Catalogue général des manuscrits des bibliothèques publiques de France,* Tome L (Paris: Bibliothèque Nationale, 1954), 221. The academy archives saved by Lamontagne are located at the Bibliothèque municipale de Bordeaux, Ms. 1696, Fonds Lamontagne, and Ms. 828, Archives de l'Académie des sciences, belles-lettres et arts de Bordeaux (107 volumes).

33. BM Ms. 1460, "Journal," 29 January 1753, 37. He was chosen to give Montesquieu's eulogy in August 1755 and February 1756. Ibid., 103.

34. Courteault, "Notice sur François de Lamontaigne," XVII–XVIII.

35. Barrière, L'Académie de Bordeaux, 48–49. In his correspondence with M. de Formey in 1750, Delphin de Lamothe remarked, concerning the academy and M. Barbot, "Cette académie n'a encore donné au public aucun ouvrage; son secrétaire, homme de beaucoup d'esprit, est un peu paresseux." Juin-Mai 1749.—Lettres de Simon-Delphin de Lamothe à M. Formey, historiographe de l'Académie royale des sciences de Berlin, sur le projet du roi de Prusse pour la réformation de la justice. Published in *Archives historiques du département de la Gironde*, vol. 32 (Paris and Bordeaux, 1898). Letter of 24 February 1750, 249.

36. "Discours de M. Paul Courteault," 71–72.

37. BM Ms. 1696 (XXVIII and XXIX), Fonds Lamontagne, Archives de l'Académie de Bordeaux. Correspondence, vols. 1–2. At times, he even made loans to the academy from his own funds. See ADG D 59, Académie de Bordeaux for an account of his loans.

hierarchy was built into the membership structure of the academy. In 1713, the regulations of the Academy of Bordeaux established three categories of academicians: *ordinaires*, *associés*, and *élèves*. The classification of student was eventually abolished, and that of *correspondent* was added in 1744.[38] The "regular" members were drawn heavily from the nobility, especially the magistrature. The academy was frequently referred to as the "daughter of the parlement," and *parlementaires* were the dominant group throughout most of the eighteenth century. This gradually shifted as it recruited more extensively from other nonnoble social and professional groups to fill the slots of regular academicians.

The class composition of the associates, the workhorses of the academy, was strikingly different.[39] Nonnobles were widely represented among the associates. The rights and greater prestige associated with the title *académicien ordinaire* led to resentment on the part of the associates, and the distinction between the categories ended in 1783.[40] Perhaps because of the scientific bent of the academy, more than half of its nonnoble members between 1713 and 1793 were from the medical field—primarily physicians, but also surgeons and even pharmacists.[41] Despite their respected position in Bordelais society, barristers played a very minor role in the academy—Delphin de Lamothe was one of very few lawyers elected before 1793.[42] Even more striking was the absence of wholesale merchants and bankers from the list of members in the heavily commercial city of Bordeaux. The traditional "notables" of Bordeaux—magistrates, clergy, landlords, doctors, and a sprinkling of lawyers—controlled the intellectual life of the city.[43]

According to Daniel Roche, the basis of recruitment to the academy

38. See Roche, *Le Siècle des lumières*, 185–255, and "Milieux académiques provinciaux," 93–184, for an analysis of the structure and composition of the Academy of Bordeaux.

39. Pierre Barrière notes that the *académiciens ordinaires* were usually amateurs, while the *associés* were the specialists of the academy. *L'Académie de Bordeaux*, 40.

40. Roche, *Le Siècle des lumières*, 109–10.

41. The "esprit de corps," "tradition savante," and public service ethic of the physicians made members of the Collège des médecins favored candidates for election to academies in most provincial cities. Roche, *Le Siècle des lumières*, 245.

42. According to Daniel Roche, the academy "n'ont fait appel qu'aux grands ténors de la compagnie" of barristers, namely Delphin de Lamothe and de Sèze. *Le Siècle des lumières*, 242. Barristers played a far more important role in the Academy of Floral Games and the Academy of Sciences of Toulouse. Berlanstein, *The Barristers of Toulouse*, 98–99.

43. Roche, "Encyclopédistes et académiciens," 85. Both Daniel Roche and Pierre Barrière discuss in detail the recruitment and composition of the Academy of Bordeaux, although there are minor disagreements between the two. Barrière includes an (incomplete) list of the names of the members

rested upon three elusive elements: "social honorability, provincial position, talents and human value."[44] Clearly, the Lamothe brothers met the
necessary criteria for membership in the Academy of Bordeaux. When
Delphin de Lamothe was elected member of the academy on 26 January
1777, he was already a respected lawyer who had served twice as syndic of
the Order of Barristers of Bordeaux, a royal professor of law, perpetual
secretary of the Academy of Painting, Sculpture, and Architecture of
Bordeaux, co-author of a two-volume commentary on the customary law
of Bordeaux, and proprietor of the *terres nobles* of Muscadet and Lyde.[45] He
had shown himself to be an enlightened man of talent. Delphin's speech
upon being elected to the academy indicated his awareness of the dignity
of the company that had accepted him—and his own.[46]

The circumstances of Victor Lamothe's election to the Academy of
Bordeaux on 20 January 1769, eight years earlier, were very different.[47] He
was only thirty-three years old, and had spent less than two years in
Bordeaux as a physician. The decision of the academy to elect Victor was
apparently based on his local social standing, powerful protectors within
the medical profession, recognition of his studies in Montpellier and Paris
and belief in his potential. At any rate, the academy chose wisely. Its
archives indicate that Victor Lamothe was a reliable member who used his
professional expertise to contribute to its collective knowledge. Like
François de Lamontagne, Victor was one of the "workhorses" of the
academy.

As with most provincial academies, the most important activity of the
Academy of Bordeaux was the *concours*, an annual call for essays on a wide
variety of topics. Voltaire lampooned the contests staged by the Academy
of Bordeaux in an often quoted passage from *Candide*: "He [Candide] was
very much grieved at having to part with his sheep, which he left with the
Academy of Sciences at Bordeaux. The academy offered as the subject for
a prize that year the cause of the redness of the sheep's fleece; and the
prize was awarded to a learned man in the North, who proved by A plus

---

between 1713 and 1793, culled from the registers. Barrière, *L'Académie de Bordeaux*, 39–46; and Roche,
"Milieux académiques provinciaux," 108–32.

44. Roche, "Milieux académiques provinciaux," 131.

45. BM Ms. 1465, "Journal," 26 January 1777, 55.

46. AM Fonds Delpit, No. 127, #3, "Compliments de Reception à l'Académie des sciences le 16
février 1777, par Lamothe p.e.d.f."

47. BM Ms. 1463, "Journal," 37.

B minus C divided by Z that the sheep must be red and die of the sheep-pox."[48] It is undoubtedly true that the majority of papers received by the Academy of Bordeaux were mediocre in quality. Nevertheless, the essay competitions offered by the academies of France, announced in the *Mercure de France* and other French and foreign journals, could bring fame and fortune to the winner, as in the well-known case of Jean-Jacques Rousseau who won the prize offered by the Academy of Dijon in 1750.[49] The prizes offered could be substantial in monetary terms, for example the 300 livre prize in physics offered by the duc de la Force.[50] In addition to annual medal competitions being offered, other "interested citizens" sometimes proposed prizes for topics of particular interest to them. In 1772, a "zealous friend of humanity" offered a prize of 1,200 l. for the best essay dealing with the slave trade, and in 1781 a woman concerned about the bed-wetting of her three daughters offered a *prix extraordinaire* of 300 l. for a paper proposing a cure for *lectio minctio*.[51]

A wide and varied range of themes was offered by the academy each year. Many dealt with some aspect of science, although history, literature, and other subjects were represented as well. With such a large number of doctors among the academicians, medical topics were of particular interest. By the second half of the eighteenth century, dissertation topics focused more frequently on practical applications of science and technology.[52] The number of responses varied greatly depending upon the topic. The technical difficulty of the question did not determine the response rate as often as did the perception of the potential utility of the topic in the eyes of the public.[53] Other topics were primarily of local interest. As

48. Ben Ray Redman, ed., *The Portable Voltaire* (New York: Penguin Books, 1977), 291. Despite his sarcasm, Voltaire was a member of eighteen academies, including that of Bordeaux. Roche, "Encyclopédistes et académicians," 74.

49. Roche, "Milieux académiques provinciaux," 157.

50. Pariset, *Bordeaux au XVIIIe siècle*, 95.

51. *Programme de l'Académie royale des belles-lettres, sciences et arts de Bordeaux*, 13 January 1772; BM Ms. 1696 (XXVIII), Fonds Lamontagne, Archives de l'Académie, No. 139.

52. Daniel Roche has broken down by subject matter the dissertation topics offered by the Academy of Bordeaux between 1715 and 1791. He counts a total of 149 topics offered during the seventy-six-year period: physics, 30 (20 percent of the total); medicine and human physiology, 27 (18 percent); botany and zoology, 18 (12 percent); history and *belles-lettres* (11 percent—no number given). The following topics were also represented: geology and mineralogy, mechanical arts, chemistry, and political economy. A total of 79 out of the 149 subjects were of a scientific nature, with those of practical application far outweighing purely theoretical topics. Roche, "Milieux académiques provinciaux," 162–63. See also *Le Siècle des lumières*, 353.

53. Projects of "public utility" became increasingly popular in the Academy of Sciences in Paris

Daniel Roche notes, the *concours* "conformed to two inclinations: it was provincial in its scholarly orientations, it sought to serve patriotism and philosophy by favoring the eulogies of great men who first gave proof of regional civic-mindedness, then national."[54] Bordeaux distinguished itself in the regularity of its academic competitions, as well as in the variety of subjects offered.[55] In 1771, enlightened citizens were invited to submit essays on no fewer than six topics, ranging from sugar refining, methods of fertilizing clay, and the medicinal properties of the animal kingdom to a eulogy of Michel de Montaigne.[56] Although medals were offered each year, they were not always awarded if the academy decided that none of the essays was worthy of the medal.[57]

While members of the academy were proud of their efforts to promote topics of potential public usefulness, an incredible amount of often tedious labor went into reading and judging these essays, constituting, as Pierre Barrière notes, a "real burden."[58] The associates provided most of the intellectual labor for the academy. With his broad knowledge in the fields of medicine and science, Victor Lamothe was particularly valuable in providing analyses of the treatises submitted in the 1770s and 1780s. An examination of his evaluations provides insight into the responsibilities of the provincial academician.

The dissertations evaluated by Victor Lamothe ranged in subject matter from physics and astronomy to sociology and public health. Some of the earliest submissions Victor reviewed concerned the epizootic diseases attacking livestock in the southern provinces of France.[59] Although it seems unlikely that Victor could have possessed expertise in all of the fields he was called upon to review, it appears that he maintained a particular interest in cattle diseases, a much discussed topic in the 1780s,

---

during the second half of the eighteenth century. Hahn, *Anatomy of a Scientific Institution*, 119–21. However, academies that offered poetry competitions still tended to attract a higher response rate than did the Academy of Bordeaux with its more practical questions. Roche, "Milieux académiques provinciaux," 160–61, and *Le Siècle des lumières*, 330.

54. Roche, *Le Siècle des lumières*, 350.

55. Barrière, *L'Académie de Bordeaux*, 83–84 and 136–37.

56. *Programme de l'Académie royale des belles-lettres, sciences et arts de Bordeaux* du 25 août 1771 au 25 août 1790.

57. BM Ms. 1696 (XXVIII), Fonds Lamontagne, Archives de l'Académie, No. 146. Out of 149 topics proposed by the academy from 1715 to 1791, only 45 were awarded prizes. Roche, "Milieux académiques provinciaux," 161.

58. See Barrière, *L'Académie de Bordeaux*, 91.

59. BM Ms. 828 (VII), "Mémoires et observations sur l'épizootie," Nos. 7–12.

when these diseases were rampant and contributing to the agricultural crisis of the prerevolutionary years.[60]

The archives of the academy indicate that Victor Lamothe was active in examining the essays submitted in competition. In 1776, he presented a flattering summary and evaluation of a pharmacological dissertation by a Monsieur Thouvenal on animal substances, and in May 1786, Victor made a joint presentation with fellow physician M. de Seze concerning a paper by the surgeon Guérin titled *L'Extraction de la cataracte*.[61] Victor and Laffon de Ladebat's report on an essay by Sieur Léglise facilitated M. Léglise's election to the academy.[62] In another case, a disgruntled candidate appealed to Victor to force reconsideration of an unfavorable evaluation of his project by another academician.[63]

Victor Lamothe was a primary evaluator of the essays submitted concerning the topic "Which would be the best methods for saving the Negroes shipped from Africa to the Colonies from the frequent and often fatal diseases they suffer during the crossing?"[64] The anonymous "friend of humanity" who offered the award of 1,200 l. for the best essay on the topic claimed that "his heart was moved when he calculated the number of these unfortunate individuals who perish in the vessels that transport them from Africa to the New World." It seems just as likely that the benefactor was a merchant concerned with his heavy losses in the slave trade.[65] Only three pieces were submitted on the subject, none of which was deemed worthy of the prize.[66]

Although Victor's remarks on the slave trade were not extensive, he commented sympathetically about a *mémoire* sent from Paris: "The author groans, along with all thoughtful individuals, to think of the unhappy servitude that the negroes suffer, both in the heart of their own countries

60. See Hannaway, "Medicine, Public Welfare, and the State," 184–218. Among the Lamothe family papers is a copy of an *Avis au public sur la maladie regnante des bêtes à cornes* from 1788. See Lamothe Family Papers, Publications, Folder #6.

61. BM Ms. 828, (LXXXVII), "Note de M. de Lamothe sur un mémoire de Thouvenel," No. 5; BM Ms. 1467, "Journal," 24 May 1786, 15.

62. BM Ms. 1696 (XXVII), Fonds Lamontagne, Archives de l'Académie, Personnel. Certificate for Mr. Léglise, 21 May 1792, No. 3.

63. BM Ms. 828 (XXII), "Vigné: Lettre à M. Lamothe," No. 24.

64. BM Ms. 828 (LXXXIX), "Rapport de M. de Lamothe 1772–1778," Nos. 5–18 contain the documents related to this topic.

65. *Programme de l'Académie royale des belles-lettres, sciences et arts de Bordeaux*, 13 January 1772. See Philip D. Curtin, *The Atlantic Slave Trade: A Census* (Madison: University of Wisconsin Press, 1969), 275–86, for a discussion of the high loss of slaves during the Middle Passage.

66. Barrière, *L'Académie de Bordeaux*, 30.

as well as among civilized people, the Europeans, who transport them to America in order to subject them to the harshest labors."[67] It is doubtful that Victor went so far as to openly advocate abolition of the slave trade, an unpopular position in the port city of Bordeaux where economic prosperity depended on slave-grown sugar. His comments suggest, however, a sympathy for the African slave and a desire to ameliorate the conditions of slavery in the West Indies as well as on the Middle Passage.[68]

However, Dr. Lamothe's evaluations of pieces submitted were not always so morally earnest. His review of the printed article submitted by Sieur Alfonse, an apothecary of Bordeaux, on the same topic, was caustic, citing numerous errors.[69] But in his comments, he did not stress the evils of the slave trade more generally. He was less bold than fellow academician and reformer André-Daniel Laffon de Ladebat, who wrote a treatise attacking the slave trade and presented it to the academy in 1788.[70]

As a doctor educated in empirical methodology, Victor Lamothe was also expected on occasion to lend his expertise to validate the proposed remedies sent to the academy. He could be adamant in his refusal to approve untested medicines. In a polite but strongly worded letter to a gentleman who submitted a secret potion to cure *lectio minctio* (bed-wetting), Victor wrote, "In good faith, you see for yourself, Monsieur, that if you made use of medication that an unknown person offered you, and you had not seen its effects on anyone, your position as surgeon assures me that it would only be in a case of the greatest urgency, of near certain death; you would not attempt a remedy that was completely unknown to you. If these very understandable reflections can persuade you, Monsieur, to entrust me with the recipe for your remedy, I give you my word of honor not to reveal it to anyone without your approval."[71]

Victor was also involved in verifying the medical solutions proposed for the academy competition that attracted one of the highest response rates

67. BM Ms. 828 (LXXXIX), "Extrait fait par M. Lamothe, le méd., de la dissertation No. I," No. 6.

68. Paul Butel and Jean-Pierre Poussou, *La Vie quotidienne à Bordeaux au XVIIIe siècle* (Paris: Hachette, 1980), 103–4. The high mortality and morbidity rate of African slaves during the Middle Passage was of concern to both the traders and European national governments, primarily for economic, although also for humanitarian, reasons. Richard B. Sheridan, *Doctors and Slaves: A Medical and Demographic History of Slavery in the British West Indies, 1680–1834* (New York: Cambridge University Press, 1985), 108–26.

69. BM Ms. 828 (LXXXIX), "Rapport fait par M. Lamothe, D.M. du Mémoire imprimé," No. 18.

70. Laffon de Ladebat was from an important Bordelais *armateur* family, and the son of a *négrier* who made his fortune in the slave trade. Paul Butel, *Les Dynasties bordelaises de Colbert à Chaban* (Paris: Perrin, 1991), 153–54.

71. BM Ms. 828 (XCV), Académie de Bordeaux, Letter dated 17 October 1780, No. 7.

for any topic proposed. The subject of feeding newborn children, particularly orphans, was of great interest in eighteenth-century France, and especially in large cities such as Bordeaux, which found themselves caring for increasingly large numbers of abandoned infants throughout the century.[72] The Hôpital des enfants trouvés made concerted efforts to recruit healthy and conscientious wet nurses, but with little success, due to low pay.[73] As a result, mortality among foundlings was alarmingly high throughout France.[74] In a *mémoire* authored in the late 1770s, the Bordelais physician M. Doazan wrote dramatically of the health hazards for the abandoned infants and the mercenary wet nurses themselves.[75]

Alarmed by the perceived dangers of depopulation in France that M. Doazan also emphasized in his *mémoire*, the royal administration was greatly concerned with providing care and feeding for the foundlings.[76] Thus, the intendant was highly supportive when the Academy of Bordeaux offered as the subject of its competition "either the means of preventing, when nursing foundlings by traditional methods, the dangers that result for both the infant and the wet nurse, and subsequently, for the population in general; or the best and most economical method to provide a substitute to breast milk for the nourishment of these infants."[77] The title indicates that the condition of the foundlings was used as a yardstick to determine the mortality of the population as a whole.

72. Eugène Mabille, *De la condition des enfants trouvés au XVIIIe siècle dans la généralité de Bordeaux* (Bordeaux: Y. Cadoret, 1909), 48.

73. Ibid., 98.

74. On the high mortality of abandoned infants, see Michael W. Flinn, *The European Demographic System, 1500–1820* (Baltimore: Johns Hopkins University Press, 1981), 40–43; and Claude Delasselle, "Abandoned Children in Eighteenth-Century Paris," in Robert Forster and Orest Ranum, eds., *Deviants and the Abandoned in French Society: Selections from the Annales*, trans. Elborg Forster and Patricia Ranum (Baltimore: Johns Hopkins University Press, 1978), 47–82.

75. ADG C 3456, Archives de l'Intendance de Bordeaux, Correspondance de Dupré de St. Maur, "Mémoire de M. Doazan, medecin de Bx., en sujet de l'administration des enfans trouvés."

76. ADG C 3456, Archives de l'Intendance de Bordeaux, Correspondance de Dupré de St. Maur. Throughout 1777, the intendant, Dupré de St. Maur, corresponded with the *directeur général* Necker concerning this issue, and interrogated his subordinates in the Guyenne concerning the facilities for *enfants trouvés*. See also BM Ms. 828 (XCIII), Letter dated 25 October 1777, No. 6. It should be emphasized that depopulation was a *perceived* rather than actual problem. According to demographic indicators, the population of France expanded rapidly during the second half of the eighteenth century. Jacques Dupâquier et al., *Histoire de la population française, Volume II: de la Renaissance à 1789* (Paris: Presses Universitaires de France, 1988), 437–38.

77. *Programme de l'Académie royale des belles-lettres, sciences et arts de Bordeaux*, 19 May 1778. See BM Ms. 1696 (XXVIII), Fonds Lamontagne, Archives de l'Académie, passim, for correspondence between Secretary Lamontagne and Intendant Dupré de St. Maur on this matter.

This topic, first proposed in 1778, and subsequently renewed in 1781, 1783, and 1785, received a total of twenty-eight responses, none of which was considered worthy of the *prix extraordinaire* of 2,000 l.[78] Various imaginative proposals were submitted. One enterprising author provided the recipe for a "nourishing powder" and a "machine to nurse infants" boasting "the bladder of a calf or a sheep" from which the children would suckle (no. 17). Another proposed substituting "the milk of an ass or mare," diluted with water (no. 13). Some of the essays bore emotional and picturesque titles, such as "Suffering Humanity Touches All Hearts" (no. 20) and "Has the Cruellest Tigress Ever Refused Milk to Her Young?" (no. 13). Despite the conscientious efforts of the authors, the comments of the reviewing academicians were often terse, even brutal: "It is barely useful to report on or to excerpt from essay no. 12, it offers nothing worthy of our attention" (no. 16); "pitiful" (no. 21); and most often, the brief comment "eliminated from competition." Victor Lamothe, who examined at least four of the works submitted, was also given to cryptic, not to say contemptuous observations: "he proposes his views; but while they take up a good third of the work, there is absolutely nothing new in them" (no. 5).[79] Dr. Lamothe would maintain medical standards.

"Always guided by the public utility," in the words of François de Lamontagne, the academy chose to test the most promising idea submitted, and asked the administrators of the foundling hospital to provide some abandoned infants for the experiment.[80] Victor Lamothe, as the official physician of the Hôpital des enfants trouvés, was placed in charge of the negotiations to choose the infants for the experiment and to care for their medical needs.[81]

A weekly journal kept by academician M. Laffon de Ladebat from 20 July through 17 August 1783 details the course of the experiment. The infants, "in conformity with essay no. 18," were to be fed a mixture of milk, water, *bouillon*, and sugar. Despite the careful medical attention given the babies by Dr. Lamothe, who examined them daily, two of the eight infants

78. BM Ms. 828 (XCIV), "Dissertations, rapports et lettres sur l'allaitement des enfants trouvés"; BM Ms. 834, "Catalogue des livres de la bibliothèque de l'Académie."

79. These extracts are from BM Ms. 828 (XCIV), Académie de Bordeaux.

80. BM Ms. 1696 (XXVIII), Fonds Lamontagne, Archives de l'Académie, "Projet de lettre, de la part de l'Académie à MM. les administrateurs de l'Hôpital des enfans trouvés, de Bordeaux," 25 February 1781, No. 119.

81. BM Ms. 1696 (XXVIII), Fonds Lamontagne, Archives de l'Académie, Lettre to M. de Lamontagne, No. 130.

undergoing the experiment had died by the week of 17 August, all were very thin, and only one child was diagnosed as "well enough [*assez bien*]."[82] The failure of the experiment was undoubtedly a disappointment for Victor, who had a particular interest in the artificial nursing of children.[83]

Victor Lamothe's intellectual contributions and dedicated work as an academician did not go unnoticed. In 1791, at a critical time, he was chosen to serve as the academy's treasurer.[84] As treasurer, Victor was responsible for a wide range of activities. The Academy of Bordeaux was a wealthy institution, possessing numerous properties that had been willed to it by earlier academicians. Victor was in charge of managing the properties and paying the employees of the academy.[85] More poignantly, he was responsible for placing the accounts of the academy in order when the revolutionary government closed it in late 1793. On the 9 Nivôse Year III of the Republic "one & indivisible," Victor Lamothe, "*ci-devant* Treasurer of the Academy," certified the accounts for the previous year, and turned the books in to the government, finalizing the dissolution of the eighty-year-old academy.[86]

Victor's participation in the Academy of Bordeaux was undoubtedly satisfying and beneficial to him. Among the members were many of his friends and colleagues from the Compagnie des médecins, and he had a friendly relationship with the perpetual secretary Lamontagne, with whom he worked closely during his tenure as treasurer.[87] The academy also provided intellectual stimulation, as Victor kept abreast of new discoveries and shared scientific observations with fellow members, such as those concerning the properties of electricity.[88] Victor demonstrated humanitarian concerns as well. His interest in African slaves and the foundlings suggests a desire to ameliorate the condition of the less fortunate, and his

82. BM Ms. 828 (XCIII), Journal maintained by M. de Ladebat, 20 July–17 August 1783, Nos. 19–23.

83. M. Capelle, "Notice sur M. le Docteur Lamothe," in *Actes de Académie nationale des sciences, belles-lettres et arts de Bordeaux*, vol. 1819, 13 May 1824, 108.

84. ADG D 58, Académie de Bordeaux, Accounts for 1791.

85. ADG, three *baux à loyer*: 3E 21736, 21 March 1792; 3E 13083, 25 January 1793; and 3E 21738, 20 June 1793. Also see D 59, Académie de Bordeaux.

86. ADG D 58, Académie de Bordeaux,"Relevé du livre de compte de l'Académie des sciences de Bordeaux: Gestion de son trésorier. Le citoyen Lamothe, 1792–3."

87. See, for example, BM Ms. 828 (XXIX), Letter from Victor Lamothe to François de Lamontagne, 11 February 1786, No. 52; and ADG D 59, Académie de Bordeaux, passim.

88. BM Ms. 828 (XXIII), "Extrait de deux lettres écrites de Paris par. M. de Ladebat à Lamothe sur le paratonnerre," September 1789, No. 12.

medical training made him sensitive to matters of public health. While today we may question the "humanitarianism" in conducting sometimes fatal experiments on abandoned babies, or in saving African slaves on the Middle Passage only to send them into the equally lethal sugar fields of the New World, the academicians viewed their efforts as serving the public utility. If they behaved as social engineers, and seemed quite callous at times—recall the exhortation of the academy to find the "most economical method" of feeding the foundlings—it was because they believed that they were serving a greater good.

Victor's title of academician contributed to his status in Bordeaux, both socially and intellectually. His attachment to the academy was reflected in his decision to participate in the reestablishment of the academy in 1797 under the Directory.[89] The scientific and utilitarian orientation of the Academy of Bordeaux suited Victor's interests and temperament. Similarly, the artistic focus of the newer Academy of Bordeaux, the Academy of Painting, Sculpture, and Architecture, attracted the attentions of his brother Delphin.

2. The Academy of Painting, Sculpture, and Civil and Naval Architecture of Bordeaux

The Académie royale des belles-lettres, sciences et arts of Bordeaux was one of the best known and most prestigious of the provincial academies. But it was not the only academy in Bordeaux. Another was established in 1768, which, for the next twenty-five years, would play an important role in fostering the *beaux-arts*.

The goal of the Académie de peinture, sculpture et architecture civile et navale de Bordeaux was to promote and support the artists and architects of Bordeaux.[90] Inspired by the discourse of a Maître Descamps of the Academy of Sculpture in Rouen, several Bordelais artists and architects,

89. The new academy was called the Société d'histoire naturelle. Jean de Feytaud, "L'Académie de Bordeaux depuis la Révolution," *Revue historique de Bordeaux et du département de la Gironde* 27 (1978–79): 193–94; Dr. Charles Dubreuilh, *Eloge académique de Victor de Lamothe* (Bordeaux: Emile Crugy, 1869), 16–17.

90. BM Ms. 1541, "Annales de l'Académie de peinture, sculpture et architecture civile et navale de Bordeaux," by Jules Delpit, 1–3. These *annales*, composed in the nineteenth century by Delpit, city historian of Bordeaux, are based on the archives and registers of the Académie de peinture, sculpture

amateur and professional, banded together in 1768 to form the Academy of Painting, Sculpture, and Architecture of Bordeaux.[91] The first meeting was held on 18 June 1768 in the *hôtel de ville*.[92] The founders, mainly artists, were soon joined by other city notables equally committed to the arts, to the public good, and no doubt to their own social standing; included among them was Delphin de Lamothe. Members were classified as honorary amateurs, amateur associates, artists, and foreign or corresponding associates. Delphin joined as an amateur associate in March 1770.[93]

A strong element of civic pride lay behind the decision of the artists and amateurs of Bordeaux to establish this academy.[94] The art connoisseurs of Bordeaux were tired of losing their most talented artists to the powerful allure of Paris.[95] Even worse, other towns had already established similar academies, leaving behind the "second city of France."[96] Urging the mayor, deputy mayor, and *jurats* to support the new academy, Delphin de Lamothe stressed that: "those of enlightened tastes and political wisdom will understand immediately the utility of this institution similar to those that Lyon, Toulouse, Rouen, and other less important cities have eagerly established, in emulation of the Capital."[97] This appeal to civic pride was important, for eighteenth-century Bordeaux was a city of merchants, not known as supporters of the arts.[98] However, the members of the academy made it their goal to persuade the citizens of this *ville marchande* that commerce and appreciation of the arts were not mutually exclusive. Men

---

et architecture civile et navale of Bordeaux. The archives of the academy are in two volumes, BM Ms. 1233–34.

91. BM Ms. 1603, Folio 3, "Notes et souvenirs d'un artiste octogénaire de 1778 à 1798": Memoirs of Pierre Lacour, 23.

92. Bernadau, *Annales politiques*, 202.

93. BM Ms. 1541, "Annales," 3. All of the original founders were Bordelais artists, except for M. Douat, *avocat général* of the Cour des aides. See BM Ms. 1603, Folio 3, Memoirs of Pierre Lacour, 23; and BM Ms. 1233, 31–33. This is dated 1769, but corrected by Jules Delpit to March 1770.

94. An earlier academy of arts in Bordeaux, founded in 1691, had lasted barely twenty years, because of lack of financial support. BM Ms. 1603, Folio 3, Memoirs of Pierre Lacour, 22; Jules Delpit, *Fragment de l'histoire des arts à Bordeaux: Académie de peinture et sculpture sous Louis XIV*, (Bordeaux: G. Gounouilhou, 1853), 528 and 551; and Charles Marionneau, *Les Beaux-arts à Bordeaux* (Bordeaux: G. Gounouilhou, 1892), 17–18.

95. BM Ms. 1233, 10 January 1778, 455–64; and Charles Marionneau, *Les Salons bordelais ou expositions des Beaux-arts à Bordeaux au XVIIIe siècle (1771–1787) avec des notes biographiques sur les artistes qui figurèrent à ces expositions* (Bordeaux: Vve. Moquet, 1883), vii-viii.

96. BM Ms. 1603, Folio 3, Memoirs of Pierre Lacour, 23.

97. BM Ms. 1233, 28(?) December 1772, 119–21.

98. BM Ms. 1233, 23 January 1774, 233–43.

of affairs were invited to participate in the academy, and by 1778, the list of eleven amateur associates included three *négociants*.[99] The academy also appealed to the general population of Bordeaux by stressing its support for architecture, opening a school for this discipline in May 1772.[100] In this heyday of city planning, when Bordeaux was celebrated for its architectural splendor, architecture was the most popular of the Bordelais arts.[101]

Despite these efforts to court the "enlightened" and wealthy population of Bordeaux, the archives of the Academy of Painting, Sculpture, and Architecture of Bordeaux chronicle the uncertainty, the financial problems, and the difficulties this academy experienced in obtaining official support during its early years, in contrast to the well-connected and substantially endowed Academy of *Belles-Lettres*, Sciences, and Arts of Bordeaux. Yet Delphin de Lamothe devoted long hours to the survival and advancement of this new academy. Why did he make this academy such a priority during the ten years that he served as perpetual secretary? His interest in the *beaux-arts* and his talent as an amateur artist were factors.[102] As a proud citizen of Bordeaux, he undoubtedly felt a desire and an obligation to promote the arts in his city. But Delphin also may have seen participation in this budding academy as a means of creating a name for himself. In 1770, he had not yet been invited to join the Academy of Bordeaux, despite the fact that his younger brother Victor had joined a year earlier. True, Delphin's interests were more focused on history and the arts than on the natural sciences so appreciated by Victor at the Academy of Bordeaux. But as a man who saw himself as a member of "enlightened" Bordelais society, Delphin must have craved the cachet attached to the

99. BM Ms. 1233, "Tableau de Messieurs de l'Académie de peinture, sculpture et architecture de Bordeaux," 507–11. Delphin de Lamothe spoke in highly flattering terms of the union of the "génie du commerce" with the enjoyment of art in his discourses welcoming *négociants* as members of the academy. See, for example, January 1777, 443. The academy also appealed to the merchants of the city by emphasizing maritime art and architecture, adding the modifier "civile et navale" to its name.

100. BM Ms. 1233, 1 May 1772, 111–13.

101. William Doyle notes the admiring comments of various visitors to Bordeaux in the late eighteenth century in *The Parlement of Bordeaux and the End of the Old Regime, 1771–1790* (New York: St. Martin's Press, 1974), 1–2. Architecture was the art most strongly encouraged and favored in eighteenth-century Bordeaux, according to Paul Butel and Jean-Pierre Poussou, *La Vie quotidienne à Bordeaux*, 240. See Pariset, *Bordeaux aux XVIIIe siècle*, 533–647, for an overview of the architectural improvements to Bordeaux throughout the century.

102. Delpit, *Notes biographiques sur les Messieurs de Lamothe* (Bordeaux: Balarac Jeune, 1846), 13. Throughout the Lamothe Family Letters, the family members, and especially Delphin, express great interest in art and painting. In 1765, he subscribed to the "Vües de Vernet," a collection of landscape paintings by Claude-Joseph Vernet, celebrated painter and future member of the Académie de peinture, sculpture et architecture of Bordeaux. Lamothe Family Letters, Delphin to Victor and Alexandre, 19 February 1765.

title of academician.[103] Moreover, did he feel a certain amount of envy for the friend of his youth, François de Lamontagne, the celebrated secretary of the Academy of Bordeaux? Upon his election in 1755, Lamontagne had referred to the "honor and especially the burden" of his new position, but Delphin may have recognized the false modesty of this formula.[104] His election as secretary of his own academy must have given Delphin a certain satisfaction and pride. Both disinterested concern for the public good and a desire to secure his own status were driving forces behind Delphin's active participation in the new academy.

The conflation of the sentiments of public service and personal honor was evident in Delphin de Lamothe's well-crafted reception address before the academy in March 1770:

> It is not then extraordinary that *belles lettres* & the *beaux arts* seek to unite; both equally children of genius; the same fire warms them; they seek the same goals, that of public utility, the only [goal] worthy of great souls.
>
> I could say, Messieurs, that it is also the only which has assembled us here; I should then pay tribute to the nobility, the unselfishness, and the patriotism of your enterprise; but the honor that you do me to invite me to join you today, in fact gives me such personal interest in that which concerns you that I hold back the truths that would become suspect from my lips: I thus confine myself to thanking you for the place that you have accorded me; I will do more, I will try to deserve it.[105]

Delphin's noble sentiments both impressed his colleagues and apparently reflected their own, for, less than a year later, he was named secretary of the new academy.[106] The next September, he was elected director, a one-year term.[107]

Delphin discussed the goals of the academy and his perceived role as secretary in a speech in which he stressed that "the principle functions of the Secretary of an Academy are to search with zeal & to propose all the means that can maintain the taste & love for work, increase knowledge &

103. In a letter to M. de Formey, Delphin referred to the members of the Academy of Bordeaux as "gens de distinction." Formey Correspondence, *Archives historiques*, Letter of 24 February 1750, 249.

104. Courteault, "Notice sur François de Lamontaigne," XVIII.

105. BM Ms. 1233, March 1770, 31–33.

106. BM Ms. 1541, "Annales," 26 February 1771, 33.

107. BM Ms. 1541, "Annales," 15 September 1771, 36.

obtain news."[108] As secretary, Delphin considered it his duty to offer practical suggestions for the conduct of the academy's sessions.[109] He advised strongly that the academy keep its deliberations private in order to encourage frank discussion and to prevent gossip.[110] He obviously preferred a clublike atmosphere. Delphin also lectured his fellow members upon their duties as academicians: to nurture "mutual affection, the bonds of esteem & of reciprocal consideration [that] are the foundation upon which the whole structure depends," to give mutual aid and support, and to practice regular attendance at the assemblies.[111] For Delphin, privacy and friendship served as ideals for the academic body.

As director, Delphin outlined three main goals toward which he urged the academy to direct its efforts: to solicit and obtain letters patent confirming the establishment of the academy; to prescribe a standard procedure for the reception of new members to avoid jealousy and accusations of favoritism; and to organize courses in architecture and anatomy to expand the academy's curriculum.[112] It was the first of these goals, as well as continuing efforts to obtain financial support and favors from the city of Bordeaux, that would occupy most of Delphin's tenure as secretary.

In the corporate society of Old Regime France, it was important for all groups, whether academic, artisanal, or professional, to have a legal existence recognized by the state. This legal existence was conferred through letters patent, establishing regulations, granting the king's protection, and giving the organization legitimacy and prestige.[113] The members of the academy recognized the need to obtain these letters patent, and appointed a four-member commission headed by Delphin de Lamothe to pursue the matter.[114] It was not an easy task. Ten years of constant effort were required before Bordeaux's Academy of Arts was accorded official existence in November 1779.[115]

---

108. BM Ms. 1233, 10 May 1771, 65–67.
109. Ibid.
110. BM Ms. 1233, 1771, 69–71.
111. Ibid.
112. BM Ms. 1233, 1772, 73–75.
113. Roche, "Milieux académiques provinciaux," 108; Mousnier, *The Institutions of France*, 430 and 455–57.
114. BM Ms. 1541, "Annales," 12 January 1772, 37.
115. The letters patent were accorded to the academy on 14 November 1779 and registered in parlement on 23 February 1780. See title page of *Lettres-Patentes et Statuts, pour l'Académie de peinture, sculpture et architecture civile et navale de Bordeaux* [du 25 Mai 1780] (Bordeaux: Chez Racle, 1780).

The assistance of powerful protectors, such as the city's *jurats*, mayor, and deputy mayor, as well as the duc de Richelieu, the maréchal de Mouchy (commander at Bordeaux), and the comte d'Angiviller, was necessary to achieve this goal, and the members of the academy courted them assiduously.[116] Even so, the academy faced difficulties obtaining its letters patent. A major problem was the objections of the members of the Academy of Painting in Paris to allowing its counterpart in Bordeaux to bear the title of Académie royale.[117] Eventually, the Bordeaux Academy forfeited some of its pride and independence by renouncing the title "royal," and accepting a subordinate association with the Académie royale de peinture de Paris.[118] These concessions allowed the Academy of Painting, Sculpture, and Civil and Naval Architecture of Bordeaux to finally obtain its letters patent in November 1779.[119] To a large extent, Delphin, in his role as perpetual secretary, was responsible for the tedious administrative work that brought the academy this new and elevated rank, a fact that surely brought him personal satisfaction as well as the appreciation and respect of his fellow academicians.[120]

Although it was a rich city, support for the arts was not a priority in predominantly commercial Bordeaux. The academy addressed the *jurats* plaintively in April 1769, pointing out the substantial expenses related to the functioning of the free school of design that the members of the academy were currently forced to fund out of their own pockets, including the payment of models, utilities, the wages of the concierge, and the purchase of antique figures, along with other essential expenses.[121] They suggested an annual contribution by the city, as well as certain privileges for academy members, including exemption from militia duty. This support would allow the academy to "acquire a solid and durable existence" and to continue to recruit professors, who, the *jurats* were reminded, received no remuneration at this time for their courses at the academy. In

116. BM Ms. 1233, April 1769, 25–26; 14 February 1772, 109; 17 December 1772, 123; 1 December 1772, 129–31; 28(?) December 1772, 119–21; 29(?) December 1772, 137–39; 1772, 133–35; 2 February 1773, 189–91; 1775, 52; 10 January 1778, 455–64; and BM Ms. 1541, "Annales," 25 August 1770, 31; 22 January 1775, 70.
117. BM Ms. 1541, "Annales," 9 May 1778, 84.
118. Pariset, *Bordeaux au XVIIIe siècle*, 650–51.
119. *Almanach historique de la province de Guienne* (Bordeaux, 1788), 221–22.
120. BM Ms. 1233, 14 February 1772, 109; "Projets de lettres patentes," from 1772, undated and 1778, 473–96; BM Ms. 1234, 12 September 1780, 39–41.
121. BM Ms. 1233, April 1769, 25–26.

a verbal response, the *jurats* expressed their distress at their inability to offer financial support at the present, but acceded to the request for exemption from guard duty for those members of the academy "who have need of it."[122] The *jurats* had also accorded the academy a room in which to hold their classes, but the city government was not willing to offer substantial financial support to a new and struggling organization.[123]

The academy, eager to obtain a promise of regular income, continued to petition the city council, and in 1771, the *jurats* agreed to provide 600 l. to help establish the free school of design.[124] In December 1772, Delphin de Lamothe requested an annual subvention of 1,200 l. to defray the costs of the establishment. In support, he provided a list of the expenses "that are absolutely necessary," mounting to 2,400 l., perhaps to impress the municipal governors with the restraint of his request. However, despite Delphin's disclaimers, the budget was not necessarily a modest one. Nearly half the expenses were associated with maintenance (including a concierge) and the cost of furnishings, while only 1,300 l. were earmarked for the necessary art supplies (see Appendix V).[125] The *jurats* declined to grant the academy 1,200 l. per year, but in March 1773 the *jurats* once again accorded them 600 l.[126]

As the academy became better established, the *jurats* began to look more favorably upon its petitions.[127] The city continued to contribute to the expenses of the academy, and in 1777, the intendant of the Guyenne, M. Dupré de St. Maur, offered 25 louis d'or (550 l.) as well.[128] The city also agreed to underwrite the cost of medals to encourage and reward six student artists of the free art school.[129] In 1778, the *jurats* asked the academy for "an account of all the expenses that it considers suitable to submit to the Assembly of Notables." As secretary, Delphin responded by outlining the many projects of the academy, including a plan to open a

122. BM Ms. 1233, April 1769, 25–26.

123. BM Ms. 1233, 28(?) December 1772, 119–21. After a series of moves, the academy was finally accorded stable lodgings. See 10 January 1777, 455–64.

124. *Archives municipales de Bordeaux, vol. 6: Inventaire sommaire des registres de la Jurade de Bordeaux, 1520–1783*, Dast le Vacher de Boisville, ed., (Bordeaux, 1896), 1:45–46.

125. BM Ms. 1233, 28(?) December 1772, 119–21.

126. BM Ms. 1541, "Annales," 14 March 1773, 50.

127. By 1774, the director of the academy, M. Laffon de Ladebat, noted, "We enjoy finally a bit more peace of mind, our existence is becoming less precarious." BM Ms. 1233, 8 May 1774, 291–97.

128. BM Ms. 1541, "Annales," 11 April 1777, 83.

129. BM Ms. 1233, 4 August 1777, 447–48.

school of naval architecture, and requested the substantial sum of 15,000 l. to encourage "the glory & the progress of the arts."[130]

With the acquisition of the letters patent in 1779, the Academy of Painting, Sculpture, and Civil and Naval Architecture of Bordeaux had finally arrived. Along with acquiring the legitimacy accorded through official recognition, the academy now had the right to claim financial assistance from the city. In 1780, it presented a budget to the city council, which demonstrated how its services and expenses had grown in the preceding ten years. Reflecting its goal of encouraging artists, the academy earmarked 1,456 l., 16 percent of the budget, for various artistic prizes and awards. In addition, 400 l. was set aside for the expenses associated with the art salons. However, in a major shift from the much more modest budget of 1772, 3,750 l.—40 percent of the total budget—was to be spent on the salaries of the professors and rector. Clearly, the professors were no longer all offering their services to the school for free. Only 400 l. were reserved for art materials, and 1,000 l. to pay the two models. The 500 l. for the concierge was now the major maintenance expense, for the city had agreed to provide heat and lighting for the school, as well as a room in which to hold classes. A final curious expense was the 1,200 l. for *jetons*, or tokens that were issued as vouchers for attendance at the academy's meetings (see Appendix VI).[131] This was a generous budget, and if provided entirely by the municipal government, undoubtedly strained the city's coffers. To supplement the financial assistance from the municipal government and the free professorial services offered by some of the artist members, the academy was forced to ask its members for periodic donations, presumably in addition to their dues.[132]

The zeal of the academicians to foster the arts in Bordeaux found two major outlets: the creation of the free school of design to encourage young artists, and frequent salons to display the works of the artists associated with the school. This *école* was the pride of the academy, and garnered the greatest support from the local authorities. In 1776, the teaching staff was composed of six painters, five sculptors, one engraver, three architects, two professors of perspective, and two professors of anatomy.[133] In

---

130. BM Ms. 1233, 10 January 1778, 455–64.
131. BM Ms. 1233, 14 March 1780, 503.
132. BM Ms. 1233, 25 July 1773, 193, and 30 March 1775, 355–57; 18 September 1775, 361; 7 January 1776, 373; "Tableau général des contributions," 451. Members were expected to pay one louis (24 livres) in annual dues. Pariset, *Bordeaux au XVIIIe siècle*, 650.
133. Marionneau, *Les Salons bordelais*, vii.

addition to teaching the art and design classes, associated professors
staffed the other courses: civil and naval architecture, geometry, perspective, and anatomy.[134]

According to Article XI of the statutes of the academy, a public
exhibition, modeled after the Paris salons, of the paintings, sculptures, and
designs of the academicians and the *agréés* was to be held biennially. In
reality, they were held in 1771, 1772, 1774, 1776, 1782, and 1787.[135] Like
the classes, these expositions were for the art students, and were expected
to "excite still more their nascent emulation."[136] They were also held to
display the fruits of the academy, and perhaps to attract the financial and
moral support of the Bordelais community.[137]

It is unlikely that many of the paintings or sculptures displayed at these
salons constituted great works of art, especially compared with the salons
of Paris.[138] With the exception of a few artists, such as Claude-Joseph
Vernet *aîné*, the celebrated painter of seascapes, members of the academy
did not go on to fame and fortune.[139] There were few masterpieces among
the works of the academy artists.[140] But the members of the academy
accomplished their goals of training budding artists, and demonstrating
that the city of Bordeaux could foster the arts independently of Paris. As
Marionneau, nineteenth-century historiographer of Bordeaux's art scene,
points out, "The Bordelais exhibitions were of real local interest; they demonstrated an autonomy [from Paris] that has completely disappeared."[141]

The free school and the salons were the most visible undertakings of the
academy, but the members also occupied themselves with other activities.

134. BM Ms. 1603, Folio 3, Memoirs of Pierre Lacour, 25.

135. Marionneau, *Les Salons bordelais*, x–xi. Salons exhibiting the works of members of the Académie
royale de peinture et de sculpture were organized in Paris beginning in 1667 and were held regularly
from 1737 on. See Michael Fried, *Absorption and Theatricality: Painting and Beholder in the Age of Diderot*
(Berkeley and Los Angeles: University of California Press, 1980), esp. 180.

136. BM Ms. 1233, 14 November 1779, 505.

137. Marionneau, *Les Salons bordelais*, x.

138. Marionneau, *Les Salons bordelais*, viii. According to Pierre, director of the Académie de peinture
of Paris in 1778, the Academy of Bordeaux consisted of "des artistes au dessous du médiocre." Pariset,
Bordeaux au XVIIIe siècle, 650.

139. BM Ms. 1460, "Journal," 14 May 1757, 168. Charles Marionneau offers a short biography of
each of the artists represented at the salons in his "Notices biographiques sur les Membres de
l'Académie de peinture, sculpture et architecture civile et navale de Bordeaux qui prirent part, dans
cette ville, aux expositions des beaux-arts de 1771 à 1787," in *Les Salons bordelais*.

140. Marionneau, *Les Salons bordelais* lists the works of art exhibited at the expositions from 1771 to
1787.

141. Ibid., vii.

Like most provincial academies, that of Bordeaux cultivated ties with fellow academies. In 1773, the academy entered into correspondence with its counterpart in Poitiers.[142] The members also contributed their expertise in critiquing and advising outside projects.[143] In addition, the academy was called upon to use its artistic knowledge to settle a dispute between two rival masonry corporations in 1773 concerning a design competition. The commission appointed by the academy restaged the competition, and diplomatically brought the contest to a close, praising the talent and the zeal of both participants and awarding a cash prize and medal to each.[144] Their deft handling of the affair won the praise and gratitude of the city.[145]

Delphin de Lamothe took his duties as both secretary and academician seriously. In addition to offering his time and energy, he presented numerous gifts to the academy, including books, prints, and poems.[146] He also assisted individual artists, many of whom were personal friends and neighbors. It was upon his recommendation that the painter Taillasson was admitted into the academy in 1774.[147] He was a stalwart defender of the position of honor due artists and amateurs, and took measures to assist two of his fellow academicians when an artisanal guild tried to include them on its tax rolls.[148] The honor of the artists of the academy reflected upon him as well.

Delphin de Lamothe's many services as well as his diplomatic skills and

142. BM Ms. 1233, 21 September 1773, 201–4. Delphin was a corresponding member of the Academy of Poitiers.

143. These included suggestions for the proposed construction of the *hôtel de ville* and reviews of a prospectus for a *journal de marine* and of a proposal for "a new architectural order." See BM Ms. 1233, 29 June 1770, 39–44; 5 August 1776, 420–27; June–July 1776, 387–417.

144. BM Ms. 1233. The Archives of the Académie de peinture, sculpture et architecture conserve numerous documents dealing with this affair in 1773 and 1774, 205–329. Local historian Jules Delpit also wrote a detailed account of the proceedings, *Un Épisode de l'histoire de l'Académie des beaux-arts à Bordeaux,* (Bordeaux: Chez Henry Faye, 1851).

145. Delpit, *Un Épisode,* 15.

146. BM Ms. 1233, 10 May 1771, 65–67. See also BM Ms. 1541, "Annales," 31 September 1772, 43; 6 March 1774, 60; 18 September 1775, 74; and 11 February 1776, 75.

147. Charles Marionneau, *Les Vieux Souvenirs de la rue Neuve à Bordeaux par un vieil enfant de cette rue* (Bordeaux: Mme. Veuve Moquet, 1890), 63.

148. BM Ms. 1233, "A Monseigneur Esmengard, intendant en la Généralité de Guienne," 15 August 1773, 195–99. The corporation of Maîtres menuisiers, sculpteurs & ébenistes had tried to include Vernet and Deschamps on its tax rolls on the pretext that as sculptors they should be taxed as members of that corporation. Delphin turned to his legal training to defend exemption for these two men, claiming that they were artists, not artisans. See also BM Ms. 1233, 1771, 69–71; 29 August 1773, 185–87; and 10 January 1778, 455–64.

eloquence were recognized by the members of the academy. For example, he was always careful to give equal credit to the arts of painting and architecture, smoothing potential discord among the members of the academy.[149] He even served as an artistic model for the painter M. Henry, whose miniature *M. xxx, Professor at the University* was his reception piece for the academy.[150] After his death, the members of the academy recognized the important services that Delphin de Lamothe had rendered.[151] As late as 1790, the painter Leupold referred to him as "one of our orators, the memory of whom will always be fresh."[152]

In the years following Delphin's death in 1781, the academy never quite lived up to the hopes of its founders, becoming less active in the 1780s. Its position of authority concerning the arts was challenged by the Musée de Bordeaux, created in 1783, which had the additional cachet and local protection of its patron, Intendant Dupré de St. Maur.[153] In 1793, the Academy of Painting, Sculpture, and Architecture suffered the same fate as all "privileged associations" under the revolutionary government and was disbanded. The arts in Bordeaux suffered with its dissolution. In 1801, despite the presence of painter Pierre Lacour, son of one of the earliest members of the academy and respected artist, a visitor to Bordeaux remarked, "In Bordeaux, art is dying of starvation."[154]

Pierre Barrière has written disparagingly of the intellectual life of eighteenth-century Bordeaux, and it is true that this port city was more respected for its commercial activity and material wealth than for cultural éclat.[155] And yet, members of the academies of Bordeaux were firmly convinced of the value of their organizations and their contribution to the public good. The practical scientific experiments and learned papers requested by the Academy of Bordeaux all aimed to improve the lot of humanity. Although we may question the actual "humanitarianism" of some of those efforts, we should not ignore the fact that the academicians

149. BM Ms. 1541, "Annales," 1 May 1772, 41; and BM Ms. 1233, 1772, 111–13. See also BM Ms. 1541, "Annales," 13 May 1780, 91–92.

150. BM Ms. 1541, "Annales," 27 August 1774, 65.

151. BM Ms. 1541, "Annales," 13 January 1781, 95; 27 January 1781, 96; and 22 December 1781, 101.

152. BM Ms. 1234, 13 March 1790, 601.

153. Pariset, *Bordeaux au XVIIIe siècle*, 654.

154. Meaudre de Lapouyade, *Voyage d'un allemand à Bordeaux en 1801* (Bordeaux: G. Gounouilhou, 1912), 42.

155. Pierre Barrière, "Bordeaux dans la vie intellectuelle française," *Revue historique de Bordeaux et du département de la Gironde* 3 (1954): 5–22.

saw their efforts as beneficial to humankind. The Academy of Painting, Sculpture, and Architecture envisioned a similarly lofty mission for itself. The "public" that this academy purported to serve may have been a narrow one—it is unlikely that the urban poor frequented the art salons of the academy—but its members believed in the civic value of nurturing a local artistic milieu.

The academies attracted and recruited a certain type of individual—an educated man, a man of the Enlightenment, dedicated to progress and the public good, with a certain amount of leisure and standing in the community—men such as the Lamothe brothers. Norman Hampson argues that these more eminent members of the liberal professions, such as barristers and doctors, formed a cultural subclass of their own and dominated intellectual life in the provinces. The nature of their professions gave them both a concern for public affairs and familiarity with abstract ideas, which made them ideal candidates for the academies.[156]

Victor and Delphin de Lamothe applied themselves wholeheartedly to the goals and missions of their academies, convinced that they were contributing to the common good and to the glory of their *patrie* of Bordeaux. Both subscribed to the values of hard work and zeal for their academy. In an essay titled "What Must Be the Zeal of the Academician for the Advancement of His Academy," Delphin stated emphatically that it could not be *trop vif*, and continued: "A noble emulation must animate them . . . a blameworthy halfheartedness in their operations announces the impending ruin of the edifice. The name of academician, far from being an honorable title for anyone who refuses to work, makes him contemptible in the eyes of his fellow members."[157] Delphin and Victor took this declaration seriously, especially the admonitions against "half-heartedness" and its call for a "noble emulation." The academician was asked to heed Delphin's exhortations to perform his civic responsibilities.

At the same time, the motives of the Lamothe brothers in joining these academies were not purely altruistic. In his definition of the academician, Daniel Roche emphasizes his privileged position, and Roger Hahn asserts that "elitism was the very essence of the institution." Despite its "utility" and contributions to the progress of science, the structure of the academy,

---

156. Norman Hampson, *The Enlightenment: An Evaluation of Its Assumptions, Attitudes, and Values* (Harmondsworth: Penguin, 1976), 136.

157. AM Fonds Delpit, No. 127, #2, "Quel doit etre le zele d'un accademicien pour l'avancement de son accademie," 1745. The date of this essay means that it was written long before Delphin joined either of the academies, and the intended audience is not indicated.

as an "aristocracy in a democratic world," doomed it in the eyes of the revolutionaries in 1793.[158] In Bordeaux as well, academies recruited the elite of society, and while the composition of the Academy of Bordeaux became progressively nonnoble as the eighteenth century drew to a close, there remained a special distinction associated with the title of academician. Despite the honors that came to him in the early 1770s, Delphin still yearned for recognition of his status and learning that would only come when he was elected to the Academy of Bordeaux. When that time finally came in 1777, he eloquently recognized the importance of this honor: "For how many years have I dared in secret to aspire to this honor? My heart, was it not ablaze . . . I said to myself, perhaps I, too, could one day show my zeal & my respect to this *corps*: perhaps I could even share its work. These wishes, I formulated them in secret: now, I am permitted to carry them out."[159] Behind the ceremonial formula was surely an authentic sense of belonging to a distinguished body.

The academies were an important manifestation of the surge in societies, clubs, salons, and circles—in a phrase, of "bourgeois sociability"—under the Old Regime. Participation in these gatherings was essential to the making of the *honnête homme* of the eighteenth century, and the Lamothe brothers benefited from the cultural brilliance of the academies. The Revolution, despite the abolition of the academies in 1793, did not bring an end to this "intellectual sociability." Academies were replaced for a time by more politically oriented clubs. Still, in 1797, the Academy of Bordeaux was reorganized under a different name, but with the same goals, values, and even membership it had had before the Revolution. In this sense, the academies were forerunners of the *cercles bourgeois* of the nineteenth century.[160]

158. Roche, "Milieux académiques provinciaux," 107; Hahn, *Anatomy of a Scientific Institution*, 225.

159. AM Fonds Delpit, No. 127, #3, "Compliment de reception à l'Académie des sciences le 16 fevrier 1777, par Lamothe p.e.d.f."

160. For a discussion of the composition and function of these "circles" of the nineteenth century, see Agulhon, *Le Cercle dans la France bourgeoise*.

"Savoir et Savoir-Vivre"

The Cultural Life of the Lamothe Brothers

"I believe that it is more essential for a physician than for many others who take up a serious profession to have *savoir-vivre*, courtesy, ease of spirit, and manners . . . [the best way to achieve this] besides observing society [*du monde*], a selected society, is through literature; I would always want a tasteful book on my table, a Virgil, a Horace, a Racine, a Rousseau, or some good Latin or French historian, to open during those idle moments."[1]

Alexis Lamothe's admonition to his younger brother Victor in 1757 betrayed a certain preoccupation with the manners, education, and life-style appropriate to a man of his position. The social circle of the Lamothe family included the intellectual elite of Bordelais society—other lawyers, doctors, noble men of leisure, and *parlementaires*. The company they sought included men and women of learning, and they were eager to be considered the equal of any individual in erudition and knowledge, if not in social rank. While the elite of Bordelais society, the richest *parlementaires*, the proprietors of the Médoc vineyards, and the wealthy overseas merchants, pursued a lifestyle to which the middle-class Lamothes, more austere and frugal, could not aspire, they still mixed together in the Academy of Bordeaux and in the salons of Madame Duplessy. To fit into this society, the Lamothe brothers carefully cultivated their public images

---

1. Lamothe Family Letters, Alexis to Victor, undated, 1757.

to conform to the ideal of the well-rounded and enlightened individual. Their social and intellectual behavior surely parallels that of other members of their social group.

And yet it is too facile to attribute the many and varied cultural activities of Delphin, Alexis, Victor, and their father only to the exigencies of polite society. While it is true that many of their endeavors took place in the public sphere and reflected a desire to secure a reputation as men of culture, they pursued other interests in private for reasons of personal cultivation, or a rather eclectic curiosity. The letters and private papers of the Lamothe family indicate a broad range of elevated interests on the part of the brothers, but also provide new evidence of the truth of Robert Darnton's thesis on the penetration of "low-life literature" in the later years of the eighteenth century among all classes of society.[2]

Provincial French society of the eighteenth century had its own way of defining a cultivated individual and, especially, a cultivated man. He was expected to demonstrate a certain *savoir-vivre*, familiarity with the right books, ideas, and political concerns. He had to have a passing knowledge of the arts, as well as of literature, history, and science. The cultivated man was further expected to be at ease in society, to show the proper politeness to women, and to fit in among people of his class.[3] The Lamothes internalized these values and sought to convey the correct impression among friends and acquaintances.

As both producers and consumers of the cultural output of the Enlightenment, the Lamothes played an active role in the creation of a political, artistic, and professional culture in prerevolutionary Bordeaux.[4] The cultural practices of the eighteenth century are of particular interest to the student of French history because of their implications for the dramatic upheavals of 1789. In his classic work on the intellectual origins of the French Revolution, Daniel Mornet argues that the diffusion and penetration of new ideas, the growth of skepticism, social and political anxiety,

---

2. Robert Darnton, "The High Enlightenment and the Low-Life of Literature," *Past and Present*, no. 51 (May 1971): 81–115. See esp. 105–12. The Lamothe Family Papers, located in the Manuscripts Division of the Library of Congress, Washington, D.C., are loosely grouped into six folders, which were given working titles, but are not classified.

3. Dena Goodman discusses the key role of salons and *salonnières* in enforcing these rules of politeness in *The Republic of Letters: A Cultural History of the French Enlightenment* (Ithaca: Cornell University Press, 1994), esp. chap. 3.

4. Roger Chartier argues that, like the producer of culture, the consumer of culture plays an active role in shaping the *mentalité* of a society. See *Cultural History: Between Practice and Representation*, trans. Lydia G. Cochrane (Ithaca: Cornell University Press, 1988), 40–45.

and a new spirit of curiosity dangerous to the established order were necessary preconditions for revolution.[5] In a modification of Mornet's thesis, Roger Chartier identifies "cultural shifts" that transformed Old Regime society and prepared the ground for revolutionary change.[6] While it is unlikely that the Lamothe brothers would have characterized their cultural activities as subversive in any way, they participated fully in the philosophical and scientific spirit of their time, following new trends, posing questions, and reexamining traditional ideas. An analysis of their interests, their activities, and their attitudes toward the cultural pursuits of their time provides new understanding of the subtle shifts in the mentality of the eighteenth-century professional—a social group whose members would play such an important revolutionary role.

1. Polite Society and the Public Persona

The members of the Lamothe family were highly conscious of their social image and the need to fit in. As Victor pursued his medical studies in Paris, his brothers frequently warned him of the importance of his public persona, especially for a provincial boy hoping to make a good impression as *honnête homme* in the brilliant capital:

> I must also recommend that you form your character as much as you can for society, where we must spend the major part of our lives, and taste the most agreeable moments; that comes only with keeping good company, studying the form that prevails, but you must not understand "good company" to be any sort of society [*toute sorte de monde*]; it is morals, politeness, and decency one must search, and they are not to be found everywhere. One can pick out a person who has associated with good company, and who has profited from it, which is nearly the same thing, as one distin-

5. Daniel Mornet, *Les Origines intellectuelles de la Révolution française, 1715–1787* (Paris: A. Colin, 1933), 469–77.

6. Roger Chartier, *The Cultural Origins of the French Revolution*, trans. Lydia G. Cochrane (Durham: Duke University Press, 1991), esp. 3–19 and 193–98. For an overview of recent historiography on the links between the Enlightenment and the French Revolution, see Thomas E. Kaiser, "This Strange Offspring of *Philosophie*: Recent Historiographical Problems in Relating the Enlightenment to the French Revolution," *French Historical Studies* 15 (Spring 1988): 549–62.

guishes a young man from Paris by the accent, a single glance or
the pronunciation of a single word is enough to determine these
things.[7]

Delphin and Alexis obviously followed their own advice, for they
figured among the "popular" set in Bordelais society. Although it is
doubtful that they were invited to the *hôtels* of the high nobility, or to the
gaming tables of the provincial governor, the maréchal de Richelieu, they
still associated with the intellectual society of Bordeaux, the traditional
professional and *parlementaire* elite of the city.[8] Delphin may have had
contact with the illustrious Montesquieu as a young man.[9] The Lamothe
brothers were not intimates of Monsieur de la Brède, but they did
participate in his social orbit as guests at the salon of Madame Duplessy.[10]

The salon was a fixture of eighteenth-century France, both in Paris and
in the provinces, and played an important role, complementing the official
existence of the academies. While primarily serving as a form of convivi-
ality, a meeting place for intellectuals to share the pleasures of conversation, reading, and gambling, the salon also became a place to critically
discuss the arts, literature, and eventually politics. Its private status allowed
much greater liberty than did the officially regulated academies.[11] The

7. Alexis to Victor, 22 January 1759. Alexis's definition of polite behavior was clearly patterned
on the courtesy of the nobility, reflecting bourgeois appropriation of certain aspects of noble behavior
outlined by Robert A. Nye in *Masculinity and Male Codes of Honor in Modern France* (New York: Oxford
University Press, 1993), 31–46. See also Goodman, *The Republic of Letters*, 111–16.

8. When he suggested to Victor in 1764 that he seek an audience with the maréchal de Richelieu,
Alexis specified that "nous ne sommes pas connus de luy." Alexis to Victor, 21 January 1764. The
maréchal's decadent lifestyle was notorious in Bordeaux, and more than one man reputedly lost his
fortune gambling at his home. Patrice-John O'Reilly, *Histoire complète de Bordeaux*, 2d ed. (Bordeaux and
Paris: Chez J. Delmas and Chez Furne, 1863), 3:303–4; A. Grellet-Dumazeau, *La Société bordelaise sous
Louis XV et le salon de Mme Duplessy* (Bordeaux and Paris: Feret et Fils and Libraires Associés, 1897),
211–14.

9. Juin–Mai 1749.—Lettres de Simon-Delphin de Lamothe à M. Formey, historiographe de
l'Académie royale des sciences de Berlin, sur le projet du roi de Prusse pour la réformation de la justice,
Archives historiques du département de la Gironde (Paris and Bordeaux, 1897), 32:249.

10. For an interesting overview of eighteenth-century Bordelais society, especially that surrounding the salon of Madame Duplessy, see Grellet-Dumazeau, *La Société bordelaise.*

11. Chartier, *The Cultural Origins of the French Revolution*, 154–55; Goodman, *The Republic of Letters.*
Jürgen Habermas identifies the salons as key to the "civil public sphere" that emerged in eighteenth-
century France, and sees them as crucial to the development of a "public opinion." *The Structural
Transformation of the Public Sphere: An Inquiry into a Category of Bourgeois Society*, trans. Thomas Burger and
Frederick Lawrence (Cambridge: MIT Press, 1989), esp. 33–34, 50–51, and 67–69. For Habermas's
views on the salons, see Benjamin Nathans, "Habermas's 'Public Sphere' in the Era of the French
Revolution," *French Historical Studies* 16 (Spring 1991): 624. For a commentary on both Chartier and

salons also provided an opportunity for the social classes to mix, so that middle-class professionals such as the Lamothe brothers were welcomed to the Duplessy household on the same footing as the daughter of the maréchal de Richelieu, Madame d'Egmont.[12] While we must not exaggerate the ties of the Lamothe brothers to the rich and powerful, their education and position allowed them contact with the elite of Bordeaux society, most notably the wealthy and influential *parlementaires* of Bordeaux. This was not so unusual, and not only because they were all members of the legal world. By the second half of the eighteenth century, professionals such as lawyers and doctors were considered valuable contributors to enlightened society, as expertise and technical skills were increasingly appreciated, reflecting the growing influence of nonnoble professionals in the cultural realm.[13]

The salon of Madame Duplessy (the former Jeanne-Marie-Françoise de Chazot) was the best known in Bordeaux. Madame Duplessy, a devotee of natural history, opened her sumptuous house near the Jardin-Public to "local celebrities, *savants*, artists, women of wit: a complete phalanx of educated persons, of quick and judicious speech, of frank and communicative good humor."[14] Partisans of the Duplessy salon argued that it ceded nothing to those of Paris in culture and erudition, and Montesquieu was in frequent attendance when in Bordeaux. Those attending in the late 1760s included "M. de Baritaut of Soulignac, who made a specialty of the study of fossils;—M. Balan, of the *Cour des aides*, renowned naturalist . . .

Habermas, see Dena Goodman, "Public Sphere and Private Life: Toward a Synthesis of Current Historiographical Approaches to the Old Regime," *History and Theory* 31 (1992): 1–20; and Christine Adams, Jack R. Censer, and Lisa Jane Graham, eds., *Visions and Revisions of Eighteenth-Century France* (University Park: Penn State Press, 1997), 1–18.

12. Carolyn C. Lougee, in an analysis of seventeenth-century salon society, demonstrates that salon society was composed of persons from a variety of backgrounds, of diverse legal status, and from various social and occupational groups and concludes that there was a certain mixing of orders and social fusion. *Le Paradis des Femmes: Women, Salons and Social Stratification in Seventeenth-Century France* (Princeton: Princeton University Press, 1976), 113–70. Roger Chartier also acknowledges the social mixing that took place at these salons in the eighteenth century in *The Cultural Origins of the French Revolution*, 157, as does Dena Goodman in *The Republic of Letters*, 5.

13. Robert Darnton, *The Business of Enlightenment: A Publishing History of the* Encyclopédie, *1775–1800* (Cambridge: Harvard University Press, Belknap Press, 1979), 446–47. Sarah Maza notes that members of the legal profession in particular were increasingly conspicuous in social and cultural life after 1750. *Private Lives and Public Affairs: The Causes Célèbres of Prerevolutionary France* (Berkeley and Los Angeles: University of California Press, 1993), 90.

14. Grellet-Dumazeau, *La Société bordelaise*, 31. In *The Republic of Letters*, Dena Goodman focuses on the key role played by women in governing the salons.

François de Lamontagne, who had the honor of giving the eulogy at the academy for the author of the *Persian Letters*—*l'avocat général* Dudon, one of those elite spirits to whom humanity owes the abolition of the *question préparatoire* [a form of torture]—the *président* Antoine-Alexandre de Gascq . . . Jean-Baptiste de Secondat, agronomist and naturalist, worthy son of an illustrious father [Montesquieu]—Jacques Pelet d'Anglade, still under the spell of the conversation of Voltaire." Included among this distinguished crowd were "the Lamothe brothers, Alexis and Delphin, eminent jurisconsults, on the eve of publishing their commentary on the customary laws in effect in the jurisdiction of the Parlement of Guyenne."[15] Participation in the Duplessy salon allowed the Lamothe brothers to indulge their taste for art, literature, and the sciences and to discuss current intellectual and political topics in a freer and more critical tone than allowed by the authorized academies. Their inclusion is further indication of their respected status in Bordeaux society.[16]

Delphin, along with his father and brothers, also hosted social and intellectual gatherings at the Lamothe household on Rue Neuve, which were comprised of his colleagues from the bar, as well as fellow members of the Academy of Arts.[17] That these gatherings could be large and boisterous, with plenty of food and drink, is attested to by Marie Lamothe, who wrote to Victor about the party held at home following Delphin's election as syndic of the Compagnie des avocats. Marie was more concerned with the culinary than the intellectual pursuits of the lawyerly guests:

> They came here yesterday upon leaving the *palais*, after dinner, about one hundred-fifty or two hundred came to visit him, the front room, the salon, half of the courtyard and a part of the hall were often full . . . we had prepared a repast for them composed of a tart as big as a plate . . . twenty-four little [ ] sweetbreads . . . macaroons, twenty-four almond cakes, and as many cream cakes . . . we were obliged to send out in search of twenty-

15. Grellet-Dumazeau, *La Société bordelaise*, 248–49.

16. M. Paul Péquigont notes that Delphin de Lamothe "fréquentait assidûment le salon de Mme Duplessis, dont il était l'un des ornements." Péquigont, *Le Barreau de Bordeaux au XVIIIe siècle* (Bordeaux, 1903), 38.

17. See Charles Marionneau, *Les Vieux Souvenirs de la rue Neuve à Bordeaux par un vieil enfant de cette rue* (Bordeaux: Mme. Vve. Moquet, 1890), 65.

four tartlets, and . . . along with that lots of orgeat of limonade, wine, and a bit of water, it was a real fair here.[18]

Delphin and Alexis also chose a more formalized social setting to take part in intellectual pursuits. Beginning in the early 1700s, gatherings devoted to specific intellectual goals were very popular in Bordeaux. A wide variety of meetings and societies dedicated to scientific studies, literature, poetry, history, and theater became increasingly common throughout France.[19] With several of his young colleagues from the bar, Delphin de Lamothe helped to found the literary society of Bordeaux in 1744, and was named secretary of the group in 1745.[20] Alexis also participated in the literary society, and, as one of its most "distinguished members," gave the keynote speech at the opening meeting on 6 February 1757.[21] Delphin also played a part in organizing discussions on law, history, geography, poetry, and other popular topics.[22]

The participation of Delphin and Alexis in the salon and literary society of Bordeaux underlines their position as enlightened men of culture. But however erudite and educated they may have been, this alone would not have guaranteed their entry into Bordelais society. Each had also carefully learned and internalized the strictures of civility—the appropriate modesty, deference, and charm that would be expected especially of men of merit, but nonnoble origins, in the company of *gens de qualité*.[23] Delphin and Alexis's obvious personal success in Bordelais society lent special force to their admonitions to young Victor in Paris. The rules of *politesse* were

18. Marie to Victor, 28 May 1757.

19. Grellet-Dumazeau, *La Société bordelaise*, 110; Pierre Barrière, *La Vie intellectuelle en France du XVI siècle à l'époque contemporaine* (Paris: A. Michel, 1961), 299–300.

20. "Autographes des personnages ayant marqué dans l'histoire de Bordeaux et de la Guyenne," *Archives historiques de la Gironde* (Bordeaux, 1895), 30:232; Pierre Meller, *Essais généalogiques: Familles du bordelais/recueil factice de brochures concernant des familles* (Bordeaux: Feret et Fils, 1897), 28; Paul Courteault, "Notice sur François de Lamontaigne, in François de Lamontaigne, *Chronique bordelaise de François de Lamontaigne, conseiller au Parlement* (Bordeaux: Imprimeries Delmas, Chapons, Gounouilhou, 1926), XVII.

21. Edmond Faurie, *Eloge des frères Lamothe, avocats au Parlement de Bordeaux* (Bordeaux: Emile Crugy, 1850), 5–6.

22. Jules Delpit, *Notes biographiques sur les Messieurs de Lamothe* (Bordeaux: Balarac Jeune, 1846), 13; Albert Dujarric-Descombes, *Deux Ex-libris bordelais: Les Frères de Lamothe et l'abbé Desbiey* (Paris: H. Daragon, 1918), 7–8; Meller, *Essais généalogiques*, 28.

23. For an eighteenth-century guide to the behavior expected of the *honnête homme*, see A. Courtin, *Nouveau Traité de la civilité qui se pratique en France parmi les honnêtes gens* [nouvelle edition] (Paris: M. Josset, 1712); and Bernard Groethuysen, *The Bourgeois: Catholicism Versus Capitalism in Eighteenth-Century France*, trans. Mary Ilford (New York: Barrie & Rockliff the Cresset P., 1968), 233–39, on the "respectable citizen" of the eighteenth century.

first and most effectively instilled at home, in the family, and later in association with the public.

First and most important, it was necessary that Victor seek out "good company," despite his youth and inexperience: "It seems to me that it would be to your advantage to go most often where you can find the best company . . . you will feel a bit out of place and confused at first, but apart from the fact that you are still very young, it is necessary to make this little sacrifice in favor of the benefit that it will bring to you."[24] His brothers also suggested that Victor carefully examine the behavior of his relatives the Cotins.[25] It was only by associating with the correct society that Victor would learn the necessary *politesse* and obtain sufficient confidence to conduct himself as an *honnête homme*.

Another important quality of the *honnête homme* was a circumspect discretion in all things. Alexis recommended to Victor, "Conduct yourself in all things as a young man of spirit who knows all and who appears to know nothing in the eyes of people."[26] Alexis and Delphin expressed approval that Victor seemed well-informed concerning the affairs of the court, but strongly suggested that, while it was good to "see and hear all," he should "have, above all, *bouche cosu*." One could never tell when one's lack of discretion could lead to social blunders.[27]

A final important point was correct behavior with women, a skill that Delphin and Alexis had undoubtedly polished at the salon of Madame Duplessy. Neither of them underestimated the influence of women in society, and Alexis cautioned Victor, "The approval of women can often make the reputation of a physician, and they do not like coarseness."[28] He acknowledged the difficulty of learning the necessary gallantry in a university setting, but noted that "in dealing with society, and especially with women, and principally in the profession that you have chosen, you must have a certain natural turn of spirit that [allows you to] banter with delicacy, to flatter without affectation, but it is the end of the game that one learns only with practice."[29]

Victor was conscious of his lack of experience and sought the advice of

---

24. Alexis to Victor, 9 October 1757. Goodman also notes the centrality of association to reputation in *The Republic of Letters*, 116.

25. Alexis to Victor, 30 November 1757.

26. Alexis to Victor, 9 October 1757.

27. Alexis to Victor, 30 November 1757.

28. Alexis to Victor, undated 1757.

29. Alexis to Victor, 19 May 1760.

his older brothers on how best to improve his self-presentation. Delphin responded with kind words about Victor's good qualities, "a good heart, justice of spirit, gentle humor, a character that is kind and obliging," but stressed that he laughed too often and sometimes inappropriately, and had an unfortunate tendency to argue with too much tenacity. Furthermore: "You do not have enough knowledge of fables, of history, that of France as well as Greece & Rome. I would like for you to have a little more familiarity with these subjects, not to know them thoroughly, but so that you do not commit anachronisms, or appear completely "green" [*tout à fait neuf*] among those people who consider them." Alexis agreed with Delphin's assessment of the need to have at least a passing knowledge of literature, history, current events, and the arts, and reproved Victor: "You read neither the gazette, nor *Mercure*, nor journals, you must try to do so, you can find out about the news or literature that one often discusses in conversation." However, Delphin did not consider Victor's social flaws irremedial, and ended his lecture teasingly: "There you have it for now, my dear doctor, all of the reprehensible things I have noticed about you; I am always pleased to do whatever I can to help improve you [*à te rendre parfait*]."[30]

Book learning and polite behavior were not the only ways in which a man could polish his image; he was also expected to travel, to taste the "curiosities" and sights of the city and countryside.[31] Both Delphin and Alexis had visited Paris as young men and used their time there to visit the public sights as well as to socialize with relatives and friends.[32] Delphin suggested strongly to Victor that he mobilize his spare hours to explore Paris and its environs: "We advise you when you have a few moments to spare & you are close by one thing or another, a church here, a library there, the Luxembourg & its *tableaux*, the gallery of the Palais-Royal, etc. . . . it is the thing to do in winter. During the *belle saison*, one goes to St. Cloud one Sunday, another to Meudon, or takes two days of holiday to go to Versailles when the King is there, then another favorable time to go to Chantilly, which must not be missed."[33] Familiarity with the sights and

---

30. Delphin to Victor, 21 August 1760; Alexis to Victor, undated 1757.

31. "Learned travel" was highly encouraged in the eighteenth century. See Robert Shackleton, "The Grand Tour in the Eighteenth Century," in Shackleton, *Essays on Montesquieu and the Enlightenment*, edited by David Gilson and Martin Smith (Oxford: Voltaire Foundation at the Taylor Institution, 1988), 363.

32. BM Ms. 1696 (II), Fonds Lamontagne, Correspondence, Nos. 37, 55, 56, 57, 60, 64; and Lamothe Family Letters, 1755, passim.

33. Delphin to Victor, 3 January 1758.

sounds of Paris and its surroundings could only increase Victor's general culture and social graces.

Despite this advice, Victor was never able to create a real stir in Parisian society. His small budget as a student prevented him from obtaining the proper wardrobe, and while they liked his good heart, his Parisian cousins considered him somewhat provincial.[34] Still, his training in Paris contributed to his acceptance among an enlightened circle of friends upon his return to the provinces.[35] For a clever young man of somewhat mediocre fortune, acceptance into polite society was an important step toward social advancement, or at least toward maintaining a respectable station in the community.

2. The Production and Consumption of Enlightenment Culture

Public functions, such as salons, societies, and other less formal social gatherings, represented one aspect of the cultural life in which the Lamothes took part. These activities allowed them to polish their social reputation and to lend luster to their external image. But other cultural pursuits were undertaken more as a matter of personal curiosity and satisfaction—to improve and edify the mind and to contribute to the inner person.[36] These activities were pursued in a more private setting, sometimes shared with other family members and friends, and represented a broad range of intellectual interests. Both scholarly topics and "curiosities" found their place among the Lamothe family papers, for in the eighteenth century, the dividing line between the two endeavors was not clear-cut.[37]

As was the case with most men of law and medicine, the male members of the Lamothe family were avid readers and put together a substantial library. By the eighteenth century, an abundant library was a sign of

34. Alexandre to Victor, 8 August 1760.

35. Lamothe Family Letters, 1773, passim. Also see Chapter 5 above.

36. See Christine Adams, "Defining *État* in Eighteenth-Century France: The Lamothe Family of Bordeaux," *Journal of Family History* 17 (Winter 1992): 25–45.

37. Robert Darnton has pointed out that the separation of the sciences from fiction in the eighteenth century was far from complete and that fantastic occurrences were often presented as scientific fact in *Mesmerism and the End of the Enlightenment in France* (Cambridge: Harvard University Press, 1968), 12–15.

membership among the social and intellectual elite, and doctors, barristers, and clergymen tended to possess extensive personal libraries.[38] The letters sent to Victor in Paris by his brothers and father, both requesting books and discussing their favorites, sketch their scholarly and literary interests in some detail.

With four barristers in the family, it is not surprising that the largest number of books requested by the Lamothes concerned the law in all its aspects.[39] Collections of *arrêts*, the *Table chronologique des ordonnances de roys de France*, the *Institutes coutumières de Loysel*, and the two volumes of the *Traité des institutions et substitutions contractuelles* are just a few examples of the works requested.[40] Medical books also found a place in their collection.[41] Father Jules occasionally asked for books related to his religious functions, and the sisters sometimes requested religious works as well.[42] Books played an essential role in the professional work of all male members of the Lamothe family. When seeking to improve their skills or increase their knowledge, Victor and Alexandre were advised to study the suitable books of their profession.[43] Their professional culture was one that relied heavily upon the available collections, manuals, and tracts on law or medicine.

Yet the reading interests of the Lamothes reached far beyond the dry texts of their professions. Humanist literature also played a role. Daniel counseled his son Victor that, when he was not perusing professional books, he should read "*belles-lettres* with which you can improve your mind" or "some little book of maxims or *pensées*."[44] The whole family read and

38. Annik Pardailhé-Galabrun, *La Naissance de l'intime: 3000 foyers parisiens, XVIIe–XVIIIe siècles* (Paris: Presses Universitaires de France, 1988), 405; Roger Chartier, *The Cultural Uses of Print in Early Modern France*, trans. Lydia G. Cochrane (Princeton: Princeton University Press, 1987), 196. The classic work on private libraries is Daniel Mornet, "Les Enseignements des bibliothèques privées (1750–1780)," *Revue d'histoire littéraire de la France* 17 (1910): 449–92.

39. Based on an examination of fifteen inventories, Lenard R. Berlanstein found that an average of 86.6 percent of the books in the libraries of the barristers of Toulouse were professional in nature. *The Barristers of Toulouse in the Eighteenth Century (1740–1793)* (Baltimore: Johns Hopkins University Press, 1975), 96. In the case of the barristers of Paris, Albert Poirot found that works of jurisprudence accounted for about 33 percent of all volumes in his study of forty-nine private libraries. Cited by David A. Bell in *Lawyers and Citizens: The Making of a Political Elite in Old Regime France* (New York: Oxford University Press, 1994), 226 n. 44.

40. Delphin to Victor, 17 December 1756; 30 April 1757; undated 1757; Alexis to Victor, undated 1763.

41. Delphin to Victor, undated 1757; 13 June 1761.

42. Jules to Victor, 27 May 1758; Marie to Victor, undated 1763.

43. Alexis to Victor, 23 September 1755; Alexandre to Victor, 17 January 1757; Delphin to Victor, 7 July 1758.

44. Daniel to Victor, 22 November 1757.

enjoyed the letters of Madame de Sévigné and felt that they profited from her sage commentary.[45] Alexis suggested that the letters of Madame de Maintenon, a woman "of spirit and reason," could also be of use in forming Victor's social character.[46] Other works that found a place in the Lamothe library included the classic works of Horace and Virgil.[47] The family was also familiar with the classical French literature of Molière, Sorel, Marmontel, and Racine and read didactic or moral works such as La Rochefoucauld's Maxims and Fénelon's *Télémaque*.[48] Delphin read the *Essais* of fellow Bordelais Montaigne and observed to his friend François de Lamontagne that it was a book "an *honette homme* [sic] cannot avoid reading."[49]

Of particular interest is the engagement of the Lamothe brothers with the literature of the Enlightenment. Historians have long debated the actual impact of the most controversial works of that period and the extent to which these books were owned and read by men of learning.[50] When recommending the books that a barrister should possess to improve his general knowledge and culture, Albert Camus, the eighteenth-century Parisian jurisconsult, certainly did not include the works of the philosophes.[51] Studies of libraries have suggested that few individuals actually owned the best-known literature associated with the Enlightenment.[52]

45. Alexis to Victor, 22 July 1755; see also Marianne to Victor, 24 January 1757.

46. Alexis to Victor, 9 October 1757.

47. Alexis to Victor, undated 1757; Delphin to Victor, 11 April 1762.

48. Alexis to Victor, 20 April 1757; undated 1757; 23 June 1758; 23 April 1765; Alexis to Victor and Alexandre, undated, 1765; Delphin to Victor, 4 July 1757. See Lamothe Family Papers, Poetry and Prose Collected by Alexis de Lamothe, 1771–88, Folder #4.

49. BM Ms. 1696 (II), Fonds Lamontagne, Correspondence, 10 October 1753, No. 26.

50. Monique Cubells observes that while the libraries of some *parlementaires* of Aix contained works by the philosophes, they tended to be those books that were "moins audacieuses," and that these men hesitated to own the most controversial books. Daniel Mornet had earlier noted the absence of the Enlightenment classics from private libraries during the eighteenth century, and Robert Darnton followed up with an attempt to define the literary culture of the Old Regime. Roger Chartier goes further in suggesting that perhaps it was the Revolution that "created" the canon of the Enlightenment rather than the reverse, giving a "premonitory and programmatic meaning" to certain books that were far less popular prior to the Revolution. Cubells, *La Provence des lumières: Les Parlementaires d'Aix au 18eme siècle* (Paris: Maloine, 1984), 343–55; Mornet, "Les Enseignements des bibliothèques privées," 463–69; Darnton, "Reading, Writing, and Publishing in Eighteenth-Century France: A Case Study in the Sociology of Literature," *Daedalus* (December 1970): 214–56; and Chartier, *The Cultural Origins of the French Revolution*, 87–89.

51. Albert Camus, *Lettres sur la profession d'avocat, sur les etudes relatives à cette profession, & sur la manière de l'exercer, avec un catalogue raisonné des livres de droit qu'il est le plus utile d'acquérir & de connoître* (Paris: Chez Méquignon, 1777), Letter #2: "Sur les études, en général, qui sont nécessaires à la profession d'avocat; l'ordre de s'y livrer; le plan d'une conférence; & la manière de se former une bibliothèque."

52. See Berlanstein, *The Barristers of Toulouse*, 99–100.

However, the Lamothe brothers, as well as their close friend François de Lamontagne (nephew of Montesquieu), evinced familiarity with both the main works and ideas of the best-known philosophes, reflecting, or perhaps explaining, their association with the intellectual elite of the Duplessy salon, where the philosophical spirit made its first inroads in Bordeaux.[53]

As loyal citizens of Bordeaux, Delphin and his brothers could be expected to have some familiarity with the works of their compatriot Monsieur de la Brède. Delphin was sufficiently knowledgeable concerning the works of Montesquieu to discuss them in detail in his correspondence with M. de Formey, *encyclopédiste* and director of the Academy of Berlin. Delphin betrayed a certain pride in the achievements of his "fellow citizen" although somewhat critical of Montesquieu's earlier works, which he believed lacked sufficient gravity for such an eminent man: "No doubt, you have seen in your city a book . . . it is *L'Esprit des lois*. The author is our *concitoyen*, former president for life in our Parlement, M. de Montesquieu, known in the republic of letters for his *Lettres persanes*, his *Temple de Gnide*, his book on *Le Grandeur des Romains et leur décadence*. These works, written with spirit and finesse, were, without excepting the last, a bit too frivolous for a president; wanting to show that he was capable of greater things, he wrote this book; you can find here some ideas that are new and daring." Delphin demonstrated an appreciation of the political views presented in Montesquieu's *chef d'oeuvre*, going on to note in a subsequent letter that "it is a book that is universally appreciated; the most solid truths are displayed there in a lively and concise manner."[54] Delphin's openness to the political ideas of Montesquieu in a book that was subsequently placed on the Index of Prohibited Books by the Vatican indicates that he was more willing to embrace the new philosophical currents than to remain true to his strict Jesuit education.[55]

One would perhaps expect lawyers to be familiar with the work of the *parlementaire* Montesquieu, and barristers occasionally made reference to him in their briefs and public pronouncements.[56] However, based on

53. Grellet-Dumazeau, *La Société bordelaise*, 10.

54. Formey Correspondence, *Archives historiques*, Letters of 26 March and 1 July 1749, 248.

55. On the censure of Montesquieu's work, see Robert Shackleton, "Censure and Censorship: Impediments to Free Publication in the Age of Enlightenment," in *Essays on Montesquieu and the Enlightenment*, 418–20; and Françoise Weil, "'L'Esprit des Lois' devant La Sorbonne," *Revue historique de Bordeaux et du département de la Gironde* 11 (1962): 183–91.

56. Berlanstein, *The Barristers of Toulouse*, 100.

analyses of private libraries, Voltaire was the philosophe most popular with legal professionals by the middle of the eighteenth century, an indication of the reception of biting satire and a critical spirit.[57]

The Lamothe brothers shared this appreciation for the works of Voltaire. While in Paris, Alexis searched eagerly for a copy of *La Pucelle d'Orléans* for Lamontagne.[58] They also possessed copies of his works at home.[59] They were aware of Voltaire's role in the celebrated Calas affair.[60] Like Voltaire, the Lamothes sympathized with the unfortunate Calas. And in his correspondence with M. Formey concerning *The Spirit of the Laws*, Delphin remarked approvingly that "M. de Voltaire . . . had the *crédit* to defend the work" against the attacks of critics such as the abbé Laporte.[61] Among their private papers is a short poem from December 1771 titled *Prédiction sur Mr. de Voltaire par Piron*, as well as a handwritten copy of *Vers de Mad. de Boufflers au sujet de la mort de Voltaire*, the final verse of which, in glowing tribute to the celebrated author reads:

> Yes, you are right, Mr. de St. Sulpice,
> Eh! why bury him, is he not immortal?
> To that divine genius, one can, with justice,
> Refuse a tomb, but not an altar.[62]

Clearly, the Lamothe brothers approved of Voltaire's crusades for tolerance and opposing censorship.

The Lamothe brothers were familiar with other examples of philosophical literature as well.[63] But the works of one philosophe held a special

57. Mornet, "Les Enseignements des bibliothèques privées," 464. Lenard Berlanstein found a work by Voltaire in one out of three of the *avocat* libraries he examined. Voltaire was also by far the most popular philosophe among the *parlementaires* of Aix. Berlanstein, *The Barristers of Toulouse*, 99; Cubells, *La Provence des lumières*, 344.

58. BM Ms. 1696 (II), Fonds Lamontagne, Correspondence, 16 September 1755, No. 56.

59. Alexandre to Victor, 19 March 1757.

60. Alexis mentioned to Victor that he had procured "a little story by Elizabeth Canneing which is a very ingenious fiction concerning that affair, it is attributed to Voltaire." Alexis to Victor, 1 January 1763.

61. Formey Correspondence, *Archives historiques*, Letter of 12 May 1750, 250.

62. Lamothe Family Papers, Poetry and Prose Collected by Alexis Lamothe, 1771–88, Folder #4; and Songs—Alexis Lamothe(?), Folder #2. John McManners provides context for this poem with his discussion of the death of Voltaire and his efforts to ensure a Christian burial for himself without renouncing his life's works. *Death and the Enlightenment: Changing Attitudes to Death among Christians and Unbelievers in Eighteenth-Century France* (Oxford: Clarendon Press, 1981), 265–69.

63. There are frequent references to the *Encyclopédie*, as well as mention of various discourses

place—those of Jean-Jacques Rousseau. Alexis and Delphin were possibly introduced to the cult of Rousseau at Madame Duplessy's salon, where Madame, along with the maréchal de Richelieu's daughter, Madame d'Egmont, shared a passion for Jean-Jacques.[64] Readers throughout France responded to the force of Rousseau's personality as it revealed itself in his books.[65] The Lamothes were no exception. Alexis obtained copies of Rousseau's popular epistolary novel, *La Nouvelle Héloïse*, and his treatise on childhood, *Emile*.[66]

However, Alexis was interested in the less "popular" works of Rousseau as well. Although few inventories of eighteenth-century libraries have turned up copies of *The Social Contract*, Alexis requested that Victor purchase him a copy of this book that would have such great impact on the discourse of the French Revolution.[67] As early as 1755, Alexis noted that he and his brother Delphin were familiar with Rousseau's discourse in *L'Origine de l'inégalité des conditions*, and that he "sometimes lost [him]self in these labyrinths."[68] Another work that he requested from Victor was the brochure *Le Projet de paix perpetuelle*.[69] The Lamothe brothers were familiar with the more radical political ideas of Rousseau.

But like Darnton's merchant from La Rochelle, Jean Ranson, Alexis appears to have been fascinated with the individual Jean-Jacques Rousseau as well as his works and ideas. He mentioned somewhat enviously that a friend from Sainte-Foy, young M. Jay, had the good fortune to see "the illustrious J. Jacques Rousseau" during a trip to Geneva.[70] He asked Victor to send him *Le portrait de J. Jacques Rousseau*, "which I am eager to know and

pronounced by well-known philosophes such as Buffon and D'Alembert, in the letters. See, for example, Alexis to Victor, 12 January 1761; 7 October 1761; 12 March 1765; Alexandre to Victor, undated 1766. See also BM Ms. 1696 (II), Fonds Lamontagne, Correspondence, Nos. 55 and 56, 2 August 1755, and 16 September 1755.

64. Grellet-Dumazeau, *La Société bordelaise*, 242.

65. Robert Darnton, "Readers Respond to Rousseau: The Fabrication of Romantic Sensitivity," in *The Great Cat Massacre and Other Episodes in French Cultural History* (New York: Vintage, 1985), esp. 232–52; Carol Blum, *Rousseau and the Republic of Virtue: The Language of Politics in the French Revolution* (Ithaca: Cornell University Press, 1986), 133–52; Chartier, *The Cultural Origins of the French Revolution*, 83–84.

66. Alexis to Victor, 27 March 1762; 26 June 1762; 26 September 1762.

67. Alexis to Victor, 26 September 1762. Daniel Mornet found but one copy of *Le Contrat social* in his survey of private libraries. "Les Enseignements des bibliothèques privées," 467; see also Darnton, "Reading, Writing, and Publishing," 215; and Simon Schama, *Citizens: A Chronicle of the French Revolution* (New York: Alfred A. Knopf, 1989), 161 and 175.

68. Alexis to Victor, 14 October 1755.

69. Alexis to Victor, undated 1763.

70. Alexis to Victor and Alexandre, 30 July 1765.

to possess, and his *Profession de foy philosophique*, containing his farewell letter to society."[71] This fascination with Jean-Jacques was not uncommon among lawyers.[72] That Delphin was also influenced by the works of Rousseau is suggested by his manuscript work *Jugements sur les ouvrages de J.-J. Rousseau.*[73]

Clearly, the Lamothe brothers read and pondered the works and ideas of the philosophes. Is it possible to ascertain their views on the philosophical ideas that many historians argue were commonplace by the mid-eighteenth century? The intensely religious attitudes of their sisters, parents, and clergyman brother Jules may have stifled conversation at home during the 1750s and 1760s, for there is no extended discussion in the letters on the merits of the various philosophes and their ideas. Daniel, the family patriarch, a deeply religious man, disapproved of some of these "new ideas," and he warned Victor to "flee the discourse and the alleged principles of certain philosophes."[74] Nevertheless, among the family's papers, carefully copied by hand, are two poems that suggest a strong interest in, and perhaps a flirtation with, Deism and materialist philosophy. The pieces are unsigned, and it is possible that Alexis, or more plausibly Delphin, who was noted as an amateur poet, may have composed one or both of the poems.

Les Systêmes is a rather whimsical piece in which God, having created his "vast machine" and placed "an impenetrable veil" over Nature, calls together all of history's great scientific and theological thinkers, "our doctors, proud children of Sophism, eternal disputers" such as Thomas Aquinas, Descartes, Malebranche, and Leibniz, among others, and asks them:

> . . . Divine my secret:
> Tell Me who I am, and how I am made:
> And, in a supplement, tell me who you are;
> What force, in every sense, moves the comets . . . ?

Following the example of the academies, God offers a prize—money, and the promise of salvation—to the man who can solve this eternal riddle.

71. Alexis to Victor, 27 November 1763.
72. Lenard Berlanstein notes that Rousseau made a strong impression on several Toulousan barristers, who sometimes formed a personal identification with him, in *The Barristers of Toulouse*, 100.
73. Meller, *Essais généalogiques*, 29n. This work is no longer among the Lamothe Family Papers.
74. Daniel to Victor, 3 February 1759.

Each thinker responds according to his philosophy, each wrong. However:

> God was not angry: he is the best of fathers,
> And without numbing us with laws too austere,
> He would like his children, those little Libertines,
> To enjoy themselves by playing with the work of his hands.

This benevolent image of God is further amplified by the closing verse, a Voltairian plea for religious toleration and freedom of thought.[75] The poem demonstrates familiarity with the main trends of thought on the essence of God, and comes down firmly on the side of the inability of human beings to know the meaning of God and Nature, and thus, the necessity to tolerate the free play of ideas.

The second piece, *Epître à Uranie*, less lighthearted, is even more forceful in its rejection of the traditional image of a harsh and unforgiving God, as well as his earthly defenders:

> . . . The priests of this temple, with a severe face,
> Offer me a God whom I must hate;
> A God who created us to be miserable

Bleak Calvinist and Jansenist views are rejected, and a more natural and reasonable religion, reminiscent of Rousseau, is proposed:

> . . . Consider that from on high that immortal Wisdom
> engraved with its hand, in the depths of your heart,
>   Natural religion:
> Believe that good faith, goodness, kindness
> Are not the objects of eternal hatred,
> Believe that before his throne in all ages, in all places,
>   The heart of the just is precious:
> Believe that a modest Buddhist, a charitable dervish
>   Will find more grace in his eyes
> Than a merciless Jansenist,
> Or an ambitious Jesuit.

---

75. Lamothe Family Papers, Poetry and Prose Collected by Alexis Lamothe, 1771–88, Folder #4, *Les Systêmes*.

In a final denial of the importance of revealed religion, the poem ends:

He judges us by our virtues,
And not by our sacrifices.[76]

Both of these poems strongly reflect the religious views of the philosophes. Peter Gay and others contend that the notions of tolerance and a certain skepticism toward religion were generally accepted in educated circles after 1750, and it is likely that Deism, materialism, and even atheism were widely debated and accepted in the salons and gatherings of the educated Bordelais.[77] This is not to say that Delphin and Alexis abandoned the outer trappings of their Catholic faith, or that their belief in God was shaken.[78] Even the gentle skeptic Montesquieu remained a practicing Catholic all of his life.[79] We can assume, however, that religious toleration and skepticism, central tenets of the philosophical movement, had penetrated even the conventional Lamothe household. That the Lamothe brothers identified with the most famous philosophers of their age is revealed in the shrine that Alexis constructed to Jean-Jacques Rousseau and to the philosophes in his *cabinet:* "I would like for Victor or Alexandre, whoever sent me the engraved portrait of Rousseau, J. Jacques, to look for another to match with that engraving; that is, a portrait of the same size . . . portraying some person of distinction of analogous character, a Fontenelle, a Locke, an Adisson, a D'Alembert . . . it would be good if he were facing Rousseau, that is to say, looking to the left, since

76. Lamothe Family Papers, Songs—Alexis Lamothe(?), Folder #2, *Épitre à Uranie.*

77. These ideas were all discussed at the gatherings of the d'Holbach circle in Paris, although the rules of "polite conversation" modified the exchange of more extreme ideas at other salon gatherings. Alan Kors, *D'Holbach's Coterie: An Enlightenment Salon in Paris* (Princeton: Princeton University Press, 1976), 92–93 and 120–46. See also Peter Gay, *The Enlightenment: An Interpretation,* vol. 2: *The Science of Freedom* (New York: Alfred A. Knopf, 1969), passim; Elinor Barber, *The Bourgeoisie in Eighteenth-Century France* (Princeton: Princeton University Press, 1955), 51–53; Mornet, *Les Origines intellectuelles,* 138–39. On the intellectual impact of atheism in the eighteenth century, see Alan Kors, *Atheism in France, 1650–1729,* vol. 1 (Princeton: Princeton University Press, 1990).

78. Barber, *The Bourgeoisie,* 53. Bernard Groethuysen speaks of the new, worldly minded Catholicism of the bourgeois that took hold in the eighteenth century. This new man was far more skeptical, but still a Catholic, a believer, and a churchgoer. See *The Bourgeois,* 9–42.

79. Robert Shackleton, "La Religion de Montesquieu," in *Essays on Montesquieu and the Enlightenment,* 109–16, esp. 111. As Alan Kors points out, few men were willing to jeopardize their respectable position in society by openly rejecting the church, even the most anticlerical and antireligious thinkers. *D'Holbach's Coterie,* 208–9.

Rousseau is facing right."[80] This small monument to the philosophical spirit in Alexis's place of work serves as testimony to the influence of the Enlightenment on the Lamothe brothers.

3. Other Intellectual Pursuits

While not so clearly linked to the direct influence of the High Enlightenment—the great names—other interests of the Lamothe brothers followed wider popular trends. Delphin, Alexis, and especially the doctor Victor shared an interest in science, the passion of the eighteenth century.[81] Bordelais historian Camille Jullian has noted the popularity of the scientific movement in the Guyenne, especially in astronomy and botany. Victor Lamothe was an amateur astronomer, and from 1778 to 1792, his meteorological observations were recorded regularly in the *Journal de Guienne*.[82] Like many Frenchmen and -women, Victor was also attracted for a time by the pseudoscience of mesmerism, which achieved a certain acceptance in Bordeaux.[83] His barrister brothers had interests in the sciences as well. It appears that these interests never went beyond the perfunctory, although Delphin did compose a *Traité de gnomonique pratique* outlining the configuration of a sundial, possibly as a school project. As a young man, Delphin competed for the prize offered by the Academy of Bordeaux on a topic titled *L'Origine et la formation des pierres figurées*.[84] Influenced by their contacts with academician Jacques de Romas, who, like Benjamin Franklin, conducted electrical experiments in the 1750s, the

80. Alexis to Victor and Alexandre, 4 September 1764.

81. Barrière, *La Vie intellectuelle en France*, 357–60; Gay, *The Enlightenment*, 2:126–28, sees passion for the sciences as a defining characteristic of the Enlightenment, and many other historians agree. See Roger Hahn, *The Anatomy of a Scientific Institution: The Paris Academy of Sciences, 1666–1803* (Berkeley and Los Angeles: University of California Press, 1971); and Thomas Hankins, *Science and the Enlightenment* (New York: Cambridge University Press, 1985), esp. 1–16.

82. Camille Jullian, *Histoire de Bordeaux depuis les origines jusqu'en 1895* (Bordeaux: Feret et Fils, 1895), 582; M. Capelle, "Notice sur M. le Docteur Lamothe," in *Actes de l'Académie nationale des sciences, belles-lettres et arts de Bordeaux*, vol. 1819, 13 May 1824, 108.

83. Charles Dubreuilh, *Eloge académique de Victor de Lamothe* (Bordeaux: Emile Crugy, 1869), 24–26. See Darnton, *Mesmerism*, on the impact of mesmerism in France.

84. AM Ms. 684, Fonds Meller, Tome I, Section on Simon-Delphin de Lamothe; Delpit, *Notes biographiques*, 13; Lamothe Family Papers, Miscellaneous Notes and Indexes, n.d., Folder #5; Faurie, *Eloge des frères Lamothe*, 6–7.

brothers had an abiding interest in the effects of lightning. They put
this interest to practical use, and their house on Rue Neuve was the first
and only one in the neighborhood to be equipped with a lightning
conductor.[85]

Of more enduring interest to Delphin and Alexis were the subjects of
history and geography. Like science, history was a popular topic in
Enlightenment France, as authors such as Gibbon promoted the belief in
the progress of civilization and sought to improve historical research.
Delphin and Alexis's interest went beyond their rather superficial dabbling
in science.[86] It is true that lawyers were expected to have an extensive
knowledge of history, but Delphin's interest was clear even in his school-
work as a youth.[87] Along with François de Lamontagne and other young
friends, Delphin helped to organize a *conférence* on history in 1744.[88]

Local history was particularly popular in eighteenth-century Bordeaux.
Both the Academy of Bordeaux and the *intendants* of the Guyenne sought to
sponsor the writing of a complete history of the region.[89] Alexis and
Delphin's friend François de Lamontagne worked all his life compiling
historical anecdotes of the province of Guyenne, although he never
published them.[90] In this spirit, Delphin published the prospectus of a
projet d'histoire ancienne et moderne de la province de Guienne in 1765, and the two
brothers used their knowledge of local history extensively in their commentaries on the customary law of the Guyenne and Bergerac.[91] Both

85. BM Ms. 828 (XXIII), Archives de l'Académie de Bordeaux, No. 12, "Extrait de deux lettres
écrites de Paris par M. de Ladebat à Lamothe sur le paratonnerre, Sept. 1789"; Marionneau, *Les Vieux
Souvenirs de la rue Neuve*, 64n. On Romas's experiments in electricity and his competition with Franklin,
see Jean de Feytaud, "L'Académie de Bordeaux sous l'Ancien Régime," *Revue historique de Bordeaux et du
département de la Gironde* 23 (1974): 77.

86. Gay, *The Enlightenment*, 2:98–100 and 368–71; Robert Shackleton, "The Impact of French
Literature on Gibbon," in *Essays on Montesquieu and the Enlightenment*, 421–35.

87. E. C. Richardson Collection, Container #8, Folder #3. Albert Camus discusses the historical
background that lawyers were expected to acquire in *Lettres sur la profession d'avocat*, 30–31.

88. AM Ms. 684, Fonds Meller, Tome I, Section on Delphin de Lamothe.

89. Pierre Barrière, *L'Académie de Bordeaux: Centre de culture international au XVIIIe siècle* (Bordeaux and
Paris: Editions Bière, 1951), 305; Jullian, *Histoire de Bordeaux*, 583–84.

90. Courteault, "Notice sur François de Lamontaigne," XX–XXIV. The text of the *Chronique*, written
by Lamontagne, illustrates his interest in local history and events.

91. Marionneau, *Les Vieux Souvenirs de la rue Neuve*, 65. Among the private papers of the Lamothe
family is a historical chronology of kings in Aquitaine that may be related to this historical prospectus.
Lamothe Family Papers, Prose Collection, Simon Delphin(?), 1745–, Folder #1. In his *éloge*, Edmond
Faurie notes that their *Commentaire* was a historical work as well as judicial. Faurie, *Eloge des frères Lamothe*,
14.

Delphin and François de Lamontagne possibly were contributors to the *Almanachs historiques de la province de Guienne*, first published in 1760.[92] In his speech to the Bordeaux Literary Society in 1757, Alexis discussed the need to study original authors and texts for a history of the province, the method used by the brothers when they wrote their *Commentaires*.[93] Among his personal papers, Alexis left a collection of *anecdotes*, with that title, concerning the city of Bordeaux, as well as the work *Recueil de morale d'histoire et de littérature*.[94] Delphin's expertise in history and his love of the subject were evident in discourses on a variety of historical topics.[95]

Extracts of historical letters and speeches were carefully copied and retained among the private papers of the Lamothe family.[96] In addition, Delphin and Alexis, as well as their father Daniel, frequently requested history books from Victor.[97] Delphin owned eleven volumes of the *Histoire littéraire de la France*, authored by the Benedictines.[98]

The Lamothe brothers considered erudition in the field of history a necessary facet of the *honnête homme*. Recall Alexis's advice to Victor to keep on his table "some good Latin or French historian," while Delphin suggested that he brush up on his knowledge of French, Greek, and Roman history. When Victor found spare time on his hands as a medical student in Montpellier, Delphin advised him to "profit from those moments that you would have used to pay visits in order to instruct and entertain yourself with things that you don't know much about yet & that you must know in this world, as you understand very well: a little history, especially modern, geography, etc."[99]

The Lamothes' love of history spilled over into a passion for geography. This interest was most clearly evinced by their ardor for collecting maps. Along with his friend M. Mel, Delphin subscribed to the *Cartes de France*

92. Courteault, "Notice sur François de Lamontaigne," XXIV–XXV.
93. Faurie, *Eloge des frères Lamothe*, 5–6; Alexandre Nicolai, *Histoire de l'organisation judiciaire à Bordeaux et en Guyenne et du barreau de Bordeaux du XIIIe au XIX siècle* (Bordeaux: G. Gounouilhou, 1892), 87–88.
94. Meller, *Essais généalogiques*, 26. These works are no longer among the Lamothe Family Papers.
95. Marionneau, *Les Vieux Souvenirs de la rue Neuve*, 65; Delpit, *Notes biographiques*, 14–15; Faurie, *Eloge des frères Lamothe*, 12–13; and BM Ms. 1233, Archives de l'Académie de peinture, sculpture et architecture civile et navale de Bordeaux, 1770, 59–61.
96. Lamothe Family Papers, Prose Collection, Simon-Delphin(?), 1745–, Folder #1.
97. Delphin to Victor, 21 January 1758; Alexis to Victor, 31 March 1759; Alexandre to Victor, undated 1766.
98. Delphin to Victor and Alexandre, 22 July 1766.
99. Delphin to Victor, 7 April 1760.

and watched the *Mercure de France* and other journals for advertisements announcing the appearance of the new Cassini maps.[100]

Delphin's fascination for maps was possibly tied to his legal work, to his interest in history, and perhaps to a desire to travel and a curiosity about other cultures. Travel, especially travel abroad, was a mania for the French of the eighteenth century. Perhaps Delphin, eager to be *à la mode*, shared this passion, although the limited resources of the Lamothe family apparently restricted the personal travels of both him and his brothers to Paris and Provence.[101]

The Lamothe brothers tried their hand at more creative arts as well. Delphin had a reputation as an excellent amateur artist and cartoonist, and his sketches grace several of his manuscripts. His caricatures, often of his colleagues, were well known, and once led to trouble when a fellow lawyer, Desplats, took offense, and the *premier président* of the parlement, Leberthon, was obliged to intervene.[102] Alexis was also an art connoisseur, demonstrating expertise in the tools and techniques of painting in a discussion of an exhibit he attended at the Louvre.[103] But more pronounced than these artistic skills and knowledge was an interest in collecting and composing songs and poetry. Poetry was a fashionable pursuit among the *beaux-esprits* of Bordeaux.[104] Delphin in particular was known as an amateur poet of some skill, but Victor tried his hand at writing poetry now and then as well.[105] Perhaps they were encouraged to appreciate poetry by their father, Daniel, who collected poems, both in Gascon and French.[106] The family as a whole seems to have enjoyed music, and sang and danced at social gatherings.[107]

<hr />

100. Delphin to Victor, 23 June 1758; 8 March 1757; 31 March 1759. See also 26 March 1757; undated, 1757. Delphin maintained his subscription to the *Cartes de France* at least through 1765. Delphin to Victor and Alexandre, 19 February 1765.

101. Paul Hazard discusses the new favor for travel abroad in the eighteenth century in *The European Mind*, trans. J. Lewis May (Cleveland: Meridian Books, 1963), 5–28. Robert Shackleton also notes the popularity of travel, but points out that it was essentially the privilege of young noblemen, while others were forced to live vicariously through an abundant travel literature. "The Grand Tour," 361–73.

102. Delpit, *Notes biographiques*, 13.

103. Alexis to Victor, 9 September 1755.

104. Grellet-Dumazeau, *La Société bordelaise*, 112–18.

105. Victor to Jules, 1 April 1758; Marie to Victor, 11 January 1763.

106. AM Ms. 519, Fonds Delpit, No. 1, "1701: Vers composé par un solitaire à l'occasion du passage à Bordeaux du roi d'Espagne"; Lamothe Family Papers, Songs—Alexis Lamothe(?), Folder #2.

107. Marie to Victor, 20 October 1757; Alexandre to Victor, 17 November 1757; Delphin to Victor, 17 December 1757; Marianne to Victor, 29 June 1764.

There is little pattern to the songs and poetry selected and preserved by the Lamothes.[108] Some were folk songs or drinking songs, such as *Le Buveur content*, and *Vive la Champagne*. While it seems unusual to find these "lowbrow" songs among the personal papers of highly educated men, the "gentry" often took notice of popular customs, proverbs, and songs, studying them as curiosities.[109]

The majority of the verses among the Lamothe papers are commonplace sentimental poems and songs of little artistic merit, some presenting a romantic view of love, as in *La tendre fleur naissante*. Others are highly cynical, such as *Eloge de l'inconstance*. Several of the poems suggest a rather jaundiced view of women, such as this *Chanson par Caron de Beaumarchais*;

> . . . Retain this witticism of a wise man,
> It's the great secret of manners [*moeurs*];
> All women deserve a tribute,
> Few are worthy of regret.

Favorite songs from operas and operettas are scattered among the family papers, including the *Vaudeville de Figaro* and the *Barbier de Seville*. Some of the music is scored, suggesting that one or more members of the family could read music, and perhaps play a musical instrument.[110]

The entire family seems to have participated in the collection of these bits and pieces as an intellectual pastime. A variety of hands copied the songs and poems in the collection, and Daniel mentioned in a letter to Victor that the family had compiled a collection of more than two hundred proverbs.[111] Their choices suggest a desire on the part of the Lamothes to stay *au courant* with popular songs and poems. Sometimes these rhymes

108. The following references are all taken from the Lamothe Family Papers, Songs—Alexis Lamothe(?), Folder #2.

109. Natalie Zemon Davis examines the waxing and waning of elite interest in popular culture in "Proverbial Wisdom and Popular Errors," in *Society and Culture in Early Modern France* (Stanford: Stanford University Press, 1975), 227–67. This was not unique to France. In eighteenth-century England, the scholarly and literary elite studied old ballads as a souvenir of the country's literature and history. See Dianne Dugaw, "The Popular Marketing of "Old Ballads": The Ballad Revival and Eighteenth-Century Antiquarianism Reconsidered," *Eighteenth-Century Studies* 21 (Fall 1987): 71–72.

110. The family sent Victor in Paris a gift of two *guimbardes*, rather primitive guitars, which suggests that he could play them. Delphin to Victor, 17 December 1757. Possession of musical instruments was still relatively rare in eighteenth-century France, although stringed instruments were those most popular among amateurs. Pardailhé-Galabrun, *La Naissance de l'intime*, 419–26.

111. Daniel to Victor, 2 December 1758.

made a commentary on current political events, as in *Le Bonheur de la France*, while others offered social satire. As taxes increased in 1763 when poor harvests were creating hardship in Aquitaine, Alexis shared a popular ditty with Victor:

> You can ruin me, oh enemy fortune,
> But make me pay, *parbleu!* I defy you to try,
> For I haven't a sou . . .[112]

One poet in particular was of special interest to Delphin de Lamothe. François-Joseph de Chancel, the seigneur de Lagrange, was the Périgord region's most celebrated poet, and lived near the Lamothe land by Sainte-Foy-la-Grande. It is possible that Delphin knew Lagrange-Chancel, who died in late 1758 or early 1759. At any rate, Delphin took a definite interest in both the compositions and the colorful private life of the poet.

Delphin copied in his own hand *Les Phillipiques*, Lagrange-Chancel's best-known work, a vitriolic attack on the duc de la Force and the regent written during the regency of Louis XV. In an *avant-propos*, Delphin chronicled the events leading to the composition of the five odes of the *Phillipiques*, an affair that led to Lagrange-Chancel's ruin. Delphin condemned the intemperate and what he considered unjustifiable attacks on the regent and his government, but praised the talent evident in Lagrange-Chancel's epic, "a work as excellent as it is malicious and reprehensible."[113]

Delphin also showed keen interest in the unedited poetry of Lagrange-Chancel, composed during a trial before parlement in 1746. In an effort to have the marriage contract of his son to a young woman from the Limousin invalidated, Lagrange-Chancel presented *mémoires* and requests to parlement, all in verse. His son, also a gifted poet, responded to his father's arguments in verse as well. Following the loss of his case, the indignant father drafted the biting *Lémovicade*. Delphin followed the battle carefully, collecting all of the different pieces composed during the trial and copying them in his own hand. He may also have been inspired to pen a sonnet chronicling the affair that appears in his dossier of documents from the trial.[114] The combination of verse and scandal in the works of

---

112. Alexis to Victor and Alexandre, 6 September 1763.

113. BM Ms. 1861, "Les Phillipiques de M. de Lagrange Chancel," manuscrit par S. Delphin de Lamothe. See also Pierre Barrière, *La Vie intellectuelle en Périgord, 1550–1800* (Bordeaux: Edition Delmas, 1936), 414 and 426.

114. According to Jules Delpit, who examined the original dossier "Ce Sonnet n'est pas signé et pourrais bien etre l'oeuvre personnelle de M. S.A.D. de Lamothe." In his dossier of pieces from the

Lagrange-Chancel proved irresistible to Delphin de Lamothe. The trial was undoubtedly a major topic of discussion at the Palais de l'Ombrière in 1746, but Delphin's dossier suggests a more intense interest.

The Lamothes consulted a variety of sources to keep up to date on current events, such as the Lagrange-Chancel trial, and demonstrated interest in a wider world beyond the confines of Bordeaux. They regularly read the gazettes of Holland, the *Gazette de France*, the *Journal des sçavants*, and the *Mercure* for the most recent literary news, as well as items about personalities and cultural events.[115] They apparently subscribed to the *Observateur* from Holland, as Delphin requested that Victor have his forty-six issues bound.[116]

But the journals were insufficient as a source of information. The Lamothe brothers recognized that the printed news was often inaccurate and demonstrated a healthy skepticism for the information provided by the newspapers. While at Goulards for the wine harvest, Delphin complained to his friend François de Lamontagne about the news concerning the Parlement of Bordeaux that appeared in the *Gazette de Hollande*: "The information that we get from it is useless."[117] Lamontagne teasingly agreed with him: "You would like some news, my dear Lamothe, and you do not want to have to rely on the *Gazette de Hollande*? You are right; I have never seen so clearly that one must be very skeptical of [that journal] concerning the accuracy of facts. Forget everything that you have heard concerning this affair; and receive from me the light of truth."[118] Lack of trust in the

---

procès, Delphin also kept a personal copy of the "Elégie de M. de Lagrange," and the "Apparition de Thémis Idille." AM Ms. 519, Fonds Delpit, No. 8. Delpit based his edition of the poems of Lagrange-Chancel on Delphin de Lamothe's private papers, which were given to him by Delphin's son Dugravier de Lamothe, and were obviously more complete than those that now exist in the Archives municipales de Bordeaux. See Delpit, ed., *Poésies inédites de F. J. de Chancel-Lagrange* (Paris: Librairie Edouard Rouveyre, 1878).

115. Jeremy Popkin has written about the evolution of the periodical press in ancien régime France, arguing that it was far livelier and more extensive than has usually been acknowledged. Figures for the *Mercure de France* in the 1780s indicate that it had the widest circulation of any periodical, reaching a level of more than twenty thousand copies per issue. Popkin, "The Prerevolutionary Origins of Political Journalism," in Keith Michael Baker, ed., *The French Revolution and the Creation of Modern Political Culture*, vol 1: *The Political Culture of the Old Regime* (Oxford: Pergamon Press, 1987), 205; Jack R. Censer and Jeremy D. Popkin, "Historians and the Press," in Censer and Popkin, eds., *Press and Politics in Pre-Revolutionary France* (Berkeley and Los Angeles: University of California Press, 1987), 22.

116. Delphin to Victor, 13 June 1761.

117. BM Ms. 1696 (II), Fonds Lamontagne, Correspondence, 30 September 1756, No. 73.

118. BM Ms. 1696 (II), Fonds Lamontagne, Correspondence, 13 October 1756, No. 75. Despite the skepticism of Delphin and Lamontagne, the "gazettes de Hollande," printed outside of France, presented a far more balanced view of politics than the *Gazette de France*, the official organ of the French government. Popkin, "The Prerevolutionary Origins of Political Journalism," 207–10; Carroll Joynes,

official news led to an informal network of news exchange between friends and family members, a system that functioned in the correspondence between the Lamothe family members in Paris and Bordeaux. For example, during his visit to Paris in 1755, Alexis sent dispatches back to his family and friends in Bordeaux.[119] The Seven Years War was a frequent topic of conversation, as it had a direct effect on the Lamothe family and their friends. The war created nervousness on the part of the Bordelais, living in a coastal city, and Jules wrote to Victor of the number of alarms in the city, the confiscation of arms, and concerns about the loyalties of the Protestants.[120] The Lamothes were shocked when their friends the Clarkes, along with all of the English, Irish, and Scottish inhabitants of Bordeaux, were expelled from the city by order of the king.[121] Alexis found this a bit extreme, noting that "not everyone, that is to say, not all natives of England or Ireland, are guilty."[122] He also expressed disapproval of the enormous costs of war to the country, as well as to the family. It made the sale of wine to Holland more difficult and uncertain, and other economic impacts of the war decreased their revenues as well.[123]

The war was of concern because of its many adverse effects—"War, war, fire, butchery, carnage," observed Alexis sadly when war threatened in 1755.[124] Other news items were of a more personal or professional interest. Delphin requested that Victor send him several brochures on the Damiens affair soon after it took place, and gave attention to other celebrated legal and criminal affairs.[125] The entire family closely followed

"The *Gazette de Leyde*: The Opposition Press and French Politics, 1750–1757," in Popkin and Censer, *Press and Politics in Pre-Revolutionary France*, 133–68.

119. Alexis to Victor and Alexandre, 23 September 1755; BM Ms. 1696 (II), Fonds Lamontagne, Correspondence, 4 October 1755, No. 57; 18 November 1755, No. 60; Discours du Roy d'Angleterre aux deux chambres du Parlement du jeudi 13 9bre 1755, No. 61.

120. Jules to Victor, 2 October 1757; see also J. Cavignac, "Les Assemblées au désert dans le région de Sainte-Foy au milieu du dix-huitième siècle," *Revue historique de Bordeaux et du département de la Gironde* 16 (July–December 1967): 109–11.

121. All those of English descent were ordered to leave Bordeaux, Bourg, and Blaye on 28 March 1762 until the end of the war. Pierre Bernadau, *Annales politiques, littéraires et statistiques de Bordeaux* (Bordeaux: Moreau, 1803), 188.

122. Alexis to Victor, undated 1762.

123. Alexis to Victor, 23 September 1755; Daniel to Victor, 2 December 1758; Delphin to Victor, 19 November 1760; Alexis to Victor and Alexandre, 16 January 1762; Delphin to Victor and Alexandre, 7 June 1763. See also Chapter 2, section 1 above.

124. BM Ms. 1696 (II), Fonds Lamontagne, Correspondence, 18 November 1755, No. 60.

125. Delphin to Victor, undated 1757; Alexis to Victor, 30 January 1762; Alexis to Victor, 21 January 1764; Delphin to Victor and Alexandre, 4 September 1764. See Dale Van Kley, *The Damiens*

the dispute over the Jesuits, a polemical religious controversy that spread throughout France.[126] They asked Victor to send a variety of *arrêts* and pamphlets on the affair.[127] However, none of the Lamothes expressed a clear opinion on these proceedings, which excited comment throughout France, perhaps reflecting conflicting emotions. Delphin had been educated by the Jesuits and had briefly considered entering religious orders as a youth. However, the parlement to which he was attached was strongly opposed to the Jesuits, and François de Lamontagne was one of the commissioners assigned to study the liquidation of Jesuit goods and property following the judgment against them.[128] Marianne revealed her uncertainty over the turn of events: "Today is the day that the Jesuits have been forced to leave . . . their *collèges*, their novitiate, their religious quarters, nothing but joy on the part of many people, and regret on the part of the others . . . what is true or false [in this affair] I do not know."[129]

They were less ambivalent concerning the celebrated Calas affair, which they began to discuss after the unfortunate Calas had already been broken on the wheel.[130] Alexis wrote to Victor, "We know quite a bit about the Calas affair, it created quite a stir here, I have most of the *mémoires*," and thereafter he and Delphin continued to request brochures and exchange updates on the case with Victor.[131] At the end of the trial, the information that they had gathered comprised two bound volumes.[132] Alexis spoke sympathetically of "the poor Calas widow and her family," and upon the vindication of M. Calas, Delphin wrote triumphantly, "Finally, finally, the

---

Affair and the Unraveling of the Ancien Régime (Princeton: Princeton University Press, 1984) for an analysis of this event.

126. Dale Van Kley's book on the events leading up to expulsion of the Jesuits is the most thorough available. Van Kley, *The Jansenists and the Expulsion of the Jesuits from France, 1757–1765* (New Haven: Yale University Press, 1975). See also Arlette Farge, *Subversive Words: Public Opinion in Eighteenth-Century France*, trans. Rosemary Morris (University Park: Penn State Press, 1994), 182–83.

127. Daniel to Victor and Alexandre, 16 March 1762; Alexis to Victor and Alexandre, 22 December 1761; Alexis to Victor, 26 December 1761; 27 March 1762; Delphin to Victor, 11 April 1762; Delphin to Victor and Alexandre, 6 July 1762.

128. Courteault, "Notice sur François de Lamontaigne," XVI.

129. Marianne to Victor, 7 August 1762.

130. See David Bien, *The Calas Affair: Persecution, Toleration, and Heresy in Eighteenth-Century Toulouse* (Princeton: Princeton University Press, 1960) on this controversial case.

131. Alexis to Victor, 1 January 1763; Delphin to Victor and Alexandre, 7 June 1763; Alexis to Victor, 23 July 1763; 21 January 1764; 29 June 1764.

132. Alexis to Victor, 24 May 1766.

Calas have been judged, they are exonerated."[133] Delphin's decision to buy an engraving of the Calas suggests sympathy with the family's position as well.[134] As enlightened men, Delphin and Alexis could really not have taken any other position. But their interest in these celebrated cases supports Sarah Maza's thesis concerning the importance of the *mémoire judiciare* in shaping public opinion.[135]

Other events of political importance caught the attention of the Lamothe brothers. Among the family papers are diverse documents concerning later political crises such as the policies of Necker and his resignation. They also collected a number of scathing poems on an issue that hit closer to home, the Maupeou Parlement. One curious piece suggests that the brothers followed the controversies associated with censorship in the theater, in particular those surrounding the plays of Caron de Beaumarchais.[136] The following extract indicates that the brothers rejected hypocrisy and censorship in the theater much as they had in literature. In response to a request by the duke of Villequier to permit use of Beaumarchais's private theater box for "two souls" who did not wish to be seen at the performance of the *Mariage de Figaro*, Beaumarchais had written:

> I have no regard, Mr. le Duc, for women who permit themselves to go see a play that they consider unrespectable, as long as they can see it secretly. I refuse to be a party to such desires. I gave my play to the public to amuse and to instruct them, not to offer hypocritical prudes the pleasure of going and thinking well of it in their private boxes, as long as they can speak ill of it in society. The pleasures of vice and the honors of virtue! Such is the prudery of this century. My play is not an equivocal work; one must acknowledge it or flee it. I hail you, Monsieur le Duc; and I will retain my box.[137]

133. Alexis to Victor, 23 March 1765; Delphin to Victor and Alexandre, 23 April 1765.

134. Delphin to Victor and Alexandre, 9 July 1765; Marie to Victor, 29 April 1766.

135. Maza, *Private Lives and Public Affairs.*

136. The drama surrounding the success and attempted censorship of *Le Mariage de Figaro* was a *cause célèbre* of the 1780s. Schama, *Citizens*, 138–44; Maza, *Private Lives and Public Affairs*, 290–95. It was banned in Bordeaux in September 1785. Bernadau, *Annales*, 18. Several pieces from this play and others by Beaumarchais are among the Lamothe Family Papers. Songs—Alexis Lamothe(?), Folder #2, and Poetry and Prose Collected by Alexis Lamothe, 1771–88, Folder #4.

137. Lamothe Family Papers, Poetry and Prose Collected by Alexis Lamothe, 1771–88, Folder #4.

A clever reply, of which we can assume that the Lamothe brothers approved.

The Lamothe brothers enjoyed the theater, a popular pastime in Bordeaux.[138] Among the family papers are selections from plays and operas.[139] Alexis was familiar with the ballet dancers who appeared in theater productions at Bordeaux and expressed approval that Victor occasionally attended the theater at Montpellier: "If it is a poor school in certain regards, and for certain persons, it is excellent in many other regards."[140] Despite the somewhat questionable morality of the goings-on at the theater, Alexis believed that it could play an important role in the education of the *honnête homme* and man of society.

The wide variety of interests on the part of the Lamothe brothers is impossible to summarize or categorize. Their tastes and ideas reflected those of other men of their social class, for many of these cultural pursuits were shared in the company of friends and acquaintances. Other interests, of a more personal nature, were undoubtedly pursued in private and shared only with family or the closest of friends.

4. The Private Side

Apparently sometime after the birth of his first child in 1773, Delphin drafted a prose piece dedicated to "my son," full of advice and common-places, detailing the need for repose and solitude, the importance of private life and spaces, and his desire "to help discover hidden charms." The tone of the piece is that of a man who is growing old—"My son, look at me weighted down by the approach of old age, my retirement is nearing, and it is time that I yield my place in the world to you"—and who wishes to impart the wisdom of his years to his child. Calling upon his

---

In the same folder is a piece titled "Vers sur la Comedie du *Mariage de Figaro*: jettés du paradis du theatre français, imprimés le ＿＿ May 1784," which ridicules the censorship of the play.

138. Theatergoers suffered when the theater burned down in 1755. The new one, designed by celebrated architect Victor Louis, was not completed until 1783. O'Reilly, *Histoire complète de Bordeaux*, 3:343–50; Bernadeau, *Annales politiques*, 166; Charles Marionneau, *Les Beaux-arts à Bordeaux* (Bordeaux: G. Gounouilhou, 1892), 22–23.

139. Lamothe Family Papers, Songs—Alexis Lamothe(?), Folder #2; Poetry and Prose Collected by Alexis Lamothe, 1771–88, Folder #4.

140. Alexis to Victor, 17 February 1761; 9 May 1761.

reading of Rousseau in younger years, he warned his son that "the world is a huge theater" and that people often hid their true motives "behind the mask of amity."[141]

The Lamothe brothers left behind numerous "scribblings" of this sort, works of their own composition with no obvious purpose other than the fulfillment of the desire to leave a personal record of certain events, similar to a diary. But did they always intend that these writings remain private? As diary-keeping, first-person narratives, and epistolary novels became increasingly popular throughout the seventeenth and eighteenth centuries, most *mémoirialistes* clung to the fiction that they were writing for their own pleasure, baring their innermost thoughts. When these authors recounted public events, the privacy of the genre supposedly insured the authenticity of the description. In a private account, what motive would the author have to lie? Alexis had internalized the formulaic language appropriate to the genre. Reminiscent of Jacques-Louis Ménétra's claim that he was keeping a journal for his own pleasure, Alexis stated at the beginning of his record of the Bordeaux earthquake of 10 August 1759: "I recall the circumstances of the earthquake that we experienced in Bordeaux in 1759, Friday, August 10th in the evening; and the impressions that it made on me and on the persons who were close to me, as well as all the impressions that it gave rise to; I will not avoid the longest details and I will include indiscriminately all that flows from my pen . . . Moreover, I am writing only for myself, therefore, censorship would be out of place."[142]

Both Delphin and Alexis left an account of the earthquake of 1759, a major event in Bordeaux.[143] Delphin's description was rather dry and straightforward, noting carefully the time it took place, the weather conditions, and the interesting tidbit that Dom Devienne, local monk and historian, had predicted it.[144] In contrast, Alexis's ten-page narrative went into personal detail on the events leading up to and following the

141. Lamothe Family Papers, Prose Collection, Simon-Delphin(?), 1745–, Folder #1.

142. Lamothe Family Letters, Alexis, Tremblement de Terre à Bordeaux, 10 August 1759. On the popularity of, and the formulas and topics discussed in, diaries, journals, and first-person narratives, see Jean-Marie Goulemot, "Literary Practices: Publicizing the Private," 363–95; as well as Madeleine Foisil, "The Literature of Intimacy," 327–61; and Orest Ranum, "The Refuges of Intimacy," 207–63, esp. 252–63, all in Philippe Ariès and Georges Duby, gen. eds., *A History of Private Life*, trans. Arthur Goldhammer (Cambridge: Harvard University Press, Belknap Press, 1989), vol. 3: *Passions of the Renaissance*, Roger Chartier, ed.

143. Lamontaigne, *Chronique bordelaise de François de Lamontaigne*, 18–20; Bernadau, *Annales*, 179.

144. AM Ms. 519, Fonds Delpit, No. 4, "Extrait d'une notice fait par M. Sm. Ant. Delphin de Lamothe. Tremblement de Terre. 10 Aout 1759."

earthquake, emotions and recollections of the tragic Lisbon earthquake evoked by the circumstances, and ultimately, resignation to the will of God. While there is no reason to doubt that Alexis was greatly moved and frightened by the powerful earthquake, his carefully phrased expression of his and Delphin's emotions suggests that he was writing for posterity as well as for himself: "Slightly recovered from our shock, my brother and I reflected on the singular effect of our fright which was to remove us suddenly from all our attachments, even those we held most dear; to us, all became insipid or unimportant, we thought that it was our great love for life that reduced us to this state in spite of ourselves, and almost mechanically; and pushing this thought further still, we found that it was not without reason, since life is the most valuable and most fragile of our worldly goods, without which we can enjoy none of the others."[145] Alexis's *mémoire* was a careful blend of religious and philosophical sentiments.

The two brothers left a number of other compositions, some detailed observations of the events of their time, others philosophical musings.[146] These personal writings, ostensibly private, remained buried in the family papers of the Lamothes. Also hidden there were a number of documents, also presumably kept private or shared only with a few trusted friends, although for a very different reason. Among the private papers of this conventional family are some poems and prose that can only be classified as seditious.

While *mauvais discours*, critical of the king, have been recorded throughout French history, it was really in the latter half of the eighteenth century that language viciously critical of royalty became widespread. The aura that had graced the kings of France gradually wore off, as the king was increasingly "desacralized."[147] Louis XVI, at first more personally popular than his detested grandfather, Louis XV, was soon ridiculed in all aspects of his person—public and private—as well as for his hated Austrian-born

145. Lamothe Family Letters, Alexis, Tremblement de Terre à Bordeaux, 10 August 1759.

146. Lamothe Family Papers, Poetry and Prose Collected by Alexis Lamothe, 1771–88, Folder #4. See also AM Ms. 519, Fonds Delpit, No. 2, "Note autographe sur le duel de MM. de Rabart et Fontayne, à Ste. Foy, en octobre 1717"; No. 3, "Extrait d'une description de Bordeaux, innaché et manuscrite, ecrite vers 1750 par M. Delphin de Lamothe, un des auteurs du commentaire sur la *coutume*"; and No. 6, "Récit du duel entre M. Rougeole, 'américain,' et le chevalier de Sèze, à Bordeaux, le 22 janvier 1777." No. 7, "Extrait d'une narration ecrite par Delphin de Lamothe au mois de juin 1780," is in Alexis's, rather than Delphin's, handwriting, despite the notation by Jules Delpit.

147. Van Kley, *The Damiens Affair*, 253–55; Chartier, *The Cultural Origins of the French Revolution*, 111–35. See also Lisa Jane Graham, "Crimes of Opinion: Policing the Public in Eighteenth-Century Paris," in Adams, Censer, and Graham, eds., *Visions and Revisions*, 79–103; and Farge, *Subversive Words*.

wife, Marie Antoinette. Gutter literature, *libelles*, brutally attacked the king, queen, and court, bringing into question the legitimacy of the government as a whole.[148]

Robert Darnton has argued that circulation of this gutter literature attacking the entire regime and decrying the moral decadence of the aristocracy and church was widespread. The Lamothe family papers would indicate that Darnton is correct.[149] Some selections, while critical of the government, are more restrained in tone and restricted to controversial topics like the Maupeou Parlement.[150] However, *Noël: sur la naissance de Mr. le Dauphin, 1781*, copied in Alexis's hand, has all the earmarks of the *libelles* described by Darnton. Seizing upon the happy occasion of the birth of the Dauphin, this poem brings into question the prince's legitimacy by mocking the king's impotence:

> The birth of a Dauphin
> Enchanted all of Paris,
> The sudden existence
> Troubled Paradise,
> What devil had produced him?
> Said the Word angrily;
> It's some turn of St. *Esprit*,
> For no one said
> That the King was his father.

The *libelle* goes on to assail other members of the court, and especially the queen for her supposedly lesbian tendencies.[151]

Where would Alexis have obtained this pornographic couplet? Possibly one of his friends or acquaintances passed it on to him, indicating the widespread popularity of scurrilous rhymes concerning the king and queen. A parody of the Lord's Prayer and the Ave Maria, copied by Victor, is no less vicious:

---

148. Darnton, "The High Enlightenment and the Low-Life of Literature," 105–15; and "Reading, Writing, and Publishing," 238–44.

149. Darnton, "Reading, Writing, and Publishing," 238–44.

150. See "Parodie des édits enregistrés en lit de justice le 12 novembre 1774 et envoyes ensuite dans les différentes cours souveraine du royaume"; "Et! Quoy Monseigneur Hu!"; "Convoi du Parlement," Lamothe Family Papers, Poetry and Prose Collected by Alexis Lamothe, 1771–88, Folder #4.

151. Lamothe Family Papers, Songs, Alexis Lamothe(?), Folder #2.

Our Father who is at Versailles,
Your name is not hallowed,
Your kingdom is shaken,
Your will is no longer fulfilled . . .

We despise you, Antoine Marie, full of vices.
    The Devil is with you . . .[152]

The fact that the Lamothe brothers possessed these compositions does not necessarily indicate that they approved the sentiments therein, or that they even opposed the regime. Nevertheless, copying and preserving them in the family papers suggests less than outright horror and rejection. Not all salacious songs and poems in the Lamothe family papers were of a political nature. Some of the more curious songs are bawdy pieces, dealing openly with sex. *L'Hirondelle de Carême* is a graphic scored piece about a man en route from Saint-Denis to Paris who seduces an attractive nun. Sexual relations with or between nuns and clergymen were a favorite topic, as suggested by this song about an Ursuline nun and a monk:

To seize our hearts,
Our confessors always
Say sweet things to us.
Ah! if you saw Father Alain,
With what ardor he kisses my hand!
    Your hand?
    My hand.
    My breast;
    Your breast?

While this is not proof of a fundamental anticlericalism, the Lamothes were irreverent enough to laugh at the escapades of nuns and priests.

Risqué and vulgar songs such as *La jeune Madelan* proliferate in the family's papers.[153] Songs of this nature were no doubt common in eighteenth-century France, and the Lamothe brothers may have collected them as "curiosities" because they found them amusing, demonstrating an

152. Lamothe Family Papers, Poetry and Prose Collected by Alexis Lamothe, 1771–88, Folder #4.
153. These songs can all be found in the Lamothe Family Papers, Songs, Alexis Lamothe(?), Folder #2.

interest in the popular culture of the Aquitaine. Certainly, this collection indicates a coarser and cruder side to the erudite and respectable La-mothes, an interest in the earthier side of life. The tendency is reinforced by the fact that Victor in Paris was requested to seek out questionable literature such as *Les Dévirgineurs* and *Mémoires par l'hermaphrodite*.[154]

This sensual and vulgar side is at odds with the more self-restrained and restrictive image that the family collectively presented in its correspon-dence. And yet, periodically, hints of earthier pleasures come through in the letters as well, especially during the family trips to Goulards: "As for the other members of the Republic of Goulards, they are all vigorous, fresh, in good spirits, alert, they do all the same things that Gargantua did, & just as well as he, that is, they drink while eating, eat while drinking, leap while dancing, dance while leaping, fart while shitting & vice versa, shit while farting, etc., etc., there you see the nonsense that Rabelais, that sober physician, is full of."[155] Their delight in food is further evidence of their pleasure in the sensual side of life.[156]

The Lamothes partook of other popular pleasures, including *carnaval*, fairs, and other curiosities in town.[157] When a giant was placed on display at the place Royale, Marie and Marianne went off to see it, accompanied by Alexis.[158] Like the rest of the Bordelais, the Lamothes prepared excitedly for the arrival and grand procession of the duc de Richelieu in 1758, inviting friends to come watch the parade with them.[159] While an interest in popular amusements and bawdy songs and poems would seem to detract from the ideal of the *honnête homme*, perhaps it helped make them well-rounded men, and indicates that they were touched by a much wider culture that in the end undermined their social conservatism.[160]

The Lamothes shared in the cultural activities of their time on many levels—high, middling—and low. Many of their activities, such as partici-pation in salons, familiarity with intellectual literature, acceptance of certain Enlightenment notions of skepticism and tolerance, and awareness of current events provided them with the patina essential to men of their

154. Alexis to Victor and Alexandre, 19 February 1765.
155. Alexandre to Victor, 17 November 1757.
156. See, for example, Jules to Victor, 11 January 1760.
157. Lamothe Family Letters, passim.
158. Delphin to Victor, 17 December 1757.
159. Delphin to Victor, 6 May 1758; Jules to Victor, 27 May 1758.
160. Robert M. Isherwood discusses the convergence of elite and mass tastes in the enjoyment of popular culture in *Farce and Fantasy: Popular Entertainment in Eighteenth-Century France* (New York: Oxford University Press, 1986).

station. Other pursuits, such as their personal writings and poetry and song collections, satisfied intellectual curiosity and personal cultivation.

The letters of the Lamothe brothers, as well as the reputations that they have left behind in public sources, suggest that they were cultivated men, conversant with the latest trends and ideas of their society, but by no means pioneers of their time.[161] While recognized as *savants*, the Lamothes cannot be considered exceptional, either in intellectual originality or in the creativity of their various projects. We can safely assume that their activities paralleled those of other men exercising liberal professions during the eighteenth century.

For the Lamothes, social acceptability and erudition were of prime importance, for they were convinced that the approbation of society was essential to the *honnête homme*. However, these literary and intellectual pursuits exposed them to controversial new ideas, and even subversive ones. Political *libelles* and the sometimes polemical literature published by foreign gazettes introduced them to the new political culture that was taking shape in the mid-eighteenth century.[162] Their own works and interests suggest that they and other men of their social group played a part in shaping this new political culture. Perhaps like other French, they came to believe that their government was becoming "despotic."[163] When revolution loomed in 1789, Alexis and Victor were familiar with the more radical ideas of the revolutionaries, although it is unlikely that they embraced them wholeheartedly.[164] A lawyer and a doctor with strong corporate ties would not have favored a radical restructuring of society, but their interests do suggest a sympathy with certain philosophic ideas that formed part of the public opinion.[165] While it is too simplistic to argue that the literature of the Enlightenment brought on the Revolution, we can

---

161. See, for example, Grellet-Dumazeau, *La Société bordelaise*; Delpit, *Notes biographiques*; Faurie, *Eloge des frères Lamothe*; Dubreuilh, *Eloge académique de Victor de Lamothe*; Capelle, "Notice sur M. le Docteur Lamothe."

162. Baker, introduction to *The French Revolution and the Creation of Modern Political Culture*, 1:xi–xxiv.

163. William Doyle, "The Parlements," in Baker, *The French Revolution*, 1:157.

164. Alan Kors demonstrates effectively that even the radical members of the d'Holbach coterie were appalled by the excesses of the French Revolution, and resented the loss of their privileged place in society. Kors, *D'Holbach's Coterie*, 261–300.

165. There has been extensive work on the development of the concept of "public opinion" in prerevolutionary France, many following on Habermas's seminal work on the public sphere. Two useful articles include Keith Michael Baker, "Politics and Public Opinion Under the Old Regime: Some Reflections," in *Press and Politics in Pre-revolutionary France*, 204–46; and Mona Ozouf, "'Public Opinion' at the End of the Old Regime," *Journal of Modern History* 60, suppl. (September 1988): S1–S21.

see the effect of the changing political culture and spread of new ideas in preparing the ground, especially when we see the extent to which these ideas penetrated even respectable households such as that of the Lamothe family. The cultural activities and intellectual interests of the Lamothe brothers provide a striking example of the changing mentality and openness to "radical" notions even among men who continued to live the life of the traditionally conservative "bourgeois" professional.

Conclusion

This study of the Lamothe family offers us a definition of the professional bourgeois family, as well as of the professional man in provincial eighteenth-century France. This definition includes a focus on family, kin, and friend networks, professional activities, cultural interests, and a desire to serve the public good. A careful balance between the demands of family life and professional and cultural pursuits was undergirded by family discipline, fiscal restraint, public image, moderation in lifestyle and work habits, and religious practice and orthodoxy. All of these elements contributed to the identity of the members of the Lamothe family.

Many of these values and norms are associated with the respectable provincial bourgeoisie of the nineteenth century, especially the emphasis on a secure and stable family life; professional status based on merit, connections and public service; and cultural activity in the service of the municipality. Certainly, the concerns of the Lamothe women reflect their counterparts in the nineteenth century, and Victor Lamothe's professional and personal outlook changed little between 1766 and 1823. Daniel Lamothe would surely have been comfortable as a nineteenth-century *père de famille*, and the sibling devotion of the Lamothe brothers and sisters finds its counterpart in the close-knit families of Victorian England.

Still, the identity and activities of the provincial professional were certainly in a process of evolution throughout the course of the eighteenth century, and indeed, into the nineteenth. In particular, the case of the Lamothe brothers demonstrates that professional and social commitments were in a state of flux and redefinition throughout the eighteenth century as the ideals of public service and utility became moral imperatives for lawyers and doctors throughout France. While for Alexis and Delphin personal cultivation and cultural pursuits were of great importance to their identity as *honnêtes hommes*, these activities were gradually receding before duty to the public good—although the good of the family never took second place. Even organizations that might appear at first glance geared to a small elite group—such as the academies of Bordeaux—carefully defined their mission as service to the public. Victor carried this new image of professional and class obligation through and beyond the Revolution, sacrificing most other cultural pursuits in favor of service to indigent mothers, orphans, and public hygiene. Still, the cultural and political importance that liberal professionals attained by the latter half of the eighteenth century—as epitomized by the important local role played by the Lamothes—foreshadowed their prominence in nineteenth-century public affairs.

Even as their cultural and political role expanded in the eighteenth century, were urban professionals like the Lamothes acquiring a sense of group consciousness? It is hard to say. Even today, we have difficulty defining social classes, especially the middle class. Were the Lamothes part of a budding bourgeoisie, equivalent to the "middling sort" in Britain, an emerging middle class, or were they better defined as urban notables? On what basis do we define this social group? How did they define themselves? In opposition to the nobility, or in opposition to the working classes?

Certainly, they associated with the nobility in the salon of Madame Duplessy and in the academies. Yet they rejected certain key values associated with the nobility of the eighteenth century, such as largesse and leisure. The frugal and hardworking Lamothes attributed little worth to these traits. But they also held themselves aloof from individuals that we today might see as members of a broader middle class—*procureurs*, lesser merchants, and the Spanish surgeon whom Alexis dismissed as of "little consequence." Difficulties in determining the precise boundaries of a "middle class" or bourgeoisie makes it difficult to discern "class consciousness."

And yet, by the nineteenth century, a discourse and consciousness of "middle-classness" had arisen, despite the fact that fissures between the various groups within that middle class remained as pronounced. And its roots lay in the eighteenth century, when urban professionals and others, in their everyday lives, were formulating, articulating, and trying to live by the values that we have come to associate with the solid provincial bourgeoisie. In part, cultivation of these conservative values was related to a certain anxiety on their part, a desire to maintain hard-won status that was not undergirded by the security of noble title. The Lamothes sought out and appreciated these values of good breeding, moderation, prudence, professional standing, and public image among their closest friends, their social group. A budding class consciousness? Perhaps.

In particular, they sought out their friends in the many professional groups and voluntary associations in which they participated. Historians have pointed to the role of voluntary associations in the formulation of middle-class consciousness in the American and English context.[1] Possibly the academies and other groupings, such as the Society for Maternal Charity, which professional men and sometimes their wives came to dominate, may have played a similar role in the French context.

This study of the Lamothe family suggests that 1789 may not be the great dividing line that historians have traditionally believed it to be. David Garrioch argues that the Parisian bourgeoisie was formed in the crucible of revolution, with the revolutionary state acting as midwife to the new local elite.[2] Clearly, the revolutionary state played a key role in fostering a sense of group consciousness on the part of urban notables. But if the "bourgeois century," and the domination of a "bourgeois" way of thinking, did not take hold until after the fall of Napoleon, the creation of a specific bourgeois mentality—with its emphasis on prudence, virtue, fiscal restraint, and a healthy sense of public worth—began among the urban professional as early as the mid-eighteenth century.[3] The Lamothe family exemplifies this "professional bourgeoisie" of the eighteenth century.

1. Most notably, Mary Ryan, *Cradle of the Middle Class: The Family in Oneida County, New York, 1790–1865* (New York: Cambridge University Press, 1981). See also Jonathan Barry, "The Making of the Middle Class," *Past and Present*, no. 145 (November 1994): 194–208, for his review of R. J. Morris's work.

2. David Garrioch, *The Formation of the Parisian Bourgeoisie, 1690–1830* (Cambridge: Harvard University Press, 1996), 244.

3. Roger Magraw, *France, 1815–1914: The Bourgeois Century* (Oxford: Oxford University Press, 1983). On page 63, Magraw describes the ideology of the Orléanist regime, "Reason tempered by Reasonableness," which could be a suitable motto for the Lamothe family as well.

Appendixes

Appendix I: Value of Lamothe family townhouses in Bordeaux

Location	Value in Livres at Time of Acquisition	Value in Livres in 1763	1790 or Time of Sale
Rue Neuve	11,120 (1737)	16,000	30,000
Rue Gensan	3,500 (1740)	6,000 (300*)	8,500 (1772)
Rue Neuve	13,000 (1751)	10,000 (500*)	unknown
Rue Neuve	7,500 (1753)	7,500 (400*)	16,000
Rue Bouquière	11,250 (1757)	9,000 (550*)	25,000
Rue Cerf-Volant	9,000 (1758)	9,000 (300*)	8,000
Sur le port	17,000 (1759)	17,000 (750*)	unknown
Rue Fondaudege (two houses)	unknown		15,000 each
Rue du Réservoir (two houses)	unknown		15,000 each

*Yearly revenue in 1763.

SOURCES: From the Archives départementales de la Gironde—2C 474, Centième denier, Bureau of Bordeaux, 21 February 1764; 2C 490, Centième denier, Bureau of Bordeaux, 19 April 1790; 3E 17827, 19 August 1737; 3E 7788, 21 August 1740; 3E 21654, 14 May 1751; 3E 21658, 20 June 1753; 3E 24241, 3 April 1757; 2C 470, Centième denier, Bureau of Bordeaux, 2 August 1758; 3E 13048, 4 February 1759. Lamothe Family Letters, Delphin to Victor and Alexandre, 7 June 1763.

Appendix II: Value of Lamothe property in Saint-Avit-du-Moiron (Goulards)

Signed Contract of Purchase	Property Value (in Livres)	Year of Acquisition
Daniel	233.68	1728
	299	1737
	1,350	1741
	160	1755
	191.16	1756
	550	1761
	192.13	1761
	304.10	1762
Alexis	140	1763
	200	1772
	150	1774
	1,484	1778
	700	1784
	180	1784
	643.3	1787
Victor	1,400	1789
Marie de Sérézac,	330	1764
Delphin, Alexis	160	1768

All of the Lamothe holdings Saint-Avit (Goulards) were worth 35,000 livres in 1790.

SOURCES: From the Archives départmentales de la Gironde—2C 3855, Centième denier, Bureau of Sainte-Foy, 1 May 1790; 2C 3825, Centième denier, Bureau of Sainte-Foy, 28 December 1728; 2C 3829, Centième denier, Bureau of Sainte-Foy, 19 November 1737; 2C 3831, Centième denier, Bureau of Sainte-Foy, 10 April 1741; 2C 3837, Centième denier, Bureau of Sainte-Foy, 25 November 1755; 3E 21121, 29 October 1756; 2C 3839, Centième denier, Bureau of Sainte-Foy, 17 August 1761 and 8 December 1761; 3E 42604, 26 November 1762; 3E 42604, 9 December 1763; 3E 42575, 10 November 1772; 2C 3846, Centième denier, Bureau of Sainte-Foy, 16 November 1774; 3E 42586, 5 February 1778; 3E 21044, 20 January 1784; 3E 42625, 24 January 1784; 3E 42628, 17 February 1787; 3E 42630, 16 November 1789; 3E 21025, 11 December 1764; 2C 3843, Centième denier, Bureau of Sainte-Foy, 21 December 1768.

Appendix III: Components of Lamothe family fortune, 1763

Income Sources	Value (in Livres)	Yearly Revenues (in Livres)	
Urban Property			
Rue Neuve	16,000	—	
Rue Gensan	6,000	300	
Rue Neuve	10,000	500	
Rue Neuve	7,500	400	
Rue Bouquière	9,000	550	
Rue Cerf-Volant	9,000	300	
Sur le port	17,000	750	
	74,500	2,800	
Rural Property			
Goulards	28,500 (?)	?	
Muscadet	28,500	?	
Rentes Constituées			
Bassoigne	6,000	300	
Corregeole	3,000	150	
Forstier	2,000	90	2 *vingtièmes* deducted
Faucher	3,000	102	3 *vingtièmes* deducted
Mestre	1,500	65.10	3 *vingtièmes* deducted
	15,500	707.10	
Total:	146,500 (?)	3,507.10	(minimum)

SOURCES: Lamothe Family Letters, Delphin to Victor and Alexandre, 7 June 1763. Archives départementales de la Gironde—2C 474, Centième denier, Bureau of Bordeaux, 21 February 1764; 3E 21673, 21 August 1760.

Appendix IV: Lamothe family tax assessments (in livres)

CAPITATION DES DOMESTIQUES DES OFFICIERS DU PARLEMENT,
DE LA COUR DES AIDES ET DU BUREAU DES FINANCES/CAPITATION
DES DOMESTIQUES DES AVOCATS, PROCUREURS ET GREFFIERS,
GÉNÉRALITÉ DE BORDEAUX

[presented here as listed in the *capitation* rolls]

1726: Au Sr. Lamothe
    1 servante — 3#
1733: Au Sr. Lamothe
    1 servante — 3#
1736: Au Sr. Lamotte
    1 servante — 3#
1747: Au Sr. Lamothe
      Sansfourche
    1 clerc et 2 servantes — 26# 10s (modéré à 9# 10s)
1748: Au Sr. Lamothe
      Sansfourche
    1 clerc et 2 servantes — 9# 10s
1750: Le Sr. Lamothe — 20#
    Un clerc et 2 servantes — 7# 10s
1751: Le Sr. Lamothe — 20#
    Un clerc et 2 servantes — 7# 10s
1755: Au Daniel Lamothe
    1 servante — 1# 10s
1759: Au Sr. Daniel Lamothe
    1 clerc, 1 cuisinère, 1 servante — 7# 10s
1763: Au Sr. Lamothe
    1 clerc, 1 cuisinère, 1 servante — 7# 10s
1767: Lamothe ainé
    Un clerc et une servante — 4# 10s
    Lamothe jeune
    Une servante — 1# 10s
1768: Lamothe, ainé
    1 clerc et une cuisinière — 6# 6s
    Lamothe, jeune
    1 servante — 1# 10s
1772: Lamothe, ainé — 28# 16s
    Un clerc et domestique — 11# 14s
    Lamothe, jeune — 28# 16s
    Domestique — 1# 16s
1773: Le Sr. La Mothe l'ainé — 24#
    Le Sr. La Mothe jeune — 24#

    Chez Le Sr. La Mothe l'ainé
    Un clerc et 1 servante — 7# 16s

Le Sr. La Mothe Jeune	
Une servante	1# 19s
1774: Le S. Lamothe L'aîné	24#
Le S. Lamothe, jeune	24#
Le S. Lamothe aîné	
Un clerc et une servante	8#
Le S. Lamothe jeune	2#
1777: (Two listings)	
Lamothe, aîné	6#
Lamothe, jeune	2#
Chez le Sr. Lamothe aîné	12#
Chez le Sr. Lamothe jeune	2#

TAILLE, SAINT-AVIT-DU-MOIRON LES GOULARDS

1711: Les h. du Me Jean Sanfourche	76# 16s 6d
1727: Mr. Daniel Sanfourche,	
Sr. deLamote, avocat	66# 16s 1d
1779: Le Sieur Simon et Alexis	
Lamothe	117# 18s 9d
1786: Les Sieurs Simon et Alexis	
Lamothe	121# 14s 11d

DIXIEME, SAINT-AVIT-DU-MOIRON LES GOULARDS

1742: Monsieur Daniel Sanfourche,	
Sieur Lamothe, avocat	18# 15s 9d

SOURCES: From the Archives départementales de la Gironde—Série C: 2696; 2718; 2719; 2722; 2723; 2724; 2725; 2727; 2728; 2729; 2731; 2734; 2736; 2760; 2766; 2781. From the Archives municipales, Sainte-Foy-la-Grande—Série CC: 14; 32, p. 13; 40, p. 10; 67, p. 13; 82, p. 13 bis.

Appendix V: Proposed budget of the Académie de peinture, sculpture et architecture civile et navale, December 1772

Pour Les gages de deux modeles . . . . 800#
[note in margin: "Note à Paris ils sont 1000#]
Pour L'huile de la Lampe & La chandelle . . . . 600#
Pour le bois . . . . 200#
Pour L'achat des livres, Bosses, estampes
desseins papier plume encore par an . . . . 500#
Pour un concierge outre Le logement . . . . 150#
Pour L'achat & entretien de tables & meubles
mannequin, drapperies pour La figures . . . . 150#
2,400#

SOURCE: BM Ms. 1233, Archives de l'Académie de peinture, sculpture et architecture civile et navale de Bordeaux, "Mémoire présenté à Mrs. Les Maire, Lieut. de Maire, jurats & conseil de ville de Bordx," 28(?) December 1772, pp. 119–21.

Appendix VI: Proposed budget of the Académie de peinture, sculpture et architecture civile et navale, March 1780*

ETAT DÉTAILLÉ

Des frais nécessaire pour L'entretien de L'académie de peinture, sculpture & architecture civile & navale; dont les jurats sont autorisé a faire les fonds par Les Lettre patents de 14 9bre 1779.

art.

1. Deux modeles a 500 chacun (independament de L'habit(*))
   . . . . 1000#

2. Huile fine pour la Lampe des Ecoles, qu'on allume 7 mois [crossed out]

3. Lumiere pour eclairer Les passages & pour les assemblé & commités [crossed out]

4. Bois pour les poeles, cheminées &c (*Nota* La ville aura la bonté de la faire fournir en nature sur les mandats de Recteur . . . . mémoire

5. Prix

   1. Un grand prix chaque année qui se distribuera alternativement a La peinture & à la Sculpture. Savoir 100# pour Les fraix de voyage de Paris, de celui qui l'aura remporté & 400# qu'on les fera comter dans cette ville (**). . . . . .500#

   2. Second prix qui se distribuera pour le genre qui
      n'aura pas concouru au grand . . . . 100#

   3. Deux medailles *d'accessit* de 24# chacune . . . . 48#

   4. Un Grand prix pour L'architecture Civile, alternativement avec L'architecture navale (**) . . . . 300#

   5. Second prix pour le genre qui n'aura pas concouru . . . . 100#

6. Prix d'Emulation

   1. Pour le dessein classe du modele, 12 medailles par an à 12# . . . . 144#
      classe de la bosse *idem*, à 6# . . . . 72#
      classe des principes, *idem*, à 4# . . . . 48#

   2. pour L'architecture civile,———, à 6# . . . . 72#

   3. ———————navale,———, ——— , ... 72#

7. Au Recteur de L'academie . . . . 300#

8. Aux douze professeurs de dessein a chacun 100# . . . . 1800#

8 bis. au professeur d'après la bosse (Le professeur principal etant stipendi par la ville . . . . 100#

9. Au professeur d'architecture Civile . . . . 500#

10. ———————————navale . . . . 500#

11. ——————— de geometre & perspective . . . . 150#

12. ——————— de steorometrie ou coupe des pierres . . . . 250#

13. ——————— d'anatomie . . . . 150#

14. pour fournir aux jettons a distribuer aux assemblis a L'acad. (20 ou 21 assemblies Le double le jour de St. Louis) . . . . 1200#

15. Au concierge de L'academie (outre son logement) . . . . 500#

16. Achat des Bosses, livres, Estampes, dessins . . . . 400#

17.   Fraix de Tenture aux Salons, sentinelles, faux fraix, papier, plumes, encre,
       & c . . . . 400#

                                                                              9200#

(*)Les modeles sont habillés de La livrie du Roy: il conviendroit qu'il Le fussent a Bordx de
la Livrie de la ville: une habit bleu veste & culotte, bouton d'or, chapeau bordé de mem.
L'habit galonné de son [page torn] arme de L'académie.
(**) Ces grands prix tant *premier* que *second* du dessein & de l'architecture ne se delivreroient
point chaque anné au Trésorier de L'académie, mais uniquement quand Les prix auroient été
veritablement remportés, & sur Le certificat des officiers de L'académie. *Nota* Cette Somme
de 9200# paraitre infiniment modique si on considere 1. que L'académie est L'unique dans
le Royaume qui reunisse une infinité d'Ecoles principales & d'enseignements particuliers 1.3
classes de dessein 2. architecture civile 3. architecture navale 4. geometrie 5. Steorometrie
ou coupe des pierres 6. anatomie, & que de simples ecoles académique comme celle de
Roüen où il n'y a qu'un professeur en titre, cedependant à 7000# de revenu. Le seul directeur
de L'ecole academique de Poitier a 12 a 1500# & L'academie Royale de Paris, qui est séparée
de L'academie d'architecture, & des principes de dessein, a 10000# du Roy.

*This document, BM Ms. 1233, Archives de l'Académie de peinture, sculpture et architec-
ture civile et navale de Bordeaux, "Arreté dans un commité particulier tenu le 14 mars 1780
par M. Bonfin, Recteur, M. Battanchon, M. Lavau, M. Lamothe secre. Presenté à MMs. les
jurst," 14 March 1780, p. 503, is torn, and therefore, the list of expenses is incomplete. As
given here, the expenses add up to 8,706 livres rather than 9,200 livres.

Bibliography

I. Manuscript Sources

Manuscripts Division, Library of Congress, Washington, D.C.

Lamothe Family Letters
Lamothe Family Papers
E. C. Richardson Collection

Archives départementales de la Gironde, Bordeaux

Série B (cours et juridictions)
Série C (administration)
    2C (registres et tables)
Série D (université et académie)
Série E (seigneuries, communes, familles)
    2E (titres de familles)
    3E (minutes notariales)
    6E (Compagnie des médecins; Compagnie des avocats)
Série G (écclésiastique)
Série J (dons et acquisitions)
    8J (Fonds Bigot)
Série L (Révolution)
Série M (administration)
    5M (santé publique et hygiène)
Série Q (domaines)
Série X (dépôt des hôpitaux)
    3X (Société de charité maternelle)
Administration de l'enregistrement et des domaines: Hypothèques. Actes civiles publics de
    Bordeaux, 1819

Archives municipales, Bordeaux

Fonds Delpit
Fonds Meller
Série GG (instruction publique; état civil)
Série I (sections populaires)

Bibliothèque municipale, Bordeaux

365: "Ordonnance de Louis XIV avec des notes de Delphin de Lamothe"
828: Archives de l'Académie de Bordeaux
834: "Catalogue alphabétique des livres de la bibliothèque de l'Académie"
1233–34: Archives de l'Académie de peinture, sculpture et architecture civile et navale de Bordeaux
1460–68: "Journal," edited by Jules Delpit
1541: "Annales de l'Académie de peinture, sculpture et architecture civile et navale de Bordeaux," by Jules Delpit
1572: "Conférence du droit romain avec le droit français sur le Code (de la bibliothèque Lamothe)," 2 vols.
1573: "Ordonnances de Louis XV—provient de la bibliothèque Lamothe"
1603, Folio 3: "Notes et souvenirs d'un artiste octogénaire de 1778 à 1798": memoirs of Pierre Lacour
1696: Fonds Lamontagne
1709: "Recueil des plaidoyers et mémoires"
1861: "Les Phillipiques de M. de Lagrange Chancel," manuscript by S. Delphin de Lamothe

Archives municipales, Sainte-Foy-la-Grande

Mainly Série CC (taille et capitation), but also Série GG and E (état civil) and an assortment of other scattered documents

Archives nationales, Paris

Série F^{10}, Agriculture, Code rural
Série R^2, Papiers Bouillon.

II. Printed Sources

Actes de l'Académie nationale des sciences, belles-lettres et arts de Bordeaux (First volume from 1819, thereafter annually).
Almanachs historiques de la province de Guienne. Bordeaux, 1760–90.
Archives historiques du département de la Gironde. Bordeaux and Paris, 1859–1932.
Archives municipales de Bordeaux. 16 vols. Includes _Inventaire sommaire des registres de la Jurade, 1520–1783_, vols. 6–13. Bordeaux, 1867–1947.
Barckhausen, Henri, ed. _Statuts et réglements de l'ancienne université de Bordeaux (1441–1793)._ Libourne and Bordeaux: Georges Bouchon, 1886.

Bardoux, Agénor. *Les Légistes: Leur influence sur la société française.* Paris: G. Baillière et Cie., 1877.

Baurein, Abbé. *Variétés bordeloises ou Essai historique et critique sur la topographie ancienne et moderne du diocèse de Bordeaux.* Bordeaux: Feret et Fils, 1876.

Bernadau, Pierre. *Annales politiques, littéraires et statistiques de Bordeaux.* Bordeaux: Moreau, 1803.

Bertrand, L. *Histoire des séminaires de Bordeaux et de Bazas.* 3 vols. Bordeaux: Feret Frères, 1894.

Boucher d'Argis, Antoine-Gaspar. *Règles pour former un avocat, tirée des plus celebres auteurs, anciens et moderns.* Paris: Chez Durand, 1778.

Caillau, J.-M. *Notice des travaux de la Société de médecine de Bordeaux depuis sa dernière séance publique.* Bordeaux: Lawalle Jeune, 1810.

Campagne, Maurice. *Histoire des Bacalan du XVe au XXe siècle.* Bergerac: Imprimerie Générale du Sud-Ouest, 1905.

Camus, Albert. *Lettres sur la profession d'avocat, sur les etudes relatives à cette profession, & sur la manière de l'exercer; avec un catalogue raisonné de livres de droit qu'il est le plus utile d'acquérir & de connoître.* Paris: Chez Méquignon, 1777.

Cazes, E. Brives. *Le Parlement de Bordeaux, Bureau de la Grande Police.* Bordeaux: G. Gounouilhou, 1875.

Chauvot, Henri. *Le Barreau de Bordeaux de 1775 à 1815.* Paris: Auguste Durand, 1856.

Corlieu, A. *L'Ancienne Faculté de médecine de Paris.* Paris: V. Adrien DeLaHaye, 1877.

Corriger, Jean. *Au fil des eaux . . . au fil des siècles: Mon village du grand coeur, Sainte-Foy-la-Grande. 700 ans de souvenirs.* Group Girondin des Études Locales, 1974.

Cosme, Léon. *Aperçu sur le barreau de Bordeaux depuis ses origines jusqu'à vers 1830.* Bordeaux: Feret et Fils, 1886.

Courtin, A. *Nouveau Traité de la civilité qui se pratique en France parmi les honnêtes gens.* [Nouvelle édition.] Paris: M. Josset, 1712.

Delaunay, Paul. *Le Monde médical parisien au dix-huitième siècle.* Paris: Jules Rousset, 1906.

Delpit, Jules. *Un Episode de l'histoire de l'Académie des beaux-arts à Bordeaux.* Bordeaux: Chez Henry Faye, 1851.

———. *Fragment de l'histoire des arts à Bordeaux: Académie de peinture et sculpture sous Louis XIV.* Bordeaux: G. Gounouilhou, 1853.

———. *Notes biographiques sur les Messieurs de Lamothe.* Bordeaux: Balarac Jeune, 1846.

———, ed. *Poésies inédites de F. J. de Chancel-Lagrange.* Paris: Librairie Edouard Rouveyre, 1878.

Dubreuilh, Dr. Charles. *Eloge académique de Victor de Lamothe.* Bordeaux: Emile Crugy, 1869.

Ducaunnès-Duval, Ariste, and Gaston Ducaunnès-Duval, eds. *Inventaire sommaire des Archives municipales de la ville de Bordeaux. Période révolutionnaire (1789–An VIII).* 4 vols. Bordeaux: F. Pech, 1896–1929.

Dujarric-Descombes, Albert. *Deux Ex-libris bordelais: Les Frères de Lamothe et l'abbé Desbiey.* Paris: H. Daragon, 1918.

Durodié, Fernand. *Les Médecins et les hôpitaux du vieux Bordeaux.* Bordeaux: A. Destout, 1924.

Encyclopédie ou Dictionnaire raisonné des sciences, des arts et des métiers, par une société des gens de lettres. Neuchastel: Chez Samuel Faulche, 1765.

Etrennes bordelaises, ou Calendrier raisonné du Palais. Bordeaux: Jean Chappuis, 1775–90.

Faurie, Edmond. *Eloge des frères Lamothe, avocats au parlement de Bordeaux.* Bordeaux: Emile Crugy, 1850.

Feret, Édouard. *Statistique général topographique, scientifique, administrative, industrielle et biographique du département de la Gironde.* 3 vols. Bordeaux and Paris: Feret et Fils and G. Masson/Emile Lechevalier, 1878–89.

Furetière, Antoine. *Dictionnaire universel contenant generalement tous les mots françois tant vieux que modern, & des termes des sciences & des arts.* The Hague: Chez Hasson, Johnson et al., 1727.

Grellet-Dumazeau, A. *La Société bordelaise sous Louis XV et le salon de Mme Duplessy*. Bordeaux and Paris: Feret et Fils and Libraires Associés, 1897.

Guignard, Fernand. *Histoire de Castillon sur Dordogne (l'une des filleules de Bordeaux) et de la région castillonnaise*. Paris: Maison Française d'Editions, 1912.

Jullian, Camille. *Histoire de Bordeaux depuis les origines jusqu'en 1895*. Bordeaux: Feret et Fils, 1895.

Lamontaigne, François de. *Chronique bordelaise de François de Lamontaigne*. Edited by Paul Courteault. Bordeaux: Imprimeries Delmas, Chapons, Gounouilhou, 1926.

Lamothe, Delphin, and Alexis Lamothe. *Coutumes du ressort du Parlement de Guienne, avec un commentaire pour l'intelligence du texte: & les arrests rendus en interprétations, par deux avocats au même Parlement*. 2 vols. Bordeaux: Chez les Frères Labottière, 1768–69.

———. *Coutumes et statuts de la ville de Bergerac, traduits de latin en français par M. Etienne Trelier, conseiller du roi en la cour de Parlement de Bordeaux, et Chambre de l'édit de Guienne, commenté par MM. de Lamothe, avocats au Parlement de Bordeaux*. Bergerac: J.-B. Puynesge, 1779.

Lapouyade, Meaudre de. *Impressions d'une allemande à Bordeaux en 1785*. Bordeaux: G. Gounouilhou, 1911.

———. *Voyage d'un allemand à Bordeaux en 1801*. Bordeaux: G. Gounouilhou, 1912.

La Violette, P. *La Plaidoirie devant la critique littéraire*. Bordeaux, 1900.

Lettres-Patentes et Status, pour l'Académie de peinture, sculpture et architecture civile et navale de Bordeaux [du mai 1780]. Bordeaux: Chez Racle, 1780.

Marionneau, Charles. *Les Beaux-arts à Bordeaux*. Bordeaux: G. Gounouilhou, 1892.

———. *Description des oeuvres d'art qui décorent les édifices publics de la ville de Bordeaux*. Paris and Bordeaux: A. Aubry and Chaumas-Gayet, 1861–65.

———. *Les Salons bordelais ou expositions des beaux-arts à Bordeaux au XVIIIe siècle (1771–1787) avec des notes biographiques sur les artistes qui figurèrent à ces expositions*. Bordeaux: Vve. Moquet, 1883.

———. *Les Vieux Souvenirs de la rue Neuve à Bordeaux par un vieil enfant de cette rue*. Bordeaux: Mme. Veuve Moquet, 1890.

Meallet, André. *Promenade dans le Bordeaux du XVIIIe siècle*. Bordeaux: Archives départementales de la Gironde, 1979.

Meller, Pierre. *Armorial du bordelais: Sénéchaussées de Bordeaux, Bazas et Libourne*. 2 vols. Marseilles: Laffitte Reprints, 1978.

———. *Essais généalogiques: Familles du bordelais/recueil factice de brochures concernant des familles*. Bordeaux: Feret et Fils, 1897: 165–72. (Brochure numbered 25–32).

———. *Mobilier d'une famille parlementaire sous Louis XIV à Bordeaux*. Bordeaux: Y. Cadoret, 1903.

Ministre de l'Education Nationale, *Catalogue général des manuscrits des bibliothèques publiques de France, Tome L*. Paris: Bibliothèque Nationale, 1954.

Nicolaï, Alexandre. *Histoire de l'organisation judiciaire à Bordeaux et en Guyenne et du barreau de Bordeaux du XIIIe au XIXe siècle*. Bordeaux: Gounouilhou, 1892.

O'Reilly, Patrice-John. *Histoire complète de Bordeaux*, 2d ed., 6 vols. Bordeaux and Paris: Chez J. Delmas and Chez Furne, 1863.

Pelleport, Vicomte de. *Etudes municipales de la charité bordelaise*. 2 vols. Paris and Bordeaux: Librairie Académique and P. Chaumas, 1869.

Péquigont, Paul. *Le Barreau de Bordeaux au XVIIIe siècle*. Bordeaux, 1903.

Péry, G. *Les Ancêtres de la Société de médecine & de chirurgie de Bordeaux: Essai historique sur la Société clinique de santé et la Société philanthropique de santé (1796–1798)*. Bordeaux, 1889.

————. *Histoire de la faculté de médecine de Bordeaux et de l'enseignement médical dans cette ville.* Paris and Bordeaux: Conseil général des Facultés de Bordeaux, 1888.

Programme de l'Académie royale des belles-lettres, sciences et arts de Bordeaux, du 25 août 1771 au 25 août 1790.

Salviat, L. F. de. *La Jurisprudence du Parlement de Bordeaux, avec un recueil de questions importantes agitées en cette cour & les arrêts qui les ont décidées . . .* 2 vols. Paris and Limoges: Arthus Bertrand and J.-B. Bargeas, 1824. Originally published in 1787.

Saulnier de la Pinelais, Gustave. *Le Barreau du Parlement de Bretagne, 1553–1790.* Paris and Rennes: J. Plihon et L. Hervé, 1896.

Société de médecine de Bordeaux. *Instruction sur les champignons vénéneux du département de la Gironde et sur les moyens de remédier leur pernicieux effets.* Bordeaux: Chez Racle, 1814.

————. *Mémoire de la Société de médecine de Bordeaux sur les moyens qu'on doit employer pour guérir l'asphyxie des noyés.* Bordeaux: Chez Racle, 1807.

————. *Opinion de la Société de médecine de Bordeaux sur l'étendue et le placement des divers hospices de cette ville.* Bordeaux: Chez Lawalle Jeune, 1810.

Sous, G. *Notice historique de la Société de médecine et de chirurgie de Bordeaux.* Paris and Bordeaux, 1895.

Valette, Jean, and Jean Cavaignac, eds. *Les Jurades de Sainte-Foy-la-Grande.* 2 vols. Bordeaux: Association pour l'édition des Jurades de Sainte-Foy-la-Grande, 1980–83.

III. Secondary Works

Ackerman, Evelyn. *Health Care in the Parisian Countryside, 1800–1914.* New Brunswick: Rutgers University Press, 1990.

Adams, Christine. "A Choice Not to Wed? Unmarried Women in Eighteenth-Century France." *Journal of Social History* (June 1996): 883–94.

————. "Constructing Mothers and Families: The Society for Maternal Charity of Bordeaux, 1805–1860." *French Historical Studies* 22 (Winter 1999): 65–86.

————. "Defining *État* in Eighteenth-Century France: The Lamothe Family of Bordeaux." *Journal of Family History* 17 (Winter 1992): 25–45.

————. "The Provinces Versus Paris? The Case of the Société de charité maternelle of Bordeaux, 1805–1820." *Proceedings of the Western Society for French History* 23 (Fall 1996): 418–30.

Adams, Christine, Jack R. Censer, and Lisa Jane Graham, eds. *Visions and Revisions of Eighteenth-Century France.* University Park: Penn State Press, 1997.

Agulhon, Maurice. *Le Cercle dans la France bourgeoise, 1810–1848.* Paris: A. Colin, 1977.

Anderson, Michael. *Family Structure in Nineteenth-Century Lancashire.* Cambridge: Cambridge University Press, 1971.

Antoine, Michel. *Le Conseil du roi sous le règne de Louis XV.* Geneva and Paris: Libraire Droz, 1970.

————. *Louis XV.* Paris: Fayard, 1989.

Arensberg, Conrad M., and Solon T. Kimball. *Family and Community in Ireland.* Cambridge: Harvard University Press, 1940.

Ariès, Philippe. *Centuries of Childhood: A Social History of Family Life.* Trans. Robert Baldick. New York: Vintage, 1962.

Ariès, Philippe, and George Duby, gen. eds. *A History of Private Life*. 5 vols. Trans. Arthur Goldhammer. Cambridge: Harvard University Press, Belknap Press, 1987–91.

Astarita, Tommaso. *The Continuity of Feudal Power: The Caracciola de Brienza in Spanish Naples*. New York: Cambridge University Press, 1992.

Baker, Keith Michael, ed. *The French Revolution and the Creation of a Modern Political Culture*, 4 vols. Oxford: Pergamon Press, 1987.

———. *Inventing the French Revolution: Essays on French Political Culture in the Eighteenth Century*. Cambridge: Cambridge University Press, 1990.

Barber, Elinor. *The Bourgeoisie in Eighteenth Century France*. Princeton: Princeton University Press, 1955.

Barrière, Pierre. *L'Académie de Bordeaux: Centre de culture international au XVIIIe siècle*. Bordeaux and Paris: Editions Bière, 1951.

———. "Bordeaux dans la vie intellectuelle française." *Revue historique de Bordeaux et du département de la Gironde* 3 (1954): 5–22.

———. *La Vie intellectuelle en France du XVI siècle à l'époque contemporaine*. Paris: A. Michel, 1961.

———. *La Vie intellectuelle en Périgord, 1550–1800*. Bordeaux: Edition Delmas, 1936.

Barry, Jonathan, "The Making of the Middle Class?" *Past and Present*, no. 145 (November 1994): 194–208.

Bell, David A. *Lawyers and Citizens: The Making of a Political Elite in Old Regime France*. New York: Oxford University Press, 1994.

Bercé, Yves-Marie. *Le Chaudron et la lancette: Croyances populaires et médecine préventive (1798–1830)*. Paris: Presses de la Renaissance, 1984.

Berkner, Lutz. "The Stem Family and the Developmental Cycle of the Peasant Household: An Eighteenth-Century Austrian Example." *American Historical Review* 77 (April 1972): 398–418.

Berlanstein, Lenard R. *The Barristers of Toulouse in the Eighteenth Century (1740–1793)*. Baltimore: Johns Hopkins University Press, 1975.

———. "Lawyers in Pre-Revolutionary France." In Wilfrid Prest, ed., *Lawyers in Early Modern Europe and America*. New York: Holmes and Meier, 1981.

Bien, David. *The Calas Affair: Persecution, Toleration, and Heresy in Eighteenth-Century Toulouse*. Princeton: Princeton University Press, 1960.

Blacker, J. G. C. "The Social Ambitions of the Bourgeoisie in Eighteenth Century France, and Their Relation to Family Limitation." *Population Studies* 11 (July 1957): 46–63.

Bloch, Marc. *French Rural History: An Essay on Its Basic Characteristics*. Trans. Janet Sondheimer. Berkeley and Los Angeles: University of California Press, 1966.

Bluche, François. *Les Magistrats du parlement de Paris au XVIIIe siècle (1715–1771)*. Paris: Les Belles Lettres, 1960.

Blum, Carol. *Rousseau and the Republic of Virtue: The Language of Politics in the French Revolution*. Ithaca: Cornell University Press, 1986.

Boissevain, Jeremy. *Friends of Friends: Networks, Manipulators, and Coalitions*. Oxford: Blackwell, 1974.

Bouwsma, William. "Lawyers and Early Modern Culture." *American Historical Review* 78 (1973): 303–27.

Brockliss, L[aurence]. W. B. "L'Enseignement médical et la Révolution: Essai de revaluation." *Histoire de l'éducation*, no. 42 (May 1989): 79–110.

———. *French Higher Education in the Seventeenth and Eighteenth Centuries: A Cultural History*. Oxford: Oxford University Press, 1987.

Brockliss, L[aurence]. W. B., and Colin Jones. *The Medical World of Early Modern France.* Oxford: Clarendon Press, 1997.

Brouillard, R. "Les Professeurs du droit et la Révolution." *Revue historique de Bordeaux et du département de la Gironde* 4 (1911): 56–68.

Brunelle, Gayle K. *The New World Merchants of Rouen, 1559–1630.* Kirksville, Miss.: Sixteenth-Century Journal Publishers, 1991.

Butel, Paul. *Les Dynasties bordelaises de Colbert à Chaban.* Paris: Perrin, 1991.

Butel, Paul, and Jean-Pierre Poussou. *La Vie quotidienne à Bordeaux au XVIIIe siècle.* Paris: Hachette, 1980.

Cassirer, Ernst. *The Philosophy of the Enlightenment.* Trans. Fritz C. A. Koelln and James P. Pettegrove. Boston: Beacon Press, 1955.

Cavignac, J. "Les Assemblées au désert dans le région de Sainte-Foy au milieu du dix-huitième siècle." *Revue historique de Bordeaux et du département de la Gironde* 16 (July–December, 1967): 97–119.

Censer, Jack R., ed. *The French Revolution and Intellectual History.* Chicago: Dorsey Press, 1989.

Censer, Jack R., and Jeremy D. Popkin, eds. *Press and Politics in Pre-Revolutionary France.* Berkeley and Los Angeles: University of California Press, 1987.

Chartier, Roger. *Cultural History: Between Practice and Representation.* Trans. Lydia G. Cochrane. Ithaca: Cornell University Press, 1988.

———. *The Cultural Origins of the French Revolution.* Trans. Lydia G. Cochrane. Durham: Duke University Press, 1991.

———. *The Cultural Uses of Print in Early Modern France.* Trans. Lydia G. Cochrane. Princeton: Princeton University Press, 1987.

Chaunu, Pierre. *La Civilisation de l'Europe des lumières.* Paris: Flammarion, 1982.

Chaytor, Miranda. "Household and Kinship: Ryton in the Late Sixteenth and Early Seventeenth Centuries." *History Workshop Journal,* no. 10 (Autumn 1980): 25–51.

Chêne, Christian. *L'Enseignement du droit français en pays du droit écrit (1679–1793).* Geneva: Libraire Droz, 1982.

———. "Simon Antoine Delphin de Lamothe: Portrait d'un professeur bordelais du XVIIIe siècle." In Gérard Aubiu, ed., *Etudes offerts à Pierre Jaubert: Liber Amicorum* (Bordeaux: Presses Universitaires de Bordeaux, 1992), 133–41.

Church, William F. "The Decline of the French Jurists as Political Theorists, 1660–1789." *French Historical Studies* 5 (Spring 1967): 1–40.

Cobban, Alfred. *The Social Interpretation of the French Revolution.* Cambridge: Cambridge University Press, 1964.

Collomp, Alain. *La Maison du père: Famille et village en Haute-Provence aux XVIIe et XVIIIe siècles.* Paris: Presses Universitaires de France, 1983.

Coornaert, Emile. *Les Corporations en France avant 1789.* 3d ed. Paris: Gallimard, 1941.

Courteault, Paul. "Une Académie des sciences à Bordeaux au XVIIe siècle." *Revue historique de Bordeaux et du département de la Gironde* 5 (1912): 145–57.

Coury, Charles. *L'Enseignement de la médecine en France des origines à nos jours.* Paris: Expansion Scientifique Française, 1968.

———. "The Teaching of Medicine in France from the Beginning of the Seventeenth Century." In C. D. O'Malley, ed., *The History of Medical Education.* Berkeley and Los Angeles: University of California Press, 1970.

Cubells, Monique. *La Provence des lumières: Les Parlementaires d'Aix au 18eme siècle.* Paris: Maloine, 1984.

Curtin, Philip D. *The Atlantic Slave Trade: A Census.* Madison: University of Wisconsin Press, 1969.

Curzon, A. "L'Enseignement du droit français dans les universités en France au XVIIIe siècle." *Nouvelle revue historique de droit français et étranger* 43 (1919): 209–69 and 305–64.

Damien, André. *Les Avocats du temps passé: Essai sur la vie quotidienne des avocats au cours des âges.* André Damien, 1973.

Darmon, Pierre. *La Longue Traque de la variole: Les Pionniers de la médecine préventive.* Paris: Librairie Académique Perrin, 1986.

Darnton, Robert. *The Business of Enlightenment: A Publishing History of the* Encyclopédie, *1775–1800.* Cambridge: Harvard University Press, Belknap Press, 1979.

———. *The Great Cat Massacre and Other Episodes in French Cultural History.* New York: Vintage, 1985.

———. "The High Enlightenment and the Low-Life of Literature." *Past and Present,* no. 51 (May 1971): 81–115.

———. *Mesmerism and the End of the Enlightenment in France.* Cambridge: Harvard University Press, 1968.

———. "Reading, Writing, and Publishing in Eighteenth-Century France: A Case Study in the Sociology of Literature." *Daedalus* (December 1970): 214–56.

Darrow, Margaret H. "French Noblewomen and the New Domesticity, 1750–1850." *Feminist Studies* 5 (Spring 1979): 41–65.

———. *Revolution in the House: Family, Class, and Inheritance in Southern France, 1775–1825.* Princeton: Princeton University Press, 1989.

Davidoff, Leonore, and Catherine Hall. *Family Fortunes: Men and Women of the English Middle Class, 1780–1850.* Chicago: University of Chicago Press, 1987.

Davis, James C. *A Venetian Family and Its Fortune, 1500–1900: The Donà and the Conservation of Their Wealth.* Philadelphia: American Philosophical Society, 1975.

Davis, Natalie Zemon. "Boundaries and the Sense of Self in Sixteenth-Century France." In Thomas C. Heller et al., *Reconstructing Individualism: Autonomy, Individuality, and the Self in Western Thought.* Stanford: Stanford University Press, 1986: 53–63.

———. "Ghosts, Kin, and Progeny: Some Features of Family Life in Early Modern France." *Daedalus* 106 (1977): 87–114.

———. *Society and Culture in Early Modern France.* Stanford: Stanford University Press, 1975.

Delbèke, Baron Francis. *L'Action politique et social des avocats au XVIIIe siècle.* Louvain and Paris: Librairie Universitaire, 1927.

Desgraves, Louis. *Evocations du vieux Bordeaux.* Paris: Les Editions de Minuit, 1960.

———. *Les Livres imprimés à Bordeaux au XVIIIe siècle (1701–1789).* Geneva: Droz, 1975.

Dewald, Jonathan. *The Formation of a Provincial Nobility: The Magistrates of the Parlement of Rouen, 1499–1610.* Princeton: Princeton University Press, 1980.

———. *Pont-St-Pierre, 1398–1789: Lordship, Community, and Capitalism in Early Modern France.* Berkeley and Los Angeles: University of California Press, 1987.

Diefendorf, Barbara B. *Beneath the Cross: Catholics and Huguenots in Sixteenth-Century Paris.* New York: Oxford University Press, 1991.

Donzelot, Jacques. *The Policing of Families.* Trans. Robert Hurley. New York: Pantheon Books, 1979.

Doyle, William. *The Parlement of Bordeaux and the End of the Old Regime, 1771–1790.* New York: St. Martin's Press, 1974.

Dugaw, Dianne. "The Popular Marketing of "Old Ballads": The Ballad Revival and

Eighteenth-Century Antiquarianism Reconsidered." *Eighteenth Century Studies* 21 (Fall 1987): 71–90.

Dupâquier, Jacques, et al. *Histoire de la population française.* 4 vols. Paris: Presses Universitaire de France, 1988.

———. *Pour la démographie historique.* Paris: Presses Universitaires de France, 1984.

Echverria, Durand. *The Maupeou Revolution: A Study in the History of Libertarianism in France, 1770–1774.* Baton Rouge and London: Louisiana State University Press, 1985.

Elias, Norbert. *The Civilizing Process: The History of Manners.* Trans. Edmund Jephcott. New York: Urizen Books, 1978.

Fairchilds, Cissie. *Domestic Enemies: Servants and Their Masters in Old Regime France.* Baltimore: Johns Hopkins University Press, 1984.

Farge, Arlette. *Subversive Words: Public Opinion in Eighteenth-Century France.* Trans. Rosemary Morris. University Park: Penn State Press, 1994.

Feytaud, Jean de. "L'Académie de Bordeaux depuis la Révolution." *Revue historique de Bordeaux et du département de la Gironde* 27 (1978–79): 193–207.

———. "L'Académie de Bordeaux sous l'Ancien Régime." *Revue historique de Bordeaux et du département de la Gironde* 23 (1974): 71–86.

Fitzsimmons, Michael P. *The Parisian Order of Barristers and the French Revolution.* Cambridge: Harvard University Press, 1987.

Flacassier, Annie. "La Société de charité maternelle de Bordeaux de 1805 à 1815." In *105e Congrès, Comité d'histoire de la Sécurité sociale,* 33–58. Caen: n.p., 1980.

Flandrin, Jean-Louis. *Families in Former Times: Kinship, Household, and Sexuality in Early Modern France.* Trans. Richard Southern. Cambridge: Cambridge University Press, 1979.

Flinn, Michael. *The European Demographic System, 1500–1820.* Baltimore: Johns Hopkins University Press, 1981.

Forrest, Alan. *Society and Politics in Revolutionary Bordeaux.* New York: Oxford University Press, 1975.

Forster, Elborg. "From the Patient's Point of View: Illness and Health in the Letters of Liselotte von der Pfalz (1652–1722)." *Bulletin of the History of Medicine* 60 (1986): 297–320.

Forster, Robert. "Family Biography." In Wolfdieter Bihl and Gernot Heiss, eds., *Biographie und Geschichtswissenschaft: Aufsätze zur Theorie und Praxis biographischer Arbeit.* Vienna: Verlage für Geschichte und Politik, 1979, 111–26.

———. "The French Revolution and the 'New' Elite, 1800–1850." In J. Perlenski, ed., *The American and European Revolutions, 1776–1848.* Iowa City: University of Iowa Press, 1980, 182–207.

———. *The House of Saulx-Tavanes: Versailles and Burgundy, 1700–1830.* Baltimore: Johns Hopkins University Press, 1971.

———. *Merchants, Landlords, Magistrates: The Depont Family in Eighteenth-Century France.* Baltimore: Johns Hopkins University Press, 1980.

———. "The Middle Classes in Eighteenth-Century Western Europe: An Essay." In Jürgen Schneider, ed., *Wirtschaftskräfte und Wirtschaftswege.* Vol. 3: *Auf dem Weg zur Industrialisierung.* Bamberg: Hermann Kellenbenz and Jürgen Schneider, 1978, 15–36.

———. "The Noble Wine Producers of the Bordelais in the Eighteenth Century." *Economic History Review* 14 (1961): 18–33.

———. *The Nobility of Toulouse in the Eighteenth Century: A Social and Economic Study.* Baltimore: Johns Hopkins University Press, 1960.

————. "Obstacles to Agricultural Growth in Eighteenth-Century France." *American Historical Review* 76 (1971): 1600–1615.

————. "Seigneurs and Their Agents." In Albert Cremer, ed., *Vom Ancien Régime zur Französischen Revolution: Forschungen und Perspektiven.* Göttingen: Vanderhoeck and Ruprecht, 1978, 169–87.

Forster, Robert, and Orest Ranum, eds. *Selections from the Annales, E.S.C..* 7 vols. Trans. Elborg Forster and Patricia Ranum. Baltimore: Johns Hopkins University Press, 1975–82.

Foucault, Michel. *The Birth of the Clinic: An Archaeology of Medical Perception.* Trans. A. M. Sheridan Smith. New York: Pantheon Books, 1973.

Fox-Genovese, Elizabeth, and Eugene D. Genovese. *Fruits of Merchant Capital: Slavery and Bourgeois Property in the Rise and Expansion of Capitalism.* New York: Oxford University Press, 1983.

Freidson, Eliot. *Profession of Medicine: A Study of the Sociology of Applied Knowledge.* New York: Dodd, Mead, 1970.

Fried, Michael. *Absorption and Theatricality: Painting and Beholder in the Age of Diderot.* Berkeley and Los Angeles: University of California Press, 1980.

Frey, Emil F. "Early Eighteenth-Century French Medicine: Setting the Stage for Revolution." *Clio Medica* 17 (May 1982): 1–13

Furet, François, ed. *Livre et société dans la France du XVIIIe siècle.* 2 vols. Paris and The Hague: Mouton et Cie., 1965–70.

Furet, François, and Jacques Ozouf. *Reading and Writing: Literacy in France from Calvin to Jules Ferry.* Cambridge: Cambridge University Press, 1982.

Garrioch, David. *The Formation of the Parisian Bourgeoisie, 1690–1830.* Cambridge: Harvard University Press, 1996.

Gay, Peter. *The Enlightenment: An Interpretation.* 2 vols. New York: Alfred A. Knopf, 1967–69.

Geison, Gerald, ed. *Professions and the French State, 1700–1900.* Philadelphia: University of Pennsylvania Press, 1984.

Gelbart, Nina Rattner. "The Monarch's Midwife Who Left No Memoirs." *French Historical Studies* 19 (Fall 1996): 997–1023.

Gelfand, Toby. *Professionalizing Modern Medicine: Paris Surgeons and Medical Science and Institutions in the Eighteenth Century.* Westport, Conn.: Greenwood Press, 1980.

Gélis, Jacques. *History of Childbirth: Fertility, Pregnancy, and Birth in Early Modern Europe.* Trans. Rosemary Morris. Cambridge: Polity Press, 1991.

Giesey, Ralph. "Rules of Inheritance and Strategies of Mobility in Prerevolutionary France." *American Historical Review* 82 (1977): 271–89.

Goldstein, Jan. *Console and Classify: The French Psychiatric Profession in the Nineteenth Century.* New York: Cambridge University Press, 1987.

————. "Foucault Among the Sociologists: The 'Disciplines' and the History of the Professions." *History and Theory* 23 (June 1984): 170–92.

Goldthwaite, Richard. *Private Wealth in Renaissance Florence: A Study of Four Families.* Princeton: Princeton University Press, 1968.

Goodman, Dena. "Public Sphere and Private Life: Toward a Synthesis of Current Historiographical Approaches to the Old Regime. *History and Theory* 31 (1992): 1–20.

————. *The Republic of Letters: A Cultural History of the French Enlightenment.* Ithaca: Cornell University Press, 1994.

Gossman, Lionel. *Medievalism and the Ideologies of the Enlightenment: The World and Work of La Curne de Sainte-Palaye.* Baltimore: Johns Hopkins University Press, 1969.

Goubert, Jean-Pierre. *Malades et médecins en Bretagne, 1770–1790.* Paris and Rennes: C. Klincksieck, 1974.

Gresset, Maurice. *Gens de justice à Besançon de la conquête par Louis XIV à la Révolution française (1674–1789).* 2 vols. Paris: Bibliothèque Nationale, 1978.

Groethuysen, Bernard. *The Bourgeois: Catholicism Versus Capitalism in Eighteenth-Century France.* Trans. Mary Ilford. New York: Barrie & Rockliff the Cresset P., 1968.

Guyon, Gérard D. "Les Textes de la Coutume de Bordeaux sur leurs éditions." *Revue française d'histoire du livre* 47 (April-May-June 1978): 399–414.

Habermas, Jürgen. *The Structural Transformation of the Public Sphere: An Inquiry into a Category of Bourgeois Society.* Trans. Thomas Burger and Frederick Lawrence. Cambridge: MIT Press, 1989.

Hahn, Roger. *The Anatomy of a Scientific Institution: The Paris Academy of Sciences, 1666–1803.* Berkeley and Los Angeles: University of California Press, 1971.

Halévi, Ran. *Les Loges maçonniques dans la France d'Ancien Régime.* Paris: A. Colin, 1984.

Hampson, Norman. *The Enlightenment: An Evaluation of Its Assumptions, Attitudes, and Values.* Harmondsworth: Penguin, 1976.

Hankins, Thomas. *Science and the Enlightenment.* New York: Cambridge University Press, 1985.

Hardwick, Julie. *The Practice of Patriarchy: Gender and the Politics of Household Authority in Early Modern France.* University Park: Penn State Press, 1998.

———. "Widowhood and Patriarchy in Seventeenth-Century France." *Journal of Social History* 26 (Fall 1992): 133–48.

Hareven, Tamara K. *Family Time and Industrial Time: The Relationship Between Family and Work in a New England Industrial Community.* Cambridge: Cambridge University Press, 1982.

Hazard, Paul. *The European Mind.* Trans. J. Lewis May. New York: Meridian Books, 1963.

Hoffman, Philip T. *Church and Community in the Diocese of Lyon, 1500–1789.* New Haven: Yale University Press, 1984.

Hufton, Olwen. "The French Church." In William J. Callahan and David Higgs, eds., *Church and Society in Catholic Europe of the Eighteenth Century.* New York: Cambridge University Press, 1979.

———. *The Poor in Eighteenth-Century France, 1750–1789.* Oxford: Clarendon Press, 1974.

———. "Women and the Family Economy in Eighteenth-Century France." *French Historical Studies* 9, no. 1 (1975): 1–22.

———. "Women Without Men: Widows and Spinsters in Britain and France in the Eighteenth Century." *Journal of Family History* 9, no. 4 (1984): 355–76.

Hunt, Margaret R. *The Middling Sort: Commerce, Gender, and the Family in England, 1680–1780.* Berkeley and Los Angeles: University of California Press, 1996.

Huppert, George. *The Idea of Perfect History: Historical Erudition and Historical Philosophy in Renaissance France.* Urbana: University of Illinois Press, 1970.

Isherwood, Robert M. *Farce and Fantasy: Popular Entertainment in Eighteenth-Century France.* New York: Oxford University Press, 1986.

Jacob, Margaret C. *The Cultural Meaning of the Scientific Revolution.* New York: Alfred A. Knopf, 1988.

Jalland, Patricia. "Victorian Spinsters, Dutiful Daughters, Desperate Rebels, and the Transition to the 'New Woman.'" In Patricia Crawford, ed., *Exploring Women's Past: Essays in Social History.* Boston: G. Allen and Unwin, 1984, 129–70.

Jones, Colin. "Bourgeois Revolution Revivified: 1789 and Social Change." In Colin Lucas, ed., *Rewriting the French Revolution.* Oxford: Clarendon Press, 1991, 69–118.

————. *The Charitable Imperative: Hospitals and Nursing in Ancien Régime and Revolutionary France.* New York: Routledge, 1989.

Kagan, Richard. "Law Students and Legal Careers in Eighteenth-Century France." *Past and Present,* no. 68 (August 1975): 38–69.

Kaiser, Thomas E. "This Strange Offspring of *Philosophie*: Recent Historiographical Problems in Relating the Enlightenment to the French Revolution." *French Historical Studies* 15 (Spring 1988): 549–62.

Kelley, Donald R. *Foundations of Modern Historical Scholarship: Language, Law, and History in the French Renaissance.* New York: Columbia University Press, 1970.

Kent, Francis William. *Household and Lineage in Renaissance Florence: The Family Life of the Capponi, Ginori, and Rucellai.* Princeton: Princeton University Press, 1977.

Keohane, Nannerl O. *Philosophy and the State in France: The Renaissance to the Enlightenment.* Princeton: Princeton University Press, 1980.

Kettering, Sharon. *Patrons, Brokers, and Clients in Seventeenth-Century France.* New York: Oxford University Press, 1986.

King, Lester S. *The Medical World of the Eighteenth Century.* Chicago: University of Chicago Press, 1958.

Klapisch-Zuber, Christiane. *Women, Family, and Ritual in Renaissance Italy.* Trans. Lydia Cochrane. Chicago: University of Chicago Press, 1985.

Kors, Alan. *Atheism in France, 1650–1729.* Princeton: Princeton University Press, 1990.

————. *D'Holbach's Coterie: An Enlightenment Salon in Paris.* Princeton: Princeton University Press, 1976.

Labatut, Jean-Pierre. *Les Ducs et pairs de France au XVIIe siècle.* Paris: Presses Universitaires de France, 1972.

Labrousse, C. E. *Esquisse du mouvement des prix et des revenus en France aux XVIIIe siècle.* Paris: Librairie Dalloz, 1932.

Landes, David. "Religion and Enterprise: The Case of the French Textile Industry." In Edward C. Carter II, Robert Forster, and Joseph N. Moody, eds., *Enterprise and Entrepreneurs in Nineteenth- and Twentieth-Century France.* Baltimore: Johns Hopkins University Press, 1976, 41–86.

Larson, Magali Sarfatti. *The Rise of Professionalism: A Sociological Analysis.* Berkeley and Los Angeles: University of California Press, 1977.

Laslett, Peter, and Richard Wall, eds. *Household and the Family in Past Time.* Cambridge: Cambridge University Press, 1972.

Lebrun, François. *Se soigner autrefois: Médecins, saints et sorciers aux 17e et 18e siècles.* Paris: Temps Actuels, 1983.

Lerner, Gerda. "Placing Women in History: Definitions and Challenges." *Feminist Studies* 3 (1975): 1–14.

Lougee, Carolyn C. *Le Paradis des Femmes: Women, Salons, and Social Stratification in Seventeenth-Century France.* Princeton: Princeton University Press, 1976.

Loupes, Philippe. "L'Hôpital Saint-André de Bordeaux au XVIIIe siècle." *Revue historique de Bordeaux et du département de la Gironde* 21 (1972): 79–111.

Lucas, Colin. "Nobles, Bourgeois, and the Origins of the French Revolution." *Past and Present,* no. 60 (August 1973): 84–126.

Lux, David. *Patronage and Royal Science in Seventeenth-Century France: The Académie de physique in Caen.* Ithaca: Cornell University Press, 1989.

Mabille, Eugène. *De la condition des enfants trouvés au XVIIIe siècle dans la généralité de Bordeaux.* Bordeaux: Y. Cadoret, 1909.

MacFarlane, Alan. *The Family Life of Ralph Josselin, a Seventeenth-Century Clergyman: An Essay in Historical Anthropology*. Cambridge: Cambridge University Press, 1970.

MacNalty, Sir Arthur Salusbury. "The Prevention of Smallpox: From Edward Jenner to Monckton Copeman." *Medical History* 12 (January 1968): 1–18.

Magraw, Roger. *France, 1815–1914: The Bourgeois Century*. Oxford: Oxford University Press, 1983.

Mauzi, Robert. *L'Idée de bonheur dans la littérature et la pensée françaises au XVIIIe siècle*. Paris: A. Colin, 1960.

Maza, Sarah. "Luxury, Morality, and Social Change: Why There Was No Middle-Class Consciousness in Prerevolutionary France." *Journal of Modern History* 69 (June 1997): 199–229.

———. *Private Lives and Public Affairs: The Causes Célèbres of Prerevolutionary France*. Berkeley and Los Angeles: University of California Press, 1993.

McManners, John. *Death and the Enlightenment: Changing Attitudes to Death Among Christians and Unbelievers in Eighteenth-Century France*. Oxford: Clarendon Press, 1981.

Medick, Hans. "The Proto-Industrial Family Economy: The Structural Function of Household and Economy During the Transition from Peasant Society to Industrial Capitalism." *Social History*, no. 5 (1976): 291–315.

Medick, Hans, and David Warren Sabean. "Call for Papers: Family and Kinship, Material Interest, and Emotion." *Peasant Studies* 8 (Spring 1979): 139–60.

———, eds. *Interest and Emotion: Essays in the Study of Family and Kinship*. Cambridge: Cambridge University Press, 1984.

Millepierres, François. *La Vie quotidienne des médecins au temps de Molière*. Paris: Hachette, 1964.

Miller, Genevieve. *The Adoption of Inoculation for Smallpox in England and France*. Philadelphia: University of Pennsylvania Press, 1957.

Mitterauer, Michael, and Reinhard Sieder. *The European Family: Patriarchy to Partnership from the Middle Ages to the Present*. Trans. Karla Oosterveen and Manfred Hörzinger. Chicago: University of Chicago Press, 1982.

Mornet, Daniel. "Les Enseignements des bibliothèques privées (1750–1780)." *Revue d'histoire littéraire de la France* 17 (1910): 449–92.

———. *Les Origines intellectuelles de la Révolution française, 1715–1787*. Paris: A. Colin, 1933.

Mousnier, Roland. *The Institutions of France under the Absolute Monarchy, 1598–1789*. Trans. Brian Pearce. Chicago: University of Chicago Press, 1979.

Murphy, Terence D. "The French Medical Profession's Perception of Its Social Function Between 1776 and 1830." *Medical History* 23 (1979): 259–78.

Nathans, Benjamin. "Habermas's 'Public Sphere' in the Era of the French Revolution." *French Historical Studies* 16 (Spring 1991): 620–44.

Neuschel, Kristin B. *Word of Honor: Interpreting Noble Culture in Sixteenth-Century France*. Ithaca: Cornell University Press, 1989.

Nicolas, Jean. *La Savoie au 18e siècle: Noblesse et bourgeoisie*. 2 vols. Paris: Maloine, 1978.

Norberg, Katherine. *Rich and Poor in Grenoble, 1600–1814*. Berkeley and Los Angeles: University of California Press, 1985.

Nye, Robert A. *Masculinity and Male Codes of Honor in Modern France*. New York: Oxford University Press, 1993.

Ozouf, Mona. "'Public Opinion' at the End of the Old Regime." *Journal of Modern History* 60, suppl. (September 1988): S1–S21.

Palmer, Robert R. *Catholics and Unbelievers in Eighteenth-Century France*. Princeton: Princeton University Press, 1947.

Pardailhé-Galabrun, Annik. *La Naissance de l'intime: 3000 foyers parisiens, XVII–XVIIIe siècles.* Paris: Presses Universitaires de France, 1988.

Pariset, François-Georges, ed. *Bordeaux au XVIIIe siècle.* Bordeaux: Fédération Historique du Sud-Ouest, 1968.

Pilbeam, Pamela M. *The Middle Classes in Europe, 1789–1914: France, Germany, Italy, and Russia.* Basingstoke: Macmillan, 1990.

Pintard, René. *Le Libertinage érudit dans la première moitié du XVIIe siècle.* Paris: Boivin et Cie., 1943.

Portemer, Jean. "La Politique royale de l'enseignement du droit en France au XVIIIe siècle: Ses survivances dans le régime modern." *Revue d'histoire des facultés de droit et de la science juridique,* no. 7 (1988): 15–43.

Poussou, Jean-Pierre. *Bordeaux et le Sud-Ouest au XVIIIe siècle: Croissance économique et attraction urbaine.* Paris: Touzot, 1983.

Ramsey, Matthew. *Professional and Popular Medicine in France, 1770–1830: The Social World of Medical Practice.* New York: Cambridge University Press, 1988.

Ranum, Orest. *Paris in the Age of Absolutism.* Bloomington: Indiana University Press, 1968.

———. "Personality and Politics in the Persian Letters." *Political Science Quarterly* 84 (December 1969): 606–27.

Ranum, Orest, and Louis d'Adhémar de Panat. "Vers une histoire de l'esthétique sociale: Le Contrat de mariage du comte de Grignon et de Marie Angélique du Puy du Fou et de Champagne." In Wolfgang Leiner and Pierre Ronzeaud, eds., *Correspondances: Mélanges offertes à Roger Duchêne.* Tübingen and Aix-en-Provence: Gunter Narr and Publications de l'Université de Provence, 1991, 355–63.

Redman, Ben Ray, ed. *The Portable Voltaire.* New York: Penguin Books, 1977.

Richter, Melvin. *The Political Theory of Montesquieu.* Cambridge: Cambridge University Press, 1977.

Roche, Daniel. *La Culture des apparences: Une histoire du vêtement, XVII–XVIIIe siècle.* Paris: Fayard, 1989.

———. *The People of Paris: An Essay in Popular Culture in the Eighteenth Century.* Trans. Marie Evans. Berkeley and Los Angeles: University of California Press, 1987.

———. *Les Républicains des lettres: Gens de culture et lumières au XVIIIe siècle.* Paris: Fayard, 1988.

———. *Le Siècle des lumières en province: Académies et académiciens provinciaux, 1680–1789.* 2 vols. Paris and The Hague: Mouton, 1978.

Ryan, Mary. *Cradle of the Middle Class: The Family in Oneida County, New York, 1790–1865.* New York: Cambridge University Press, 1981.

Schama, Simon. *Citizens: A Chronicle of the French Revolution.* New York: Alfred A. Knopf, 1989.

Schneider, Robert A. *Public Life in Toulouse, 1463–1789: From Municipal Republic to Cosmopolitan City.* Ithaca: Cornell University Press, 1989.

Sewell, William. *Work and Revolution in France: The Language of Labor from the Old Regime to 1848.* Cambridge: Cambridge University Press, 1980.

Shackleton, Robert. *Essays on Montesquieu and the Enlightenment.* Edited by David Gilson and Martin Smith. Oxford: Voltaire Foundation at the Taylor Institution, 1988.

———. *Montesquieu: A Critical Biography.* London: Oxford University Press, 1961.

Sheridan, Richard B. *Doctors and Slaves: A Medical and Demographic History of Slavery in the British West Indies, 1680–1834.* New York: Cambridge University Press, 1985.

Slater, Miriam. *Family Life in the Seventeenth Century: The Verneys of Claydon House.* Boston: Routledge and Kegan Paul, 1984.

Smith, Bonnie G. *Ladies of the Leisure Class: The Bourgeoises of Northern France in the Nineteenth Century.* Princeton: Princeton University Press, 1981.

Spencer, Samia I., ed. *French Women and the Age of Enlightenment.* Bloomington: Indiana University Press, 1984.

Sperber, Jonathan. "Bürger, Bürgertum, Bürgerlichkeit, Bürgerliche Gesellschaft: Studies of the German (Upper) Middle Class and Its Sociocultural World." *Journal of Modern History* 69 (June 1997): 271–97.

Stone, Bailey. *The French Parlements and the Crisis of the Old Regime.* Chapel Hill: University of North Carolina Press, 1986.

Stone, Lawrence. *The Family, Sex, and Marriage in England, 1500–1800.* London: Weidenfeld and Nicolson, 1977. Abridged edition. New York: Harper and Row, 1979.

Tackett, Timothy. *Priest and Parish in Eighteenth-Century France: A Social and Political Study of the Curés in the Diocese of Dauphiné, 1750–1791.* Princeton: Princeton University Press, 1977.

Taton, René, ed. *Enseignement et diffusion des sciences en France au XVIIIe siècle.* Paris: Hermann, 1964.

Taylor, George V. "Noncapitalist Wealth and the Origins of the French Revolution." *American Historical Review* 72, no. 2 (1967): 469–96.

Tilly, Louise. "The Family Wage Economy of a French Textile City: Roubaix, 1872–1906." *Journal of Family History* (Winter 1979): 381–94.

———. "Individual Lives and Family Strategies in the French Proletariat." *Journal of Family History* 4 (Summer 1979): 137–52.

Tocqueville, Alexis de. *The Old Regime and the French Revolution.* Trans. Stuart Gilbert. Garden City, N.Y.: Doubleday, 1954.

Traer, James. *Marriage and the Family in Eighteenth-Century France.* Ithaca: Cornell University Press, 1980.

Trumbach, Randolph. *The Rise of the Egalitarian Family: Aristocratic Kinship and Domestic Relations in Eighteenth-Century England.* New York: Academic Press, 1978.

Van Kley, Dale. *The Damiens Affair and the Unraveling of the Ancien Régime.* Princeton: Princeton University Press, 1984.

———. *The Jansenists and the Expulsion of the Jesuits from France, 1757–1765.* New Haven: Yale University Press, 1975.

Vess, David M. *Medical Revolution in France, 1789–1796.* Gainsville: University Presses of Florida, 1975.

Vollmer, Howard M., and Donald L. Mills, eds. *Professionalization.* Englewood Cliffs, N.J.: Prentice Hall, 1966.

Vovelle, Michel, ed. *Bourgeoisies de province et Révolution.* Grenoble: Presses Universitaires de Grenoble, 1987.

———. *Piété baroque et déchristianisation: Les Attitudes devant la mort en Provence au XVIIIe siècle.* Paris: Plon, 1973.

Wade, Ira O. *The Structure and Form of the French Enlightenment.* Princeton: Princeton University Press, 1977.

Wahrman, Dror. *Imagining the Middle Class: The Political Representation of Class in Britain, c. 1780–1840.* New York: Cambridge University Press, 1995.

Watson, Alan. *Roman Law and Comparative Law.* Athens: University of Georgia Press, 1991.

Weil, Françoise. "'L'Esprit des Lois' devant La Sorbonne." *Revue historique de Bordeaux et du département de la Gironde* 11 (1962): 183–91.

Weiner, Dora. "French Doctors Face War, 1792–1815." In Charles K. Warner, ed., *From the*

Ancien Régime to the Popular Front: Essays in the History of Modern France in Honor of Shepard B. Clough. New York: Columbia University Press, 1969, 51–73.

Weisz, George. "The Politics of Medical Professionalization in France, 1845–1848." *Journal of Social History* 12 (Fall 1978): 3–30.

Wheaton, Robert, and Tamara K. Hareven, eds. *Family and Sexuality in French History.* Philadelphia: University of Pennsylvania Press, 1980.

Woloch, Isser. "The Fall and Resurrection of the Civil Bar, 1789–1820s." *French Historical Studies* 15 (Fall 1987): 242–62.

Zeldin, Theodore. *France, 1848–1945: Ambition and Love.* New York: Oxford University Press, 1979.

IV. Unpublished Theses and Papers

Andrieu, Marie. "Les Paroisses et la vie religieuse à Bordeaux de 1680 à 1789." 2 vols. Thèse de troisième cycle, Université de Bordeaux, 1973.

Daffos, Agnès. "L'Enseignement supérieur à la fin de l'Ancien Régime: Exemple de la Faculté de droit de l'Université de Bordeaux." D.E.A., Bordeaux, 1988–89.

Dietle, Robert. "Salvaging the Everyday: The *Bon Bourgeois* of Paris." Ph.D. diss., Harvard University, 1991.

Hannaway, Caroline. "Medicine, Public Welfare, and the State in Eighteenth-Century France: The Société royale de médecine of Paris (1776–1793)." 2 vols. Ph.D. diss., Johns Hopkins University, 1974.

"Hommage à nos concitoyens, Mestre, Jay, Garrau, députés aux assemblées révolutionnaires: Exposition des Archives Municipales du 17 au 31 juillet 1989." Archives municipales of Sainte-Foy-la-Grande, 1989.

Index

relatives in, 31, 88, 91, 92, 93, 98–101, 104
Victor's studies, desire to remain in, 6, 23,
 26, 28, 36, 69, 75, 157–67, 168, 175,
 181, 186, 200, 223, 230
Parlement of Bordeaux (Parlement of
 Guyenne), 18, 46, 97, 107, 124, 128,
 129, 144, 168, 244, 245, 247
 and the Academy of Bordeaux, 195, 198,
 199
 barristers of the, 6, 19, 94, 118–20, 121, 126,
 127, 130, 131, 134, 147–48
 jurisprudence of the, 132, 134, 139, 226
 magistrates of the, 28, 63 n. 60, 67 n. 87,
 106, 118, 143, 233, 242
 See also Order of Barristers
patronage, 8, 89, 106–10, 113, 127, 128, 164,
 196. *See also* friendship; friends
Phillipiques, Les, 244–45
philosophes, 32, 181, 189, 232–38
 and academies, 193, 197, 198
 legal reform, ideas on, 140, 142, 144–45
physicians. *See* medicine
poetry, 189, 202 n. 53, 217, 227, 234, 236–38,
 242–45, 248, 251–54, 255
Polignac, cardinal de, 196
priesthood, 6, 19, 33–35, 41, 53, 123. *See also*
 clergy
professeur royal en droit français (royal professor of
 French law), 28, 134
 Delphin as, 126–28, 136, 139–40, 147, 149,
 200
professional culture, 11, 113, 231
professionalism; professionalization, 5, 6,
 8–12, 116 n. 2, 148, 153 n. 8
property, 17, 18, 28, 51–54, 67, 68, 71, 84,
 104, 129, 176
 division of, 79–83
 joint management of, 72–75, 85
 rural, 59–62
 urban, 56–59
Protestantism, 18, 36, 36 n. 20, 246
Provence, 35, 42, 242
public service; public utility, 10, 11, 13, 257
 and the academies, 193, 194, 206, 208, 211,
 219
 and law, 139, 148
 and medicine, 152, 153, 176, 178, 186

Rabelais, François, 151, 254
Reign of Terror, 83, 117, 172, 176, 187

religion/religiosity, 5, 12, 13, 19, 22, 38, 146,
 247, 251
 books, religious, 231
 of Jules, 26, 34–37, 236
 of medical students, 155–56, 159–60
 practices, religious, 31–33, 169, 257
 skepticism, 235, 254
 toleration, 36, 142 n. 138, 237–38
 of the women, 7, 34–35, 44–48, 236
René, vicomte de la Faye, 104
rentes, 57, 67, 81, 83
Richelieu, duc de, maréchal (Louis-François-
 Armand du Plessis), 102, 108, 135, 165,
 196, 213, 224, 225, 235, 254
Robespierre, Maximilien, 117
Roche, Daniel, 199, 202, 219
Roche, Madame de la, 169–70, 196
Roman law, 20, 52, 118, 119, 137, 139, 140
Rousseau, Jean-Jacques, 201, 221, 235–36, 237,
 238–39, 250

Saint-André, cathedral, 32
Saint-Avit-du-Moiron, 35, 60, 79, 94
Sainte-Foy-la-Grande, 35, 36, 83, 88, 91, 94–
 96, 101, 109, 128, 129, 235
 as Protestant stronghold, 17–18, 36
 vintage season, 63
Saint-Magne, 33, 36, 37, 41, 92
Saint-Michel, parish church of, 32, 33, 35, 47,
 56
salons, 13, 189, 192, 224–26, 227, 230, 238,
 254. *See also* Academy of Painting, Sculpture, and Civil and Naval Architecture of
 Bordeaux: art salons; Duplessy, Madame:
 salon Duplessy
Salviat, L.F. de, 131–32, 134
Sérézac, Marie de (1699–1773), 6, 15, 32, 42,
 87, 91, 128
 death of, 52
 familial role, 7, 21–23, 43–45, 47–48
 management of resources as widow, 73–76,
 79
 marriage to Daniel, 18–19, 27–28, 56, 90
Seven Years War, 64, 65, 246
slavery/slave trade, 145, 201, 203–4, 207–8
smallpox, 180–81, 183
social mobility, 54, 68, 84–85, 89 n. 9, 116
Société de charité maternelle (Society for
 Maternal Charity), 11, 178, 184–86, 259

Société de médecine de Bordeaux (Society of
Medicine of Bordeaux), 176–77, 181
Société d'histoire naturelle de Bordeaux, 176
Société royale de médecine (Royal Society of
Medicine), Paris, 152, 170, 176, 179,
186
songs, 242–43, 253, 255
syndic, of the Collège des médecins, 169; of
the Order of Barristers, 122, 123, 126,
200, 226

Tableau des avocats, 94, 119
taxation, 56–57, 59–60, 70, 71–72, 83, 145,
151, 217, 244
theater, 102, 227, 248–49, 250
torture, 144, 226
Tourny, marquis de, Louis-Urbain Aubert, 196
Turgot, Anne-Robert, 145

University of Bordeaux, 28–29, 121, 126, 127,
135, 139, 141, 167
usury, 76, 76 n. 134

vaccination (smallpox), 177, 178, 180–83, 186
venality, venal offices, 54 n. 10, 75, 126, 146,
149
Vernet, Claude-Joseph, 216
vol domestique (thievery by servants), 144
Voltaire (François-Marie Arouet), 193, 200,
226, 234

wet nursing, 170, 172, 173 n. 98, 205
widowhood, 58, 73–74, 104 n. 104
wine harvest; production, 30, 45, 60, 61, 63,
65–66, 79, 91, 245
sales, 63–65, 246
women, 7, 8, 35, 135, 162, 225, 243, 248, 257.
and Lamothe brothers, 101–5, 222, 228
role in the "family economy," 43–48, 66,
75–76
See also childbirth; domesticity; gender
roles

Zola, Emile, 4